ROAD TO THE KILLING FIELDS

53

TEXAS A&M UNIVERSITY
★ MILITARY HISTORY SERIES ★

indd·

ROAD to the
KILLING FIELDS

The Cambodian War of 1970–1975

WILFRED P. DEAC

Foreword by Col. Harry G. Summers, Jr.

TEXAS A&M UNIVERSITY PRESS
College Station

The paper used in this book meets the minimum requirements
of the American National Standard for Permanence
of Paper for Printed Library Materials, Z39.48-1984.
Binding materials have been chosen for durability.

Library of Congress Cataloging-in-Publication Data

Deac, Wilfred P., 1934–
    Road to the killing fields : the Cambodian war of 1970–1975 / by
Wilfred P. Deac ; foreword by Col. Harry G. Summers, Jr. — 1st ed.
        p.   cm. — (Texas A&M University military history series ; 53)
    Includes bibliographical references and index.
    ISBN 0-89096-750-4 (cloth); 1-58544-054-X (pbk.)
    1. Cambodia—History—Civil War, 1970-1975.   I. Title. II. Series.
DS554.8 D397   1997   97-13661
959.604'2—dc21   CIP

History . . . is indeed little more then the register of the crimes, follies, and misfortunes of mankind.

—EDWARD GIBBON, 18TH CENTURY

American assistance can be effective when it is the missing component in a situation which might otherwise be solved . . . It can not furnish determination, it can not furnish the will, and it can not furnish the loyalty of a people to its government.

—DEAN ACHESON, 1950

CONTENTS

ILLUSTRATIONS

MAPS

FOREWORD

In Hanoi on April 25, 1975, five days before the fall of Saigon, to negotiate the terms of the U.S. withdrawal, the North Vietnamese kept guaranteeing that there would be no bloodbath after their takeover of the South. Reminding them of the terrible stories of just such a bloodbath taking place in Cambodia, which had fallen two weeks earlier, I said their reassurances were hard to believe.

They reacted in outrage. "We're not Cambodians!" they shouted. "We're not barbarians! We're a civilized people who would never do such horrendous things." At the time their comments were dismissed as evidence of the centuries-old Vietnamese antipathy toward their Khmer neighbors, but history would prove them all too correct.

While the Communist takeover of South Vietnam was not without its human costs, it did not begin to compare with the killing fields in Cambodia, where one million (some say three million) men, women, and children were brutally murdered by Pol Pot and his Khmer Rouge forces in the name of ideological purity—a greater proportion of the population than in any other revolution in this century.

Over two decades later, that cancer has still not been completely expunged. In August 1996, it was revealed that Ieng Sary, foreign minister in Pol Pot's murderous 1975–79 regime—and who had been sentenced to death in absentia for his part in the massacres—had defected to the government in Phnom Penh, weakening the surviving Khmer Rouge strongholds in northwest Cambodia. Tellingly, that story was buried on page seventeen of the *Washington Times,* for Cambodia still does not register high among American concerns.

Most accounts of what has been called the Second Indochina War concentrate on Vietnam and the period of intense U.S. involvement there and end with the Tet Offensive of 1968. Slighted are the last seven years of the war in Vietnam, and ignored almost completely are the wars that raged simultaneously in Laos and Cambodia. As former CIA director William Colby noted, that's like ending the study of World War II with the battle of Stalingrad, the Allied landing in North Africa, and the battle of Guadalcanal in the Pacific.

My own belated education on Cambodia was provided by the series of articles on the war there written by Wilfred P. Deac for *Vietnam* magazine. His over thirty-three years of government service in posts around the world included a stint in the political section of the U.S. Embassy in Phnom Penh in 1971. Now he has expanded his articles into *Road to the Killing Fields,* focusing on the crucial 1970–75 period that led to the Khmer Rouge victory and the holocaust that followed.

Except for the "secret" bombing campaign that was ended by Congress in August 1973, direct U.S. military involvement was limited during this time. Although the April–June 1970 "Cambodian incursion" would take place in the first part of that period, the incursion was actually part of the U.S. withdrawal plan that had begun in July 1969. By August 1972, all U.S. ground combat forces had been withdrawn from Vietnam, and by March 1973, under the terms of the Paris Peace Accords, all remaining forces had been withdrawn as well. Other than for U.S. military equipment delivery teams, Cambodia was on its own for the final two years of the Second Indochina War.

Deac sets the stage with Operation Eagle Pull, code name for the evacuation of the U.S. embassy at Phnom Penh on April 12, 1975. It is yet another indication of the level of U.S. concern for Cambodia that, unlike the tens of thousands of South Vietnamese who were evacuated from Saigon some eighteen days later, only 203 Cambodians and other nationalities along with 84 Americans were airlifted from Phnom Penh.

In the first three chapters, Deac traces the ethnic, cultural, and historical differences between Cambodia and its neighbors. Unlike the Lao, Thai, and Vietnamese peoples who originally descended into Southeast Asia from China, Cambodia's Khmer people migrated northward from Indonesia and were under Javanese rule until their independence in 802. From then until the fall of its capital at Angkor to the Thai in 1431, Cambodia dominated Southeast Asia. For the next four centuries Cambodia descended into the dark ages, ending in 1867 when it became a French colony to avoid absorption by Siam (Thailand) and Vietnam. Becoming part of French Indochina in 1887, Cambodia won its independence with the 1954 Geneva Accords, which ended the First Indochina War.

Deac also examines the career of Cambodia's Norodom Sihanouk. A prince of the royal family, he was crowned king by the French in 1941. Early on, Sihanouk demonstrated his ability to play both sides of the street, becoming the self-proclaimed "father and first citizen of the Khmer nation" in 1953 when the French withdrew from Indochina. Abdicating in favor of his father in 1955 to escape parliamentary supervision, Prince Sihanouk established the *Sangkum Reastr Niyum* (People's Socialist Community), which won all ninety-one seats in the national assembly in the September 1955 election, the last freely contested election until 1993. He dubbed his opponents from the right of the political spectrum "Khmer

Bleu" and those from the left "Khmer Rouge," thus giving name to what would become one of history's most murderous groups.

Recognizing, as Deac points out, "one overriding fact of life," that his rule and his country's peace and prosperity were at the mercy of his neighbors and of the major Cold War powers, Sihanouk loudly proclaimed a policy of neutralism. But he soon realized that his effort to steer a neutral course on the international scene between the warring powers was becoming impossible. Domestically, his favorite ploy was the "retreat-return" tactic, where he would leave the country, allow the domestic situation to fester, and then return to power when opponents came around to his way of thinking. First adopted in 1953, then again in 1969, "retreat-return" was employed once again in 1970, when Sihanouk left for France for "medical treatment." But this time the tactic backfired, turning into an act of abdication.

With the beginnings of the road to the killing fields established, Deac turns to the road itself, detailing the journey to the holocaust, with the overthrow of Sihanouk on March 18, 1970, as the "most crucial turning point of Cambodia's modern history." Deflating the myth that the coup d'etat was instigated by the United States, Deac writes, "the best available evidence indicates that [Sihanouk's cousin] Sirik Matak provided the brains and [prime minister and defense minister] Lon Nol the brawn." That individual mid-level members of the U.S. military may have encouraged Khmers to depose the prince, Deac offers as a likely scenario. But, he asserts, it is all speculation that misses the main point: "Even without firm [American] backing, the Khmer plotters surely could assume that America would not stand idly by while one of the much-talked-about Southeast Asia dominoes fell to the Communists."

That does not mean, as some have claimed, that the United States was responsible for the holocaust that followed. For that, Sihanouk must assume a large share of the blame. Taking refuge in China after the coup, Sihanouk met with Premier Phan Van Dong of North Vietnam and then gave legitimacy to the communist Khmer Rouge (K.R.) opposition in Cambodia by becoming its titular head. In radio broadcasts, Sihanouk made appeals for the dissolution of the Phnom Penh government, and audio tapes of this "call to arms" were widely circulated throughout Cambodia, exploiting the peasants strong loyalty to their god-king.

"The convergence of events and national aspirations made the Cambodian War inevitable," argues Deac. "The root cause . . . was the illegal PAVN-PLAF [People's Army of Vietnam (the North Vietnamese regular army) and the People's Liberation Armed Forces (the Viet Cong guerrillas)] presence in Cambodia." This presence led in turn to cross-border commando operations by the U.S. Military

Advisory Command Vietnam's super-secret Studies and Observations Group and to Operation Menu, the so-called secret bombing of PAVN-PLAF sanctuaries in Cambodia. Typical of the convoluted nature of U.S. involvement in Cambodia, this bombing was no secret to Sihanouk, who in fact had given his tacit approval to the operation.

Sihanouk's "island of peace" was no more. In March 1970, with Lon Nol as commander-in-chief, the Cambodian Army took to the field to eject the Vietnamese Communists from their border sanctuaries. These border sanctuaries also prompted a U.S.–South Vietnamese "incursion" into Cambodia in April 1970, ostensibly to protect the ongoing U.S. withdrawal from Vietnam. The real reason, Deac explains, "was to prevent the fall of Cambodia, the White House nightmare of a 'Communist-dominated Sihanouk government providing a secure (and nation-wide) sanctuary and logistics base' for the PAVN-PLAF."

While the incursion had some short term favorable consequences, these were far outweighed by its long term negative effects. "In addition to proving that America was desperate to end the Vietnam War without knowing how," the incursion led to the Senate's Cooper-Church Amendment which prohibited the use of funds for "United States personnel in Cambodia who furnish military instruction to Cambodian forces or engage in any combat activity in support of Cambodian forces." Although sometimes honored more in the breech than in the observance, this and other congressional restrictions greatly hampered U.S. ability to help the Cambodians in their increasingly deadly struggle.

Another limiting factor was the January 1973 Paris Peace Accords between the United States and North Vietnam and the withdrawal of all U.S. forces from Vietnam three months later. That month would also see the first directly unassisted major operation by the Khmer Rouge. Flying from bases in Thailand, the United States would mount an intensive bombing campaign to turn back the offensive. This would end with a congressional mandate, effective August 15, 1973, to stop funding to finance "directly or indirectly, combat activities by U.S. military forces in or over . . . or off the shores of Cambodia, Laos, North Vietnam and South Vietnam."

"After the summer of 1973," said Henry Kissinger, "I knew that Cambodia was doomed." Yet the war would continue for another year and a half—a drawn out affair in part because the United States was prohibited from active combat there, and both the North and South Vietnamese were now occupied almost exclusively with their own struggle. Cambodia was on its own.

Cambodia's war was set off by outsiders. But it was the Cambodian people that ultimately paid the price. On April 15, 1975, the Communists swarmed over

Phnom Penh's last defenses, and the government collapsed the next day. The Khmer Rouge's Year Zero had begun. Sihanouk, in Beijing, said the Khmer Rouge victory was "the most glorious in Kampuchea's two-thousand-year history." Not until the early 1980s, notes Deac, did Sihanouk learn that his children and grand-children were among the million or more who perished in the killing fields.

Wilfred Deac's powerful recounting of how it all came to be is a cautionary tale that should be required reading for policymakers as evidence of how even the best of intentions can have horrible consequences.

Col. Harry G. Summers, Jr.
Editor, *Vietnam* magazine

PREFACE

America's military commitment in Southeast Asia during the 1960s and 1970s consisted of three wars. The Vietnam War was the largest and is justifiably the best known. The second war, in Laos, though less publicized, has received its share of attention in books and articles. The third, Cambodia's conflict, is another matter. There, general knowledge is limited to the 1970 incursion and the postwar killing fields. What has been published about this third war has treated the subject as part of a larger picture. To date, there has been no book whose primary objective is to detail the course of the war.

One of the three main purposes of *Road to the Killing Fields* is to fill this gap in the history of America's involvement in Southeast Asia. In addition to being the first book to focus specifically on the war from a historical point of view, this is the first study of the conflict by an "insider." During my overseas-oriented government and private sector career, I served as an officer attached to the U.S. Embassy in Phnom Penh in 1971. As a member of the embassy's multiagency contingent, I benefited from, in addition to daily personal observations and conversations, close professional contact with Cambodian civilian and military personnel at various levels; interviewed a great number of persons, including refugees, ralliers, and prisoners not available to outsiders; and had access to American, Cambodian, French, and captured documents.

As part of its role in filling a historical gap, this book attempts to resolve certain controversial issues as much as available and releasable facts allow. For example, while the United States certainly must bear a great part of the burden for the Khmer war tragedy, claims that America was responsible for the overthrow of Sihanouk, for the beginning of the Cambodian War, and for the Khmer Rouge victory are simplistic and inaccurate. A U.S. desire to destabilize the Sihanouk regime had long wound down by the time internal problems and the Vietnamese Communist occupation of eastern Cambodia led to the prince's ouster.

It also was the illegal Vietnamese Communist presence in and military use of Cambodian territory that triggered Allied counteractivities and that led to the outbreak of the war before the publicized U.S. incursion. And however much American military action and support of an increasingly unpopular government contributed to the prolonging of the war and to the dislocation and dissatisfaction of Cambodians, the Pol Pot victory was owing to support given to the Khmers

Rouges by North Vietnam, Communist China, and Sihanouk himself, as well as to the Lon Nol regime's incompetence and corruption. Although Hanoi did not create the Khmer Rouge movement, it did establish the Khmer Communist Party, and it did assure the success of an active dissidence that otherwise might never have grown beyond its prewar strength.

Equally erroneous is the emotional and illogical claim that American bombs caused Khmer Rouge brutality. The latter was a direct result of the Pol Potist obsession with creating an agrarian-based "pure communism." It was a Utopian mentality that was introduced into the earlier multi-interest Khmer Rouge movement and pursued with such a ruthless singleness of purpose that it soon spread like a cancer. As in 1917 Russia, it was the case of a determined Communist minority taking over a revolutionary movement and viciously consolidating its misguided power.

Other controversial questions—such as the Khmer Republic's chances of victory if its government had been less corrupt and Cambodia's postwar fate in a Hanoi-dominated Indochina if Sihanouk had remained in power—remain moot. What remains clear, however, is that, as in the case of America's World War II enemies, it is time to move forward beyond the enmity of the conflict.

The second purpose of this book is to contribute to the understanding of not only the Cambodian War but also the dynamics of military and civilian policy making and warfare. In terms of the military and political progression of events, the war was a predictable offshoot of the widening conflict in Southeast Asia, just as various countries were drawn into past major wars. However, Cambodia's war had unusual aspects, the most notable one being the development of the fanatical Khmers Rouges. Their leaders—apparently determined to outdo Stalin's and Mao Zedong's internal "cleansings" while fighting perceived threats—steered a self-destructive course.

This book's third aim, admittedly an optimistic one, is to provide future leaders with a historical example of how not to conduct politico-military policy. Obvious moral issues aside, the Cambodian example demonstrates that the pursuit of short-term goals improperly perceived and selfishly conceived often rebounds to the detriment of the long-term national interest. The domestically pressured American withdrawal from Southeast Asia and the Vietnamization program were by then no-win situations, however much time bought for them by the Khmer Republic's fight for survival. Nor did Washington's Realpolitik dancing with Beijing and Moscow require Phnom Penh's abasement to succeed.

America's role in the Cambodian War was part of a miscalculated Southeast Asia policy, if such it could even be called, based on combating communism by snatching up France's Indochina relay baton in an already lost postcolonial race.

It was not without good reason that President Charles de Gaulle of France, during a 1966 visit to Phnom Penh, warned the United States of the perils of military involvement in Indochina. Each reactive step U.S. policymakers took—failing to learn from the French defeat and failing to look ahead to where those steps were leading—moved their country nearer to moral and physical exhaustion. Instead of either refusing direct involvement or seeking full commitment, responding to situations real and imagined, the often well-meaning but fumbling American leadership tried to attain increasingly divergent short-term goals with unrealistically ambitious measures.

One result was that, whereas Hanoi was fighting one Indochina war, Washington was pursuing three, each in a different manner but all with self-imposed limitations that made them unwinnable. A second result was one of the most traumatic periods in American history. Domestically, the Indochina experience left the country divided and shaken, with political careers and reputations left for the sweeper's broom. Internationally, it besmirched American honor and credibility. On a human level, the tragedy included the avoidable killing and maiming of young Americans and countless Asian men, women, and children. The Indochina fighting also left Cambodia shattered, its pieces more fragmented than those of already war-torn Vietnam and Laos. If the war produced any heroes, they were among those whose names will probably never be known. For certainly there were none among the leaders of any of the nations involved.

Three of this book's chapters deal with events preceding the war itself. These are included to provide a context for understanding the Cambodian fighting in historical, cultural, and human terms rather than seeing it as a detached sequence of events.

Purists will quickly note that compromises have been made regarding Cambodian names and terms. Despite recent progress toward standardization, the spelling of Cambodian words remains greatly subjected to spellings and usages simultaneously affected by the Khmer, French, and English languages. I have tried to use the most popular spellings of the war period. In place names, for example, I use the common name rather than the U.S. Board on Geographical Names designation. Similarly, for simplification I have taken liberties in other areas, treating "Khmer" used as an adjective and as a noun denoting the Cambodians; treating "Cambodia" and "Kampuchea" as interchangeable, although I use the latter as preferred by the antigovernment side; and using "Khmer Rouge" consistently for the insurgent side, although, since being coined by Sihanouk, the precise meaning of the term has changed with the evolution of the government opposition groups involved.

In general, contrary to the Western practice, surname precedes given name in Cambodia. Thus, using Lon Nol as an example, Lon is the family name. Because of their frequent appearance in place names, the following terms justify translation: *kompong* (raised bank, such as a river bank), *phnom* (hill or mountain), *prek* (waterway), *prey* (forest), *tonle* (river), and *wat* (pagoda or temple).

Having already stated the primary purposes of this book, I can add another reason it was written. It seems that wartime service in Southeast Asia, however long it lasted, left most Americans with personal ghosts to exorcise. One of my personal ghosts was well defined by Colonel Dennison Lane (who served in Cambodia during the 1970–75 war) in Al Santoli's *To Bear Any Burden:* "The Cambodians really believed in us. I'm not so sure the Vietnamese did. That's why Cambodia troubles me more than Vietnam or Laos. The Cambodians were the most trusting."

ROAD TO THE KILLING FIELDS

Operation Eagle Pull

THE OPERATION BEGAN AT 6:07 A.M. on Saturday, April 12, 1975.[1] Twelve aircraft of Marine Heavy Helicopter Squadron 462 lifted from the USS *Okinawa's* long flight deck. Like hornets swarming from their nest, they climbed to orbit positions above Amphibious Ready Group Alpha. Except for the aircraft carrier *Hancock,* which had arrived late the day before, the flotilla of landing operation ships and their four escorts had been steaming in circles in the Gulf of Thailand for forty-three days. The warm-up, check-out flights completed, the CH-53D helicopters descended at spaced intervals toward *Okinawa* and the smaller amphibious transport dock ship *Vancouver.*

Shielding their eyes from the wind blast of the six-bladed main rotors of the Sea Stallion choppers, 360 marines of the 2nd Battalion, 4th Regiment began filing up the rear ramps—the command group and elements of Companies H and F on *Okinawa,* and Company G elements on the aft helipads of *Vancouver.* Expecting to face enemy fire and angry mobs in less than two hours, the helmeted, armor-jacketed leathernecks nevertheless embarked with a sense of relief. It was the end of six monotonous weeks of alert status at sea broken only by what they derisively called MODLOC liberty—MODified LOCations of the ships' operating areas, all within the gulf. Fuel tanks were topped off to feed each twenty-ton helicopter's dual-turboshaft engines.

One after the other, the Sea Stallion pilots grasped the collective-pitch levers low to the left of their seats. Easing up on the pivoted lever changed the pitch of the main rotor blades spinning overhead, allowing the helicopter to rise. Simultaneously rotating the handgrip to full power, like increasing the speed of a motorcycle by twisting the handlebar throttle, enabled the prop lift to overcome the weight of the fully-loaded aircraft. To keep a chopper from spinning out of control like a top, the pilot gradually pushed down on a left floor pedal to neutralize the torque effect with the CH-53's smaller, four-bladed tail rotor. A turn in the right direction was accomplished by the use of the floor pedals. Finally, moving forward the between-the-knees cyclic-pitch control stick tilted the main rotor blades to give the machine its forward movement. Throbbing above the naval flotilla, the olive-green helicopters formed into four divisions of three to circle and wait for the green light. At ten-minute intervals, like projectiles released from a slingshot, three Sea Stallions left their orbit and sped north.

Meanwhile, in the besieged Cambodian capital of Phnom Penh 130 miles to the northeast, preparations were being completed to receive them. The U.S. ambassador, forty-nine-year-old John Gunther Dean, gave the nod to pre-designated embassy personnel to assemble the people who would be evacuated by the approaching helicopters. The country, after just over five years of full-scale war, was about to fall to the Communists. Since only U.S. military, economic, and political support had kept them from overwhelming the Cambodian government before now, getting American officials out before they were captured was high on the Washington, D.C., priority list. Evacuation by fixed-wing aircraft from the city's Pochentong Airport, earlier used to fly out families and some personnel, was now out of the question because of communist shells and rockets. The Mekong River, flowing east of the surrounded capital, had been Phnom Penh's main transportation artery. It, too, was now closed. Helicopters were the only sure way out—provided that the enemy didn't shoot them down or shell the landing field during the withdrawal. And provided that Cambodian government troops, in panic or anger, didn't interfere. Speed and surprise were essential.

A ten-man, ground-based evacuation command group led by marine Colonel Sydney "Tom" Batchelder drove one thousand yards along the main road leading northeast from the embassy. Its destination was a fence-enclosed soccer field barely three hundred yards west of the junction of the Mekong and the Bassac Rivers and just below the uncompleted Cambodiana luxury hotel. A six-storied apartment building on the east side shielded the field from enemy eyes across the river, not to mention from direct gunfire. It was there, designated Landing Zone (LZ) Hotel, that the Squadron 462 helicopters were to land.

Each driving a vehicle, the command group team members parked so as to block all road access to the LZ, with the exception of the primary one leading from the embassy complex. Distributor caps were pulled to immobilize nine of the vehicles' motors. The tires were another matter, since anyone trying to block the evacuation could simply roll the cars and trucks aside or onto the landing field. As dramatic as shooting them out Hollywood style would be, the noise would only call unwanted attention to the operation. The team's G-3 (operations) officer, Major George Cates, had the answer ready in a plastic bag on a chain around his neck. He distributed the valve stem extractors to use in deflating the tires of all the vehicles except a pickup truck fitted with a winch and cable. If necessary, it would serve to tow aside disabled helicopters. Assisted by the embassy security guards, the command group swiftly disabled the vehicles. Three more tasks remained to be done—establish radio communications, first with the choppers' command element, code-named Cricket, then with the four-engined air force HC-130, designated King Bird, which would control the helicopters from high overhead; and finally, to lay out marker panels to guide the whirlybirds three at a time onto their touchdown points.

Landing Zone Hotel now was initially secure. The helicopters were en route, and the evacuees were converging on the embassy. A squadron of 7th Air Force jets based in neighboring Thailand was in position to provide air cover if necessary. Triggered one day shy of two years since it was conceived in the dying hope of the Cambodian republic's survival, Operation Eagle Pull was the first of two final, major noncombatant evacuations of America's Southeast Asia war. The second, larger and more publicized, was Operation Frequent Wind, the abandonment of Saigon only seventeen days later.[2]

Minutes before the Eagle Pull choppers began lifting off from the helicopter assault ship *Okinawa* that fateful April 12, notes from Ambassador Dean were being hand-carried to four leading Cambodian officials. We're officially leaving your country, they were told; do you and a few you select want to join us? Cambodia's leader, Marshal Lon Nol, accompanied by twenty-nine family and government members, had already left. His successor as acting president, slim, balding Lieutenant General Saukham Khoy, pulled up to the embassy's closed gates in his official car shortly after receiving his note. Despite the unfavorable political climate created by a recent change of government in Bangkok, Washington hoped to form an exile government around Khoy in Thailand. Once the anti-Vietnam War furor died down in America, the United States intended to generate the conditions necessary for the return of the exile government to Cambodia. Those closer to the situation in the field were less optimistic than Washington about the viability of such a plan. Undersecretary of Sports Long Botta also decided to leave his country. But, to the surprise of the ambassador, who knew their lives to be in danger, all of the others turned down the American invitation.[3]

Prime Minister Long Boret, unaware of Khoy's departure, said he would stay to continue the struggle against the Communists. Prince Sisowath Sirik Matak, the sixty-one-year-old former prime minister who probably had been closer to the Americans than any other Cambodian leader, expressed his bitter feelings in a letter handwritten in French and delivered to the ambassador at 9 A.M.:[4]

Dear Excellency and Friend,

   I thank you very sincerely for your letter and for your offer to transport me toward freedom. I cannot, alas, leave in such a cowardly fashion.
   As for you, and in particular your great country, I never believed for a moment that you would have this sentiment of abandoning a people which has chosen liberty. You have refused us your protection and we can do nothing about it. You leave and my wish is that you and your country will find happiness under the sky.
   But mark it well that, if I shall die here on the spot and in my country that I love, it is too bad, because we all are born and must die one day. I have only committed this mistake of believing you, the Americans.
   Please accept, Excellency, my dear friend, my faithful and friendly sentiments.

                                                              Sirik Matak

The evacuees began arriving at the wall-enclosed compound at around eight o'clock. They were issued tags bearing their names and aircraft-boarding priorities. Only when the helicopters were making their final run in did they begin to file nervously out the back of the embassy grounds into waiting trucks for the short drive to the LZ. A cable classified "Confidential" flashed from the embassy. It read EMBASSY PHNOM PENH IS CLOSING DOWN ITS COMMUNICATIONS FACILITIES EFFECTIVE 120100Z HOURS APRIL 1975. DEAN. The wire recorded in cablese language that, as of 1 A.M. Greenwich Mean Time, that April 12, the U.S. government presence in Cambodia officially had cut itself off from the rest of the world.[5]

At 7:43 A.M., the first division of three helicopters passed over the surf breaking against the shoreline just north of Cambodia's only deep sea port, Kompong Som. Once over land, they came under the control of the commander of the U.S. Support Activities Group/7th Air Force (COMUSSAG) in Thailand. As the Sea Stallions bopped onto a northeasterly course toward Pich Nil Pass in the malarial Elephant Mountain range, a top-priority "Flash" message was relayed to U.S. President Gerald Ford, informing him that the aircraft had penetrated foreign airspace. The marine copters paralleled Highway 4 toward their final approach point, code-named Oscar, about thirty miles west of Phnom Penh near embattled Kompong Speu. They checked in with their aerial HC-130 control post; King Bird told them to "proceed directly to the landing zone." They were six minutes ahead of schedule. The inbound helicopter trio then switched radio frequency to coordinate the landing directly with the ground command group waiting at LZ Hotel. Their powerful engines propelled the Sea Stallions, shadows racing behind them across the riceland, toward the city beneath a sunny sky broken by billowy cumulus clouds. Their pulsating throb soon was slicing the almost tangible tension pervading the 3.7-acre soccer field.[6]

It was 8:54 A.M. when Squadron 462 commander Lieutenant Colonel James Bolton eased down the first helicopter. Its giant rotor blades whirred up loose dirt and grass and bent back the palm fronds edging the field. As the initial group of evacuees hurried toward it, the command element CH-53 briefly lifted back up. A second chopper touched down to disgorge its load of defense perimeter marines. The three Sea Stallions soon formed a perfect triangle on the LZ, all the latter could safely accommodate at one time. The on-board gunners remained alert behind their .50-caliber machine guns as the first increment of troops sprinted to one end of the LZ. Their battalion commander, Lieutenant Colonel George Slade, strode over to Colonel Batchelder, who had overall operational control of the marines while they were on the ground, and reported in.

Cambodian civilians, with more arriving on bicycles and motorcycles, crowded the sidelines. Although Slade's leathernecks stood with M-16 rifles defensively raised to chest level, it immediately became apparent that the onlookers were curious, not hostile. Some at first thought that the aircraft were bringing in troops to save the city at its eleventh hour. Happily, there was no repetition of the brutal chaos that preceded North Vietnamese General Le Trong Tan's Easter Sunday occupation of Da Nang barely two weeks earlier. Then, with a million refugees crowding into South Vietnam's second largest city, swarms of panicked soldiers and civilians rushed aircraft trying to leave the main airport. The Eagle Pull marines slowly and firmly moved the Cambodians back to keep the landing area clear.

Although the evacuation proceeded with remarkable efficiency, the planners had not been blessed with crystal balls. There were, for example, far fewer passengers than anticipated. A total of 590 people, including 146 U.S. citizens, was expected; in fact, 84 Americans, and 203 Cambodians and other nationalities were evacuated aboard the Sea Stallions. A dozen of the embassy's local employees refused to leave. Also turning down the chance were *New York Times* correspondent Sydney Schanberg and his assistant, Dith Pran, whose saga was to be depicted in the Oscar-winning film *The Killing Fields*. As the operation gained momentum, a filled helicopter immediately roared skyward, soaring high to avoid possible gunfire before making the seventy-minute return trip to the Gulf of Thailand. Other CH-53s, with no one to embark as the trucks made further round-trips to the embassy, had to rise into a holding pattern to give incoming birds space to disembark their marines. Whereas Eagle Pull started six minutes early, it now fell behind schedule as succeeding waves of rotary-winged aircraft were detained at Point Oscar until preceding helicopters cleared the LZ. Close radio contact enabled Sea Stallions to be called in as evacuees reached the soccer field.[7]

Nearly half an hour after the last Squadron 462 choppers were released from Point Oscar for the hop to the LZ, a second wave of Sea Stallions began lifting off from the carrier *Hancock*. They belonged to Marine Heavy Helicopter Squadron 463, commanded by Lieutenant Colonel Herbert Fix. Having left Hawaii in late March and been temporarily diverted to Vietnamese waters, the squadron had plenty of time to prepare for the worst scenario, including the reported threat of Soviet-made SA-7 anti-aircraft missiles. Maintenance crews had spray-painted the CH-53s with low infrared-reflecting paint and installed decoy flare dispensers to confuse the missiles' aiming systems. Twelve of the Squadron 463 helicopters were assigned to airlift the marine landing force back to the Alpha group ships at the end of the operation. An additional two were launched as backups. This second wave was held up at Point Oscar for about half an hour while its sister squadron completed pulling out the last of the evacuees.

At 10:15 A.M.—thirty minutes after the official closing of the embassy—Ambassador Dean, taut-faced, wearing a dark suit with matching striped tie and pocket handkerchief, boarded a Sea Stallion. The embassy country team, including Military Equipment Delivery Team Brigadier General William Palmer and the Central Intelligence Agency chief of station (whose reporting to Washington predicted a "bloodbath" after the Communist takeover), joined the ambassador in the helicopter. Confirmation that Dean and Khoy were on their way released the Squadron 463 whirlybirds for the run in to Phnom Penh.[8]

Soon the 2nd Battalion marines were methodically boarding the incoming aircraft. The operation was winding up when the expected Communist reaction finally came. Shortly before eleven o'clock, 107mm rockets began streaking in to burst uncomfortably close. Word was radioed to the U.S. Air Force 23rd Air Support Squadron forward air controllers circling overhead. While one of several twin-engined OV-10 Broncos screamed down toward the grassy far bank of the Mekong, where the firing was thought to be originating, 82mm mortar rounds started thudding around the LZ. One high-trajectory shell detonated near the Cambodians watching the evacuation. A teenaged boy was killed, another wounded. A marine corpsman did what he could for the wounded youth before leaving. The spotter plane was unable to locate the source of the firing.

Exploding projectiles and the deafening helicopter noise made communication so difficult that two Company G leathernecks nearly remained behind. Captain William Melton, the company commander, ran to the tailgate of the last helicopter as a noncommissioned officer was making a head count. Melton later recalled that "the sergeant's eyes grew wide in disbelief and horror." Mouthing the words and raising two fingers, the non-com indicated marines were missing. The captain, accompanied by the platoon leader and the sergeant, "ran around the long building on the edge of the soccer field to the entrance gate the platoon had been guarding. We saw two marines standing in their original positions almost catatonic." Melton slapped one on the shoulder, shouting for the pair to leave. Turning and realizing that their comrades were long gone, they needed no persuasion.

The last squadron 463 chopper rose from LZ Hotel at 10:59. At 11:15, two air force HH-53C Super Jolly Green Giants (air force name for its search-rescue version of the S-65 family of Sikorsky company aircraft) hovered into position above the LZ. The "Super Jollies" of the 40th Aerospace Rescue and Recovery Squadron, based in Thailand, alit to pick up Colonel Batchelder and his ground command group. They were the last scheduled Americans to fly out. It was not a moment too soon. Either the Communists had gotten their act together or resentful government troops had decided to give the Americans a lethal send-off. Small arms fire punched into the first air force chopper, causing only superficial damage. A machine gun round, however, slammed into the second helicopter's tail rotor as it rose above LZ Hotel. Buffeted by heavy vibrations, the Super Jolly nevertheless made it back to Thailand. As the last aircraft soared above the low Phnom Penh skyline, enemy shells began exploding directly on the now-empty soccer field. The Americans had not fired a shot in anger during the entire operation.

One after the other, the evacuee-carrying Sea Stallions crossed about a hundred miles of hostile territory to return to their floating bases. The final one landed on *Okinawa* at 12:15 P.M.—six hours and eight minutes after the first had lifted off. Most of the evacuees were assigned overnight bunk space as the small fleet steamed northwestward across the gulf. At 2:50 that afternoon, Dean and seventeen others boarded Squadron 462 helicopter No. 10. A couple of hours later, the ambassador stepped through the forward doorway and down a ramp onto Thai soil. The furled, plastic-wrapped American flag that had flown over the embassy in Cambodia the day before was bundled beneath his left arm. The next day, the rest of the evacuees were helicoptered to Thailand and the naval force turned about to steam to the Philippine Islands.

Eagle Pull marked the end of the most crucial phase ever of U.S. involvement in Cambodia. That phase—spanning the period between the establishment of the Lon Nol government and the beginning of the aptly named killing fields—lasted just over five years. It was a tragic direct offshoot of the strife that tore apart Vietnam. Yet, although their nation played a key role, many Americans are unaware that a full-scale war was fought in Cambodia between 1970 and 1975.

CHAPTER ONE

A Land
and Its People

AS THE DRONE OF THE EAGLE PULL HELICOPTERS moved seaward from Cambodia, it left behind a country whose future was as uncertain as its recorded past. Although the land had been inhabited for thousands of years, its first history was recorded by Chinese brushes. Unfortunately, the Chinese, already a dynastic empire expanding southward at the inception of the Christian era, did not produce accurate records of ancient Cambodia. They uncritically accepted unverified reports concerning foreigners who paid them tribute, traded forest products, and occasionally asked for military assistance. Even the archaeological evidence left by the early Cambodians had crucial gaps: it provides intriguing details without the overview necessary to fit them together into a complete picture. The national boundaries themselves would remain indistinct and changing until the late nineteenth century. And even then questions would remain.[1]

Modern Cambodia, its shape bringing to mind a paws-on-the-ground koala bear, claims over 69,000 square miles, approximately the size of Missouri. In 1970, its population was about seven million, of whom some 87 percent lived in the countryside. Only 10 percent spoke a Western language, generally French. Another 750,000 Cambodians lived in Vietnam and Thailand. The latter embraces the country's west and northwest frontiers. Laos lies to the northeast. Vietnam, which has the longest border with Cambodia, is to the east and southeast. On the southwest is the Gulf of Thailand. The Mekong River snakes for about 196 miles from the Laotian border to Vietnam, roughly forming the western edge of the eastern third of the nation.

Kratie, significant to the Communists during the 1970–75 war, is on the river about 110 miles below the Laotian frontier. Near this provincial capital

were the headquarters of the Cambodian Communists and, from the time of the controversial American incursion, of the elusive Central Office for South Vietnam (COSVN, North Vietnamese control point for the People's Liberation Armed Forces, or Viet Cong as they were commonly known). Farther downstream on the Mekong lies Kompong Cham, the nation's third largest city. Chup, once the world's largest rubber plantation, was just to the east. Nearly eighty miles beyond the provincial capital of Kompong Cham is the national capital of Phnom Penh, with a 1970 population of approximately 500,000. Phum Prek Neak Luong, where southeast-bound Highway 1 ends at a ferry crossing before resuming on the other side of the river to continue on to Saigon, rests some forty miles above the Vietnamese border. The country's only ocean port, Kompong Som on the Gulf of Thailand, was built between

May 1956 and April 1960 with French assistance and originally called Sihan-oukville, a name it was to regain in the mid-1990s.

In the west central third of the country is the vast, elongated Tonle Sap. The Great Lake, as it is known, long has been one of the world's richest fresh-water fishing areas. The Sap River (Tonle Sap) flows southeastward from the lake to empty into the Mekong, except during the wet, soil-enriching south-west monsoon season. Between about mid-May and October or November, bloated with rain and with melted Himalayan snow filling the Mekong, the Sap reverses to flow back into the Great Lake. The latter's size swells from just over 1,000 to 3,000 or more square miles (or considerably more if the Mekong Delta flooding is included) and its depth increases five to ten times. The fall reversal of Sap River flow and the onset of the dry season traditionally has been celebrated by an elaborate water festival. Where the Sap and the Mekong meet, an extension of the former, the Bassac River (Tonle Bassac), forms to run generally southward west of the Mekong to empty into the South China Sea after traversing lower Vietnam. The juncture of the three rivers—appro-priately called the Four Arms (Four Faces to the Cambodians) because of the gigantic crooked X they form—is the site of Phnom Penh. The only other cities with over 300,000 inhabitants at the outbreak of the 1970–75 war were Battambang in the west and Kompong Cham.

Tropical Cambodia, three-quarters lowland (Tonle Sap Basin, Mekong Delta, and a coastal strip in the southwest), has three mountain chains: the Kravanh (Cardamom) and Damrei (Elephant) Ranges in the southwest and the inward-facing sandstone escarpment of the Dangrek along the northern Cambodian-Thai border. Phnom Aural, over a mile high and ranking as the country's highest point, is at the eastern end of the Cardamoms. Northeast-ern Cambodia rises to merge into the Central Highlands of Vietnam. For-ests, in 1970 covering over half the land, comprised open grassy woodlands of the plains, upland rain forest, and dense deciduous areas mainly east of the Mekong. Wildlife ran the gamut from mosquitoes, exotic birds, and reptiles to tigers and elephants, with the latter widely used for transportation and labor tasks. Cambodia was noted for its rice, rubber, and corn, with a grow-ing demand also for its wood, pepper, and gemstones.

In 1970, the nation had about twelve thousand miles of roadway, less than 14 percent of it paved. Most of it was built by the French before World War II as part of the Indochina network. The only subsequent major addition came with the July 1959 inauguration of U.S.-funded Highway 4 between the capi-tal and Kompong Som. Cambodia had two single-track railroad lines leading out of Phnom Penh. One, laid down between 1960 and 1969 with French, West German, and Chinese aid, ran 168 miles to Kompong Som. The other, built by the French during the 1930s and 239 miles long, was to Thailand via Battambang. International airports were only in the capital (Pochentong); at Siem Reap, near the historical ruins of Angkor; and at Ream, near Kompong Som. Twenty-three other landing fields handled limited air traffic.

Ethnic Khmers made up about 85 percent of the people in 1970. The largest minorities were Chinese and Vietnamese. Both tended to be urbanites, the Chinese dominating the commercial sector and the Vietnamese often being middle-class artisans and clerks. The other minorities were Moslem Cham and mostly northeastern hill tribes officially known as Khmer Loeu and unofficially as *phnong* (savages). The infusion of Chinese and Vietnamese blood over the years tended to lighten the dark-skinned Khmers.[2] As the calendar reversed from B.C. to A.D., the ancestors of the ethnically-mixed Khmers began a millenium of Indianization. It was a peaceful assimilation of myths, religious beliefs, an alphabet, dress and etiquette, political institutions, and even the early name *Kambuja*. Old Cambodia apparently followed the development pattern of medieval Europe and pre-Christian—era China, individual fiefdoms joining or brought under control of their most powerful elements. Funan, overlapping what today is southeastern Cambodia and Vietnam's Mekong Delta, now is believed to be less what historians initially called the first coherent "mighty kingdom" than a group of states. The same holds for Chenla, whose name was to be given to two ill-fated twentieth-century military campaigns.

The past history of Cambodia is still being written. Continuing research often not only adds to existing knowledge but changes the conclusions and theories of earlier historians. Indeed, precise dates and details remain so shadowy that the definitive history of ancient Cambodia may never be written. Funan gave way to Chenla in the seventh and eighth centuries. Khmer domination spread over part of the Mekong Delta and sections of present-day Cambodia, Thailand, and Laos. Centralization, the political-economic coherence necessary for unification, evolved through military campaigns, population growth, and improved agricultural technology, to name three factors. The result was to be Cambodia's "golden age," its claim to historical fame and national pride, the period of Angkor between 802 and 1431.[3]

Pirates from Java, Sumatra, and Malaya had, by the end of the eighth century, brought an internally divided Chenla under the control of the Sailendra dynasty of Java. The head of one Chenla state decided to do something about it. In a decades-long series of military operations and political alliances, Jayavarman II liberated Cambodia from Java and founded the country's first true kingdom, stretching from China, Champa (today's south central Vietnam), and the sea to land in the west. In 802, in rites presided over by a Brahman priest, Jayavarman became a *chakravartin* (imperial monarch) and formally declared Cambodia's independence. He named present-day Roluos, on the north shore of the Great Lake, as his capital. For the next 629 years, Cambodia dominated Southeast Asia.

Just over half a century later, a subsequent monarch, ambitious Yasovarman I, decided to create a grand metropolis as the center of his kingdom. A raised highway was built northwestward from Roluos along the alluvial plain toward the site of his proposed city ten miles away. There he had a temple, a suitable future tomb, erected atop one of the area's few hills. The elevation, over two-hundred-foot-high Phnom Bakheng (Mighty Ancestor Hill), would become a battleground in 1972. In 899, Yasovarman, surrounded by bodyguards, priests, and parasol bearers, a pointed golden helmet on his head, stood atop Phnom Bakheng and showed where he wanted his royal palace built a short distance away. It would stand in the northwest quadrant of reservoir-flanked, moat-surrounded Angkor Thom (Great City), which would not be completed until the twelfth century. Yasovarman also ordered temples established to honor Siva, Vishnu, and Buddha. One of these, cliff-perched Preah Vihear on the Thai-Cambodian border, became the scene of perhaps the last shots fired in the war that ended in 1975.

The Angkor complex of communities and agricultural projects grew under succeeding kings until it covered an area more than fifteen miles east to west and five miles north to south, over twice the size of New York's Manhattan Island. In 1113, just south of the stockaded Great City, Suryavarman II began construction of the world's largest religious building, the towered temple that would become Cambodia's national symbol—Angkor Wat. The temple, too, was to be turned into a combat zone during the 1970s. Worse perhaps, from a historical point of view, its archaeological treasures became a target of looters.

As Cambodia moved to the zenith of its turbulent history, successive Angkorean kings expanded their realms' borders, mostly to the west. Trade flourished, more cities were planted to accommodate a growing population and the kingdom fluctuated between times of unity and periods of instability. With religion an integral part of politics and everyday life, temple building continued. Warfare, though sporadic, was another constant, with the Chams being among the empire's most consistent enemy. In the early twelfth century, Suryavarman II, the builder of Angkor Wat but also an ambitious militant, led the Khmers eastward into Champa, taking its capital and capturing its ruler. However, the next war with Champa, not three decades later, proved devastating for the Cambodians. Neither side, both relying heavily on elephants, appeared to gain an edge. The deadlock was broken when Cham King Jayaindravarman IV switched from elephants to crossbow-armed warriors on horseback. This produced victories but not enough to reach the Khmer capital. The Cham ruler thereupon sent oar-propelled warships, their prows decorated with half-man, half-bird carvings and tusk battering rams, into Cambodia's Great Lake. Bas reliefs in the Angkor ruins attest to the fierce naval battle that raged on the huge lake. More than one spear-wielding combatant foundering in the water fell victim to voracious crocodiles.

The Chams sacked the Khmer capital in 1178 and executed its ruler. A Cambodian prince raised new armed forces to rout not only the Chams but also the Vietnamese from Annam to the north of Champa. As King Jayavarman VII, he had the capital rebuilt, its wooden palisades replaced with stone walls. Harnessing a record labor force, perhaps Jayavarman's only feat that the later Pol Pot would applaud, he oversaw the country's largest public works program, ranging from roads and temples to canals and reservoirs. With Champa, most of Laos and part of Thailand conquered, Khmer power had reached its peak by the mid-thirteenth century. Two major evolutionary changes affected Cambodia during this period. One was the growing adoption of the Theravada variant of Buddhism, more austere than the Hindu cults that gave rise to the ornate Angkorean buildings and arts. The second was a weakening of political and military power vis-à-vis its neighbors. The only external threat to Cambodia now lay to the west. Again echoing twentieth century hostility, the Khmers clashed with the Thais, who besieged the Angkorean capital in 1357; sixteen months later, the city-temple complex fell. The Thais, having pulled back, repeated the conquest five decades later. The incursions continued until, sapped by the death of its king and the work of traitors, the Angkorean capital fell for the final time in 1431 after a seven-month-long siege. Cambodia's golden age faded as the Khmers, ceding their greatest architectural creations to the embrace of the jungle and habitation by bats, moved their capital to the southeast. While the Thai sackings, accompanied by the removal of thousands of prisoners to Siam and the turning of the Angkor area into a frequent battleground cannot be ignored as factors, other reasons—political, economic, and natural catastrophe, for example—have been put forward for the move.[4]

Cambodia thereupon entered what historians perhaps inaccurately called its "dark ages," more than four centuries of gradual decline that ended when the country traded its independence for colonial domination to avoid absorption by Siam and Vietnam. The kingdom's "stagnation," however, was anything but quiet and uncomplicated. Post-Angkor Cambodia at first remained strong enough to sustain its on-off, seesaw combat with the Thais. If the warfare was nothing new, the shift in economic emphasis at the time was. Agriculture remained vital. However, an increasing percentage of revenue came from commerce—a development underlined by the establishment of the new capitals (they relocated more than once) on major water transportation routes. Since the traditionally self-sufficient Khmers had little experience with trade, foreigners, especially Chinese, quickly filled the void. More modest and short-lived commercial interests were pursued by the Portuguese, British, and Dutch, while the French initially concentrated on missionary work.

Europe's first direct introduction to Cambodia came in the sixteenth century with the visit of a Portuguese friar. Contact then became frequent enough so that, when the Thai threat seemed overwhelming, the current Khmer ruler felt he could turn to the newcomers for help. Portugal, already overextended abroad, could do nothing. Expansion-hungry Spain eagerly stepped forward, in the process introducing firearms into Cambodian history. Addled by the Asian country's internally confused state, however, the Spaniards so thoroughly mishandled affairs that by the time the door was slammed on them in 1603, Cambodia was a vassal state of Siam. Fifteen years later, with the Thais busy fighting the Burmese to their own west, the Khmers ousted their invaders and declared independence anew. The Cambodians and the Thais were still at loggerheads when the Vietnamese reappeared on the scene. Viewing the Khmers as barbarians ripe for civilization and colonization, they began to squeeze Cambodia from the southeast. Before long, turning Khmer internal strife to their advantage, Vietnam gobbled up what had once been the lower Chenla states, including present-day Ho Chi Minh City. Civil wars and invasions had laid the country low by the end of the eighteenth century. Cambodia's days as a significant Southeast Asian commercial center were over, and the nation fell into a more than seventeen-decade period of isolation, dominated by its neighbors.

While Khmer royalty, split into pro-Vietnamese and pro-Thai factions, squabbled over succession to the throne, Cambodia's traditional enemies gnawed away at the hapless kingdom's edges. In the second half of the eighteenth century, and again during the 1830s, the Vietnamese and the Siamese were at each others' throats as well, with the Khmers caught in between. In 1845, Vietnam and Siam compromised by placing Cambodia under their "joint protection." It was a case of two foxes biding their time with one rooster before one or the other pounced on it. The new Khmer king, Ang Duong, adopted a modus operandi that later would be used by his great-great-grandson, Norodom Sihanouk, against the United States and Vietnam. The ruler walked a tightrope between his neighbors, careful to give neither an excuse for further aggression. It had been an ignominious slide from most powerful Southeast Asian kingdom to buffer state at the mercy of peoples it had once bested.[5]

The multifaceted, often contradictory aspects of Cambodian culture had become firmly anchored by the end of the Angkor period. Military conquest as a foundation of the kingdom left a heritage of warrior qualities, real or imagined, to inspire national strength and character. The foundation, however, had the self-inflicted flaw of self-defeating high-level divisiveness. Where the nation's neighbors once had offered potential for expansion, they now posed a threat to survival. During the ensuing years, foreign influence continued as military, political, and economic necessities. Domination by and payment of tribute to Vietnam and Siam were followed by occupation and rule under the French and the Japanese. Not inclined to engage in business activities and lacking a middle class, the Khmers grew to rely on the Chinese as merchants and bankers and on the Vietnamese as craftsmen and small businessmen. This led to a fear of "cultural extinction," which, coupled with fantasies of Angkorean greatness (dormant until aroused, ironically, by the French), ultimately bred distrust, resentment, nationalism, and xenophobia. The absence of internationally recognized modern accomplishments was compensated for by, in the words of a Khmer scholar, "chauvinistic belief in the superiority of Cambodian culture." The seeds of their ultimate expression would bloom in the Khmer Rouge killing fields, with Pol Pot boasting, "If our people can build Angkor, they are capable of anything."

A religio-political concept of god-king (the revered mortal source of military and moral strength) was bequeathed by Angkor, whereas a more flexible and practical system of national administration would have been more desirable to deal with both internal and external challenges. There existed, in essence, two classes: the few in power, with the royal family at the top, and those without power. There were no political, professional, or social groups like those associated with the Western middle class. As the center of all authority and mediator with the gods, the king was the people's paternal protector (hence the *varman,* meaning "armor" or "protection," common as the suffix of Angkorean kings' names). Where national loyalty existed, it became unquestionably identified with whoever was in power; the question of subservience to the more powerful, of trading obedience for protection, became entrenched. It did not matter that various factions within the royal families frequently connived against each other, allying themselves with the Vietnamese or the Thais to retain or grab power. While belief in the king's divine power ebbed in the cities, the rural population relied on it as a distant stabilizer to keep their everyday living "decent." This accounts to a great degree for the general lack of enthusiasm shown for the nation's subsequent conversion from monarchy to republic. It also underscores the impact on the average Khmer of Sihanouk's 1970 alignment with the Khmer Rouge.

The system, with its sharp delineation of social status and urban-rural differences, also left an unbridged chasm and stoked hostility between the city dwellers and the more numerous farmers. The latter, as long as they paid their taxes, received the protection of a remote government and were allowed to subsist undisturbed (as long as peace reigned) in virtual detachment from the concerns of the capital or the nation. The gap between urban advantages and rural poverty endemic to ancient societies widened with the country's exposure to Western influences, felt largely in the cities. The Khmer leadership's failure to integrate various parts of the nation, ethnically as well as socially and economically, resulted in a lack of collective social responsibility.

Religion, more of a life philosophy and a moderating social force than a simple form of worship, was and remains a key factor in Cambodian culture. After the family, Buddhism is the center of the rural community. Not only did each town have its own temple, but until the 1970–75 war most of the young men temporarily went into the monkhood before settling down. While Buddhism superimposed itself on the worship of Hindu deities and the ancient belief in ancestral spirits, and in fact became somewhat diluted by them, it did not eliminate them. On the here-and-now level, the average Khmer's fate was placed in the hands of supernatural occult powers, on spirits and astral influences.

The result, a search for protection by supernatural as well as by human rulers, was an odd mixture. During the 1970s conflict, for example, a Buddhist leader led a largely Buddhist army. Yet he was swayed by mystical aspects of ancient Angkor, relying to an incredible degree on guidance from seers and priests, and his soldiers went into battle wearing magical tattoos and carrying amulets and potions to make them invulnerable to enemy bullets. As a 1980s White House occupant demonstrated, however, Cambodian leaders were not the only ones to turn to an astrologer to enhance decision making. Where the beneficent tenets of religion clashed with the basic political and economic challenges of everyday life that created dishonest or antisocial acts, Cambodia is little different from other countries. The difference has been one of degree.

Corruption is an aspect of all multilayered societies. Cambodia's is a precolonial inheritance. In ancient times, officials made up for a lack of salary by siphoning wealth from people and land under their control. Bribes became the rule. French attempts to change this only added sophistication and new means to continue the old ways. The population accepted corrupt practices as part of its recognition of the omnipotence of its rulers and the existent patron-client arrangement. Cambodia's corruption level, however, became suicidal, where common sense and survival instincts were overwhelmed by greedy rationalization and spurious justification. At the higher levels, royal family members accepted all manner of remuneration for favors granted. The future leader of the Khmer Republic opportunistically sold rice to and received payoffs from the North Vietnamese while at the same time suppressing Khmer Communists. It therefore seemed only natural for even those with minimal power to divert what little they could. City clerks assured a service in return for financial consideration. Simple soldiers set up roadblocks to charge travelers a toll payable in riels or goods. What Cambodian leaders refused to accept was the basic fact that everything has a limit.

A nation is the product of its experiences. Each adopts a philosophical veneer determined by events, beliefs, educational levels, and technological developments, to name but four factors. Cambodia has been called a "gentle land"—optimism with a feeling of "all will be well," the face seen by most visitors, the smiles that welcomed the Khmers Rouges into Phnom Penh in 1975. However, this surface is easily roiled by violence and callousness, especially toward those viewed as enemies, reminding one that the "gentle land's" past has been an extremely violent and unstable one. A workable conflict resolution process has yet to arise; as Cambodia's recent past has shown, the use of power or a withdrawal have been the usual reactions to conflict. This situation, of course, is not unique to Cambodia, as events in the Balkans and elsewhere have so graphically demonstrated.

The Cambodian culture has tended to make the individual, especially the rural dweller, a conservative and a fatalist who, although affable and sociable, avoids risks and confrontations, often concealing contention or resentment.

The Khmers have been described as nationalistically independent, concerned with appearances and social standing, and, in context of the latter, generous. Although aggression may not be part of the individual Khmer's makeup, this trait has been aroused and manipulated by leaders playing on deep-seated, history-tied fears, needs, and prejudices. A striking example was provided by the 1970–75 war in the contrasting handling of troops by Pol Pot and by Lon Nol that contributed to the Khmer Rouge victory. Both, however, effectively aroused latent aggression that led to the mass killing of Vietnamese. If folklore is any indication of national character, it is enlightening to note that Cambodia's ancient tales, often humorous, do not tout dramatic heroes like those common to European, American, and Japanese storytelling. The Khmers tell of animals and simple people using their wits to survive and get the better of other, usually more powerful, characters, the type found in many Western fairy tales.[6]

CHAPTER TWO

The French Connection

KING ANG DUONG FEARED THAT HIS KINGDOM of Cambodia was doomed to eventual extinction at the hands of Siam and, especially, Vietnam, and he himself felt threatened by internal usurpers. The only salvation appeared to be, once again, turning to Europe. A secret letter from the king to Emperor Napoleon III in 1853 opened the door to diplomatic relations with France. The door abruptly closed because of Gallic ineptness and Thai pressure on the Khmer ruler. However, the French, outmaneuvered by their British rivals on the Asian subcontinent, were determined to get their share of the Far East's reported untapped wealth. Their interest was heightened by the travels of naturalist Henri Mouhot, who called the rediscovered Angkor ruins "an architectural achievement which perhaps has not and never will have an equal in the world."

France, citing Vietnam's persecution of its Catholic converts as justification, moved first against Cambodia's eastern neighbor. In mid-1862, the French acquired southeastern Vietnam, including Saigon. Just over a year later, in a treaty forcefully concluded with a wavering King Norodom (his father, Ang Duong, died in 1860), the French emperor consented to convert his "rights of suzerainty (given over by the Vietnamese) over the kingdom of Cambodia into a protectorate." In 1867, Siam renounced all control over Cambodia in exchange for the two western provinces of Battambang and Angkor (now Siem Reap). The Khmers finally were free of Vietnamese and Thai oversight thanks to the French, but the cost was high—their independence and four provinces, two in the east already having been added to French Vietnam. For better or for worst, France was to reshape Cambodia's military, political, economic, educational, and social institutions in ways that would change the nation forever.

Gunboat diplomacy, overcoming mid-1880s rebellion that at one point even threatened the capital, rode roughshod over the Khmer way of life and tightened French control. In October 1887, Cambodia and Vietnam became part of an Indochina Union; Laos was added after being wrested from the Siamese six years later. *Résidents* (local governors) reporting to a *résident superieur* (resident general), who in turn answered to the Union's governor-general, were posted in the provincial capitals to assure that French wishes prevailed. Although the king had become a virtual figurehead, Cambodia's new masters were taking few chances. When ailing, opium-addicted Norodom died, they installed the more pliant Sisowath branch of the royal family on the throne. Frenchmen occupied the key positions in the burgeoning bureaucracy.

France, disappointed to find that Cambodia lacked abundant natural resources, nevertheless decided to exploit those that did exist. They transformed the country's primitive self-sufficient economy into one dependent on the outside world. To the growth and export of rice was added that of corn. Toward the end of the nineteenth century, rubber trees from South America were introduced and over the years responded to the growing demand for rubber with increased acreage. Roads were built and a railroad soon connected Phnom Penh with Battambang and Siam. These changes, in turn, affected settlement patterns and encouraged urban development. The French presence also brought peace and hygienic methods. The population rose from just under a million in 1863 to more than four million in 1950. Further demographic changes came as Vietnamese migrated to Cambodia to work in the plantations, to become fishermen, to open small businesses, and to join the government as lower- and middle-level functionaries. The Vietnamese influx was owing largely to the initiative of the French, who considered the Khmers indolent and incompetent.

In 1907, the French pressured Thai King Chulalongkorn to return the rice-growing provinces of Battambang and Angkor to Cambodia. As part of its cultural *mission civilisatrice,* rationalizing its search for power and wealth as a noble civilizing mission, France sent scholars to translate Cambodia's royal chronicle (the only locally written history), bring the Angkor ruins to the light of day, and explore the country. This would prove, for the French, to be a Pandora's box that produced Khmer nationalism, a revival of the glory of Angkor later warped to become inspiration for Lon Nol's grandiose and Pol Pot's twisted dreams. The lopsided modernization France brought to Cambodia, like that of other colonial conquests, retained a village-based economy. Within that economy, however, the taxes levied on the Khmers were the highest per capita in all of Indochina despite the fact that their country received considerably less developmental attention than less easygoing Vietnam.[1]

The Khmers—allowed to keep their symbolic royalty, inured by centuries of often harsh domination and generally uneducated—moved into the twentieth century with stoicism. But, while French rule appeared to be relatively unchallenged,[2] the seeds of nationalism were germinating beneath the surface among the educated urban minority. In 1936, the first Khmer language newspaper was established by a Khmer Krom (member of southern Vietnam's Cambodian minority) judge named Son Ngoc Thanh, who would play a significant role in the country's subsequent history. Not surprisingly, the newspaper was called *Angkor Wat*. Any assumption of a lasting French colonial presence was shattered by World War II.

Japan's desire to become the leading power in Asia was abetted by the 1940 defeat of France, whose overseas armed forces were left demoralized and weakened. Bolstered by a treaty of friendship with Thailand (whose name was changed from Siam in 1939) and the support of Nazi Germany, Tokyo easily obtained the use of Indochinese transportation centers for its military arms. By the summer of 1941, about eight thousand Japanese troops were shouldering aside their French counterparts in Cambodia alone. Thailand, exploiting the situation to reclaim land it had lost earlier, sent its Japanese-trained and equipped army across the borders of Cambodia and Laos. U.S.-built Curtiss Hawk H75N fighters flown by Thai pilots overwhelmed French air defenses. France's ground forces, whose loyalty since the defeat in Europe was to the pro-Nazi Vichy regime, were pushed back. Only at sea were the defenders victorious. In a January 1941 battle off Chang Island in the Gulf of Thailand, French naval units led by the light cruiser *Lamotte-Picquet* battered the aggressors, who lost their two battleships. Whereupon Tokyo stepped in with the smile of the mediator. As a result, Battambang and Siem Reap Provinces (except for the Angkor area) reverted to Thailand, and Cambodian King Monivong turned his back on everyone and everything French. Thailand, alternately collaborating with, playing dumb for, and betraying the Japanese, continued to display the talents that kept it the only country in that part of Asia to have permanently retained its independence.

In Cambodia, needing its troops for the great battleground of the Pacific war, Japan allowed the acquiescent French to play the colonial masters while at the same time encouraging Khmer national feelings. When the king died in April 1941, the French selected as Monivong's successor his shy eighteen-year-old nephew, who appeared pliable and free of independent ideas. Norodom Sihanouk went from a *lycée* (secondary school) in Saigon to the throne in Phnom Penh's royal palace. If he needed any reminder of where the real power lay, the youth received his crown in October 1941 from Admiral Jean Decoux, the governor-general, who let Sihanouk know that his great-grand-father also had been crowned by a French naval officer. The new monarch took as his crown-name Norodom Sihanouk Varman, meaning Norodom the Protected (by Buddha) Victorious Lion. Meanwhile, archaeologists contin-ued to work on the Angkor sites, an area that for centuries had remained a Buddhist sanctuary. Emphasis at the ruins, since 1908 overseen by the *Ecole Française d'Extrême-Orient* (the area-specialized French government research institution), now had shifted from studying artwork to investigating the Angkorean way of life. Excavation began at Angkor Thom, the Great City, only in 1944.

With the ebbing of their fortunes of war, the Japanese acted on their needs of rallying the Indochinese to their cause and assuring that the French did not turn their guns on them. On March 9, 1945, French forces in Indochina, except for a few thousand who fled, were disarmed and interned by the Japa-nese; the colonial administration was abolished. Cambodia was encouraged to declare its independence from France and join Japan's Greater East Asia Co-Prosperity Sphere. Four days after this tour de force, King Sihanouk an-nounced Cambodia's independence and promised to cooperate with the cur-rent occupiers of his country. Son Ngoc Thanh, who had sought asylum in Japan after the French quelled a major 1942 anticolonial demonstration he was involved in, returned from Tokyo to become foreign minister. The day the war ended, thirty-eight-year-old Thanh was promoted to prime minister. French efforts to supplant the forty-seven-letter ancient alphabet with a Ro-man one and to replace the Buddhist lunar calendar with the Gregorian one were overturned. Street names were changed and national holidays were cre-ated. The whiff of freedom, albeit a limited one, lasted several months. The short period was heady (patriotic gatherings and the formation of political groups) but not trouble-free (Khmer-Vietnamese clashes and an abortive antiroyalist coup in August 1945).[3]

The British-led Allied Land Forces in Cambodia unit arriving in Phnom Penh in early October 1945 was tasked with taking "command of all Japanese forces in the area, . . . maintaining law and order, . . . safeguarding all Allied nationals, ensuring the stability of the Cambodian government (in accordance with a French directive), and disarming all Vietnamese." A source of Allied fear was the Viet Minh, Communist-led Vietnamese nationalists who already were resisting the European return and infiltrating both Cambodia and Laos. Two French army companies shortly followed to reestablish their nation's supremacy. French Far East commander General Philippe Leclerc flew into Cambodia on October 15 to arrest, with a simple nod reinforced by his bodyguard, Son Ngoc Thanh for "collaboration with the Japanese." Sihanouk, feelings split between dislike of foreign domination and hostility toward Thanh (whom he connected with the August coup attempt), made sure he was away on a three-day pilgrimage when his prime minister was arrested and sent into exile. France seemed ready to pick up where it had left off in 1940.

Times had changed, however. Far from reclaiming the past, France found itself now concentrating on simply holding on. To the east of Cambodia, the French and the Viet Minh were engaged in the First Vietnam War. A pattern was set for the future as Ho Chi Minh's infiltrators began to organize a Khmer People's Liberation Army. On the opposite frontier, the heterogeneous Khmer Issarak (Free Khmer) guerrilla movement backed by Thailand set up a government-in-exile with a base in Battambang Province. Before long, the east-west nationalist elements were cooperating in an effort to oust both Sihanouk and the French. The latter made a few concessions in a futile attempt to fend off Khmer nationalism: political parties could be formed for the first time, elections to a consultative assembly were held, a constitution was drafted, and an indigenous military force was created. At the same time that they eroded colonial hold, these developments also set a precedent for weakening the nation's traditional royal authority.

Cambodia's post–World War II army had a modest beginning. A single battalion overseen by French officers was approved in November 1945 and set up soon afterward. On the first day of 1946, an officer candidate school was opened to train both potential officers and noncommissioned officers. The Franco-Cambodian Modus Vivendi and the Franco-Khmer Military Convention of January and November 1946, respectively, more clearly defined the existence, organization, and mission of the new Cambodian army. As an "autonomous state within the French Union," Cambodia was required to use its military units to help defend the rest of Indochina in addition to protecting itself. Although the king, acting through a defense ministry, was acknowledged as the army's "supreme commander," the French retained a controlling hand. The army's growth paralleled that of the Viet Minh and Khmer Issarak threats. By the end of 1946, Khmer forces numbered approximately one thousand men organized into two rifle battalions and three thousand in a constabulary. Over the next two years, the hard-pressed French permitted the addition of two thousand troops. Cambodian soldiers participated directly in France's Indochina war.

In 1947, under French and American pressure and desiring to join the United Nations, Thailand returned Battambang and Siem Reap Provinces to the Khmers. At the end of 1949, as its unending war further drained France's resources and will, a treaty advanced Cambodia from its "autonomous" status to what Sihanouk called "50 percent independence." While the treaty did give the Khmers greater say in their military, political, economic, and judicial affairs, the French continued to hold decisive control. In 1950, most non-Communist nations, including the United States, were able to extend diplomatic recognition to Cambodia as an "independent state in the French Union."

The 1950s saw the emergence of Cambodia as a player on the international scene and the setting of the stage for the tragic drama of the killing fields. At the beginning of the decade, not unjustifiably given the blinding glare of the East-West confrontation, Southeast Asian nationalism and communism merged into one in the eyes of the cold warriors of both sides. America, itself sucked into the black hole of the Korean War, formalized its aid to the French in Indochina. Within three or four years, the United States was paying for about 80 percent of France's war effort against Ho Chi Minh's communist nationalists. Sihanouk, meanwhile, proved to be far from the harmless colonial puppet everyone expected. He had gained enough confidence to exploit skillfully the post–World War II situation and the character of his people to increase his power. In June 1952, he staged what was called a "royal coup d'état" and began a Royal Mandate period of direct rule that lasted until February 1955. He suspended the constitution and even led army operations against the Khmer Issarak in western Cambodia. Sihanouk's next step was to nudge the French toward the exit door.

In February 1953, Sihanouk fertilized the seed of an approximately nine-month-long "royal crusade for independence," which included a round-the-world trip. Offered little more than lunch by the French president, the king went to North America. There, the U.S. secretary of state warned him that independence would mean a Communist takeover. John F. Dulles's pontificating and President Dwight D. Eisenhower's standoffishness exacerbated the Cambodian leader's resentment of what he considered America's smugness and uncaring attitude. Sihanouk came home in May, taking his bruised ego into self-imposed exile near the ruins of Angkor under the protection of a local commander named Lon Nol.

The retreat-return tactic was one Sihanouk often would use successfully until it finally backfired in 1970. When major crises occurred, he would leave Phnom Penh, usually for France, and let the domestic situation fester. Then, when his opponents finally "saw the light" and came around to his way of thinking, be would return to take charge once more. Between Sihanouk's lobbying efforts, changing times that assured public support for self-determination, and France's falling fortunes in Indochina, the seed planted earlier by the king finally brought forth the bloom of independence. Sihanouk, self-proclaimed "father and first citizen of the Khmer nation," returned to the capital in triumph to accept the transfer of political power from the French. The highlight of Cambodia's Independence Day, November 9, 1953, was the parade of colonial troops leaving Phnom Penh. The last of the French forces, engaged in combat in eastern Cambodia, departed in late 1954 as a result of the Geneva Conference.[4]

France's colonial army was replaced by the 17,000-strong *Forces Armées Royales Khmères* (FARK, the Royal Khmer Armed Forces). Once again, as Viet Minh and Khmer Issarak elements launched attacks, Sihanouk personally commanded a counteroffensive, this time in the northeastern part of Cambodia. An independent FARK conducted its first unilateral operation in March 1954, when a Viet Minh battalion speared out of Laos to overrun a French-led Khmer unit. The invaders then moved deeper into Cambodia. This Vietnamese Communist advance finally was stemmed by a FARK counteroffensive in July. The Geneva Conference that month resulted in an end to hostilities, an amnesty decree for the Khmer Issarak insurgents, and the transfer of the remaining Cambodian military elements under French control to FARK. The latter action, along with national mobilization and conscription of males between the ages of fifteen and thirty-five, raised FARK's strength to nearly 47,000 men. A number of factors, however, led to a drastic military manpower cutback by the end of the year.

Several major players besides Sihanouk were establishing their roles during this period. Bespectacled Son Ngoc Thanh came back from exile in 1951. If the king thought him neutralized or the French wrote him off as a "spent force," they were wrong. An antiroyalty, anticolonial iconoclast who had American support, Thanh quickly dropped out of sight to join Khmer Issarak holdouts. Labeled by Sihanouk first as a communist and then as a traitor beholden to "his CIA patrons," he took charge of a faction of the splintered and fading Issaraks called the Khmer Serei (also meaning Free Khmer). Thanh's ambition to establish and use a united resistance to climb to national power, however, never would be realized.

Two conservatives had assured themselves key parts in the developing drama by the mid-1950s: Lon Nol as army chief of staff and Sisowath Sirik Matak as minister of national defense and foreign affairs. Born on November 13, 1913, of Khmer-Chinese parentage in Prey Veng Province, the dark-skinned Lon Nol entered civil service after completing his secondary school education in Saigon and early allied himself with the king. He transferred to the army as a lieutenant to fight the Viet Minh. Lon Nol would become defense minister in 1960 and, the following year, would attain the rank of lieutenant general. Aloof and polished Sirik Matak, born in 1914 and Sihanouk's cousin, was a prince in the rival Sisowath branch of the royal family. He and Lon Nol became friends at the Saigon *lycée,* where both were enrolled. Embarking on a civil service career, he had occupied a number of military and civilian government positions.

Personalities far to the other side of the political spectrum were active as well. These had the goal of a communist Cambodia; only their approaches differed. In eastern Cambodia, one arm (the People's Revolutionary Party of Kampuchea) of Ho Chi Minh's three-tentacled Indochina Communist Party was forming a Khmer guerrilla force under Vietnamese tutelage. This group was expanding its influence (even to the point of collecting taxes from Khmer peasants) and laying the foundation for a Hanoi-dominated Cambodia. Other leftists, such as Khieu Samphan, overtly were supporters of the king. Still others were students at the *Cité universitaire* in far-off Paris, where communism was fashionable in intellectual circles. This group was straining the teachings of Marx and Lenin through the sieve of its unique concept of a Kampuchean Utopia.

Among these radical students were Saloth Sar and Ieng Sary, both of whom joined the French Communist Party. The duo, with a handful of Khmer educators and bureaucrats, would create the most extremist element of Cambodia's Communists. Although touting a credo built on a rural foundation, neither had experienced extensive manual labor or national leadership. They became related by marriage when Sar wed Khieu Ponnary and Sary married Ponnary's younger sister, Khieu Thirith. Both women were to play vital roles in the radical communist movement. Sar left France to join the rebels in eastern Cambodia and enroll in the Indochina Communist Party. He was to remain a mystery figure to the world until his emergence after the 1970–75 war as Pol Pot. Ironically, Sar's best friend at junior high school in the early 1940s was Lon Non, the younger brother of Lon Nol, who would wield considerable power before fatally entrusting his life to his former school buddy. Sar would be no more flexible or compassionate with those of his Communist comrades who had received their training from the North Vietnamese.[5]

CHAPTER THREE

The Sihanouk Years

FOR TWO MONTHS IN MID-1954, delegates of Cambodia, Laos, and the two Vietnam factions met in Geneva, Switzerland, with representatives of the United States, Soviet Union, People's Republic of China, Great Britain, and France (just defeated in its Vietnam War) to discuss "a lasting peace in Indochina." The result was four documents: individual cease-fire agreements for Cambodia, Laos, and Vietnam, and an unsigned final declaration. The conferees agreed, according to Chapter II, Article II, of the July 20 Cessation of Hostilities in Vietnam agreement, to a "simultaneous cease-fire throughout Indochina." As regards Cambodia, the Communist People's Army of Vietnam (PAVN, also known as the North Vietnamese Army, or NVA) forces, including several battalions that Sihanouk's modest army had been unable to dislodge after their invasion in April, were to get out within ninety days. Khmer rebels were to be demobilized within thirty days.

While going nearly the full route toward avoiding military alliances and the stationing of foreign troops on its territory, Cambodia was allowed to "seek whatever military aid it desired" despite North Vietnam's strong objection. Sihanouk insisted on the clause because he already had requested direct American aid. General elections were to be held in 1955 under the watchful gaze of a newly created, multipurpose International Control Commission (ICC) consisting of Canadian, Indian, and Polish representatives. The Geneva Conference marked the end of French rule in Indochina.

That Cambodia emerged from the Geneva sessions with a unity denied to Vietnam and Laos was owing to both Khmer stubbornness and U.S. backing. A significant insight into the Cambodian attitude and its overreaching aspirations was provided by Khmer delegate Tep Phan's comments about "Cambodian lands in South Vietnam" on the final declaration's statement regarding Vietnamese territorial integrity. Phan said that the declaration provision "does not imply the abandonment of such legitimate rights and interests as Cambodia might assert as regards certain regions of South Vietnam."[1]

The last of the French and most of the Viet Minh forces left Cambodia by October 1954. Accompanying the latter to northern Vietnam, which the Geneva agreements separated from southern Vietnam along the 17th parallel pending the never-held elections, were the majority of the estimated two thousand members of the People's Revolutionary Party of Kampuchea. Other Cambodian Communists, including Pol Pot, secretly returned to Phnom Penh to work for their candidates in the upcoming elections. They felt that the Soviet, Chinese, and Vietnamese Communists, each with their own agenda, had betrayed them by compromising at Geneva.

Norodom Sihanouk, born October 31, 1922, the son of King Norodom Suramarit and Queen Kossamak Nearireath, was a modern version of his Angkorean antecedents. He had a regal view of his people as "children" who "know nothing about politics, and they care less."[2] All they needed, he believed, was an "authoritarian, conservative, paternalistic form of government." Capable of bonhomie and outwardly warm, he also demonstrated callousness and a cynical view of human nature. He condoned illegalities, including violence, when doing so enhanced his power. Foreigners generally saw him as a short, chubby, and amiable multilingual nationalist who womanized, played a hot saxophone, and made grade-B movies. His 1945 marriage to a cousin ended in divorce when, in the prince's words, "she got fed up with my unfaithful behavior." He married Monique Izzi, whose father was European, in 1952. Monique, her mother, and her half-brother would subsequently be accused of playing a key role in black market and illicit land sale activities. Sihanouk was egocentric, mercurial, and emotional, and interpreted Angkorean grandeur according to his preconceived notions. He was, in fact, a dynastic ruler in the classic tradition, the ultimate source of all power in his kingdom. Few took the time to recognize that, as a calculated ploy or merely to avoid confrontation, he had a way of telling most people what they wanted to hear, a trait common to successful politicians.

Admirers saw Sihanouk as the betrayed patriot, the founder of modern Cambodia, who kept his homeland out of the Vietnam maelstrom for more than fifteen years. The charisma he displayed as he frequently moved among his people, coupled with the national concept of god-king, made him the idol of the majority of the population, those inhabiting the countryside. Ever hypersensitive to criticism, he once said that his countrymen "venerate me as a divinity and regard my character as sacred . . . To insult me, to wound me, is to strike at the Cambodian nation." Among many of the educated city dwellers (the 10 percent who spoke French), however, he was an anachronism. Chhang Song, later information chief for the Lon Nol government, recognized Sihanouk's talents but concluded that "he was not a good manager of the country . . . he dragged the country to its demise."[3] In any case, by the mid-1950s the king, braced by French advisers, had evolved from insecure schoolboy to monarch who, apparently convinced that he had gained his nation's independence single-handedly, felt he could run the country as he wished. He was willing to do whatever was necessary, to seek accommodation with anyone, as long as it helped him and Cambodia.

Although Cambodia was, after World War II, a constitutional monarchy, imprecisions in the 1947 constitution allowed Sihanouk to rule without parliamentary supervision. To preserve legality, he tried and failed to change the constitution. Therefore, in March 1955, he shocked everyone by abdicating in favor of his father. He did this, he said, to avoid being reduced to a monarch "called upon to countersign decrees" produced by others. Rid of his ceremonial title but retaining all of its prerogatives, *Samdech* (Prince) Sihanouk now was free to enter the political arena. The prince's first significant move was establishment of the *Sangkum Reastr Niyum* (People's Socialist Community), an "assemblage of the people" designed to replace a party system by absorbing or smothering opposing political parties.

Sihanouk's confidence as he entered the September 1955 elections was not misplaced. His *Sangkum* won all ninety-one seats in the assembly with 83 percent of the votes. It was to be the last "freely contested" election until 1993; both, though, were marked by what politely can be termed irregularities. Using manipulative tactics that ranged from clever political juggling and cajolery to threats and violence, as well as capitalizing on his general popularity, Sihanouk achieved a virtual monopoly of power. Those who opposed him and were repressed to seethe underground he dubbed *Khmers Bleus* (Blue Khmers), if they were rightists, and *Khmers Rouges* (K.R., Red Khmers), if they were on the political left. The prince later narrowed his use of Khmers Rouges to denote the followers of Pol Pot, calling the pro-Hanoi element Khmers Viet Minh. He also adopted three constants that dominated his thinking, the convictions that (1) he was not responsible for his country's problems, (2) only he could solve these problems, and (3) "all the misery of Cambodia comes from the United States."

The prince's loudly heralded embracing of neutralism and his playing of one side against the other recognized one overriding fact of life: his rule—in effect his nation's peace and prosperity—was at the mercy of his neighbors, on one hand, and of the major Cold War powers, on the other. An agreement with the People's Republic of China (PRC), wary of Vietnamese nationalism, brought in capital for commercial projects. Another with the Soviet Union garnered industrial equipment, technicians, and a hospital. Still another with the United States reaped military aid, agricultural and road-building programs, and rice when the local harvest failed. The try-to-please-everyone policy ultimately pleased no one. Cambodia had begun a tightrope balancing act that Sihanouk's artful skills and other nations' more pressing priorities would merely prolong until the inevitable fall.

Sihanouk's ambitious program of economic, financial, educational, and health care reforms outpaced the country's capabilities. Nationalization of banks and international trade in 1963 replaced foreign investments with corrupt state monopolies. Agriculture, initially prospering, slumped in 1964 as peasant taxes were diverted to the cities. The 1958, 1962, and 1966 elections were one-party travesties. Expanding educational facilities fostered unrealistic hopes among the rural poor and idealistic resentment among the urban young. Despite these corrosive undercurrents, the decade ending in 1965 marked what more than one observer called Cambodia's modern golden age. The nation was at peace. The *samdech euv* (prince father or papa, as he commonly was called), visiting his "children" or addressing them on the radio in his high-pitched, singsong voice, had the support of his silent majority. The questionable goal was a nonconfrontational, authoritarian status quo.[4]

Cambodia's road to the killing fields of the mid-1970s began at the juncture of two other paths—one the centuries-old ambitions of neighboring states, the other the small nation-crunching competition of the East-West giants. U.S. interest in Cambodia grew from the fear of Communist expansion. Whether the threat in Southeast Asia was viewed as a monolithic or a nationalistic communism was deemed irrelevant. It was the question of police state communism, made possible by the two largest Communist countries, trying to take over an area of the world believed by the Western democracies to be of strategic importance. Had not the North Vietnamese leader studied in the Soviet Union and served as a Comintern agent in China? And wasn't he one of the founders of the French Communist Party? Furthermore, like Stalin in Russia, Ho Chi Minh had conducted a purge, killing and imprisoning thousands, only a decade after taking over the Vietnamese nationalist movement by convincing his opponents he had American support.[5]

In mid-1955, President Ngo Dinh Diem broadcast his refusal to discuss nationwide elections with Ho Chi Minh's Communists, stating that his Republic of Vietnam "did not sign the Geneva agreements. We are not bound in any way by these agreements." With further conflict on the horizon and the last French troops withdrawing in 1956, American advisory groups took up the task of training and equipping the South Vietnamese. Meanwhile, cadres left behind in violation of the Geneva agreements when the Communists regrouped to North

Vietnam built up the political-military movement its opponents called the Viet Cong (V.C.). The V.C. launched an escalating insurgency against the Diem regime. A sign of things to come, the heaviest concentration of insurgents was along the Cambodian border, where the terrain favored guerrilla warfare and from where the Communists could cross the sparsely-populated frontier to find sanctuary if necessary. In mid-1959, North Vietnam took steps to turn the insurgency into a war. Group 599 was activated to develop the increasingly sophisticated system of supply lines called the Truong Son (High Mountains) Trail, popularly known as the Ho Chi Minh Trail. As existing paths were enlarged and supplemented in Laos and Cambodia, infiltration of men and supplies into South Vietnam began in earnest. A second unit, Group 579, was created to smuggle personnel and goods into the south by sea. Hanoi would decide to move regular army units into South Vietnam in 1964.[6]

No more than a person can remain unaffected when a neighbor's house is ablaze could a reluctant Cambodia avoid becoming embroiled in the Second Vietnam War. Sihanouk's efforts to retain control and maintain neutrality resembled the awkward jumps of someone trying to avoid rain puddles. He gladly entered into a May 1955 agreement for U.S. aid—which was to total $392.6 million between 1955 and November 1963. The military portion of this money comprised 30 percent of the small country's defense budget by the time Sihanouk cut it off.[7] A thirty-man American Military Assistance Advisory Group (MAAG)—initially part of the MAAG Indochina Command established to provide advisor support to Vietnam, Laos, and Cambodia—was set up in Phnom Penh "to supervise the distribution and use of equipment." The group established personal contacts with and armed the Khmer army but stopped short of training it. That the French did until 1971.

America apparently hoped to use its assistance to encourage Cambodia's acceptance of protection offered by the Southeast Asia Treaty Organization (SEATO), one of several military pacts initiated by Secretary of State Dulles to contain Communist expansion. At first the *samdech* reacted favorably to the SEATO "umbrella of protection" over Southeast Asia. But, while the prince realized that the greatest threat to his realm was Communism, he believed that North Vietnam would win the war flaring to Cambodia's east. He also thought that the nearby PRC would be the dominant force in Asia after the Vietnam War ended, that the Americans ultimately would pull out. As the Khmer leader told a reporter, "All of Southeast Asia is destined to become Communist. All that I am trying to do is this: when it happens in Cambodia, I want it to happen without breakage." Warned by Prime Minister Jawaharlal Nehru of India against being "too pro-Western," Sihanouk received further pressure while attending the Afro-Asian Bandung Conference in Indonesia. There, in April 1955, Prime Minister Zhou Enlai of China and Foreign Minister Pham Van Dong of North Vietnam let the prince know that they would respect his country's integrity if he "followed a neutral course."[8]

These factors, plus Sihanouk's resentment of American favoritism toward his traditional enemies (Thailand and South Vietnam) and unsubtle pressure to accept the SEATO offer, prompted the prince to tilt into a left-leaning neutrality. In September 1955, Sihanouk assumed his country's premiership. Cambodia was admitted into the United Nations in December. February 1956 saw the first of Sihanouk's visits to Beijing, where he was promised assistance to counterbalance U.S. aid. Four months later, after the signing of an economic assistance pact, the Chinese came through with $22.3 million, their first aid to a non-Communist country. Reversing his initial stand, the prince now formally rejected SEATO's "umbrella of protection." In the months ahead, he added the USSR, Czechoslovakia, and Poland to his new relationships. Neutrality—"noncommitment to a military alliance or ideological bloc"—became Cambodian law in September 1957. All of this served to confirm America's suspicion that Khmer leadership consciously was playing into Communist hands; the Cold War tolerated no middle ground.[9]

The anti-Communist reaction to Sihanouk's left-leaning neutralism started with temporary economic blockades imposed by South Vietnam and Thailand. The former's action deprived Phnom Penh, then Cambodia's sole commercial port, of its vital Mekong River access to the sea. Concurrently, the U.S. Central Intelligence Agency (CIA) increased its funding of Son Ngoc Thanh's two-thousand-strong anti-Sihanouk Khmer Serei group, which had been making an in-country nuisance of itself from a base near the Thai border. Sihanouk, whose book *My War with the CIA* emotionally expressed views he held during his exile years, considered America's first resident ambassador, the very conservative and blunt Robert McClintock, and his chief assistant, Martin Herz, to be "CIA agents."

Early in 1958, the Thais crossed the northern Khmer border to occupy the clifftop tenth-century Preah Vihear temple ruins. More than three years would pass before an International Court of Justice (then called the World Court) decision coaxed the invaders out. To the east, in June 1958, some three thousand South Vietnamese troops sought to cover their 8.5-mile-deep invasion of Cambodia's Stung Treng Province by moving border markers inland. The Vietnamese were to accuse the Khmers of also playing with frontier markers in 1962. With three to four hundred thousand Vietnamese residing in Cambodia and four to five hundred thousand Khmers in South Vietnam, the eastern threat appeared more serious. America's reaction, when Sihanouk complained, was a reminder that U.S.-provided arms were intended for use only against Communists. The prince used this slap to justify granting de jure recognition to Communist China in July 1958. Full diplomatic relations were established the following month when Sihanouk again visited Beijing. A joint declaration signed in August provided for Chinese commercial and industrial assistance in return for Cambodian political support and "respect" for the Chinese community in Cambodia. North Vietnamese violation of Khmer sovereignty still was low-key, though very real, as supply lines and depots grew at the lower end of the Ho Chi Minh Trail. Although the Khmer leader was disturbed, his early complaints to the intruders were mild.[10]

Sihanouk had little success justifying his self-preservation strategy to President Eisenhower and Secretary Dulles during a September–October visit to the United States, where he also twice addressed the UN. The prince returned home under the mistaken impression that, despite their differences, his visit had improved relations between the two countries. In fact, the visit had merely reaffirmed Washington's decision covertly to encourage anti-Sihanouk Khmer dissidents, mainly by financing and channeling their activities. Sam Sary, onetime royal adviser and ambassador, then considered by the State Department as America's "staunchest friend," worked with Thai and South Vietnamese officials, as well as with the ubiquitous Son Ngoc Thanh, to destabilize the prince. When Sihanouk bared what he called the Bangkok Plot, Sary's scheming with Thailand, in January 1959, the forty-two-year-old Sary fled Cambodia. He mysteriously disappeared for good in 1962. Sihanouk suggested that U.S. officials knew about the plot but didn't inform him.

Just as shadowy as Sary was the mystical, skeletal Brigadier General Chhuon Mchulpich, also known as Dap Chhuon. A former Khmer Issarak who defected to Sihanouk, he subsequently became, in turn, governor of Siem Reap Province, interior minister and commander of Military Region IV, headquartered in Siem Reap city. The ambitious Chhuon won points with Washington, Bangkok, and Saigon for his vehement anti-Communism. He ran his region almost as an independent fiefdom and more often than not was at odds with his national leader. While the convoluted details of the so-called Dap Chhuon Affair remain clouded by contradictory accounts and archival secrecy, Chhuon apparently received gold, arms, and communication equipment from Thailand and Vietnam. What better way to undermine the left-tilting Sihanouk regime than to effect the secession of Siem Reap and adjacent provinces to form an anti-Communist "free state"? The festering Siem Reap boil was lanced in late February 1959, when Lon Nol (now wearing the hats of defense minister and army chief of staff) was sent by Sihanouk with two armor-supported battalions to arrest Chhuon before he put his plan into effect. Chhuon, initially acting in an unconcerned manner that suggests Lon Nol's complicity in the conspiracy, fled toward Thailand. He was chased, wounded, and captured, then summarily executed while en route back to Siem Reap. Although Saigon initially denied involvement, two Vietnamese were arrested in Chhuon's villa, which also contained arms and gold bullion. Thailand insisted that its hands were clean.

American intelligence involvement was peripheral, its presence on the scene once more opening it to accusations of initiating action. Aware of and skeptical about Chhuon's ambitious plan, the CIA tried dissuading the plotters from pursuing the affair. Failing to do so, the agency continued to monitor developments. A CIA case officer assigned to the Phnom Penh station in the embassy lent Slat Peou (Chhuon's brother and the Siem Reap representative in the national assembly) a radio to communicate what was going on to the embassy. Slat Peou was arrested and confessed his role. A military court in September sentenced thirteen conspirators to death. Sihanouk reprieved eight and ordered the rest shot. While the prince and others accused America of being behind the scheme, it was the U.S. intelligence agency that talked Premier Field Marshal Sarit Thanarat of Thailand out of invading Cambodia.

In Phnom Penh, anti-U.S. feeling surged. Americans and their Khmer friends were subjected to surveillance and harassment. Sihanouk made the Dap Chhuon incident the centerpiece of *Shadow over Angkor*, one of his three movies shown at Cambodia's first film festival several years later. In it, the prince played the lead. His wife was the romantic costar. Meanwhile, the Soviets did what they could to stoke the *samdech*'s anti-American fire even further. In early 1960, for example, *Blitz*, a Bombay, India, weekly publication consistently used as a Communist propaganda outlet, "exposed" the existence of a letter purportedly written by Sam Sary to Phnom Penh embassy Deputy Chief of Mission Edmund Kellogg. The letter, "proving" U.S. involvement in the Lap Chhuon Affair, was a forgery, clever except for the fact that Kellogg had been transferred elsewhere more than two weeks before the date on the alleged letter.[11]

On August 31, 1959, in the king's bedroom of the royal palace in Phnom Penh, Chief of Protocol Prince Vakrivan began to open a gift. An accompanying card purporting to be from "Micael [*sic*] Baker company [the U.S. firm that engineered the highway between the capital and Sihanoukville]" bore an unsigned wish in French that the "humble gift might give the queen [Kossamak] pleasure." A plastic bomb inside a small lacquered box, "mailed from an American military base in South Vietnam," according to Sihanouk, suddenly exploded, shattering Vakrivan's upper body. The blast, punching a hole in the cement floor, also killed King Suramarit's valet and wounded two others. The royal couple, having gone into the adjoining throne room to receive Prime Minister Son Sann, who had been talking to the prince, were unhurt. They believed Sam Sary, then in Vietnam, was responsible. Sihanouk later expanded the blame to include Son Ngoc Thanh, also in Vietnam at the time, and the CIA. The British Embassy saw the Communists behind the outrage, since they were the only beneficiaries. Sixteen and a half months later, a military court sentenced Phan Vinh Tong, a Cambodia-born Vietnamese former newspaper editor, to death for his role in delivering the bomb to the palace.

At the end of the year, Reath Vath, whom the *samdech* called a Khmer fanatic manipulated by Thanh and the CIA, mingled with a crowd greeting Sihanouk during one of his frequent visits to the provinces. Guards, detaining Vath because of his nervous behavior, found a pistol and a hand grenade on the youth. Violence was directed elsewhere as well. On the night of October 10, 1959, the editor of the Khmer Communist newspaper *Pracheachon,* Nop Bophann, was assaulted in Phnom Penh. He died two days later. The Communists pointed an accusing finger at Lon Nol, who, they said, was acting on the prince's complaints regarding *Pracheachon*'s antigovernment statements.[12]

By the beginning of the new decade, a prison complex at the edge of the capital held more than two thousand political prisoners, the majority accused of participation in the 1959 plots. With his right-wing opponents thus neutralized for years to come, Sihanouk now was more firmly than ever in control. Sixty-four-year-old King Suramarit's death in April 1960 was followed by a farcical national referendum that, in one historian's words, "in effect dismantled Cambodia's thousand-year-old monarchy." In June, after a staged constitutional crisis, the Sangkum-dominated national assembly made Sihanouk chief of state "during the vacancy of the throne." In late September, his political horizons outwardly untroubled, Sihanouk revisited the United States. He attended a UN session and met with President Eisenhower. A month later, Lon Nol, elevated to prime minister, traveled to Washington to discuss American aid and Cambodia's differences with Thailand.

Further indications of improved relations came with America's support for Cambodian claims to the Thai-occupied Preah Vihear temple when hearings opened in Holland in April 1961. Then, on August 27 of that year, the arrival of the mine sweepers *Excel* and *Leader* marked the U.S. Navy's first visit to Cambodia. Months later, Phnom Penh accepted delivery from America of four T-37 Tweet jet trainers and two transport aircraft. A half dozen *Aviation Royale Khmère* (ARK, the Cambodian air force) pilots returned from training in the United States. Cambodia about this time also received four Fouga CM 170 Magister jet trainers from France. Internally, during a roughly three-year period, *Samdech* Sihanouk cultivated popular approval while deftly continuing to pound down potential opposition. But if the lid temporarily had been placed on the political pot, the military pot holding the war in Vietnam was boiling over.[13]

Fighting along the eastern frontier increased in intensity as the Vietnamese Communist presence in Cambodia grew larger. In September 1961, in one of a series of such clashes, two Khmer battalions and local militiamen battled several hundred intruders. The Vietnamese Communists were driven back out at the cost of eight Cambodian dead. Most of the frontier action, however, was between the Communists and the U.S.–South Vietnamese forces. From their vulnerable point of view, the Khmers could more easily overlook the intrusion of the Communists, who started trouble in Vietnam and dashed across the border to their Cambodian sanctuaries; that alone did not hurt them physically. Furthermore, the Communists provided moneymaking opportunities—goods smuggled from the American-replenished warehouses in Saigon and victuals for the insurgents, for example. By 1966, between 25 and 50 percent of Cambodia's falling rice crop would be sold or traded to the PAVN and its South Vietnamese pawn, the People's Liberation Armed Forces (PLAF, the military arm of the Viet Cong). There was little concern among villagers or corrupt officials that this commerce also was throwing their country's budget out of kilter.

The heavy weapon-backed U.S. and South Vietnamese reaction to the Communist abuse of national boundaries, however, was another matter. It brought physical destruction to frontier villages. As a result, Sihanouk began loudly protesting the increasing Allied incursions into Cambodian in pursuit of their attackers, while remaining low-key about Communist violations. Khmer complaints and Allied recriminations spiraled upward and outward. On August 27, 1963— citing border crossings, and the Diem regime's persecution of Buddhists and discrimination against the Cambodian minority in the Mekong Delta—Phnom Penh severed political relations with Saigon. Cambodia's diplomatic ties with Thailand already had broken in 1961 over the latter's verbal attacks on Sihanouk and support of the Khmers Sereis.[14]

Concurrently, Cambodian-American relations abruptly deteriorated. On November 20, 1963, Sihanouk ended U.S. economic and military aid, "kick[ing] out some 300 American . . . officials who moved around our country as if they already owned it," as he put it. The Khmer leader's decision was based on three broad reasons bolstered by specific incidents, Chinese pressure, and the conviction that the Communists would be the ultimate victors. One reason was his belief, not entirely unjustified, that the United States wanted to replace him. There were the foiled plots of 1959. There also was the May Day double-assassination attempt earlier in 1963. Shortly before the state visit of PRC President Liu Shao Chi, two Taiwanese rented a house beside the airport road near the popular *Nakry Bopha* Restaurant. They burrowed a tunnel beneath the two-lane highway. A large explosive charge was to be detonated inside the cramped tunnel at the moment Liu and Sihanouk drove over the spot on their way to the capital. Tipped off by Beijing, the Khmer security service arrested the Taiwan Chinese duo, whom the prince called "CIA-hired criminals."

The murder of President Diem of South Vietnam in a U.S.-condoned coup on November 1 seemed further evidence to Sihanouk of what American ill will could lead to. Khmer Serei activity also was becoming intolerable. The group's antigovernment radio broadcasts originated in Thailand and Vietnam, which the prince considered puppets of Washington. Just the day before casting off U.S. aid, Sihanouk announced the arrest of two Khmer Serei men traveling from Vietnam with the presumptuous intention of negotiating with him in Phnom Penh. The widely publicized execution of one of the men quickly followed. Sihanouk's paranoia regarding American intentions also was focused on FARK, his armed forces. Its officers, virtually all right-wing, had gained increased power over the years. This was acceptable to the *samdech* only as long as he had their undivided loyalty. The problem was that the canceled military aid program had fostered close ties between many Khmer officers and their American counterparts.

A second reason Sihanouk further alienated Cambodia from the United States was the burgeoning of cross-border incidents. Not only had South Vietnamese hot pursuit operations increased, but American aircraft, which had dropped bombs on Khmer territory as early as 1962, now were flying regular reconnaissance and fire control missions over Cambodia. The third reason was Washington's growing commitment to the Thais and Vietnamese, whom Sihanouk termed "eaters of Khmer soil." The Cambodian chief of state would have been even angrier had he known that the U.S. Joint Chiefs of Staff in the Pentagon were pushing for presidential approval "to attack supply lines and storage sites in Laos and Cambodia."

Although his country's economy was sliding backwards, the prince was confident that his "sweeping economic reforms"—the ill-fated "Buddhist socialism" that further widened the gap between Sihanouk and his urban subjects—and other foreign assistance would compensate for the cutoff of U.S. aid. He said that "France will continue to have a much more privileged position in Cambodia than anyone else." De Gaulle's France welcomed the opportunity to regain a leading role in Southeast Asia at Anglo-Saxon expense. A Franco-Khmer military assistance agreement was signed shortly afterward. However, neither French aid, nor that of the PRC, which the prince called "Cambodia's best friend," would prove as generous as America's in keeping the Khmer budget balanced.

In the face of worsening relations between the United States and Cambodia, President John Kennedy was considering shortly before his death two moves to defuse the situation. One was to send a personal representative to assure the Khmer leader of American support for the sort of neutrality Sihanouk espoused. The second would dispatch Dean Acheson, who had represented Cambodia during World Court deliberations over the Preah Vihear temple dispute, to Phnom Penh to "clear the air by denying any continuing complicity" with the Khmer Serei movement. Any hope for détente was set back when a December 1963 Sihanouk radiocast was justifiably taken as rejoicing over the deaths, over a two-week interval, of President Diem, Thai Premier Sarit Thanarat, and "the great boss" (Kennedy), who were "all going to meet in hell!" Reactions included the recall of the U.S. ambassador and the closing by Sihanouk of Cambodia's embassies in Washington and London.[15]

Like the huge Angkorean sculptures of god-kings with four faces back-to-back, Sihanouk looked everywhere for the direction that most suited his current concept of survival. He now was turning from West to East. In denying his reputation for fickleness and unpredictability, the prince explained, "In the final analysis [my] policy consists in acquiring the maximum number of friends and in making the minimum number of enemies." This meant eschewing the politics and ideologies of other nations as long as they "refrain from meddling in our internal affairs." Cambodia, he said, had to be reactive because "of our size." Certainly true, but Sihanouk's condemnation of Allied transgressions while overlooking those of the Communists smacked as much of hypocrisy as of Realpolitik. Neither the prince nor the outside world then realized that the Communist front was anything but united.

The Khmers Rouges, increasingly repressed by the prince, were dedicated to eliminating the country's monarchic trappings but were divided on what to replace them with. Their most rabid faction, the Marxist-Leninist Workers' Party of Kampuchea (the renamed People's Revolutionary Party of Kampuchea), in 1963 chose Pol Pot as central committee secretary to replace its missing and presumed dead leader, Tou Samouth.[16] Without the Chinese, North Vietnamese, and Soviets behind them, however, the KR, like the South Vietnamese Communists, were little more than gnats irritating giants. Mainland China pursued a multifaceted policy that was consistent only in its anti-Americanism. It both embraced the Cambodian Communists and armed the government that was killing them. And—never mind China's role in arming North Vietnam—the Chinese and Vietnamese remained historical rivals. Beijing unquestionably preferred an independent Khmer insurgent movement over one controlled by Hanoi.

The North Vietnamese, for their part, considered the Khmer Communists as protégés, yet held as tight a rein as possible on them and overtly supported Sihanouk; they needed a neutralized Cambodia successfully to pursue their war in South Vietnam.[17] Only after that was won could they unleash the K.R. to subvert the prince, but even then only under their control. This Pol Pot would not accept. Like the prince and Lon Nol after Sihanouk, the anti-Vietnamese Cambodian Communist had his own concept of a revived Angkorean glory. His, inspired by the brutal China of Mao Zedong, called for a new atheistic civilization built atop a totally destroyed past.

In early March 1964, placard-toting, stone-throwing demonstrators organized by the Cambodian government extensively damaged the American and the British embassies in Phnom Penh. They were protesting the type of action that was repeated only days later. On March 19, U.S. military advisers were present when a South Vietnamese column assaulted the village of Chantrea, four miles inside Cambodia. Khmer civilian casualties numbered thirty-seven. It was during this operation that the *Aviation Royale Khmère* scored its first and only aerial victory. Two American-built T-28 Nomads (Trojan trainers converted into fighter-bombers) pounced on a U.S. Air Force O-1 Bird Dog observation aircraft. Whatever its location when struck by the T-28 machine gun slugs, the slow and unarmed O-1 crashed in Vietnam. Chantrea was only the then most publicized incident of many involving violations by all sides and costing several American lives.

United Nations efforts to ameliorate Cambodia's problems in 1964 died stillborn. Sihanouk went on protesting and calling for an international conference to assure Cambodia's neutrality. American attempts at rapprochement, including an unsuccessful bid to install a new ambassador, were deflected by the *samdech*. In March 1965, Sihanouk chaired an Indochina People's Conference "to condemn United States activities in southeast Asia." Matters were made even worse by an article in the April 5, 1965, issue of *Newsweek*, which stated that Sihanouk reportedly had "one to several concubines" and referred to his mother as "money man" Queen Kossamak, who owned "bordellos at the edge of the city." She actually owned the land, not the buildings. An orchestrated mob responded on April 28 by once more attacking America's embassy. That same day, coincidentally, Allied planes hit two Cambodian villages suspected of containing enemy troops. The magazine article and bombing incidents, the Khmer leader said in a May 3 broadcast, had convinced him to end diplomatic relations with the United States. With the closing of the American Embassy, Australia agreed to look after U.S. interests in Cambodia.[18]

By this time, the U.S. had allowed itself to be irretrievably sucked into the Vietnamese maelstrom. In the wake of an August 1964 naval incident in the Gulf of Tonkin off North Vietnam, President Lyndon Johnson persuaded a like-minded Congress to empower him "to take all necessary measures to repel an armed attack against the forces of the United States and to prevent further aggression." By the beginning of 1965, there were 23,300 American military personnel in Vietnam. Escalation continued with extensive aerial bombing operations over Vietnam and Laos, but not yet Cambodia. In March 1965, the first U.S. combat units landed in Vietnam, an action Sihanouk called "aggression." The following month, these units were green-lighted to switch from defensive to offensive actions. Autumn saw the first significant American public protests against the administration's Southeast Asia policy.

The official taboo against American crossing of the often ill-defined Cambodian border underwent gradual erosion in 1965 as a compromise was sought between political objectives and military necessity. In April, the Pentagon gave U.S. forces permission for limited "self-defense" penetration. The air force, for example, could chase enemy aircraft into Cambodian air space if the enemy struck first and "only if still engaged in combat." Revising the restrictive rules of engagement still further after the major clash of American and PAVN units in Vietnam's Ia Drang Valley, the Joint Chiefs of Staff on November 21 authorized hot pursuit "air strikes, ground artillery firing and troop maneuvering into Cambodia as necessary to defend against enemy attacks from that country." The day after Christmas 1965, Cambodia accused the U.S. and South Vietnam of conducting "almost daily" operations on its territory and causing civilian casualties. One of the most publicized raids—the August 2, 1966, attack by American F-105 fighter-bombers on Thlok Trach—was witnessed by representatives of the International Control Commission, several embassies, and the press. Snapping that the Americans "must first recognize that Cambodia is a country that has a border," Sihanouk canceled a scheduled peace pipe meeting with U.S. Ambassador-at-Large W. Averill Harriman.[19]

Like a highwire artist buffeted by constantly changing crosscurrents of air, Sihanouk found his efforts to steer a neutral course between the warring powers growing more frenetic. The Communists were entrenching themselves more deeply in the eastern part of his country, even shifting the North Vietnamese–controlled Central Office for South Vietnam (COSVN, a movable military-political command headquarters) from Vietnam into Cambodia. The *samdech* again appealed for international respect of his nation's boundaries. Hanoi and its National Liberation Front (NLF) puppet in South Vietnam submitted positive written responses to the appeal in June 1967; the United States did not until April 1969.

On June 13, 1967, Cambodia established relations with the NLF and quickly elevated its representation to embassy level. Two months later, the Democratic Republic of Vietnam (DRV, North Vietnam) opened an embassy in Phnom Penh. When the NLF became the Provisional Revolutionary Government of South Vietnam (PRG) in June 1969, Cambodia was among the first to recognize it. In addition, Sihanouk was the only foreign chief of state at the funeral of Ho Chi Minh. This tilt toward the Communists, helped to no small degree by pressure from Beijing, resulted in the prince formally authorizing the PAVN/PLAF sanctuaries inside Cambodia and their resupply through Sihanoukville, Cambodia's only ocean port, to counter Allied attacks on the Ho Chi Minh Trail and South China Sea shipping.[20]

Under the watchful eye of a Vietnam-born Chinaman named Hak Ly, growing stacks of Soviet and Chinese arms, munitions, and other supplies were transferred from ships to canvas-covered trucks at Sihanoukville. The heavily laden vehicles then motored northwestward along Route 4 to depots at Kompong Speu near Phnom Penh for breaking down into distribution lots to be hauled both eastward and northward toward the Vietnamese border. Ironically, the 144-mile-long, 59-bridge Cambodian-American Friendship Highway, as Route 4 was called, was laid down in the late 1950s with U.S. funds. This major supply line, whose own transportation network blended into the Ho Chi Minh Trail in southern Laos, became known as the Sihanouk Trail. By 1970, it was funneling an estimated 80 percent of the material reaching the Communists in South Vietnam. The traffic also benefited high-level Cambodian military and civilian officials and FARK, the first financially and the second through a percentage of the goods passing through. To help cover his collusion with the Communists, Sihanouk ordered a clamp-down on foreign journalists and terminated the mandate of the International Control Commission in Cambodia.[21]

Allied hot pursuit strikes continued—Cambodia filed 851 protests between May 1 and October 31, 1967, alone. Khmer statistics recorded 1,864 ground and 5,149 air violations, resulting in 293 Cambodian deaths and 690 injuries, by Allied forces by the end of April 1969. Despite this, the growing Communist presence, South Vietnam's unexpected staying power and his own internal problems convinced the Khmer leader that he should mend his fences with the West. Washington was amenable. President Johnson, who had limited cross-border activity as much as possible, thought that Sihanouk "runs a wonderful country, he's a great little man . . . and I don't see why we can't find some way to get along with him." His predecessor's widow, Jacqueline Kennedy, received a jasmine petal welcome during a November 1967 visit to Cambodia. It was a diplomatic démarche passed off as a "childhood dream" trip to see the ruins of Angkor. The following January, as the Communists were massing in Cambodia for their Tet offensive, an American delegation arrived in Phnom Penh. Its head, Ambassador to India Chester Bowles, was told that Cambodia was "not opposed to hot pursuit in uninhabited areas" and wished "to reestablish normal relations with the United States." Sihanouk also told Bowles that he would "send troops to engage any Vietnamese" in Cambodia.

During the ensuing months, in arrangements code-named Vesuvius, U.S. intelligence dossiers containing irrefutable evidence of Communist sanctuaries inside Cambodia were provided to the Khmer defense ministry through Ambassador Noel St. Clair Deschamps of Australia. Among the information garnered by American intelligence was the fact that North Vietnam had gotten bold enough to risk its small air force along the border. U.S. electronic intelligence confirmed that Soviet-made aircraft were flying air drop sorties from Cambodia to South Vietnam. A PAVN defector told of other flights to evacuate wounded soldiers from small fields in east and north central Cambodia to North Vietnam. Still further flights, using both fixed and rotary-winged aircraft, sometimes with Russian crewmen, were reported to be making limited, multimission flights to sites on both sides of the frontier.

While the Bowles visit was to have an indirect impact on justifying upcoming U.S. air activities, its positive aspects were diluted by strong statements from Washington about the right to enter Cambodia, by Thai and South Vietnamese intransigence, and by further Khmer casualties during hot pursuit actions. President Johnson directed a policy of "responding gradually" to "recent moves by Sihanouk aimed at improving relations." U.S.-Khmer diplomatic ties were not to be renewed until June 1969, and then only by exchanging chargés d'affaires rather than ambassadors.[22]

Intensification of the Vietnam War pushed the United States into more complex cross-border activities, which, its leadership felt, required secrecy. Indigenous troops were recruited and, usually led by Americans, sent on various missions into North Vietnam, Laos, Cambodia, and even southern China. The first Cambodians widely targeted for recruitment were the four to five hundred thousand living in the southern extremity of Vietnam—the Khmers Kroms (K.K., Lower or Lowland Khmers). Some of them belonged to the Khmer Serei movement, which had been bedeviling Sihanouk since the 1950s. Others adhered to the largely defunct Khmer Kampuchea Krom (KKK) group, originally created by Sihanouk to counter the Khmers Sereis and dedicated to the return to Cambodia of Vietnam's Mekong Delta provinces. Numerous KKK, their loyalties mixed, had turned to banditry.

As part of the effort to defeat the PLAF guerrillas in South Vietnam, KK were recruited for incorporation into Civilian Irregular Defense Groups (CIDGs). These initially were intended as local defense forces ostensibly under Vietnamese control but actually run by Americans (first the CIA, then the Army Special Forces) until 1971. The paramilitary CIDG program, which involved between fifty thousand and eighty thousand troops defending thousands of square miles in Vietnam and Laos, was a natural manpower pool for small-scale clandestine cross-border operations. Recruits also came from a little-known group called the *Front Unifié de Lutte des Races Opprimées* (FULRO, the United Front for the Struggle of Oppressed Races). Composed of mountain tribesmen living principally in Vietnam's Central Highlands, but also in Cambodia's Mondolkiri and Ratanakiri Provinces, FULRO was founded in 1964. Displaying sometimes uncertain loyalties, unanimous only in its anti-Vietnamism, the group maintained on-and-off contacts with the K.R. Its founder, Y'Bham Enuol, was to become a victim of the 1975 killing fields. FULRO gave up its long, lonely struggle only in October 1992.

American military need systematically to cross the frontier came in 1965 when Sihanouk severed diplomatic relations with the United States and the North Vietnamese presence in Cambodia was confirmed. The Pentagon authorized the establishment of a closely controlled cross-border capability in mid-1966. Operations would be performed by the Studies and Observation Group (SOG), a military element created two years earlier and kept secret for political reasons. Nominally under the U.S. Military Assistance Command, Vietnam, (MACV), the unified command overseeing America's war and answering to the Commander-in-Chief, Pacific Command, (CINCPAC) headquartered in Hawaii, SOG actually reported to the Special Assistant for Counterinsurgency and Special Activities in Washington. SOG, originally formed to operate on a small scale in the Vietnam-Laos border area, ultimately employed more than two thousand Americans (mostly military personnel) and more than ten thousand multinational indigenous troops. It set up specialized internal groups to meet its expanding needs, including a mini air force of helicopters, transports and electronic warfare aircraft, and a fleet of fast patrol boats.

SOG was tasked with: (1) cross-border activities, chiefly intelligence-gathering; (2) missions concerned with missing, downed, and captured Americans; (3)underground operations in North Vietnam; (4) psychological warfare; and (5) ad hoc assignments ranging from kidnapping and assassination to booby-trapping enemy munitions and retrieving lost documents and equipment. Headquartered in a two-story house on Saigon's Pasteur Street, SOG, in November 1967, absorbed other active clandestine programs and, for its ground operations, established three field components: Command and Control North (covering North Vietnam, Laos, and the PRC), Command and Control Central (Cambodia-Laos-Vietnam tri-border area), and Command and Control South (Cambodia and South Vietnam). The latter, smallest of the trio, inherited the recently created Operation Daniel Boone. Daniel Boone—subsequently renamed Salem House and, when South Vietnam took over ground reconnaissance activities, Thot Not—was the designation for sorties into Cambodia. Some cross-border missions were led by members of the Australian Army Training Team, Vietnam. In addition, independent activities were conducted by the CIA.

Operation Daniel Boone went into action in 1967, its geographical operating area at first restricted to the northeastern tip of Cambodia, but later broadened. Between June 1, 1967, and October 4, 1968, SOG completed 157 missions into Cambodia, more than 80 percent of which encountered enemy troops. Small U.S.-officered units were helicoptered from Vietnam and Thailand under a number of so-called projects, such as the Greek operations, so named because of their Greek letter code names. One, Detachment B-57 Project Gamma, sought information on Communist bases and the Sihanouk government's complicity with the enemy. It became what one historian called "the finest and most productive" American intelligence collection effort in Southeast Asia. In 1969, Gamma's sources inside Cambodia suddenly started drying up. An internal investigation pointed the finger at a Vietnamese asset secretly working for the enemy. The result was the execution of the suspected double agent, followed by the sensationalized Green Beret murder case and trial.

One of SOG's so-called Blackjack missions, mobile strike forces operating at the same level as PLAF units, involved an American U-2 spy plane that crashed in eastern Cambodia in December 1966, two and a half years after the first high-altitude reconnaissance flight over the country. The 185-man Third Mobile Strike Force, a U.S.-led team of Khmers, was sent into Communist-occupied territory to recover the U-2's "black box" with its sensitive technical data. Contrary to most published accounts, the box was retrieved from the crash site without incident and not from an enemy encampment after a shootout. Other missions insinuated Khmer teams into Cambodia dressed as K.R. to gather information (operations code-named Pike Hill) and to conduct guerrilla warfare (Cedar Walk). SOG Bright Light sorties to rescue reported U.S. prisoners of war provided Hollywood-like assaults on camps in Cambodia and elsewhere between 1966 and 1972 but resulted in only one partial success, a wounded airman dying soon after recovery from captivity. One reason for this lack of success, according to the SOG command history, was that "by the time intelligence worked its way through the Byzantine maze of bureaucracy and diplomatic complications [i.e., coordination with three military levels and two embassies to conduct each operation inside Cambodia], any POW or downed airmen were long gone."

SOG missions relied heavily on the group's Ford Drum program. The latter consisted of backseat U.S. or Vietnamese photographers equipped with 35mm cameras and telephoto lenses flying in O-1 Bird Dog or O-2 twin-tailed aircraft over Cambodia and Laos. These slow, high-winged airplane sorties not only performed reconnaissance tasks but also participated in tactical air strikes. Ford Drum flew 368 treetop missions for more than three years before incurring its first loss. A single-engined O-1G overflying enemy sampan and bicycle supply routes in Kompong Cham Province in December 1970 was downed by small arms fire. Overflown by gunships and converted jet trainer A-37 Dragonflies, a U.S.-led team recovered the bodies of the pilot and the photographer. In January 1971, a SOG roadwatch element observing Route 13 in Kratie Province reported the first appearance of North Vietnamese tanks during the Cambodian conflict. It had been a SOG maritime group commando raid in North Vietnam that inadvertently triggered the controversial Tonkin Gulf Incident. According to the Pentagon, SOG "also contributed greatly to the success of the Cambodian incursion of mid-1970." At least 1,885 increasingly hazardous SOG actions supported by 4,890 air sorties (including 2,305 by helicopter gunship) were completed in Cambodia before the group's U.S. participation wound down to deactivation in April 1972. SOG was credited with killing more than 1,300 Communists at the cost of an estimated 300 or more Americans lost. Its functions were taken over by the South Vietnamese. However, U.S. Special Forces continued to be involved in limited cross-border activities until the Vietnam War cease-fire of January 1973.[23]

Despite the official taboo against border crossing, American military units other than SOG and the air force occasionally entered Cambodia on purpose or accidentally to pursue or ambush an enemy unhindered by such militarily unrealistic restrictions. Navy SEAL (Sea, Air, and Land) veteran James Watson recalled capturing two Chinese intelligence officers inside Cambodia and returning them to Vietnam for interrogation. The U.S. Navy's multifaceted effort to interdict enemy supply lines in the brown water maze of the Mekong Delta along the Cambodian border also provided Sihanouk grounds for complaint. In November 1968, for example, three helicopter-escorted, fifty-foot Swift patrol craft engaged in two actions on a canal paralleling the frontier between the Gulf of Thailand and the Bassac River. Ten men and ten women, allegedly KKK, were reported killed in the second clash.

Numerous times during the 1960s, U.S. trespassers were bagged by the Khmers. On March 21, 1968, for instance, the Philippine tug *Bream,* operating under American contract, was detained after crossing the border on the Mekong. Its two American guards, along with eight crewmen, were later released as "a gesture of respect to the memory of the late senator Robert F. Kennedy," in Sihanouk's words. On April Fool's Day, a navy P3 VI Orion electronic surveillance aircraft was downed, apparently by a Khmer vessel, in the Gulf of Thailand. The dozen American crewmen perished. In mid-December 1968, after personal messages from the lame duck President Johnson, Cambodia released the more fortunate crews of an army river craft and a downed helicopter. Three months later, four airmen from a U-1A Otter were let go upon receipt of an apology and explanation from newly installed President Richard Nixon. The following month, two U.S. Navy helicopters were brought down in Svay Rieng Province; four crewmen died, four were injured.

Less measurable aspects of the Vietnam War affecting Cambodia involved defoliation and weather alteration along the frontier. The chemical spraying of vegetation that could conceal the enemy was carried out by the air force and the navy during the 1960s; it ceased in 1971. The first known use of weather warfare in history began in March 1967 and ended in July 1972. Thailand-based U.S. aircraft dropped 47,409 canisters of rain-producing silver dioxide or lead iodine in 2,602 missions over Indochina to bog down Ho Chi Minh Trail traffic. Although a Pentagon spokesman later said that the cloud seeding increased local rainfall up to 30 percent, it safely can be concluded that any results proved more an annoyance than a deterrent to the recipients of the chemically-induced water drops.[24]

Of higher profile was the growing use of U.S. air power over Cambodia. The fighter-bombers and helicopter gunships were joined in 1969 by the Strategic Air Command's largest bomb carriers. It was an escalation, hidden from the American Congress and public, that was to set off a series of events leading to the nation's first forced resignation of a president. Convinced that, as the freshly inaugurated president said, "the only way we could get things going on the negotiation front [in the virtually stalled Paris peace talks] was to do something on the military front," Nixon, in March 1969, decided to bomb Communist sanctuaries inside Cambodia. It was a decision U.S commanders in Vietnam had been urging since 1965. Washington did not feel it necessary to consult with the Cambodian leader "in view of Sihanouk's earlier indications [e.g., the Bowles mission] that he would tolerate them." The *samdech,* although he resented *any* violation of his nation's boundaries, had made clear his desire to remove the Vietnamese. His ill-armed, ill-trained army of thirty to thirty-five thousand was incapable of doing anything about the Vietnamese Communists—numbering forty to three hundred thousand, according to various sources—occupying eastern Cambodia.

During the night of March 17–18, 1969, forty-eight Strategic Air Command B-52 bombers from Guam Island thundered high above the Philippine and South China Seas on a five-hour flight to drop twenty-four tons of high explosives on an enemy border base area designated 353 and believed to house COSVN headquarters. A thirteen-man Daniel Boone team helicoptered into the still-smoldering target area to collect prisoners and documents instead found an angry hornets' nest; only four survived the Communist gunfire. The bombing was the first of 3,875 sorties that dropped 108,823 tons of bombs over a fourteen-month period on six sparsely populated target areas code-named Breakfast, Lunch, Snack, Dinner, Dessert, and Supper—together comprising Operation Menu. Given that Soviet spy trawlers immediately radio-relayed B-52 takeoffs from Guam and Okinawa, that enemy spies often learned of bombing plans in advance, that key U.S. codes were compromised, and that COSVN was mobile, Menu was a questionable undertaking, despite the cost to the Communists in lives and supplies. The air raids, according to onetime Communist official Truong Nhu Tang, produced "undiluted psychological terror" and "caused significant casualties generally [but] did not kill a single leader in the headquarters complexes."[25]

New York Times reporter William Beecher exposed Operation Menu in a May 9, 1969, article. Largely ignored by the public, it staggered the White House. Already concerned about other leaks to the media, the president launched a spying operation—complete with twenty-one months of wiretapping government officials and reporters—that culminated in the Watergate scandal of 1972–74. Nixon would have been better off ignoring the Beecher article. It was not until years later, when air force officers brought the matter to congressional attention, that the secret bombing powder keg was ignited. So it was that Richard Nixon's first major presidential decision, the bombing of Cambodia, set off the domestic abuses of authority that led to the downfall of his administration.

Interestingly, the congressional resolution calling for Nixon's impeachment was over the bombing of Cambodia, not Watergate. It also was ironic that Cambodia's leader, whose perceived political sensitivity was a consideration in the decision to keep the bombing under wraps, made no protest when the B-52 activities became public. He told Senate majority leader Mike Mansfield in August 1969 that "it is in one's own interest, sometimes, to be bombed—in this case, the United States kills foreigners who occupy Cambodian territory and does not kill Cambodians." Although an unknown number of Khmers indeed were killed, Sihanouk had become anxious for a rapprochement with the United States—to the point of providing intelligence on Communist bases. Menu was still on the table when the prince reestablished relations with America and invited Nixon to visit his country.[26]

Communist activity in Cambodia was becoming increasingly intolerable for the nationalistic Sihanouk. The Vietnamese posed the gravest threat. They, in effect, had taken over the country's eastern frontier. In addition, their nurturing of Khmer Communists had caused an intensification of K.R. activity. When Khmer insurgents conducted sabotage and violent hit-and-run operations in seventeen of Cambodia's nineteen provinces in 1968, for example, it appeared part of an overall North Vietnamese strategy. Hanoi was disturbed by Phnom Penh's rapprochement to the United States and did want to keep FARK dispersed and tied down. In general, however, North Vietnam sought to keep its protégés on a leash by feeding them only enough arms to keep the Cambodian government off balance and to sustain them for future use.

This was made evident during an earlier visit by Pol Pot to Hanoi. The central committee secretary of the most radical element in the K.R. movement was received with icy reserve before being sent on to Beijing. When Pol Pot returned to his headquarters in eastern Cambodia, he had assurances of Chinese backing, and a bitter determination to dominate the K.R. and ultimately boot the North Vietnamese. His Workers' Party became the Communist Party of Kampuchea (CPK). Two years later, in 1968, the Revolutionary Army of Kampuchea—forerunner of the People's National Liberation Armed Forces of Kampuchea (PNLAFK)—was established.

Sihanouk's FARK could cope with the Khmer Communists in Battambang Province, far from Hanoi's protective wing. The situation in northeastern Cambodia was far different. One reason, of course, was the Vietnamese Communists who hampered government anti-K.R. operations. But there also were the Khmers Loeus (Upper or Upland Khmers), the isolated, dark-skinned highland tribesmen who long had resented Phnom Penh's intrusion into their lives. They were easily recruited by the K.R. and would make up a significant part of the victorious army that years later entered the capital. By 1970, for reasons as varied as simple proselytizing, peasant dissatisfaction, government repression, and border bombardments, the insurgents had gained telling strength in the northeast frontier region. Estimates of K.R. manpower ranged from a modest four hundred to a hefty ten thousand. Although outnumbered and outgunned, they were eliminating perhaps two dozen of FARK's thirty to thirty-five thousand troops each month.

Nor were neighboring and internal Communists Sihanouk's only left-wing headaches. In 1967, the tumultuous PRC tried to spread its ongoing Cultural Revolution to ethnic Chinese in other countries, including Cambodia. The prince publicly castigated Beijing. Stating that "if we ever turned communist, we would prefer Khmer Communism," Sihanouk stifled internal Chinese dissent and threatened to seek direct American help. In this case, things rapidly cooled down and, for the sake of mutual interest, the two countries were reconciled by year's end.

Whatever their differences, the North Vietnamese, their South Vietnamese cohorts, and the K.R. all were Communists undermining the Khmer nation. In the fall of 1968, an exasperated Sihanouk for the first time openly admitted the existence of the Communist sanctuaries and ordered his army—which had once been called by their own commander-in-chief "less effective than the Paris police"—to mount a major offensive to clear the undesirables from Route 19, running from Stung Treng and Ratanakiri Provinces toward Pleiku in Vietnam. The Vietnamese Communists vigorously resisted this new threat to the Ho Chi Minh Trail sections passing through the area. Violent clashes resulted. Like it or not, Cambodia was becoming more deeply involved in the Vietnam War.

In 1969, as Operation Menu drove the Communists farther in-country, there were instances of active FARK cooperation with American and South Vietnamese forces just across the border. Next, Phnom Penh rescinded Communist use of Sihanoukville, arousing mixed feelings among the military and civilian Khmer officials profiting from the arms transfers. To increase pressure on the Communists to vacate their sanctuaries, delivery of their last authorized arms shipment, which arrived in April 1969, was stretched out over a six-month period. Also in April, the prince instructed Defense Minister Lon Nol "to give up the defensive spirit and adopt an offensive spirit . . . to deal with the Viet Cong and Viet Minh."

On May 24, 1969, the Khmers sat down with Vietnamese Communist representatives to request them "to desist from committing violations against Cambodian territory." No official response was forthcoming. In fact, North Vietnamese defense Minister General Vo Nguyen Giap already had ordered his PAVN to expand border operations and move still deeper into Cambodia. The following month, Sihanouk told press conference attenders that "at present there is war in Ratanakiri between Cambodia and Vietnam." Four months after that blockbuster, he charged that thirty-five to forty thousand Vietnamese Communists occupied parts of seven Cambodian border provinces. But, even with air superiority ensured by Soviet-made MiG jets and U.S.-supplied T-28s, the Khmers could do little about it.

As the decade neared a close, the *samdech* publicly was lambasting both the Communists and the U.S.-Vietnamese allies. Yet he secretly abetted many of their actions. And at the same time that he was establishing relations with North Vietnam, Sihanouk reknotted diplomatic ties with the United States in exchange for a pledge to "respect Cambodia's independence and sovereignty within the present boundaries." The American diplomatic mission that arrived in Phnom Penh in August 1969 consisted, two months later, only of Chargé Lloyd Rives, a political officer, an administrative officer, a three-man defense attaché office, and an air attaché. This apparent vacillation was all part of Sihanouk's strategy for survival, as he earlier put it, "by playing off rival external influences against one another in such fashion that they cancel each other out."

Allied border violations generally were not aimed at the Cambodian government. Growing K.R. guerrilla activity, however, was. That the K.R. were ideologically tied to Hanoi and Beijing, and directed from an area occupied and protected by the Vietnamese, made the Communist threat a dire one. Hanoi's aim was a communist Indochina under its domination. The more modest K.R. goal was ramified by its various elements. While the Khmers trained in Hanoi sought a Cambodia along the lines of North Vietnam, for example, Pol Pot's followers envisioned nothing less than a xenophobic "purist" state along Maoist lines. Whichever K.R. goal prevailed, it could not be attained without Vietnamese help. In any case, the events of 1967–69 provide compelling evidence that it was neither U.S. bombing nor Allied incursions that brought Cambodia into a full-scale war or led it to the infamous killing fields. By the time of America's heightened profile on the Cambodian landscape, the Khmer nation already had been invaded by the Communists and its people already were involved in a budding civil war.[27]

CHAPTER FOUR

1970: Cambodia's Turning Point

DURING THE LATTER HALF OF THE 1960s, Cambodia's internal situation insured that, even without the Vietnam War, the nation was in trouble. Economic decline, exacerbated by the nationalization of various sectors of the economy, had not been reversed. Agriculture, the economy's foundation, was stagnant. The historical gap between rich and poor, urban and rural, had broadened into a chasm. Khmer politics were, if such was possible, even more unstable, with polarization to the right and left increasing pressure on and further eroding the power of the regime. Government administration was marked by Byzantine maneuvering, incompetence, corruption, and insensitivity to the public.

In the 1966 elections, Sihanouk stood aside for the first time in over a decade. As a result, the pro-American rightist politicians made gains that enabled them to name General Lon Nol as prime minister. Nol, himself as much a politician as a soldier, was outwardly obedient, not overly impressive professionally, and cunningly ambitious. Sirik Matak, the *samdech*'s elitist cousin and royal rival, became Nol's deputy. Matak resented the prince for at least two reasons. One was the fact that the French had selected a Norodom, Sihanouk, to be king in 1941 instead of a Sisowath, Matak's uncle Monireth, as almost everyone expected. The second was Sihanouk's erratic and unpredictable method of governing. Rumors had it that, probably in collusion with Lon Nol's younger brother, Matak was scheming to usurp the prince's position.

Early in 1967, clumsy government efforts to end the illicit diversion of rice (mostly to the Vietnamese Communists) and to regain control of lost revenue ignited existent unrest near Samlaut in the western province of Battambang. Violence spread from the rice bowl province. The government responded with brutal repression. By June, the insurrection officially was over, but reprisals continued. While casualty figures remain obscure, the uprising took many hundreds of lives. Sihanouk subsequently mentioned fatalities of ten thousand, one thousand, and "under one hundred," depending on the occasion he uttered them. During the political crisis generated by the Samlaut uprising, the urban-based Communist networks were virtually eliminated and Lon Nol resigned, ostensibly for medical reasons resulting from a jeep accident eight weeks earlier. More likely, he was removed because, with the army as his power base, he posed a threat to the prince's own power and, having had a leading role in suppressing the uprising, he provided Sihanouk with an excuse to replace him.

Whatever their initial role, the Communists exploited the rebellion and built on it to stage a more closely controlled insurgent campaign the following year. Ambushes, raids, and the "rounding up" of peasants that was to become a K.R. trademark began in January 1968 at the scene of the failed 1967 insurrection, Battambang. Other provinces soon were affected. The psychological impact of the K.R. "offensive" was all out of proportion to its strength, reflecting both the confusion of the times and the enfeeblement of the Sihanouk regime. Whereas government circles feared the worst, Cambodia's Communists actually were leading a hand-to-mouth existence barely assisted by Vietnamese mentors still intent on assuring Khmer neutrality.[1]

After a six-month "retreat" in France, Lon Nol returned home and, in 1968, became Cambodia's defense minister. The prince, his popularity greatly eroded in the cities, reacted to the deteriorating situation by virtually relinquishing his leadership during the summer of 1969. Sihanouk's stepping back this time opened the door for a swiftly established rightist Government of National Salvation, with Lon Nol once more prime minister. Nol also retained his defense minister title. Sirik Matak, ambassador to Japan at the time, came back as Nol's first deputy. For the *samdech,* it was very nearly, in one historian's words, "an act of abdication." Sihanouk escaped into moviemaking (nine films in three years), pursuing musical interests, entertaining foreign dignitaries, and touring the countryside to keep up his rural support as his nation's instability worsened. In Cambodia's worst balance of payments deficit, for example, imports at the end of the decade totaled seventy-seven million dollars compared to fifty million dollars in exports.

Lon Nol, who had just lost his first wife, returned to Europe for medical treatment in late October. Shortly afterward, in early January 1970, it was Sihanouk's turn to leave. His reason, as given, was for treatment of "obesity, blood disease and albuminuria" at Grasse on France's Côte d'Azur. The prince undoubtedly hoped that, as in past crises, he could manipulate people and events to his advantage and recoup his losses. After visiting France, he planned to return via Russia and China, where he intended to ask Moscow and Beijing "to curb the activities of the Viet Cong and Viet Minh in my country." This time, though, Sihanouk would find that his highwire act had lost its safety net.[2]

Shortly after Sihanouk flew out of Pochentong with his wife, Monique, and eleven others, the Phnom Penh gambling casino he had legalized in 1969 to generate desperately needed revenue was shuttered. The Government of National Salvation, with Sirik Matak as its driving force, had already denationalized several state enterprises (including banks) and devalued the riel currency to encourage foreign investment. Cambodia's alienation from North Vietnam accelerated, this at least with the *samdech*'s approval. The prince met with Lon Nol while both were in France to discuss, among other matters, the strategy they would pursue regarding the Communist presence in eastern Cambodia. Lon Nol then flew back to Phnom Penh.

In March 1970, the National Bank of Cambodia announced the recall of five hundred riel banknotes because of Vietnamese Communist forging. In addition to countering the bogus bill problem, the move stemmed the outflow of currency by preventing both the exchange of old notes for new ones by illegal groups and their reimportation from outside the country. Since these notes were the standard currency used by the Communists to buy goods in Cambodia, the North Vietnamese reportedly lost over seventy million dollars. Their loss would have been greater except for the fact that Communist agents in the national bank provided enough warning to enable the Vietnamese to convert a large part of their holdings before the measure went into effect. Another anti-Communist move was the establishment of ties in South Vietnam with Son Ngoc Thanh, Sihanouk's old adversary who was helping the Allies raise military units of ethnic Khmers to fight in the Vietnam war.[3]

During January and February 1970, FARK artillery lobbed shells into the PAVN-PLAF sanctuaries. Khmer civilian involvement began on March 8 in the area known as the Parrot's Beak, an arm of Svay Rieng Province that stabs southeastward only thirty-three miles from South Vietnam's capital. Peasants and soldiers massed in front of the modest governor's mansion to protest both the Communist presence and Allied incursions. Demonstrations in other eastern communities, all orchestrated of course, were accompanied by a "sympathy turnout" in Phnom Penh on March 9. It took little effort to stoke the average Cambodian's anti-Vietnamese feelings into a lively blaze. By 9 A.M.

on March 11, between ten and twenty thousand students, soldiers, and monks were gathered at the ornate Independence Monument in southern Phnom Penh. Then, marching beneath a fiery sun with banners and Sihanouk portraits held high, they trooped less than a mile along Norodom Boulevard to congregate in front of first the PRG Embassy and then North Vietnam's. The well-organized demonstration quickly shifted into high gear. Both buildings were stormed, furniture and papers flew from shattered windows, and cars were overturned. Flames soon engulfed the litter. Only when it was over did the police, commanded by Oum Mannorine, the *samdech's* brother-in-law, move onto the scene.

One document taken from the PRG Embassy further hardened Phnom Penh's stand against Hanoi. It was a contingency plan for extending Vietnamese occupation of the border areas to all of Cambodia. Other papers, containing information on U.S. and South Vietnamese activities, were so detailed that one American concluded that the North Vietnamese Embassy was the elusive COSVN. While disturbances targeted ethnic Vietnamese homes, businesses, and churches for another two days, there were no fatalities. And, although major public events in the country never were staged without official sanction, the Khmer government called the rioting "an expression of the real sentiment of the Cambodian people fed up by the occupation of Cambodian territory."

The next day, Lon Nol issued letters of apology to the Vietnamese—accompanied by demands that they vacate their sanctuaries within three days. Sirik Matak abruptly canceled the nation's trade agreements with the Communists that had allowed them to be resupplied through Sihanoukville. Cambodia watchers were divided between those who insisted that the embassy sackings were part of a plot to undermine the prince (as Sihanouk himself charged in a 1981 book) and those who believed that the *samdech* had ordered them. Reliable information reaching the U.S. Embassy indicated that Sihanouk planned controlled demonstrations to strengthen his hand in Moscow and Beijing but that, with secret police help, they got out of hand. Soon afterward, Lon Nol's brother, Lon Non, took credit for the sacking of the embassies. In any case, Sihanouk's outward reaction was anger. Publicly lashing out at those who would "throw our country into the arms of a capitalist imperialist power" and, at the same time, warning that if Vietnam remained in Cambodia, the Communists "must not complain if we join the American camp," the prince apparently presumed an ability to continue juggling matters to his and his country's advantage. He might well have been able to do so—if he had returned to Phnom Penh directly instead of adhering to his schedule.

On Friday, March 13, the same day Khmer border troops and Vietnamese Communists were fighting their 164th skirmish since the beginning of the year, Sihanouk left for communist Eastern Europe. At the Paris airport before his departure, he said in English, "I don't believe I am being threatened by a coup d'état." Informed that the prince would be back in his capital the following week, the Cambodian government ordered national flags put up along the highway between the airport and the city. Then Sihanouk changed the date of his return to March 24.[4]

Three days after the *samdech* left Paris, Mannorine, the secretary of state for surface defense and chief of the national police, was hauled before the national legislature, along with Major General Sosthene Fernandez, the secretary of state for national security. They were questioned about corruption. It was an indication of how far Sihanouk's stock had fallen. It would have been unthinkable in the past to treat a royal relation in this manner. Anti-Vietnamese slogan-toting students and mufti-clad paratroopers stood between the building and Mannorine's police during the tense legislative session. That night, fearing the worst, Mannorine attempted a coup against Lon Nol and his deputy. The army proved stronger than the police and the prince's brother-in-law was arrested. With Lon Nol in charge of the army as defense minister, Sirik Matak now took over the police. General Fernandez fared much better. Although a past supporter of Sihanouk and Mannorine, he also was an associate of Lon Nol. Within two months of being questioned, then forced to resign, he returned to the army with a higher rank.

The best available evidence indicates that Sirik Matak provided the brains and Lon Nol the brawn (that is, the army) for the most crucial turning point of Cambodia's modern history, the removal of Sihanouk from power. Nol, ever the mystic with roots in the traditional past, envisioned only absorbing more of the *samdech*'s power and forcing Sihanouk into an even greater anti-Communist stance. Matak, backed by other political leaders, on the other hand, wanted the prince out. Presuming the accuracy of historian David Chandler's sources, during the predawn hours of March 18, Matak used a death threat to extract a tearful Lon Nol's agreement to overthrow the prince. Other sources stated that Nol joined the conspiracy only after learning that Sihanouk intended to have him arrested along with the principal conspirators when he returned. Whatever the truth, the army was ordered to surround the national assembly, post office, and radio station. Communication lines to the outside world were severed, and the airport was closed.

Later that Wednesday morning, the national assembly and the council of the kingdom (senate) reconvened in joint session. At 11 A.M., after unanimously approving the suspension of various civil rights under a "state of danger" article of the constitution, the legislature began a two-hour meeting to accuse the Norodom family of "unwholesome activities" ranging from deception to corruption and treason. Outside, many of the soldiers assigned to maintain order were lying on the grass with their boots off; some of their armored vehicles had white cloths tied to the gun barrels. Just after noon, using color-coded ballots, the ninety-two delegates voted to adopt—"in accordance with Article 122 of the 1974 constitution"—a resolution to withdraw, as of 1 P.M., "confidence in Prince Norodom Sihanouk in the function of chief of state." Ironically, Article 122 was Sihanouk's own creation. In 1960, the prince had been instrumental in amending the constitution to allow him to become chief of state based on that year's popular referendum. The Article 122 amendment permitted the general assembly president to assume chief of state power if the chief was "temporarily absent from Cambodia or unable to exercise his powers."

Any doubts the assemblage may have had about correctness of their action or even of retaining Sihanouk as a figurehead should have been removed by a cassette tape freshly arrived from Paris. Secretly recorded a week earlier at the Cambodian Embassy by either a disaffected Khmer or a foreign intelligence service, it preserved the prince's threat to have the entire Government of National Salvation executed upon his return. Sihanouk's twenty-nine years of rule ended as Assembly President Cheng Heng became acting chief of state, the title being more potent than the actual position. Furthermore, although Sirik Matak was the prime mover behind the change of leadership, Lon Nol, with his brother's help, quickly elbowed him aside to become Sihanouk's successor.

The diplomatic community was taken by surprise. U.S., British, and Australian officials pooled information to find out exactly what was going on. There was some French input as well, with military representatives expressing sympathy for the new government. Because of his own primitive communication setup, American Chargé Rives used British facilities to inform the State department of fast-developing events. News of Sihanouk's ouster shocked the Cambodian masses, urban and rural alike. They certainly were anti-Vietnamese, but only an urban minority was anti-Sihanouk. Most Khmers felt they had been manipulated by the Phnom Penh elite and regretted the prince's departure. There was a lot of head-shaking, but initially no action.[5]

Sihanouk, in Moscow, had days earlier refused to receive a delegation the national assembly wanted to send to brief him on the situation and to ask him to hurry home. Although talks with the ruling Kremlin triumvirate of Brezhnev-Podgorny-Kosygin about Cambodia's border problem proved fruitless, the prince actually delayed his departure for one fateful week. Whatever the reasons—uncertainty, overconfidence, fatalism, or fear for his own safety—it wasn't until the day of his overthrow that he climbed into a limousine for the drive down the Kiev Highway to Vnukovo II Airport. En route, Soviet Premier Alexei Kosygin informed Sihanouk that he no longer was Cambodia's leader.

One can only imagine Sihanouk's tormented thoughts during the long flight to Beijing. He clearly was unsure of his future when he disembarked from the quad-jet Ilyushin-62 to be greeted by Prime Minister Zhou Enlai. Since the prince's first inclination was to seek asylum in France, his decision to remain in the PRC suggests manipulation of his fears by the Chinese, who surely realized Sihanouk's value as a counterweight to North Vietnamese influence in Cambodia. Sihanouk soon met with North Vietnamese Premier Pham Van Dong as well. Shortly, an alliance was created between the prince's supporters and his old enemies, the K.R. The alliance was given legitimacy by placing Sihanouk at its head. Press declarations and radio broadcasts followed. On March 19 and again on March 23, the prince made radio appeals for the dissolution of the Phnom Penh government. It would be replaced, he said, by a government under his leadership. He also called for the formation of a liberation army and the creation of a National United Front of Kampuchea (FUNK, for *Front Uni National de Kampuchea*). The prince, for whom revenge now was an obsession, became a key element of K.R. success. Upon hearing the royal appeal, for example, the FARK commander at the provincial capital of Kratie dismissed his battalions and turned east central Military Region 6 (Kratie and Mondolkiri Provinces) over to the K.R. Similar scenes were repeated in other parts of Cambodia. In return, the K.R. gave Sihanouk the weapon to avenge his ouster.

The establishment of FUNK and Sihanouk's government-in-exile, the Royal Government of National Union of Kampuchea (GRUNK, for *Gouvernement Royal d'Union Nationale de Kampuchea*) was announced from Beijing on May 5, 1970. GRUNK was recognized by a number of Communist states, with the exception of the USSR and most of East Europe. FUNK was composed of four major elements with little in common and enough disparity to assure the eventual fracture of their alliance of convenience. The Sihanouk loyalists were known as the Khmers Rumdos (Liberation Khmers). Two elements comprised the diehard, no-compromise Communists driven underground by Sihanouk before the events of March 18, 1970. The group led by Pol Pot had hidden in the Cambodian hinterland and was vehemently anti-Vietnamese. The other consisted of those who had fled to North Vietnam for succor, training, and indoctrination. Feeling superior to the Pol Potists, these Khmers Viet Minhs, as they were called, were to pay dearly for underestimating the ruthless efficiency of their rival Communists. Both groups were atheistic and anti-Sihanouk. Finally, there were the so-called moderate intellectuals who expected to use the prince to gain power, then drop him. The only significant thing these disparate factions shared was the desire to cast out the new Phnom Penh regime. Over the next two years, FUNK's People's National Liberation Armed Forces of Kampuchea—numbering around fifteen thousand by the end of 1970—would be recruiting and organizing, and undergoing training by the PAVN, with Chinese and Soviet instructor assistance. Small units gradually would join the PAVN-PLAF as auxiliaries.

Reminiscent of Khomeini's later cassette campaign in Iran, tapes of the prince's "call to arms" were circulated widely throughout Cambodia. In addition, beginning in August 1970, Sihanouk participated in FUNK radio programs broadcast from a transmitter in southern China. This was a clever exploitation of the age-old loyalty to royalty of the peasants, who had no way of knowing that their beloved *samdech* was merely a figurehead and a pawn. In the meantime, a Summit Conference of Peoples of Indochina was convened under Chinese auspices in Guangzhou (Canton) "to coordinate the struggle of the Cambodian, Laotian and Vietnamese peoples." The Communists now had expanded the Vietnam War even further and unwittingly prepared the stage for the ascendancy of the K.R. Back in Cambodia, Sihanouk's actions had earned him a flood of media denigration and the government's promise of arrest for treason if he returned.[6]

Contrary to the black-and-white view of events held by some, reality usually is composed of varying shades of gray. This is true of the controversy over American involvement in the prince's overthrow. To the question of whether the United States was behind it, the answer is no. Did Americans have foreknowledge of the event? A qualified yes, because, although some were aware of ongoing agitation, even Cambodian participants did not all expect actual deposition of the *samdech*. Did the United States have contact with anti-Sihanouk elements and encourage them? Yes and no.

"Lon Nol's coup came as a complete surprise to us," stated President Nixon, who was enraged that he had received no forewarning from his intelligence community. Henry Kissinger, his assistant for national security affairs, said, "We never encouraged Sihanouk's overthrow nor knew about it in advance. We did not even grasp its significance for many weeks." Despite the political shadow subsequently and justifiably cast over both men, there is little reason to doubt their words. Available documents, including contemporary internal memoranda, indicate, as Kissinger said, "that Cambodia scarcely was a high priority concern." Foremost on the administration agenda—its focus on strategic history-making issues often to the detriment of "lesser" ones—was rapprochement with both the USSR and the PRC. Overthrowing Sihanouk would have worked against this goal. In Southeast Asia, U.S. attention centered on the critical situation in Laos, where the CIA-backed Montagnard forces were facing defeat, and, more important yet, on pulling out of Vietnam. Again, it was not in the American interest to upset the Cambodian status quo. No matter how mercurial Sihanouk was or how much he was distrusted, he had, for the first time in years, adopted a pro-U.S. position. Furthermore, the problems that came in the wake of the 1963 Diem overthrow in South Vietnam and the earlier unsuccessful attempts to tumble Sihanouk were warning to leave well enough alone.

Only after March 18 did the president order, "I want [CIA Director Richard] Helms to develop and implement a plan for maximum assistance to pro-U.S. elements in Cambodia." By resorting to covert means, the administration hoped to avoid giving the Communists pretext for military action against Cambodia. The CIA responded with some suggestions but explained that it couldn't properly comply without a station in the country. Since the 1965 embassy closedown, the agency's interests had been looked after by the Australian Special Intelligence Service station in Phnom Penh. It was owing to Sihanouk's CIA-phobia that, when the American Embassy reopened in temporary quarters in 1969, not only were no CIA employees assigned, but effort was made to select State Department personnel who had never served in Southeast Asia.

At the time of the prince's unseating, the embassy consisted of a chargé d'affaires, a junior foreign service officer, an air force attaché, a sergeant, a communicator, and two secretaries. Chargé Rives, using cardboard boxes as file cabinets, and his staff were working out of the two-story servants' quarters of his house near the Bassac River. They shared the mission's two telephones, which, in turn, shared a single incoming line. Lacking mechanical coding-decoding equipment, the communications gear was tied to the commercial service in Phnom Penh, from where all traffic was routed to Manila for retransmission. "Hardly the task force for the overthrow of Prince Siha-nouk," observed Andrew Antippas, who arrived on April 28, 1970, as politi-cal affairs officer and became the first U.S. official to visit the national assembly, the center of opposition to the prince.

Over strong State Department objections, Nixon on April 1 directed the immediate establishment of a CIA station. The latter became active twenty-four days later with the arrival of Chief of Station John Stein, who had served in Belgium and Africa, and a communicator. Following a subsequent tour in Libya, Stein briefly became deputy director of operations, in charge of over-seas clandestine activities, before retiring. Another assigned intelligence officer was Thomas Ahern, a veteran of the Caribbean area, Vietnam and Laos. Ahern had the later misfortune of being the Tehran station chief when Khomeini's minions overran the U.S. Embassy and made hostages of most of its staff. At the end of April, the embassy had only six people able to communicate with the French-speaking Khmers; none of the staff spoke Cambodian. Another French-speaker, an army colonel, arrived weeks later to be the military's eyes and ears in Phnom Penh. After about a month of pithy observations, such as that the Vietnamese Communists are "on the run everywhere . . . [they're] whipped," the colonel was recalled.[7]

Although the CIA had relied on Australia for its Cambodia-watch, as well as on its own posts in other Southeast Asian cities, it still had a lot of in-coun-try catching up to do. Its competitors, both friendly and hostile, had enjoyed uninterrupted information-gathering. The French, for example, had a uni-formed *Deuxième Bureau* (military intelligence) colonel and his adjutant oc-cupying desk space inside Cambodian army headquarters. According to Count Alexandre de Marenches, head of France's CIA counterpart between 1970 and 1981, French intelligence had an even more sensitive source in Cambodia, one "who was born there and spoke Khmer." At the Soviet Embassy in northern Phnom Penh, even the ambassador, Sergei Yemelyanovich Kudryavtsev, con-sidered intelligence-gathering his primary mission. His heavy-drinking mili-tary attaché once left his document-filled briefcase in the car taking him home from a social function. Its sensitive contents were photocopied before being returned by the American military officer who "found" it.[8]

Much was made by antiestablishment critics and Sihanouk of the March 14 hijacking of the 7,500-ton American freighter *Columbia Eagle,* which was car-rying $10 million in 500- and 750-pound bombs, igniters, and fuses for U.S. aircraft based in Thailand. Two Californians, steward Clyde McKay, aged twenty-five, and stoker Alvin Glatkowski, twenty, self-professed Marxists, used a bogus bomb threat to trick all but a dozen of the other crewmen to abandon ship. Leaving the evacuees bobbing in two lifeboats in the Gulf of Thailand to be picked up later, the hijackers forced Captain Donald Swann at gunpoint to turn the ship toward Cambodia. The next day, the ship anchored near Sihanoukville. McKay and Glatkowski asked for and received political asylum.

When Sihanouk was ousted later that week, there was an outcry of "CIA plot" from the left, including communist newspapers the world over. *Columbia Eagle,* conspiracy theorists insisted, was "low in the water when it arrived and high in the water when it left, indicating its cargo [including M-16 rifles to arm Lon Nol's soldiers] had been unloaded." These accusations provided little comfort to the hijackers, whose poor timing landed them in a sweltering Landing Ship Tank (LST) converted into a prison docked at Phnom Penh's Chrouy Chang War naval base. After allowing diplomatic observers and reporters aboard to verify that the ship's cargo was untouched, the Khmers released *Columbia Eagle* in April. The vessel, still unloaded, steamed to a U.S. naval base in the Philippines.

The hijackers, moved into Phnom Penh where they could be taken "off drugs on which [they] have been existing for some time" (to quote a U.S. Embassy official), were indicted in absentia by a Los Angeles grand jury. On October 31, 1970, McKay and a U.S. Army deserter, Larry Humphrey, eluded their Khmer guards in a restaurant. Abandoning Glatkowski, they roared off on a motorbike. They were believed to have then joined the K.R., ultimately marrying and taking up farming in northeastern Ratanakiri Province. Glatkowski had a nervous breakdown and spent some time in a Khmer mental institution. Then, unable to get asylum in the USSR, he turned himself in at the American Embassy. Flown out of Cambodia on a military flight on December 18, 1970, he was arrested by U.S. marshals just before landing in California. Tried in 1972 and sentenced to ten years imprisonment, the unrepentant Glatkowski was paroled five years later.[9]

Uncertain as to how events would turn out, afraid to give the Communists an excuse to blitzkrieg Cambodia and expecting Sihanouk's return, the White House reacted to events in Cambodia with caution. Relations with the new government were established on "a temporary basis" and Nixon called for a respect of Khmer neutrality in a March 21 news conference. Ten days later, Secretary of Defense Melvin Laird expressed concern to Secretary of State William Rogers that "we may not be taking all the steps that we could or should to prevent the Cambodian situation from developing in a way which we would wish to avoid. It would obviously undermine our position in Vietnam if the present government were overthrown." He suggested three areas of action. First, build up Khmer faith in the Lon Nol government, perhaps by helping settle a border land dispute with Vietnam. Second, reduce external military threats, such as removing Thai frontier troops to free Khmer border units to fight the Communists. Third, provide military assistance without involving U.S. forces.

The method of and delay in providing arms to the Cambodians lend further weight to indications that the United States was reacting to an unexpected event. In late March, air force Lieutenant Colonel Robert Riemensnider, then the only military officer in the American Embassy, was invited to Cambodian air force headquarters. There, officers "speaking for Lon Nol" made the first Khmer request for material assistance. They didn't want any American soldiers, they added, but would like the release of Khmer Krom troops in South Vietnam so they could be integrated into the Cambodian army. On April 9, Lon Nol's brother, Major Lon Non, personally asked the embassy for an immediate "100,000 to 150,000 weapons, and ultimately for 200,000 to 250,000" to meet the Khmer army's expected expansion.

White House reaction was reflected in an April 27 Nixon-to-Kissinger memorandum: "I do not believe he [Lon Nol] is going to survive," but "we must do something to help him survive." Even two antiwar Senate investigators (James Lowenstein and Richard Moose) visiting Cambodia observed "considerable [local] support" for Lon Nol and popular mystification at "American hesitancy in arming them [the Khmers] to defend against an invading force armed by China and the Soviet Union." A hesitant Washington instructed Chargé Rives to encourage France, which maintained a limited in-country military presence, to increase aid it already had been giving Cambodia.

On April 14, Lon Nol broadcast an appeal for "all unconditional foreign aid from all sources" to counter escalating Communist "acts of aggression." A week later, he made a direct plea to President Nixon. A meeting of the Washington Special Actions Group, the National Security Council subcommittee for contingency planning and crisis management, was convoked. Its recommendations resulted in the transfer of three thousand seized enemy AK-47 rifles to the Cambodians on April 23 by Vietnamese C-47 transport planes. Word even went out to American military installations in Vietnam to turn in "liberated" AK-47s, whether in personal possession or displayed in offices and service clubs, so that they could be given to the Khmers. On the overt level, Nixon decided to establish a small, civilian-led military assistance program to provide American weapons. Thus, by the end of its first full month, the new Khmer government had received nothing beyond a token shipment of small arms. Only on May 22 was the Joint Chiefs of Staff chairman able to submit to the defense secretary an if-needed air interdiction program covering eastern Cambodia.[10]

The foregoing further indicates an absence of American encouragement and foreknowledge of Sihanouk's overthrow at the policymaking level. As for other American abetment and precognition, however, a number of sources and "insider knowledge"—that amalgam of security lapses, leaks, rumors, and boasting—point strongly to unofficial encouragement by U.S. personnel, some with ties to Khmer counterparts dating back to the earlier American aid program. Henry Kissinger was quoted as telling European journalists at a 1977 luncheon that the United States was not involved in the change of governments, "at least not at the top levels." General William Rosson, onetime MACV deputy commander, is cited by writer William Shawcross as telling him "that United States commanders were informed several days beforehand that a coup was being planned" and that "American support was solicited."

Frank Snepp, a CIA analyst in Saigon between 1969 and 1971, is quoted as saying that there were "links between the Defense Intelligence Agency in Saigon and Lon Nol." Special Forces Captain Forrest Lindley, head of a SOG team involved in cross-border operations, has stated that in February 1970, "I was told that there would be a change of government in Cambodia." Half of his command, he said, was later transferred to another army element to replace "Khmer Serei units that were going into Cambodia." Australian author Richard Hall wrote in a 1978 book that although Sihanouk's removal was "generally attributed to the CIA," he had "heard that disputed in both Canberra and Washington," that "an old boy network of Cambodian officers trained in the U.S. enabled the coup to be organized with American army support bypassing the CIA."

Other allegations aired after Sihanouk's ouster were used to "prove" American connivance, but addressed purported earlier schemes, not the 1970 event. The most probable scenario is that individual U.S. military mid-operating levels, including an air force general, did encourage Khmer counterparts to depose the prince in the interest of their Vietnam War effort. Furthermore, U.S. military and civilian contacts of pro-American officers and politicians— though not advising such an action—assured the Cambodians of support if anti-Communists replaced Sihanouk; such assurances, given cultural nuances and human nature, could have been wishfully interpreted by a Khmer opposition that hoped to replace the *samdech*. Looking at the earlier South Vietnamese plotting against President Diem, it is easy to visualize the even less coup-adept Khmer cabal bumbling on and off a zigzagging path toward the precipice over which it ultimately would nudge itself. And, as in the Vietnamese case, the plotters dared not take the final plunge without some assurance of a U.S. safety net.

Son Ngoc Thanh, the Khmer Serei leader who was in contact with Lon Nol and Sirik Matak, later told an interviewer that "only after I was able to provide assurances that the U.S. would send the Khmer Krom troops did Lon Nol act." Thanh said that he wasn't part of the original conspiracy to oust Sihanouk, that it was organized inside Cambodia. Regarding Lon Nol's meetings with him to get assurance of Khmer Krom support, Thanh said that he informed a CIA officer and that "they [the CIA] said go ahead." This certainly indicates reactive U.S. support rather than the active fomenting of a coup, as many have charged. Assuming American backing, Thanh insisted that even if U.S. support had not been forthcoming, national assembly "deputies would have overthrown Sihanouk anyway." While the contextual intent of these assurances remains a moot point, it would not be the first time Americans said they would not support a coup but would recognize the successor government if it succeeded. Even without firm backing, the Khmer plotters surely could assume that America would not stand idly by while one of the much talked-about Southeast Asia dominoes fell to the Communists. As the late former CIA director William Colby said, "I don't know of any specific assurances [Lon Nol] was given, but the obvious conclusion for him . . . was that he would be given United States support."[11]

Meanwhile, the convergence of events and national aspirations made the Cambodian War inevitable. The root cause, of course, was the illegal PAVN-PLAF presence in Cambodia, which Hanoi had increased in early 1969. Not unexpectedly, the Vietnamese Communists failed to evacuate the border areas by sundown on March 15, the unrealistic deadline set by Phnom Penh. Representatives from both sides met at the Cambodian foreign affairs ministry the next day but accomplished nothing after two hours of talk. A week after Sihanouk's removal, Phnom Penh again asked Hanoi for a discussion of the problem of Vietnamese forces on Khmer territory. March 27 was agreed upon for another meeting. Instead, on the day of the scheduled parlay, the North Vietnamese and the PRG embassies' staffs left Phnom Penh for Hanoi aboard an ICC transport, thereby severing relations. Lon Nol and Sirik Matak in the meantime had officially stated that there would be no change in the nation's policy of "independence, sovereignty, peace, strict neutrality and territorial integrity."

Although the action was consistent with his statement and came only after the Communists refused to vacate their sanctuaries, Lon Nol's complete closure of Sihanoukville to the Vietnamese convinced Hanoi that Phnom Penh was playing a new and hostile game. On March 22, having already blamed Sihanouk's departure on "the U.S. imperialists," Hanoi radio announced its backing of "the just struggle that Sihanouk and the Cambodian people are waging" against the new regime. Saigon reacted two days later by pledging support for the Khmer government. The PRC, while forging a Sihanouk-K.R. alliance and, on May 5, breaking diplomatic relations with Cambodia, also let Phnom Penh know that it would consider "the matter between Sihanouk and the Khmer government . . . nothing more than an internal problem" if Cambodia accepted the presence of the PAVN-PLAF sanctuaries and supply lines, as well as provided propaganda support to the Vietnamese Communists. In contrast, the Soviet Union retained its representation in Phnom Penh.

The Nixon administration's stand was that "the question of recognition does not arise." However, this official position masked a division within Washington's ranks. The State Department, although not enamored of Sihanouk, was less than enthusiastic about supporting his successors. With Sihanouk's popularity and possible return, a widening of the Vietnam War and congressional reaction in mind, the department used bureaucratic stalling tactics to slow an increase in the U.S. presence in Phnom Penh. The Pentagon, on the other hand, was focused on the war and welcomed the installation of the strongly anti-Communist Lon Nol. These differences were to carry over to the embassy level, where the top military officers adopted a hear-no-evil stance against the State-CIA acknowledgment of the Khmer government's fatal flaws.

With the change in leadership came an immediate alteration of the Khmer government's attitude toward the U.S. Embassy. It was low-key at first, so as not to jeopardize Cambodia's last-minute attempts to seek an accommodation with the Communists. Intelligence on the location of enemy units was passed to the embassy via the British and the Australian military attachés, through whom the Khmers also requested information from Saigon. In late March, in a clandestine meeting initiated by the Cambodian intelligence service, the U.S. Air Force attaché met with a Khmer area commander on a houseboat on the Bassac River just outside the capital. The American was given valuable military intelligence. After North Vietnam broke relations, Khmer-American meetings became open and broached political subjects. U.S. personnel were allowed unrestricted access to a war room (later upgraded to a joint operations center) that the Cambodian high command set up to coordinate its activities. The war room's usefulness, however, was limited, mostly because of inadequate communications at every level of the Cambodian military machine, which also began to deluge the embassy with target information and air strike requests. American military commanders, meanwhile, overwhelmed the embassy for clarification of the Cambodian situation. To aid in communication, a mobile facility consisting of two huge white equipment vans was flown into Phnom Penh for embassy use in June 1970.

Sihanouk's continued popularity with the rural classes was underscored two days after his call for a general uprising against the Lon Nol government. On March 26, in the first significant domestic opposition to the new regime, peasant-dominated demonstrations erupted in the country's third largest city, Kompong Cham, forty-eight air miles northeast of the capital. The governor's mansion was sacked; dozens were killed or injured. One of the dead was another of Nol's brothers, rubber plantation owner Lon Nil, whose liver was cut from his sliced-up body to be cooked and distributed for eating. It was a long-accepted primitive belief, not unique to Cambodia, that the liver eater absorbed his enemy's strength.

Violent unrest rocked other towns in southeastern Cambodia. Commandeered vehicles carrying angry protesters from Kompong Cham and Svay Rieng Provinces were stopped short of Phnom Penh. It took army troops, brutally clamping down, to quell four days of pro-Sihanouk, anti–Lon Nol riots. Hundreds died or were arrested. Evidence of Vietnamese Communist involvement in the demonstrations included the apprehension of several PAVN-PLAF cadre members among the agitators. Furthermore, all of the disorders occurred in provinces housing border sanctuaries. Whatever the degree of Communist incitement, which did exist, the disorders were symptomatic of deep-seated unease permeating Khmer society at one of the most critical times in its history. These first and last pro-Sihanouk demonstrations of the Cambodian War sharpened the unforgiving polarization that led to the killing fields of 1975.[12]

CHAPTER FIVE

A Nation at War

SIHANOUK'S "ISLAND OF PEACE" WAS NO MORE. The war it had avoided for so many years hit Cambodia like a splash of boiling water. Phnom Penh's avowal of neutrality was drowned out as soldiers of both sides, confused by the political developments, suddenly found themselves caught up in intensifying fighting along the border from the Gulf of Thailand northeast to Kratie Province.

Even as Sihanouk was being cast out, howitzers of the Army of the Republic of Vietnam (ARVN) were lobbing shells from Chau Doc Province over the frontier onto Communist targets west of the Mekong in response to Khmer calls for assistance. The first coordinated Allied military effort of the Cambodian War came on March 20. It was a preview of the pattern the conflict would follow in the months ahead. A FARK outpost in southeastern Takeo Province was assailed by a PLAF company of about 150 men. The Cambodian commander radioed for help from ARVN artillery positions in An Phu, ten miles to the south in Chau Doc Province. Incoming rounds persuaded the attackers to pull back. The outpost commander then requested air spotter support while his men made a sweep of the area. Shortly, an American forward air controller (FAC) plane buzzed over the border and sighted the enemy. The South Vietnamese howitzers again opened up. There also were Vietnamese and U.S. fighter-bomber strikes against enemy positions in the same area.

Neighboring Kandal Province, astride the Bassac River and bordered on the east and north by the Mekong, was the scene of the next noteworthy Allied effort. Following conferences between the Vietnamese and the Cambodians, an ARVN ranger battalion stabbed two miles over the frontier against a three-hundred-man Communist sanctuary on March 27. U.S. Huey Cobra gunships provided covering fire. A reported fifty-three enemy died to three of the rangers; an American observation helicopter was damaged. Later that day, the Pentagon said that U.S. participation in the operation had been "without

[its] prior knowledge or consent." It added that while continuing to adhere to a policy of not widening the Vietnam War, American incursions into Cambodia would "continue for self-defense purposes." When ARVN rangers made another cross-border assault the next day, U.S. helicopters assisted them from Vietnamese air space. But just west of Svay Rieng Province's Parrot's Beak, a senior American military adviser crossed over with a group of ARVN officers to talk to the Khmer area commander. His orders, the U.S. colonel explained, were "to encourage meetings between Vietnamese and Cambodians."

The Cambodian government belatedly recalled veterans and reservists to the armed services, now renamed *Forces Armées Nationales Khmères* (FANK). Other armed elements, such as the national police's provincial guard units, were absorbed by the army, the *Armée Nationale Khmère* (ANK). In addition, all males aged eighteen to forty-five were asked to volunteer. Enthusiastic belief that Cambodia could readily regain control of its eastern frontier allowed FANK to grow quickly during the succeeding months, reaching a year-end strength of about 150,000. Young Khmers—barely, if at all, trained—went off to war cheerfully waving from commandeered buses and commercial trucks. Sandbags appeared around government buildings and hastily constructed bunkers in Phnom Penh.

At the mid-March upsurge of fighting, Lieutenant General Lon Nol, as FANK commander-in-chief, had a thirty to thirty-five thousand–man army of thirty infantry battalions, thirteen to fifteen infantry companies, support battalions, an armored regiment, an artillery battery, and an anti-aircraft battery. The army was concentrated primarily in the east and around the capital. FANK's air force, renamed *Armée de l'Air Khmère* (AAK), of 1,250 men was stationed at its only permanent base at the southeastern end of Pochentong Airport. The equally small FANK navy, the *Marine Nationale Khmère* (MNK), was based at Chrouy Chang War, on the Mekong just outside the capital, and at Ream, on the Gulf of Thailand near Sihanoukville, which was renamed Kompong Som. Ill-trained, haphazardly equipped, misused, poorly led, and poorly adapted to the different countries that had assisted it, FANK lacked cohesion. In its desperation to build new military formations, the government reduced recruit training time by half and created understrength components. During FANK's hasty reorganization, a dozen infantry brigades consisting of several battalions were created and concentrated in the southeastern part of the country. These were divided into two main forces—a general reserve (the 1st Brigade) in the Phnom Penh Special Military Zone, and the territorial forces under regional commanders in six existent military regions. Paramilitary units also were created for local defense.

On the international political front, Lon Nol instructed his UN mission to ask the Security Council to send observers to verify the Communist in-country presence. Accusing the intruders of attacking Cambodian outposts, the prime minister also called for the ICC, withdrawn in 1969 at Sihanouk's request, to return and "investigate Cambodia's charges of North Vietnamese and Viet Cong incursions." Beyond proposing an international conference "to end fighting in Cambodia" (which Hanoi rejected), the UN would be as responsive to Lon Nol's appeals and complaints as it had been to Prince Sihanouk's.

North Vietnam, determined to protect the supply lines and sanctuaries essential to its priority goal of conquering South Vietnam and assuming Cambodia now was in the enemy camp, decided to neutralize the Khmer regime before it grew into a real threat with the inevitable nourishment of U.S. aid. A COSVN document that reached anti-Communist hands on March 24 indicated that, if negotiations between Hanoi and Phnom Penh failed, the PAVN would invade Cambodia and would pursue a crash program to militarily and administratively enhance the Khmer Communists. On March 29, four PAVN divisions—the 1st, 5th, 7th, and 9th, between forty-five and sixty thousand battle-steeled men against Lon Nol's raw and inadequately armed thirty to thirty-five thousand—turned 180 degrees and began a multipronged offensive toward the center of Cambodia. Big gun support was provided by the 69th Artillery Division. A fifth infantry division, the PAVN-PLAF C40 (reflecting the Communist military region designation), also moved into place. Encamping in Kompong Thom and Siem Reap Provinces, respectively north and northwest of Phnom Penh, it took control of the ruins of Angkor. If Hanoi merely was trying to secure its sanctuaries, as some have claimed, it did not need such a systematically aligned and formidable force.

If the United States had any doubt about Hanoi's intentions toward the new Khmer regime, these were made clear on April 4 during the drawn-out peace talks in Paris. North Vietnamese delegation leader Le Duc Tho told his American counterpart that "as long as the Lon Nol–Matak government remains in Cambodia, then the Cambodian question cannot be settled." He also refused to discuss neutrality for Cambodia or a "cease-fire anywhere in Indochina." An ad hoc inter-agency group convened in Washington to study the situation and to discuss aid to Cambodia. Its belief that the fall of Phnom Penh was not imminent—based on political factors and the onset of the rainy season rather than on faith in FANK—was bolstered by a State Department report. The latter, dated April 22, stated that instead of attacking the capital, "the Communists intend to protect their interests in the border area while applying a range of pressures . . . against the current regime in hopes of bringing it down."

In Beijing when Sihanouk fell, Pol Pot hastened to Hanoi. Finally, after years of being virtually shunned by them to placate Sihanouk, he was going to receive North Vietnamese help. He immediately requested the return to Cambodia of the approximately one thousand Khmers who had been in North Vietnam since the Geneva Agreements almost sixteen years earlier. The Pentagon, learning of these developments that threatened to worsen the border situation, stepped up its years-long pressure for White House approval of an incursion against the Communist sanctuaries in Cambodia. The CIA, however, privately believed that, while an invasion had "some potential for disruption of VC/NVA efforts," any effects would be "neither crippling nor permanent." As Communist attacks spread throughout Cambodia's southeastern provinces, President Nixon leaned more toward the military viewpoint.[1]

Between April 3 and 24, there were at least twenty-nine major Communist attacks in Cambodia's eight south and central eastern provinces. FANK abandoned frontier outposts in, among other areas, the strategic Parrot's Beak area. On April 17, Phnom Penh admitted that in two weeks the PAVN-PLAF had "more than doubled its area of control" despite assistance its troops were receiving from South Vietnam's armed forces. Shortly after that admission, the enemy ran roughshod over a Khmer battalion only 25 miles south of Phnom Penh. Two days later, they were overrunning a hamlet fifteen miles from the capital. Another twenty-four hours and Route 2 between the capital of southern Takeo Province and Phnom Penh was cut. On April 23, Route 1 linking Phnom Penh and Svay Rieng was severed west of the latter's provincial capital. Route 13 between the frontier and Kratie Province's capital also was snipped. The next day, the FANK chief of staff estimated that, since the beginning of the Communist offensive, "about 3,500 Khmers" were killed, wounded, or missing. Mekong River traffic came under attack. Soon the country's northeastern provinces of Kratie, Mondolkiri, Ratanakiri, and Stung Treng were almost totally isolated and under enemy control.[2]

Media representatives, accustomed to a relatively free hand in South Vietnam, discovered an entirely new ball game as they sought news stories in the outbreak of heavy fighting across the border. Over a four-day period, eight news seekers disappeared in Svay Rieng. Two were American: photographers Sean Flynn, son of movie star Errol Flynn, and Dana Stone, freelancing for *Time* and the CBS network, respectively. The two, riding on rented red Honda motorcycles, were cruising along Cambodia's Route 1 when soldiers of the PAVN 9th Division stopped them. Moved about to foil rescue attempts, the two photographers were turned over to the K.R. and executed in June 1971, in Kompong Cham Province, far from where they had been captured. Contemporary pressure to locate the missing pair was such that the U.S. Embassy was tasked with using its contacts and assets to locate them. A famous playboy/actor-turned-photographer, the twenty-nine-year-old Flynn had gone to Vietnam in 1966. There he said, "I'm finally living the last great adventure, that of war and death." Many of the journalists then began to cover the war vicariously in, as novelist John Le Carré put it, "an encapsulated, self-defining world whirling in its own eccentric orbit." With justification perhaps, since at least twenty-three of them would permanently disappear in Cambodia by mid-1974.[3]

Khmer anger, frustration, and military impotence found a scapegoat in a traditional enemy. The first manifestation of irrational blame-shifting occurred in Svay Rieng as thousands of Cambodians fled the Communists debouching from their border sanctuaries. When ethnic Vietnamese civilians tried to join the Khmer exodus, they were forced back. Other Vietnamese civilians living farther inside Cambodia soon were herded into barbed wire-enclosed compounds. At one site, nearly a hundred were killed "in the crossfire" that accompanied a Communist advance into the area. Refugees said that the crossfire came from FANK soldiers who told the civilians to run and then started shooting. In Phnom Penh, a 6 A.M. to 6 P.M. curfew was announced for the capital's 120,000 Vietnamese, ostensibly to avert an increase in "subversive activities." It also helped stem the flight of *Yuon* (Annamites, but used pejoratively for all Vietnamese) back to their country.

On April 21, Cambodian troops tried to wrest Saang, a quaint village on the Bassac just below Phnom Penh, from the enemy, who had occupied it two days earlier. When the attack failed, a new commander was brought in, the recently reinstated and promoted Lieutenant General Sosthene Fernandez. His initial approach was to prod about a hundred Vietnamese Catholic civilians armed with a bullhorn and a white flag to enter the town and ask the invaders to surrender. Not surprisingly, gunfire broke out, pinning down the civilians. "We now know where the Viet Cong positions are," explained Fernandez. During the next few days, Cambodian artillery, complemented by MiG jets and T-26s, lambasted Saang. Then ANK troops, half of them in uniform less than a month, moved into the smoldering town.

In mid-April, a Khmer police official was hurriedly summoned to the ferry landing at Neak Luong, where Highway 1 crossed the Mekong on two barges about thirty-seven miles downstream from the capital. Civilian corpses, hands tied, were floating downriver. During the next four days, as Cambodians saw in *Chaul Chhnam,* their new year, the incredulous official counted four hundred bloating Vietnamese bodies in the river. Local residents later reported that the dead came from an isle a few miles above Neak Luong. The arrival of a large boat carrying Cambodian soldiers and Vietnamese civilians from the direction of Phnom Penh on April 10, they said, was followed by five nights of shooting. Other reports told of Cambodian troops, police, and even civilians killing Vietnamese in Phnom Penh and other parts of the country. The government-instigated pogrom officially was explained away as a difficulty in determining "whether Vietnamese were Viet Cong or peaceful citizens," as civilian anger at "collusion between Vietnamese residents" and the invaders or as the unavoidable result of combat. The government, however, did admit arresting approximately thirty thousand local Vietnamese. The United States condemned the "massacre of innocent civilians." Saigon issued an appeal for international intervention and asked for the repatriation of its citizens from Cambodia.

Approximately 190,000 Vietnamese, including those who had fled to Cambodia to escape fighting in their own country, were evacuated to South Vietnam over the following month. Cambodia suddenly found itself with a shortage of skilled labor, although an estimated 250,000 Vietnamese remained. About 20,000 of these lived on Phnom Penh's northern rim among the Catholic churches near the Sap River. The uncounted victims of the April killing spree cracked Lon Nol's fragile alliance with Saigon. South Vietnamese soldiers furthermore would exact random revenge from Cambodian citizens during the seesaw warfare that ravaged the frontier area in the months ahead.

If the government was persecuting its Vietnamese residents and refugees, it also was calling for Khmer unity. Reversing Sihanouk's policy of putting a "traitor" label on dissidents of both left and right persuasion, Phnom Penh appealed for all exiles to return to their homeland and released nearly five hundred political prisoners. Leniency did not extend to the Norodom family, however. After a three-day deliberation, a military tribunal on July 5 sentenced the *samdech* to death in absentia. The nine counts included allowing the Communists to settle in border sanctuaries, furnishing rice and arms to them, and embezzling. Monique, Sihanouk's wife, was given a life sentence, also in absentia. Others in the prince's entourage were condemned to either death or long prison sentences. Son Ngoc Thanh, the Khmer Serei leader, returned to

Phnom Penh on July 20. Thanh had ordered his group, its raison d'être gone with Sihanouk's ouster, dissolved. Lon Nol rewarded him for his support by appointing him a senior adviser. Name changes continued to be made to mark the transfer of power. The capital's main street, Monivong, became Boulevard 18 Mars (in honor of the date of Sihanouk's overthrow). Le Royal, the city's best hotel, was renamed Le Phnom (The Hill), although signs, documents, and nearly everyone long retained the old designation.[4]

Meanwhile, on April 1, the Cambodian government issued a "curse on all your houses" communiqué, striking out at America's hot pursuit policy, South Vietnam's incursions, and the continuing presence of the Vietnamese Communists. Whatever its sincerity, it was the proverbial cry in the wilderness. The Communists would not leave, and the Americans and South Vietnamese were shortly to unleash their biggest cross-border operation without consulting the Cambodians beforehand.

Operation Menu's B-52 missions were nearing an end when, on April 20, the Pentagon approved the MACV commander's request to complement the heavy bomber sorties with tactical air strikes against "maneuvering enemy personnel and supplies" within a limited area inside northeastern Cambodia. Operation Patio, as the tactical raids were called, was to last for only thirty days. Six F-100 Super Sabre jets lashed a 125-man enemy column eight miles inside Cambodia four days later in the first Washington-sanctioned tactical air operation of the Khmer war. On May 14, using phony cover targets to conceal the depth of the penetration from the American public, a 32-sortie Patio mission flamed a truck park/storage depot at the Cambodia-Laos border. In all, 156 sorties were flown and 263 tons of munitions were dropped before Patio was terminated on June 30, 1970. The code name for U.S. tactical combat flights over Cambodia then was changed to Freedom Deal. Within four months, the limitation of 28.8 miles into northeastern Cambodia on Freedom deal had been stretched far to the south and west. Even then, quietly made exceptions permitted strikes beyond the limited area. These, like the earlier B-52 raids, resulted in dual reporting until February 1971, with sorties outside the Freedom Deal zone before that date being falsely reported as within bounds. Of the more than eight thousand tactical sorties flown between July 1970 and February 1971, about 44 percent were outside the Freedom Deal boundaries. After Operation Menu's closure in May 1970, the electronically directed B-52 missions over Cambodia continued under Operation Arc Light, begun in 1965 to support ground actions and interdict supply lines in Vietnam.

Monivong, Phnom Penh's main street, with the popular Monoram Hotel at the right. The thoroughfare was renamed after Prince Sihanouk's ouster. Photo by author

On April 20, Nixon announced "the withdrawal of another 60,000 U.S. troops from Vietnam in 1970 and another 90,000 in 1971." In apparent contradiction, ten days later he informed the American public of a massive offensive into Cambodia against "the headquarters for the entire Communist military operation in South Vietnam." He explained that enemy actions in Cambodia "clearly endanger the lives of Americans who are in Vietnam now." He also said that, while the United States would continue interdiction bombing of Communist targets, there would be no close air support of FANK or ARVN elements in Cambodia. For three days, beginning on April 29, Allied forces, including Cambodian contingents attached to the U.S. Special Forces, poured across the frontier, igniting a 21.7-mile-deep, thirteen-operation incursion aimed principally against two areas that jutted into Vietnam (the so-called Parrot's Beak and Fishhook). American troops would remain in Cambodia until the last day of June.

Two U.S. Navy warships were stationed off Kompong Som until June 13 to prevent the surreptitious entry of supplies for the Communists. Other vessels blockaded the rest of the coast to the eastern border. A U.S.-Vietnamese flotilla, the largest Allied naval task force of the Vietnam War, pushed up the Mekong under strong air cover on May 9, clearing the river banks as it moved upstream. The armada disembarked South Vietnamese marines to retake the strategic ferry crossing town of Neak Luong, captured by the enemy barely a week earlier. While the bulk of the vessels remained at Neak Luong, thirty Vietnamese craft continued on to unload supplies at Phnom Penh, provide fire support to Kompong Cham farther upstream, and return with thousands of countrymen fleeing the earlier Cambodian pogrom. Neak Luong became a vital base from which South Vietnamese forces supplied and coordinated their activities in Cambodia. B-52s supported the ground advance without pause through the Menu-to–Arc Light transition on May 26.

Ironically and embarrassingly, the U.S. Embassy was one of the last to learn of the incursion, because of White House secrecy and inadequate decoding equipment. Chargé Rives heard the news over commercial radio as he was manually decoding a State Department instruction to inform Lon Nol. The latter already had held a press conference on the Allied incursion by the time Rives got to him.

The primary reason for the invasion—the one around which all others, including forestalling enemy threats to Vietnamization and the U.S withdrawal from Vietnam, revolved—was to prevent the fall of Cambodia, the White House nightmare of a "Communist-dominated Sihanouk government providing a secure (and nation-wide) sanctuary and logistics base" for the PAVN-PLAF. Washington had two outside choices: intervene directly or face a suddenly worsening political-military situation. It was a Catch-22 dilemma without a truly satisfactory solution.

The COSVN, North Vietnam's headquarters for operations in South Vietnam, which American policymakers didn't seem to realize was a multiunit element that could be moved easily by trucks, remained intact. Accurately located by U.S. intelligence in Base Area 353 (the Breakfast target of the Menu raids), the COSVN had been operating in the Mimot rubber plantation just west of the Fishhook section of Kompong Cham Province. Then, in mid-March, seeing the risk of being vised between the Cambodians behind them and the U.S.-ARVN forces in front, the COSVN staff had begun an approximately fifty-mile move northward to a new site near Kratie city on the west bank of the Mekong. They were long gone when American troops overran the old site. The COSVN soon was joined in its new location by South Vietnamese Communist headquarters units and Pol Pot, who commanded only between two and three thousand soldiers scattered throughout the western, southern, and eastern parts of Cambodia.

In addition to proving that America was desperate to end the Vietnam War without knowing how, the incursion resulted in immediate temporary benefits in Southeast Asia, and long-term political and psychological losses, both domestic and international. The Communists were dealt a blow, but one softened by both knowledge of the operation at least a few days before-hand and the realization that the incursion was limited in time and space. Although able to avoid a major confrontation and conserve its main forces, the enemy lost thousands of men. Thousands more were held up in the Ho Chi Minh Trail pipeline. The flow of supplies and munitions from North Vietnam was interrupted. Mountains of weapons, ammunition, vehicles, and supplies (an estimated 40 percent of the stockpile in Cambodia) were cap-tured or destroyed. Tons of documents, including plans for the defeat of the Lon Nol government, were seized. There was little question that the Com-munist offensive capability was blunted, gaining time for Cambodia, Viet-namization, and, although Hanoi didn't intend to interfere, America's departure. However, as one Khmer officer observed, the multipronged incur-sion "merely pushed . . . enemy sanctuaries deeper" into a part of the country that had been abandoned by FANK.

The violent reaction in the United States against the incursion reassured the Communists that ultimate victory in Southeast Asia was theirs. Ameri-can antiwar demonstrations were capped by the Kent State University trag-edy, in which four students died, and by a massive march on Washington. Three of Kissinger's own staff resigned; 250 State Department employees signed an objection to the administration's action. International protests followed, ignoring the fact that the Communists had long before made a mockery of Indochinese national boundaries and considered the wars in Cambodia, Laos, and Vietnam as one.

The Cambodia invasion also led to congressional restrictions on future ac-tivities in Southeast Asia. The Senate's Cooper-Church Amendment to the Foreign Military Sales Bill prohibited the use of funds for, among other things, "United States personnel in Cambodia who furnish military instruction to Cambodian forces or engage in any combat activity in support of Cambo-dian forces." It was the first restriction of a president's military action during wartime. This limitation was only the first, new ones subsequently joining each supplemental bill for assistance to the Phnom Penh regime. The divisive conflict between the White House and Capitol Hill was to go on until Nixon stepped down.[5]

Although daily Khmer-U.S. Embassy discussions on American assistance followed the initial March contact with the air attaché, military aid for the reeling Cambodians was slow in coming. A number of considerations aggravated the traditional bureaucratic crawl. Information coming out of Cambodia often was imprecise and inconsistent, in large part because of the intelligence hiatus of Sihanouk's anti-U.S. years. Initial reports were pessimistic enough to shadow the benefits of sending matériel to a country seemingly about to collapse. Not least were the possibilities that Sihanouk might return at any time or that Lon Nol was not the real power in Cambodia. In any case, vis-à-vis American policy, Cambodia was important only inasmuch as it affected the U.S. role in Vietnam.

With the decision to start sending arms to Cambodia came another to accede to the Khmer request to release Khmer Krom troops trained by the U.S. Special Forces to fight in Vietnam. During April and May, about four thousand of them, organized into eight battalions, were flown in their camouflage uniforms into Phnom Penh to augment Lon Nol's army. Their commanders almost immediately met with an American Embassy official to present their combat requirements. The Khmers Kroms would form FANK's spine during the first of their country's five years of war.

America's embrace of the Cambodian tar baby was clinched in May 1970, and not only by the incursion and the transfer of arms and Khmer Krom troops to Cambodia. Early in the month, Brigadier General Alexander Haig, Kissinger's military assistant, flew into Phnom Penh for a firsthand look at things. He returned to recommend that administration of the low-key military assistance program, then one of the tasks of the embassy's defense attaché, be given as a full-time assignment to a retired army officer. The recommendation was approved, and Jonathan Ladd was selected. Ladd had served with Haig as an aide to General Douglas MacArthur during the Korean War, commanded the U.S. Special Forces in Vietnam, and retired as a lieutenant colonel that January. Appointed a reserve foreign service officer in the State Department and assigned to Phnom Penh as the embassy's political-military counsel, he reached Cambodia in early June. Ladd reported directly to the White House and to the MACV commander, even after the arrival of an ambassador. These direct lines to Washington and Saigon enabled him, in the words of a colleague, "to wring equipment out of the depots in Vietnam" and "give the Cambodians useful tactical advice." The in-country assistance program staff numbered six officers and four enlisted men by year's end.

Having told the White House that he "did not want the job if Cambodia was to become another Vietnam" and having been assured that it wouldn't, Ladd believed that the war should be fought by the Cambodians using guerrilla methods. General William Yarborough, deputy commander-in-chief, U.S. Army Pacific, before his 1971 retirement, agreed with Ladd. Seeing "plans for bolstering the conventional [Khmer] forces with artillery, armored personnel carriers [and] the weapons of infantry . . . I could see so clearly the same old pattern of Vietnam on an austere basis, but without the help of the Yanks." He pointed out that "our philosophy was to fill the gap [in Khmer capabilities] with material, to give them bigger and better, more bang . . . and yet this was the very thing that the enemy machine was designed to cope with and counter." Seeing only failure in that course of action, Yarborough, who earlier had been in the field with Cambodian soldiers, "proposed an irregular warfare defense of this country." The Khmer G.I., he felt, "would make a superb irregular warfare soldier, the guerrilla warfare type." Supported along the chain of command, he worked up a "complete system of defense of Cambodia." Any plans for a low-profile guerrilla warfare approach to the Cambodian War were crumpled in the hands of the conventional warfare-oriented Joint Chiefs of Staff in Washington.

In mid-May, MACV created a Special Support Group, made up largely of U.S. military volunteers, to study the Cambodian picture, then plan and coordinate the delivery of matériel to the Khmers. Americans in mufti soon were shuttling between Vietnam and Cambodia to determine FANK needs, help the Khmer air force with training and security requirements at Pochentong and at a site in Battambang Province, and establish delivery procedures. Also that month, an initial group of FANK volunteers was flown into South Vietnam to train at two U.S. Special Forces camps. As others arrived, a third camp was opened. By November 1, four battalions of recently recruited Khmers Kroms and four of native Cambodians—4,096 men in all—had been trained "from the ground up." Fresh green troops began reaching the camps that month, followed by thousands more, all scheduled to be formed into thirty additional FANK battalions by the following summer. Khmer unconventional warfare forces training was conducted both in Vietnam and at a base in Lopburi, Thailand. Paracommando instruction was given in Indonesia. Khmer aircrews underwent training with the U.S. 56th Special Operations Wing at Udorn in Thailand.

When the 5th Special Forces Group left Vietnam in March 1971, most of those instructing the Cambodians stayed behind. Joined by Australian and New Zealand instructors, they received a third wave of Khmer recruits in August 1971. The U.S. training mission expanded in early 1972. It declined later in the year with the shaping up of the last Khmer battalions and Vietnamese need for the camps. In any case, the January 1973 Paris Agreements intended to end the Vietnam War precluded further Cambodian training in Vietnam. By the time it formally closed down in February 1973, the Special Forces program had trained eighty-five Khmer infantry battalions and a marine fusilier battalion. The basic training of FANK soldiers by then had shifted into Cambodia, where existing centers were improved and new ones built. They were located at Kampot, Kompong Speu, Lovek, Prey Sar, Ream, and Sisophon. Various specialized training programs continued in other countries, notably Thailand and the U.S., until the later stages of the war.

A July 24, 1970, U.S. presidential determination provided $7.9 million for Cambodia, principally for thousands of captured Communist weapons and twenty-three thousand surplus American M-1 carbines and Garand rifles, for the fiscal year ending June 30. An earlier determination allotted $1 million for "aircraft repairs" and "arms and ammunition for a Cambodian Army Mobile Strike Force." This contingency fund commitment was supplemented by an additional $40 million in State Department–handled Military Assistance Program (MAP) funds. The latter amount drained money away from aid packages intended for countries in Latin America, the Mediterranean area, Africa, and the Far East. America's low profile dissolved on August 19 with the signing of a U.S.-Cambodian military aid agreement providing for $185 million during the fiscal year beginning in mid-1970. The next fiscal year's assistance pledge would increase to about $200 million.

CIA-contracted Continental Air Services set up a charter service to help the Khmers move arms and ammunition into Cambodia. To counterbalance the powerful transmitters beaming propaganda from Hanoi and Beijing, an American company was hired to put up a million-watt radio station in Phnom Penh. What this multifaceted windfall meant to Cambodia and to the United States was unclear at the time. But the comment of one FANK officer seemed apropos. On a visit to Pentagon East, MACV's sprawling, air-conditioned headquarters on Saigon's northern rim, the officer smiled and said, "Oh, how very nice. You bring America to Vietnam."[6]

Vietnamese assistance to Cambodia was assured by two secret visits by South Vietnam's Vice President Nguyen Cao Ky to Lon Nol in April 1970 and an official one in early May. In turn, Major Lon Non, as national police chief as well as representing his older brother, made several trips to Saigon's presidential palace. The results were a military assistance agreement signed on May 27 and the restoration of diplomatic relations between the two countries. Liaison officers were exchanged to serve in each other's headquarters. The South Vietnamese were authorized to establish a base at strategic Neak Luong. There, in June, Vietnamese President Nguyen Van Thieu had a solidarity meeting with Lon Nol, Sirik Matak, and Acting Chief of State Cheng Heng. He treated the Cambodians on their own territory to food and wine helicoptered in from Saigon's Caravelle Hotel.

ARVN, which had conducted numerous cross-border operations to assist FANK even before the controversial incursion, kept about thirty-four thousand men (the number varying according to operation needs) in Cambodia after the end-of-June U.S. withdrawal. Vietnamese aircraft were given the nod to operate out of Pochentong. By August, twelve A-1 Skyraider bombers, six U.S.-loaned UH-1H helicopters, two AC-119 Shadow gunships, and several observation planes flown in from Vietnam were sitting on the Phnom Penh flight line. The helicopters were turned over to the Khmers once aircrews were trained to fly them. These aircraft were augmented by AAK's current air force of Soviet-made MiG 15 and 17 jets, and U.S.- and French-supplied models. Vietnam also agreed to help train FANK soldiers and to allow Cambodian recruitment efforts among ethnic Khmers living in South Vietnam.

Although Cambodia and Vietnam needed each other to fight the Communists, their cooperation was a rather bumpy road. Official Cambodian spokesman Major Am Rong, for example, speaking in a room adorned with anti-Vietnamese posters, complained on May 22 of two invasions of Cambodia, by "the North Vietnamese and the South Vietnamese." After one particularly blatant instance of ARVN vandalism and looting, Major Soeung Kimsea, FANK 22nd Battalion commander, said that "the population now fears the South Vietnamese more than they do the V.C." Later Khmer complaints addressed the resettling of Vietnamese peasants inside Cambodia, continuing criminal acts, and collusion between North and South Vietnamese troops. The United States sought to sandpaper the rough edges between its reluctant allies. One way was the inauguration of monthly tripartite meetings in early July 1970. America was represented by the MACV deputy commander, Cambodia by FANK Chief of Staff Lieutenant General Sak Sutsakhan.

Meetings with Cambodia's other traditional enemy, Thailand, also resulted in a resumption of diplomatic relations and the offer of training facilities, as well as the loan of five T-28 aircraft. Thai planes began aerial reconnaissance, supply, and combat missions over Cambodia. Despite promises to send troops, Bangkok decided not to unless Washington promised completely to finance them and to come to Thailand's assistance if the Communists won and threatened it. The United States agreed to fund a five-thousand-man contingent. Once trained, however, the Thai soldiers were sent to fight not in Cambodia but in Laos.

If Thailand gave the new Khmer government only halfhearted support, in the case of Laos it was Cambodia that declined close cooperation when it was first offered. In May 1970, a Royal Laotian Air Force C-47 landed at Pochentong. Former Prime Minister Prince Boun Oum led a delegation of southern Laotian anti-Communist leaders from the plane to waiting vehicles. They were driven into Phnom Penh to meet with the Lon brothers. Speaking in French, the visitors asked Lon Nol to station troops in southern Laos to head off PAVN forces they expected would be sent down the Ho Chi Minh Trail against Cambodia. Left unsaid was the fact that Khmer soldiers also would help the Laotians in their own war. In any case, according to a participant in the meeting, Lon Nol brushed aside the suggestion with an optimistic, "Ils vont se casser" [They, the North Vietnamese, will break themselves, if they attack us].[7]

Throughout May 1970, as U.S. and South Vietnamese forces advanced into the essentially flat land of southeastern Cambodia, vicious fighting kept FANK off balance. Towns fell. Some were retaken; too many remained in Communist hands. Fortunately for the Khmers, ARVN units were on hand to keep southeastern Cambodia from being lost. Enemy troops broke into Kompong Som on May 16 but were evicted the next day. A few days earlier, elements of the PAVN 9th Division took over the Michelin Company's seventy-square-mile Chup plantation across the Mekong from the provincial capital of Kompong Cham. They then directed their attention at the city.

Kompong Cham was defended by four understrength FANK battalions when it was besieged by the North Vietnamese. Two ARVN task forces were dispatched to relieve it on May 23. Capped by U.S. tactical aircraft and helicopter gunships, the South Vietnamese broke through the enemy forces to occupy the heavily napalmed Chup rubber plantation. Then, coordinating in a broad pincer movement with the naval vessels that had helped liberate Neak Luong and continued up the Mekong, they continued their advance toward Kompong Cham. After linking up with Khmer G.I.s pushing east out of the city to break the siege, the ARVN units turned back toward the border. At Chup, they told the French management that they weren't occupying the plantation and proceeded to strip it of all moveable assets, leaving behind a nonproducing ruin that was quickly reclaimed by their northern opponents. Chup again was under fire during the first week in June, this time by B-52s.

The provincial capital of Kompong Speu, twenty-five miles southwest of Phnom Penh on Highway 4, was overrun by the enemy on June 13. The action blocked fuel supplies normally trucked to the capital (which had only a two-week reserve) from the country's sole refinery in Kompong Som. Once more, the Cambodians called for ARVN help. An armor-led Vietnamese force joined six FANK battalions to recapture the town, which also was the site of the French military mission commissary. At fifty miles from the frontier, the operation marked South Vietnam's deepest penetration into Cambodia. That fighting also halted Japanese-supervised construction on the huge nearby Prek Thnaot (Sugar Palm River) dam and power plant complex. The latter was the first phase of a planned $60.5 million multination Mekong River irrigation and 18,000-kilowatt power project.

About thirty-five miles to the north, short hours before Allied troops retook Kompong Speu, the enemy severed Cambodia's single-track east-west railroad line. They had cut the north-south line to Kompong Som two months earlier by blasting a bridge. It was nearly 4 A.M. on June 16 when a rice-laden Phnom Penh–bound freight train chugged onto a siding at Krang Lovea to let a westbound passenger train pass. Both were stopped when Communist soldiers surged into the station. Shooing away the passengers, crews, and station master, they sent rockets into the steam locomotives. Rounded-up villagers were forced to unload more than two hundred tons of rice and other food. The raiders, who earlier had interdicted Route 5, then returned north to maintain pressure on the provincial capital of Kompong Chhnang.

Across the Great Lake to the northwest, some two hundred tourists were fleeing Siem Reap as the PAVN-PLAF C40 Division prepared to attack from the adjacent Angkor ruins. The ensuing assault on Siem Reap failed because of an unusually spirited Cambodian defense, including mobilized civilians, and South Vietnamese fixed and rotary-wing gunship support. In the northeastern Ratanakiri Province, a dramatic U.S.–South Vietnamese land-and-air operation in June enabled 7,571 encircled Cambodian soldiers, dependents, and refugees to be snatched from under the noses of the Communists. The rescued Khmers were taken into Vietnam for transfer to Phnom Penh.

As Communist assaults spread throughout Cambodia, American and Vietnamese aircraft went beyond their support of the ongoing incursion to assist beleaguered FANK G.I.s as far away as Kompong Thom in the center of the country. The provincial capital seventy-nine air miles north of Phnom Penh was viewed by the invaders as a strategic link in controlling Cambodia and in maintaining supply lines extending down from Laos. Between July 31 and August 9, 182 U.S. fighter-bomber and 37 fixed-wing gunship strikes were flown and, in Lon Nol's words, "turned the tide at Kompong Thom." At least one American plane apparently was downed during fighting near Tang Kauk, an agricultural village of several thousand southeast of Kompong Thom. Two crewmen in the forward seats died in the crash, according to a K.R. regional political-economic committeeman who defected to the government in 1971. He said that a third crewman was captured and refused "to answer questions, drink or eat." Ka Savuth, the rallier, described how the captors thereupon nailed the American's hands to a wooden cross with "his feet touching the ground." The crucified man died in agony after a week on the cross.[8]

By June, after a tedious journey down the malarial, air-harassed Ho Chi Minh Trail through Laos, Pol Pot was back at his headquarters in Cambodia's Ratanakiri Province. Soon after the government began its first offensive in the late summer, he moved his staff across Kratie Province past North Vietnam's COSVN to a site on the Chinit River in Kompong Thom Province, where he had been born in May 1928. Still primarily in the recruiting and organizing stages, the Pol Pot Communists had yet to consolidate, control, and standardize the activities of adherents scattered throughout the five geographical administrative zones into which they had divided the country. CPK elements often came into conflict, sometimes bloody, with both their Vietnamese backers and the K.R. who had been trained by Hanoi.

The Pol Potists skillfully wheedled their way into the K.R.'s most critical administrative positions and exploited Hanoi's concentration on the Vietnam War to erode Vietnamese control and gain ascendancy. With increasing power came the confidence to establish the CPK's inane form of communism and ruthlessly to eliminate perceived threats to that power. Proximity to the rural masses, Sihanouk's appeal, the overall better behavior of the Communist armies, and the widespread Allied bombardments facilitated K.R. recruitment tasks. Intelligence reports indicated that, by the fall of 1970, up to thirteen thousand Cambodians were fighting in more than two dozen Khmer Communist or Khmer-Vietnamese battalions. Thousands more belonged to irregular units. Subtle and devious CPK methods insured that outsiders would not get a coherent picture of events deep inside Cambodia for years to come. Most of the Allies' intelligence sources were the so-called ralliers, those who for any number of reasons defected with small pieces of a complex jigsaw puzzle.[9]

Cambodia's capital was left hemmed in on three sides by the 1970 enemy onslaught. Westbound Route 5 to Battambang, the province that provided the nation with 70 percent of its rice, was the only highway still open. Then, hurt by the Allied incursion and Khmer resistance, in need of rest and resupply, the Communists suddenly eased their pressure. The slowdown in fighting gave the Khmer government, a groggy combatant saved by the bell after being mauled in the opening round, time to react in a more organized fashion. A three-stage strategy was adopted in June. The Lon Nol Line, an imaginary one, was drawn northwestward across Cambodia from the Fishhook area to cross the Mekong near Prek Kauk and then pass Kompong Thom along Route 6 to Siem Reap before veering sharply north to the Thai border near Samrong. Stage one of the strategy realistically called only for survival south of the Lon Nol Line. Most of the population and arable land lay there. During the second phase, this territory would be consolidated. The optimistic last stage called for retaking the lost ground north of the line.

On June 1, the government imposed martial law. On the June 25, a general mobilization was announced, with everyone between eighteen and sixty instructed to "perform military service or join supporting organizations." As Phnom Penh's population doubled from a refugee influx and supply lines became increasingly threatened, the regime asked the capital's inhabitants to raise chickens and plant vegetable gardens. On July 1, a new political cabinet was named, marking the first of numerous high-level governmental rearrangements. The only selections of consequence were Lon Nol and Sirik Matak, the first to remain as prime minister and national defense minister, the second to be his deputy.[10]

Military action now generally was reduced to enemy harassment and government counterblows. American aid finally was flowing in. FANK was growing. Nevertheless, at the height of the 1970 wet monsoon season, marked by steamy morning hazes and late afternoon downpours, the Communists controlled all of the eastern and central parts of northern Cambodia, sections in the east central area, most of the southwest and highlands in the south. In all, the government had lost more than half of the country during a roughly four-month period.

It seemed time to think about Phnom Penh's first offensive of the war, not only to regain ground but also to reassure the public, the military ranks, and the world that the government could win. An ambitious goal was selected— open the land route to and relieve surrounded Kompong Thom, the capital of the province of the same name whose loss had been averted by Allied air power. Sitting on Highway 6 about midway between Phnom Penh and Siem Reap, the city was being hit by on-and-off ground assaults and mortar fire from an enemy whose lines often were only six hundred feet from FANK defensive positions.

FANK's projected offensive was given three parts, two following land routes and the third the Sen River. A major objective of the first two was Kompong Thmar (near which Pol Pot was headquartered) in southern Kompong Thom Province. Kompong Thmar, situated just south of the Lon Nol Line about sixty-six air miles north-northeast of Phnom Penh, is the apex of a rough triangle of highways. Routes 6 and 21, merging into a continuation of Highway 6 at the town, form the respective left and right legs of the triangle. The latter's base is Route 7 from Skoun, where it starts at its juncture with Highway 6, to Traeung, where Route 21 to the northwest begins. Route 7 then continues eastward to the provincial capital of Kompong Cham and crosses the Mekong en route to the frontier's Fishhook area.

Skoun, recently retaken from the PAVN-PLAF with the decisive assistance of U.S. airpower after months of battering during seesaw warfare, was to be the logistical base and jumping-off point for FANK's main thrust. When FANK began its drive north on the curvy thirty to thirty-five miles of Route 6 to Kompong Thmar, a secondary force simultaneously would advance up Route 21 from Traeung toward Bos Khnoar village and the Chamcar Leu rubber plantation. There would be artillery and armored support, but the key to success was Allied air might. Short, cane-wielding, and eccentric Brigadier General Um Savuth was placed in charge of the land offensive's 10–12 battalions (including battle-tested Khmer Krom troops). The river operation would ferry reinforcements and supplies to Kompong Thom and return with refugees. Appropriately, the offensive was named *Chenla Dey Teuk* (Chenla, after the sixth-century states, Earth and Water, as the nation has been known because of the importance of these two elements).

There was a festive air about the FANK units gathering in Skoun in late August. Soldiers and their families—the latter a familiar sight in battle zones, given the low army pay and haphazard, corrupt supply system—chatted and laughed as they disembarked from gaily painted buses and other civilian vehicles that mixed incongruously with olive drab military trucks and M-113 armored personnel carriers (APCs). Raised in a culture that blended Buddhism and animism, the average Khmer G.I.s believed in the power of amulets and tattoos. They wore monk-blessed scarves, waist-girdling strands of

U.S.-equipped soldiers of the FANK 7th Brigade. Photo by author

metal prayer discs, beads, and small bags around their necks. The bags, placed in the mouth for strength and protection when going into combat, contained tiny ivory Buddhas and coins bearing ancient Hindu figures. The American-trained Khmers Kroms often were more self-conscious, tucking their scarves inside their helmet liners. These beliefs were encouraged by Lon Nol, who established a mobilization bureau committee to promote "cultural warfare using traditional Mon-Khmer *vethamon* [occult practices]."

On Monday, September 7, Brigadier General Neak Sam ordered the first battalions to move out. Rested and enthusiastic, they started up Highway 6 as a U.S. spotter plane weaved or circled over the raised two-lane asphalt ahead. The FANK motorized column inched nine miles to Prakham, arriving there on September 10. The offensive was slowed by blown bridges, felled trees, and trenches dug across the road rather than by enemy combat action. Then, a few miles farther on during the morning of September 13, the troops experienced their first real resistance at a tumbled bridge just outside Tang Kauk. Since the low-lying fields flanking the highway were inundated by monsoon rains, there was no way for vehicles to circumvent the obstacle. Engineers repaired the span under sporadic mortar fire, and the column moved closer to Tang Kauk. Suddenly, it came under heavy shell and machine gun fire from fortified bunkers and trenches. A call for air strikes was radioed up to a twin-engined OV-10 Bronco orbiting overhead. As aircraft thundered in with rockets and bombs, confirmation of the presence of "sizeable" forces brought in to ambush the Chenla column was provided by a captured PAVN soldier.

A Communist mortar barrage began around midnight on September 14, peppering the dug-in FANK soldiers. It was followed by a 9th PAVN Division assault that failed to overrun the Khmer positions. Having repelled the Communist charge, the government troops moved forward. They reached the southern part of long, narrow Tang Kauk village, only to be forced back with significant losses. Meanwhile, a repaired bridge to their rear went up in flame and smoke. Civilian workers dispatched to fix it were attacked. At this point, the principal field commanders were recalled to Phnom Penh "for consultation."

The waterborne element of the Chenla operation had been having more success. It churned northwestward from the Sap River port of Kompong Chhnang. Then, at the lower tip of the Tonle Sap Lake, it veered sharply northeastward up the Sen River. By midmorning on September 9, the force had wound thirty-four miles up the waterway virtually unchallenged, with an identical distance still to go. The troop-carrying boats were receiving harassing fire, which killed an officer, by the time they chugged into Kompong Thom late that evening. Three days later, the naval vessels returned to their base as Communist guns intensified fire on the reinforced city. By September 15, the riverine flotilla had evacuated approximately six hundred refugees to Phnom Penh. Another three days and the hardworking seamen disembarked a fresh battalion, munitions, rice, and flour from twenty-five boats to bolster Kompong Thom's defenses. The Sen River operation continued until early October with varying degrees of enemy interference. Any plans for the city's enlarged garrison to break out to the southeast to join up with the Chenla ground element obviously had to be shelved, now that the Highway 6 advance was stalled some forty miles away.

Fresh battalions moved north from Skoun amid reports of a large enemy force preparing to cut off the troops already stretched out along Route 6. As these reinforcements drew closer to them, the main column near Prakham was showered with shells howling in from Tang Kauk. It was the first PAVN-PLAF artillery barrage on Cambodians during the war. The next day, the fresh troops linked up with the main body, bringing the Chenla attack force to fourteen battalions totaling more than seven thousand men. Further reinforcements subsequently increased the Chenla army "to about 32 battalions, many untrained," as U.S. observers noted. On the other side, the defenders of Tang Kauk were buttressed by an influx of soldiers from rubber plantations east of Highway 6. They soon numbered an estimated three to four thousand, at most. Miles below Tang Kauk, PAVN sappers penetrated Khmer lines again to flame a bridge freshly repaired by engineers. The span, and others, would be fixed and destroyed again in a few days. Harassment raids pecked at sections of the long, unmoving FANK column.

On September 21, Lon Nol helicoptered to Skoun. After reviewing the still uncommitted troops there, he flew on to Prakham "to straighten things out." The next day, a government announcement stated that General Neak Sam, "suffering from malaria," was replaced by Brigadier General Thong Van Phan Moeung, the commander of western Military Region 3. That same day, eleven FANK battalions resumed the offensive. Paratroopers, strengthened by infantrymen, left the highway blacktop to slog east and north behind Tang Kauk. Other G.I.s sloshed into the rice paddies to the west to complete a flanking maneuver, while an APC-supported element moved up the roadway. An American FAC fired smoke rockets to mark enemy strong points for circling U.S. 7th Air Force jets and Khmer T-28s. The enemy defense gradually dissolved northward in the face of the coordinated assault. Over the next month, Allied aircraft pounded the foe's principal base of operations, the Chamcar Andong plantation just southeast of Kompong Thmar. The last of Cambodia's five largest rubber-growing tracts to continue operating, Chamcar Andong quickly was shut down by American bombs. Tang Kauk finally fell to FANK on September 25.

For the moment, the heavy fighting was over. A Khmer army spokesman said that only four Vietnamese bodies had been left among the broken red tiles, fire-sooted walls, and blast-stripped palm trees of Tang Kauk. He added, "We did not have many losses." FANK admitted to forty-three dead and more than three hundred wounded in the final drive to take the town, placing Vietnamese dead at more than three hundred. In a quote worthy of a similar one from a U.S. officer in Vietnam, a ground-based Khmer forward air guide (FAG) who coordinated air strikes with airborne American FACs said, "We had no choice. We had to bomb Tang Kauk to liberate it."

Tang Kauk was FANK's "first major victory." It also was the PAVN-PLAF's first departure in the war from strictly hit-and-run tactics. More important, perhaps, was the fact that Chenla did not get past Tang Kauk, fourteen miles from its starting point. In the days ahead, Cambodian soldiers would conduct sweeps in the jungle to the east, leading to renewed, but limited, fighting in October. Civil and military pacification teams arrived to resettle the roughly five thousand inhabitants of the half dozen cleared hamlets between Skoun and Prakham, and to form self-defense militia units. The enemy resorted to peck-and-flee stabs against the Highway 6 forces and rear supply lines, while at the same time trying to dilute the FANK concentration by attacks on Kompong Thom and along Route 7 around Kompong Cham. By November, although the government called it a victory, Chenla was dormant.

There was little letup in the renewed fighting elsewhere as the Communists concentrated on land arteries linking Phnom Penh to its provincial capitals (thirteen of nineteen were in government hands) and the outside world. On November 20, the enemy cut Highway 4, which had been reclaimed by FANK. Isolated from the two-year-old refinery in Kompong Som, the capital had to institute its first gas rationing of the war. As 1970 neared its end, the Communists intensified their attacks on the umbilical cord connecting the Chenla column with its supply sources. They hit Route 6 where it wove through the lake-strewn area between Skoun and the capital. Two vital bridges were destroyed. Until they could be repaired, the Chenla soldiers had to rely on air-dropped supplies to maintain their positions. On November 30, the PAVN-PLAF even temporarily occupied the Prek Kdam ferry landing and southeastern terminus of Route 6 on the Sap River.

PAVN 9th Division elements, reinforced by units sent from the border area, jabbed at FANK outposts along the approximately thirty-mile-long stretch of Highway 7 between Skoun and Kompong Cham to the east. It took the South Vietnamese, flying a forty-helicopter airmobile operation into Kompong Cham's airport, and U.S. Air Force jets and Shadow gunships to help FANK reopen the highway. As intended, the enemy actions along Routes 6 and 7 prevented Chenla from reawakening. Communist determination to defeat Lon Nol was made clear by the fact that by the end of 1970 the North Vietnamese had some ten thousand troops targeted against FANK. While their 1st Division sat astride Route 4, units of the 5th, 7th, and 9th operated from plantations far to the northeast.[11]

American warplanes by now had become an integral part of the Cambodian War, a fact those involved desperately sought to keep from public attention. Fixed-wing gunship sorties, for example, increased measurably during the second half of 1970. The AC-119G Shadows out of Saigon's Tan Son Nhut field soon were joined by K-model Stingers, upgraded with two 20mm cannons to supplement the standard four 7.62mm mini-guns. The Stinger also had side-looking radar and infrared gear in addition to the night observation sight. The aircraft—thousands of rounds per minute spewing from the boxy fuselage between twin engine-to-tail booms—buzz-sawed enemy threats to the capital, Kompong Cham, Kompong Thom, and Skoun. As a primary air interdiction element, the gunships hammering night and day at road and river traffic constantly refined their methodology. For instance, they augmented their ground-based tactical air center with the use of FACs and electronics-crammed EC-121 aircraft monitoring such devices as movement-sensing instruments planted alongside enemy supply routes. Between July 1970 and March 1971, AC-119s killed an estimated 3,151 Communist troops and hit 609 vehicles and 731 sampans. In all, of the U.S. Air Force's 201,484 sorties in Southeast Asia in 1970, 16,624 were over Cambodia. Operation Arc Light B-52 sorties that year totaled 15,103, of which Cambodia absorbed 2,906. In addition, U.S. Army helicopter gunships, working with observation helicopters, flew hunter-killer missions over the country east of the Mekong.[12]

In early September 1970, the burgeoning American embassy began its move from Chargé Rives's modest quarters in southeast Phnom Penh to a nearby wall-enclosed, multistory white building. At midday on September 12, Emory "Coby" Swank, a slender native of Maryland whose previous postings included the USSR, Laos, East Europe, and China, arrived at Pochentong from Saigon aboard a military transport to become the first American ambassador to Cambodia since 1965. The forty-eight-year-old chief of mission was widely believed to be in line for either the State Department's senior career foreign service officer position in Washington or the ambassadorship in Moscow. "However," recalled one of the embassy officers, "Swank had no specific strategy for operating the U.S. Mission except that Americans were not going to tell the Cambodians how to run their war. Nor, as he said when told of rampant corruption, were they there to reform the Khmer society." Swank was about to find Phnom Penh a political minefield.

A case in point was the evolution of military assistance to Cambodia. Whether a result of Nixon's desire to accelerate Cambodia's arming (what the U.S. Army called a need for an administrative "single point of contact" for the growing aid program) or the Defense Department's bureaucratic determination to control it, the creation of a Military Equipment Delivery Team, Cambodia (MEDTC, pronounced "medtack"), was approved on December 28. A continuation of activities performed by MACV and Fred Ladd's office, MEDTC accompanied the switch in aid financing from presidential contingency funds to Foreign Assistance Act resources, making assistance a part of the Military Assistance Program (MAP). MEDTC was to be head-quartered in Saigon and initially limited to sixty people. Ten of these would be permanently assigned to Cambodia, with the others shuttled in on a temporary duty basis as required. Not only did this bulldoze Ladd's low-profile program, but it also bypassed Saigon, whose commanding officer believed his MACV could best coordinate military aid. The MEDTC chief would report directly to CINCPAC commander Admiral John McCain, Jr.

Cambodian workmen were renovating the embassy when the new ambassador moved into his second-floor office. With the sense of war yet to contaminate completely Phnom Penh's stubbornly held aura of colonial serenity, security was a secondary priority. Two Khmers were in the partly lit courtyard of the embassy compound guarding the front gate. Inside the mission were a U.S. Marine guard, a clerk, and a teletype operator. It was just before dawn on December 1. A sudden brilliant flash of light inside a section of the building still undergoing remodeling was immediately followed by a thunderous blast punctuated by spraying glass, wood, and masonry. Part of the front wall was blown out, four rooms were damaged, windows were smashed, and the new switchboard was a shambles. No one was hurt, a fortunate contrast to the day-time car bomb that inflicted two hundred casualties at the Saigon embassy in March 1965. A Communist agent was believed to have smuggled plastic explosive and a timing device into the embassy the evening before in either a briefcase or a worker's tool kit. Despite a number of earlier terrorist attacks that killed twenty-five people in the city, this was the first general one directed at Americans. Twenty-nine days later, two U.S. noncommissioned officers assigned to the defense attaché's office were shaken but unhurt when an explosive detonated yards behind their car as they drove to work.[13]

Developments during the second half of 1970 persuaded the Cambodian government to upgrade its military goals to an unrealistic level. For example, an October 4 defense ministry paper entitled *Strength and Organization of the Khmer Armed Forces* envisioned a FANK force of 610,000. A regular army of 350,000, air force and navy each of 25,000, and territorial force of 210,000 would be supplemented by a 53,000-strong local paramilitary self-defense arm. A political goal was achieved on October 7 when the joint houses of the Cambodian legislature enacted a law establishing the nation as a republic, effective at 7 A.M. two days hence.

Shortly after dawn on October 9, the assembly president read the republic-creating proclamation. Then the triumvirate that had taken over from Siha-nouk earlier that year—Chief of State Heng, Prime Minister Nol, and Deputy

Prime Minister Matak—led dignitaries to Republic Square. There a new flag—blue with three white stars in the upper right and a white silhouetted Angkor Wat in a red upper left quadrant—was raised to the martial strains of an equally new anthem. Nol and Matak were promoted to general-of-the-army and lieutenant general, respectively. A parade and three days of festivities followed. The creation of the republic marked the official end of a 1,168-year-old monarchy, established with the ascension to the throne of Jayavarman II in 802 A.D. and the transition from the Java-dominated Chenla era to the unified Angkor period.

Although Heng was to remain chief of state pending a presidential election, the real power remained in the hands of Lon Nol, who, with the support of the military establishment and his younger brother's help, had elbowed aside both Heng and the more capable Matak. Nol wound up the eventful year by writing a letter to his American counterpart. A summary of Cambodia's military situation and needs, it was the start of a personal correspondence that, by mid-August of 1972, would number sixteen letters and two telegrams. President Nixon's responses were five letters and a number of oral messages. Washington saw it as allowing the Khmer leader the opportunity to vent steam and, at the same time, give the U.S. ambassador frequent access to him.[14]

CHAPTER SIX

1971:
The Decisive Year

WITH THE CHENLA OFFENSIVE BEATEN DOWN on Highway 6 northwest of the capital a mere fourteen miles from its jumping-off point, the only factors standing between the new republic and military defeat on New Year's Day of 1971 were U.S. aid, Allied air power, and about 11,000 South Vietnamese troops then in southeastern Cambodia. On January 18, finally ending the sham that all U.S. air activity was interdictory, but still hedging, the Pentagon announced its intent to employ the "full range" of air power against enemy troops and supplies that "ultimately" might threaten American forces in Vietnam. There would be no use of U.S. ground troops or military advisers, it added.[1]

Six days earlier, an Allied offensive was launched to reopen Route 4, the vital artery connecting Phnom Penh and the Gulf of Thailand seaport of Kompong Som. For two months, the Communists had been harassing road traffic and using units of the ANK 13th and 14th Brigades as punching bags. Capitalizing on their success, they dug in where the highway zigzags across the rugged, tree-canopied Elephant Mountains about midway between the capital and the sea. Unable to reopen the key road, the Cambodians again turned to the Americans and the Vietnamese for help. Allied planners agreed on the U.S. air-supported, two-pronged Khmer–South Vietnamese operation that got under way on January 13.

Lieutenant General Sosthene Fernandez of Cambodia issued a move-out order to the northern prong of the offensive from his command post at Kompong Speu, on Highway 4 some twenty-five miles west of Phnom Penh. Eight thousand troops, spearheaded by the 1st Paratroop Brigade and armored personnel carriers, started southwestward along the dual-lane hardtop. The general's situation illustrated a key weakness of the U.S. effort in Southeast Asia—sponsoring Third World nations to fight according to world power standards. As commander of Military Region 2, Cambodia's southwestern front, the small, wiry-haired general had an army totaling approximately thirty thousand, of whom only 60 percent were properly armed, and which included barely trained women and children. His command post was in a claustrophobic, windowless room boasting recently installed air conditioning. But, unlike the super-equipped American military nerve centers he tried to emulate, his sometimes was torrid and well lit and other times frigid and dimmed out because it lacked enough electricity to sustain both air conditioning and lighting.

On the other side of the mountain range, U.S.-trained Lieutenant General Ngo Dzu,[2] in charge of the ARVN's southern Cambodia operations, unleashed his 4th Armored Brigade, with two armored cavalry regiments, three ranger battalions, an artillery battalion, and an engineering group—a total of about five thousand men—northward along Route 4 and, as a secondary operation, eastward on Route 3. The main Allied armies were to meet at seven-mile-long Pich Nil Pass, which was defended by an estimated three battalions of the PAVN 1st Division supported by a Khmer Rouge PNLAFK battalion. Two days into its advance, the ARVN force ran into an ambush at Stung Chhay Pass in the lower mountain range. Its 16th Armored Cavalry Regiment quickly smashed through, leaving the rangers to mop up. A second ambush was better organized. PAVN gunners hit the first and last vehicles of the 12th Armored Cavalry Regiment's lead squadron to block the road, trap the unit, and wipe it out. They were thwarted when the lead armored vehicle accelerated and, a blazing torch, cleared the highway before blowing up. The timely arrival of a ranger battalion and U.S. aircraft crossfired and obliterated the bushwackers.

Planning role aside, U.S. involvement unquestionably stretched congressionally imposed no-combat restrictions. Like all violations of congressional bans during the Southeast Asian conflict, it was the inevitable result of the unrealistic demands of a nation hoping to win an unwanted war with half-hearted means. Despite government efforts, it was a dichotomy impossible to conceal in an open society. A media photographer reported American helicopter gunships chattering overhead at Stung Chhay, the first of the ARVN's two major encounters before climbing to Pich Nil Pass. To the north, U.S. F-4 Phantom jets were spotted dropping napalm tanks on Communists confronting the Cambodians. B-52s, strategic bombers in a tactical role, left clear evidence of the elephantine loads they dumped on enemy positions. The *New*

York Times even ran a photograph of a bareheaded, camouflage-uniformed American, identified by a Saigon-based spokesman as "a logistics officer," running toward a Cambodian Bell Huey helicopter in the battle zone.

A major American support element consisted of two 7th Fleet vessels—*Iwo Jima,* a helicopter amphibious assault ship, and *Cleveland,* an amphibious transport dock—steaming fifteen to twenty-five miles offshore in the Gulf of Thailand. The world's first ship designed specifically to operate rotary-winged aircraft, the flat-topped *Iwo Jima* could carry a fully equipped marine landing team, a reinforced helicopter squadron, and supporting personnel. The over 18,000-ton ship had twenty-four aircraft aboard to provide air support. The slightly smaller *Cleveland,* with two large landing spots on the flight deck aft, was carrying a full complement of six two-rotored CH-46 Chinooks. The latter ferried supplies from *Iwo Jima* to the ARVN soldiers ashore. *Cleveland,* with forty army communications specialists aboard, also served as a floating gas station for trios of Huey Cobra AH-1G gunships and Cayuse OH-6 light observation copters flying control and strike missions from a base just over the border in Vietnam.

The U.S. Air Force's daily sorties against the well-entrenched enemy blocking the highway numbered about a dozen. These included, in addition to two Strategic Air Command Stratofortress missions of several planes each, 7th Air Force fighter-bomber and quad-gunned AC-119 gunship strikes. No American losses were reported during the official duration of U.S. support for the operation. However, American planes continued to be involved as enemy activity resumed. Two days after American participation in the Route 4 offensive officially ceased on January 25, an F-100 Super Sabre went down near the road, owing to "unknown causes"; the pilot was killed.

In the meantime, the Cambodians had been slow in building up an effective final assault against the Communists atop Pich Nil. It was only the commitment of the U.S.-trained, battle-tested 7th Khmer Krom Brigade that broke a threatening stalemate at the northern end of the mountain divide. On January 22, the Allies decisively broke the enemy hold on the Route 4 summit and shortly afterward linked up. Khmer troops joyously raised their temple-emblemed flag above the napalmed ruins of Prince Sihanouk's onetime summer home. An ARVN officer put the number of enemy killed in the battle for control of the crest at 115, with 2 captured. South Vietnamese casualties, he said, were 10 dead and 49 wounded. The Cambodians did not release their casualty figures. Bridges and ravine-sided roadway blown up by the Communists to delay the Allied advance remained to be repaired, and bomb and shell craters had to be filled, before supply trucks could once more use the highway.[3]

The modest Route 4 victory was overshadowed by events in the Cambodian capital. Only hours before the Allies took control of Pich Nil Pass, the enemy bombarded Phnom Penh with rockets and mortar fire for the first time during the war. Worst of all, despite an intelligence warning eight days earlier that an attack was imminent, Vietnamese Communist *Dac Cong* (Special Task) Command sappers virtually obliterated AAK, the Khmer air force.

At 2 A.M. that January 22, under cover of a mortar barrage, fewer than one hundred black-clad enemy infiltrated the defense perimeter of Pochentong, the country's largest airport situated 4.5 miles west of the capital center. They fanned out and dashed from plane to plane laying lethal satchel charges. One reportedly climbed atop the terminal's restaurant to fire rockets at an ammunition dump. A second munitions storage facility was volcanoed. Pochentong trembled beneath a series of further detonations. Ten MiG-17 jets (all Cambodia possessed), five T-28 armed trainers, ten C-47 transports, and eight helicopters became instant scrap during the four-hour assault. The pride of Air Cambodge Airline, a Caravelle jet in which Prime Minister Lon Nol had returned from a Saigon conference the evening before, rested beneath a collapsed hangar roof. Ironically, none of the twenty South Vietnamese aircraft at the field was hit, probably because they were closely guarded by Vietnamese sentries. Disorganized gunfire added an anticlimactic exclamation mark to the raid. The first official announcement put the Cambodian dead at 13 soldiers and 26 civilians, with 170 wounded (mostly military dependents). The U.S. Embassy believed losses were higher. Unconfirmed reports claimed that three attackers had been slain.

There were other targets that night. Rocket and mortar rounds thumped into the naval base on the Chrouy Chang War Peninsula across the Sap River just east of Phnom Penh. Other projectiles slammed into the city itself, as well as on surrounding villages. Probing attacks were made against the capital's outer defense perimeter. Sunrise filtered through a pall of smoke drifting aloft; fires still crackled at the airport and at the naval yard. Then the terrorist activity began, three in daily succession between the January 22 and 24. Ambassador Tran Van Phouc of South Vietnam was injured by glass shattered in a bomb blast at his house. A bomb shook the immigration service office that processed applications from Vietnamese. Finally, an explosion gutted the Phnom Penh offices of the national electrical power utility, injuring six but failing to disrupt service. It was a preview of things to come. All this time, rockets and mortar rounds continued randomly to arc into the capital. Two

Author's car being checked by mirror for possible terrorist explosives before being allowed into the U.S. Embassy courtyard.

AAK T-28s circling overhead and the resumption of daily U.S. military assistance flights—which had brought in 1,400 tons of equipment since November 12, 1970—did little to reassure the shaken public. The city was subjected to its first public dusk-to-dawn curfew since the war began ten months earlier.

Three days after the raid on Pochentong, a group of armed Americans in shirtsleeves led by a muftied colonel landed at the airport in three U.S. Army helicopters. The objects of their attention were two of several damaged UH-1 rotary-winged aircraft. The choppers had no national insignia but bore U.S.-type tail numbers. The newcomers, identified as belonging to the 520th Transportation Battalion in Vietnam, spent about an hour the next day rigging the two damaged aircraft to be airlifted out by a pair of larger CH-47 Chinook helicopters. Pochentong was to continue to figure heavily in the war, and not only as AAK's primary base. Vietnam Air Force FACs, with Khmer backseat coordinators, operated routinely from the airport's military area, American FACs only until August 1973. American technicians completed a radio control center there to improve air support coordination for ANK. In September

1971, a downed American UH-1B Huey gunship recovered in a search and recovery mission was flown into Pochentong. In late November of that year, U.S. Army helicopters were diverted from Mekong Delta strike sorties to assist aircraft that had already been scrambled to recover a downed air force pilot. These whirlybirds refueled at Phnom Penh's airport before proceeding north to provide cover for the pilot's rescue. Finally, of course, Pochentong played a key role in resupplying the capital.

A second significant enemy commando raid further wet-blanketed satisfaction over the reopening of Highway 4. On March 2, Vietnamese Communist raiders penetrated the government defense perimeter at Kompong Som. Their target was the country's oil refinery. Explosions and fire gutted 60 percent of the installation's storage capacity. Buildings and equipment also were damaged.[4]

The enemy raiding had two direct and two indirect effects. It frightened the government into pulling even more units away from its idle Chenla operation and elsewhere to defend the capital. This, in turn, reinforced a siege mentality that sacrificed offensive action for urban defense. Further, the existent officially declared state of emergency was extended for another six months. Finally, Lon Nol's health was pushed beyond its limit. The Cambodian leader, already exhausted from sleeping only three hours a night, spent six hours on February 8 reassuring the national assembly about his military policies. At about 5 P.M. that day, while emerging from the shower, he suffered a stroke. Two days later, he signed a decree turning over his political powers to Deputy Prime Minister Sirik Matak.

Since local medical facilities were inadequate, U.S. Secretary of State William Rogers approved air evacuation of the stricken prime minister to Hawaii. A Medevac VIP-configured jet flew Nol, his wife, and ten other Cambodians northeastward across the Pacific. The patient was admitted to Tripler General Hospital in Honolulu on February 13 with a diagnosis of "diabetes, hypertension, and a cerebral thrombosis of the right middle cerebral artery with complete paralysis of the left arm and partial paralysis of the left leg. His speech was moderately impaired and he was nonambulatory." Doctors predicted recovery to the point of walking with a left leg brace and cane upon discharge in three weeks. Released from the military hospital in March, the Khmer leader moved to Hickam Air Force Base under Secret Service protection to convalesce and await follow-up tests.

There was little doubt that, given the army's fallen fortunes under Lon Nol's generalship, members of the high command encouraged their chief to stay away as long as possible. In fact, in a tame version of the plotting against President Diem of South Vietnam eight years earlier, Nol's political foes were scheming to depose him while, at the same time, his allies maneuvered to strengthen his rule. Nol's 1970 coup co-conspirator Sirik Matak, for one, told the U.S. ambassador that "the general had to go." On another level, the traditionally superstitious Khmers interpreted the stroke as a bad omen. In any case, Lon Nol's political opponents failed to get the American encouragement they felt was necessary to act, and the Cambodian leader returned to Phnom Penh at 11 A.M. on April 12 aboard a Viscount turboprop. Welcomed at the bottom of the disembarkation ramp with a kiss from his deputy, he shook hands with a number of diplomatic corps representatives. Nol was helped first into a wheelchair and then into a limousine to be driven to temporary quarters at the defense ministry. Although obviously showing the effects of his stroke in posture and speech, he appeared to be in high spirits as he again reached for the reins of power.

One long-lasting aspect of Lon Nol's Hawaiian convalescence provided a humorous insight into the Khmer leader's personality. While watching television on Oahu one day, he excitedly reacted to an advertisement for Geritol. Nol shared the typical Asian male's concern with virility and, having been chided by his wife for being less sexually active in his mid-fifties, saw the high-potency product as just what he needed. I want Geritol, he told his American benefactors. Its apparent beneficence resulted in his receiving a steady supply through the U.S. Embassy. A *New York Times* reporter in 1974 wrote that the then sixty-year-old Nol attributed the birth of his fourth child to the rejuvenator.[5]

The prime minister's stroke gave his short, paunchy, and mustached younger brother the opportunity further to increase his political clout. Lon Non was ambitious, wily, and unusually aggressive for a Cambodian. Unpopular and distrusted, even in the circles that formed his brother's power base, Non was (to quote Sihanouk) "known for his 'strong arm' methods and as a contender for power at the top in case his ailing brother becomes incapacitated." A U.S. Embassy appraisal considered Non to lack "good political judgment" and "moral scruples." *Petit Frère* (Little Brother), as he was known, owed his graduation from military academy, where he failed, and his army commission to his brother. As far as religion was concerned, he was less than devout. He surrounded himself with sycophants. With the spread of hostilities, Non went from police official to instant army officer, becoming a lieutenant colonel in charge of a brigade. There he sought maximum public exposure and minimum exposure to the enemy.

Lon Non also kept a controlling hand on the nation's police forces and on what passed for an intelligence service. His claim of "6,000 agents in K.R. territory" produced a few inaccurate reports and suspicions that he was in contact with the enemy for unpatriotic reasons. Non's reaction to the internal political rumblings that accompanied military defeat, continuing economic decline, and Nol's stroke was twofold: convince his brother, who said he was considering resigning, not to do so, and play potential rivals against each other to keep power in the family. He eyed American aid as a chance for further power and enrichment. According to one embassy observer, Non tried "to insert himself into the U.S. MAP by getting involved in the illicit arms trade."

Little Brother also played a role in a controversial CIA–Defense Department program code-named Copper. The program envisioned using Khmer troops in Laos to interdict the southern end of the Ho Chi Minh Trail. Lieutenant Colonel Lim Sisaath, a military academy classmate of Lon Nol, was placed in charge of two battalions of Cambodian recruits flown to Pakse, Laos, during the fall of 1970. The men were trained at a nearby site and were fighting the PAVN early in 1971. Poor combat performance, with subsequent desertions and a mutiny, clouded Project Copper. The primary reason for the problems apparently was inadequate leadership. Sisaath had "led" from behind, and his deputy was more interested in heroin smuggling than fighting. Lon Non took over Copper in February 1971. This time, the Khmer troops acquitted themselves well until the program suddenly was terminated in mid-year. The accepted reason was that Non recalled the Khmers to participate in ongoing combat across the Mekong from the capital. An unconfirmed report, however, said that the project crashed when Non was found to be using aircraft flying between Laos and Cambodia to transport heroin.[6]

Heroin abuse by U.S. servicemen in Vietnam had increased frighteningly after its initially detected existence in the late 1960s. The opiate's source was the Golden Triangle where Burma, Laos, and Thailand meet. The area long had supplied much of the opium, morphine base, and various grades of the processed powder to the world's drug markets. Traffickers, chiefly Chinese and French, had exploited the area's vast illicit drug potential even before World War II. It was a simple matter to bolster production to meet the demands of disillusioned or bored G.I.s caught up in a badly supported war. Along with this demand came a new wave of traffickers—North and South Vietnamese, Laotian, and American military and civilian officials.

The Cambodian conflict merely provided an additional playground for the traffickers as wartime chaos prevailed and soldiers of both sides crisscrossed

Khmer territory. From a minor market (mainly for smoking opium) and transit point, Phnom Penh became a major way station for drugs. Khmer officials were added to those who profited from the lucrative trade. At the end of 1971, twenty kilograms of Number 4 heroin sold in the Cambodian capital for 60–80 thousand riels (55 riels to the dollar was the official rate before the January 17, 1972, devaluation jumped it to 120 to the dollar).

Heroin reached Phnom Penh in various ways. Some was shipped from Laos to Bangkok, then east to Aranyaprathet on the Thai-Cambodian border. There it reportedly was transferred from Thai army to ANK trucks and driven along Route 5 to the capital for resale or direct on-shipment to such destinations as Saigon and Hong Kong. A preferred method was aerial delivery, often by Laotian planes, to Pochentong. From there it went by land, sea, or air to Vietnamese and Americans in Saigon. South Vietnamese Air Force (SVNAF) 5th Air Division transports flew daily round-trip supply flights into Cambodia, which proved convenient for traffickers. There also were the SVNAF AC-47s assigned Phnom Penh defense perimeter missions and the Vietnamese helicopter contingent at Pochentong. South Vietnamese vessels helping MNK guard the Mekong line of communication (LOC) were reported as drug carriers as well. Ironically, overproduction and demand reduction accompanying the dwindling American presence in Vietnam resulted in the drop of heroin prices ($1,700 in mid-1971 to $650 in February 1972 for a kilogram of Number 4 heroin in the Golden Triangle) and stockpiling. The obvious next step for the drug dealers was to unload their bloated stocks overseas, principally to the United States.[7]

The evolving military situation, including the debilitating January Pochentong raid, intensified U.S. air operations over Cambodia, both tactical support for Khmer and Vietnamese ground elements, and the interdiction of enemy land and water supply routes. On March 10, the American defense secretary legitimized ongoing action by designating the "total land area of Cambodia, including inland waters and the adjacent sea areas," a "hostile fire area effective 1 January 1971." The rationale given was that this was "in direct support of military operations in the Vietnam combat zone." Seven weeks later, with minor modifications, Secretary Laird, in one of many extensions, continued the sanction of air operations over Cambodia through November 1, 1971. He also okayed continued B-52 sorties along Highway 4.

While the total number of U.S. aircraft operating from Vietnam, Thailand, and aircraft carriers in Southeast Asia dropped from 1,584 in October

1970 to 833 on December 31, 1971, a growing proportion was being allotted to Cambodia missions. In 1971, 14 percent of the air force's total combat sorties were directed against Cambodian targets, as compared to 8 percent the previous year. Navy jets were called in when requests for support overwhelmed the air force. The 61,000 American and South Vietnamese sorties flown over the country accounted for 10.5 percent of all the bombs dropped in the overall war theater that year. During the first six months of 1971 alone, 1,100 fixed-wing gunship sorties were directed at Cambodia.

The Allies did not always see eye to eye on strategy and capabilities, however. On July 1, 1971, for example, U.S. 7th Air Force commander General John Lavelle withdrew tactical air, FAC, and helicopter support from Cambodian southwestern Military Region 2, except for emergencies, to prod the Khmer air arm to carry a greater share of the responsibility for assisting ANK operations. The ploy succeeded. In another instance, U.S. Army Major General John Cushman, chief of the Delta Region Aviation Command (DRAC) at the Allied Support Operations Coordination Center in Vietnam, complained that while "we are making every effort to assist [Cambodian General Fernandez] within our means," there was a "disparity of [helicopter] gunship vs. TAC [tactical fixed-wing] sorties." Comparing seventy-one gunships to thirty-six tactical sorties during the last week in November 1971, Cushman insisted that "Cobras, though effective, can't substitute fully for TAC air . . . Fernandez, who despite our urging and instructions, refrains from requesting TAC air on an immediate basis to support his forces."

A more serious downside of the air strikes first came to American public attention in 1971. Angkor Borei, a capital of eighth-century Chenla near the Vietnam border, was visited by a three-plane cell of high-flying Stratofortresses that boxed it with bomb loads equal to those of sixty fighter-bombers. By the time the town also received the attention of Khmer T-28s, more than one hundred of its inhabitants were dead, many buried beneath the more than two hundred leveled houses. Allied bombings were to provide the K.R. with many hundreds of angry new recruits. Part of the problem apparently lay with the inadequate communications that accompanied the less than ideal coordination of air strikes involving military partners with different languages, methods, and outlooks. For example, the Khmer high command would request a raid on an enemy "training camp." The latter, it was discovered too late, was simply the site of a political indoctrination session by Communist cadres who left their peasant audience immediately after giving their spiel. Implicit in this actual example is the fact that while most American airmen adhered to strict rules of engagement designed to protect noncombatants, their Allied counterparts were far less scrupulous.

Even observing the rules of engagement left open such questions as how aviators were to respond to the deliberate Communist placement of military units in villages and the use of Khmer porters in battle zones. The movement of peasants, often displaced by the fighting, further aggravated the problem. Finally, the devastating weapons of modern warfare are much less precise than their introducers would like to believe. The Cambodian government, which believed civilian casualties during the first year of the war to be five hundred dead and one thousand hurt, said that 20 percent of the nation's combat damage was owing to air bombardment. A U.S. congressional report placed Khmer casualties "in the thousands" during the first months alone, blaming most on tactical air strikes.

The American defense secretary, after their first public exposure, defended the widespread air operations as consonant with the Nixon doctrine and the December 1970 military aid bill. The first, enunciated by President Nixon at a July 1969 press conference, said that "our Asian friends" would have to take an increasingly greater responsibility for their own defense. However, in the case of non-nuclear aggression and noninternal subversion, the U.S. "shall furnish military and economic assistance when required and as appropriate." The second, in which Congress voted a $1 billion military aid supplement, proscribed the use of American ground troops and advisers, not air power.[8]

It was inevitable that growing U.S. aid would be accompanied by a swelling of the American presence in Phnom Penh. From 11 persons in April 1970, the embassy's American staff increased to 91 in March 1971, and to 137 seven months later. On January 31, the Military Assistance Program inaugurated in 1970 officially was taken over by the tri-service Military Equipment Delivery Team, Cambodia, under Kojak–look-alike Brigadier General Theodore Mataxis, who had been acting commander of the 23rd American Division in central Vietnam. The low profile efforts of Political-Military Officer Fred Ladd, working with a small staff inside the embassy, gave way to a ballooning program administered by a growing group ultimately housed in "temporary" metal structures erected behind the building.

MEDTC's mission was to oversee the congressionally approved military assistance program by "evaluating requests, coordinating delivery, observing and expediting distribution, and reporting on and monitoring the use" of American matériel. Beyond this benign mission statement, American soldiers would try to reorganize FANK from a modest infantry-based force able to hold its own to an independent 220,000-man machine capable of overcoming the Communists. Hastily implemented to meet an unexpected situation, this goal mirrored uncertainties about enemy intentions, capabilities, and potential.

MEDTC was divided into a Saigon rear echelon and a Phnom Penh forward unit to comply with congressional limitations on the number of U.S. personnel in Cambodia. Military in-country assignees didn't take long, however, to increase in number from an original ten to sixteen (with the forty-four others in Vietnam) in January 1971. MEDTC reached its authorized personnel ceiling of twenty-three in Phnom Penh in May, with another ninety allowed for the rear echelon. Defense Department pressure to raise the number still further paralleled the increase in aid. The State Department reluctantly consented to fifty in the Cambodian capital. By late summer of 1971, the in-country MEDTC group numbered nearly that many. In December, after more Pentagon pressuring, it totaled sixty-two. This was in addition to the twenty-five servicemen reporting to Defense Attaché Colonel Harry Amos.

With the encouragement of CINCPAC in Hawaii and the Chairman of the Joint Chiefs of Staff (CJCS) in Washington to "act independently," Mataxis soon was, in his own words, "sidestepping around the ambassador [his nominal boss]" to perform his perceived tasks. He moved his staff from Saigon to Phnom Penh in August. Additional manpower, on "temporary duty" assignments to circumvent the in-country personnel restrictions, were flown in from Vietnam as needed. Americans "available [to FANK] for discussion" actually were advising and engaged in combat activities; wounds were incurred. MEDTC skirted other rules, as when shotgun shells, tabooed by the ambassador as in violation of the Geneva Convention, were smuggled in. Mataxis admitted that "this did not lead to a happy headquarters, but that's the way it worked—you do what you have to do to make it work."

While Mataxis apparently agreed with Ladd that bureaucratic accountability (for example, U.S.-style administrative paperwork and requesting additional support personnel) was an "overly restrictive" requirement, he nevertheless "followed orders and built the beginnings of a conventional army," as a civilian embassy official observed. And although Washington touted its aid program as "the Nixon Doctrine in its purest form," FANK overreliance on the United States and the nature of MEDTC assistance produced results that were more American than Cambodian. One embassy officer, pointing out the relatively small dimensions of the battleground and enemy successes without sophisticated equipment, remarked that FANK had been strapped into a "technological strait jacket." Cambodia indeed had become a replay of the Vietnam War, but at a Spartan level.

On January 5, 1971, Congress approved Public Law 91-652, an authorization bill for $85 million additional military assistance for Cambodia, $70 million for "special" economic aid, and $100 million to reimburse funds diverted from other programs to meet Khmer emergency needs. In March, $8.5 million in further economic aid and $10 million more in counterinsurgency funds (to total $20 million) were earmarked for Cambodia. By the end of the year ending on February 28, 1971, America had supplied $33 million in military aid: thirty thousand carbines, twelve thousand M-1 Garand rifles, sixty trucks, six howitzers, four hundred radios, six helicopters, and air support. The military assistance program alone, excluding ad hoc support at the onset of the war, would total $1.18 billion by the end of the conflict. In January 1971, eight U.S. thirty-one-foot-long, fiberglass river patrol boats (PBRs) were transferred to the Khmer navy in Saigon. Five-man crews to man the machine gun and grenade launcher–armed PBRs were trained by the Vietnamese. On March 26, twenty-five U.S. Army–furnished M-113 APCs were off-loaded in the capital after being brought up the Mekong from Vietnam. Later, another half dozen T-28s were transferred to the Khmer air force. Disturbingly, the initial shipments of modern M-16 rifles coming into the country were going not to the troops fighting the war but to the soldiers protecting the government in Phnom Penh.[9]

Aside from the Route 4 operations and clashes around the capital, the most significant fighting in Cambodia during the first seven and a half months of 1971 was between Vietnamese. On January 17, several hundred ARVN paratroopers under Lieutenant General Do Cao Tri (corrupt, but militarily competent, it was said) helicoptered across the border to an enemy encampment near Mimot on a rescue mission. Whether owing to faulty intelligence or to their removal earlier, the twenty Americans reportedly held prisoner in the camp were not there. The choppers returned to Vietnam with thirty Communist captives instead.

ARVN launched two noteworthy offensives in 1971 in hopes of retaining the initiative gained during the preceding year's incursions. The controversial *Lam Son 719* advance into Laos between January 30 and April 6 was a costly test of the Vietnamization of the Vietnam War. While it upset PAVN plans for further offensives that year, it also foreshadowed a gloomy future for the South Vietnamese once they lost American air support. A simultaneous division-strength stab at the Chup plantation in Cambodia was cut short when its commander, General Tri, died in a helicopter crash. The other offensive, *Toan Thang 01-71,* was a disaster. Late in May, the fourth month of this offensive into eastern Cambodia, an ARVN task force was surrounded on Route 13 southeast of Snoul. Its attempted breakout toward an armored brigade coming to the rescue turned into a rout. While ARVN continued to operate in eastern Cambodia—often in joint, not always friction-free missions with ANK—throughout the rest of the year, these operations were mostly in-and-out punches with limited objectives and equally limited successes.[10]

It quickly became apparent that, volumewise, the principal line of communication for getting supplies to Phnom Penh, the key to the Khmer Republic's survival, was the Mekong River. The Cambodian government, struggling for balance while being pummeled by an experienced opponent, was ill-prepared to meet its own needs. U.S. Rear Admiral Herbert Matthews, Jr., naval force deputy commander in Vietnam, was credited with organizing and radio-monitoring from Vietnam a forty-five-vessel South Vietnamese convoy that brought the capital critically needed fuel on January 17, 1971. Short weeks later, the South Vietnamese Navy (SVNN) undertook systematic river trains based on bow-doored, 328-foot-long tank landing ships. The task was relinquished to chartered civilian ships and barges soon afterward, with SVNN thereafter limiting itself to an escort role.

The Mekong route from Tan Chau, just over the border, to Phnom Penh shimmied through jungle, overhanging banks, and several narrows. After the oiler *Mekong* was sunk by enemy fire early in 1971, the Cambodians asked for systematic escort assistance. The result was a cooperative effort, involving nine armed services of three nations, to organize and coordinate air and river bank protection. Air cover responsibility was broken down geographically: SVNAF for the Vietnam portion; USAF, in cooperation with AAK, for the border-to-Neak Luong stretch; and AAK for the relatively trouble-free final section. In their assigned area, SVNAF T-37 counterinsurgency jets and T-28s, working with American FACs and DRAC Huey Cobra gunships, flew at 1,500 feet during the day. At night, two each of the U.S. Navy's UH-1B helicopters and OV-10 twin-engined aircraft provided a low-level umbrella. All these were supplemented by around-the-clock SVNAF fixed-wing gunships when convoys were scheduled. C-119 Shadow gunships of the 7th Air Force circled river trains at 3,500 feet night or day in their protective zone until mid-August 1971. U.S. fighter-bomber strikes were called in as required.

On the ground, armor-backed ARVN units worked with the Khmer 4th

Infantry Division to secure the Mekong embankments between the frontier and Neak Luong. A monthly average of three convoys was established. The Gulf of Thailand LOC would be tested only on New Year's Day 1972, when the American charter ship *Transglobe* delivered twenty-five two-and-a-half-ton trucks to Kompong Som. As a resupply point, Kompong Som never reached its full potential because of the inability of FANK to keep open the Route 4 artery to the capital.

Aerial resupply, to become the primary LOC in the dying days of the republic, began early with South Vietnamese C-119 and C-123 transport runs; U.S. four-engined C-130s provided a backup. It became an all-American show when SVNAF ceased ground-to-ground supply operations in Cambodia in October 1971. Air drops remained a joint Allied chore, with Americans flying seven emergency missions to embattled Khmers between February 1971 and the end of the year. By 1972, MEDTC could even count on direct Military Airlift Command flights from the United States to Phnom Penh. To improve Cambodian ground supply capabilities, six hundred Dodge and International Harvester trucks, with one hundred trailers, were transported to Vung Tau, Vietnam. These were distributed among five road convoys and, with U.S. air cover, driven to Phnom Penh between April and September 1971. These trucks proved invaluable, especially along Highways 1, 4, and 5, during the war, even though the enemy intermittently cut the roads.[11]

Cambodia's armed forces seemed unable to cope with the reality that victory and glory cannot simply be plucked like ripened fruit from a tree secured by a protector. They had numerous weaknesses that gradually were being overcome—an olio of arms, mixed organizational systems, and inadequate training. But one weakness ignored by Cambodian leaders, the one probably most easily corrected, was FANK's most serious: corruption. FANK's ten-month increase in size from around 40,000 to about 200,000 by January 1971 lost meaning because anywhere from 10 to 50 percent of the number consisted of nonexistent "phantom soldiers" conjured up to fill greedy officers' pockets. A July FANK census discovered that at least 22,000 "phantoms" were on its rolls and that another 46,000 real soldiers were "untraceable." Later in the year, American auditors reported that 6 to 8 percent of FNK's salaries were being dispensed to national troops.

The incompetence and avarice permeating Cambodia's armed forces filtered down to create demoralization and undiscipline. On August 8, 1971, to cite an example, a group of paratroopers fought military policemen over an unpaid restaurant bill in the central market area of Phnom Penh. A grenade was tossed, killing an M.P. and injuring three other persons. In September, an army lieutenant led about 100 G.I.s from Skoun in Kompong Cham Province south to the capital to protest that they had been enlisted to fight in their own province of Kompong Chhnang to the west. When their officer was arrested, the mutineers and their families camped out on the outskirts of Phnom Penh. They refused to move until the lieutenant was freed and named battalion commander.

Even the alliance between Cambodia and South Vietnam remained shaky. Only a common anti-Communist cause and U.S. stick-and-carrot methods kept problems under control after the preceding year's Khmer massacre of ethnic Vietnamese and ARVN's retaliatory looting, burning, and raping in the southeastern provinces. Proof that tension remained came on January 30, 1971. An argument between Vietnamese sailors and Cambodian soldiers escalated into explosions and wild gunfire in downtown Phnom Penh. It went on for perhaps fifteen minutes before armor-backed troops restored calm. Fortunately, only a bystander was killed; ten others were injured. Following a visit by U.S. Under-Secretary of State John Irwin in May, Lon Nol invited Vietnamese Prime Minister Tran Thien Khiem to Cambodia for a discussion that included bettering relations. In midsummer, a Khmer official optimistically, and not without acidity, announced that FANK would be so well equipped and organized by June 1972 that the South Vietnamese troops could go home.

It was while investigating reports of South Vietnamese infiltration and settling in Svay Rieng Province that First Vice–Prime Minister In Tam was almost killed in July. As his convoy neared the frontier, the lead truck detonated a mine and blocked the road. Mortar and automatic weapon fire peppered the FANK armored vehicles and jeeps from prepared ambush positions. In Tam and most of the others sought shelter in a roadside ditch while the armored vehicles returned fire. The attackers withdrew after a three-hour shootout that killed at least one Khmer and a reported ten ambushers.[12]

Nor was the nation's internal political-economic situation any more reassuring. While the two parties, the Republicans and the Democrats, pecked at each other, Lon Nol used divide-and-conquer tactics to destabilize them and protect his power. In a move reminiscent of his predecessor's methods, Lon Nol resigned his posts as prime minister, defense minister, and FANK chief of staff on April 20 "for reasons of health." A carnival ride crisis followed, with no one willing to form a new government. It was, as historian David Chandler called it, a "somnambulistic ballet" during which national sentiment flowed away from Lon Nol to Sihanouk. When the dust finally settled,

Nol, still holding power, had acquired the super rank of marshal and Sirik Matak was his prime minister.

By October, after cabinet and assembly reshufflings (with the two-house parliament transformed into a constituent assembly), Nol headed a new government whose power was concentrated in the executive branch. Decrying "the sterile game of outmoded liberal democracy," he promptly established the legal framework for ruling by decree. Economically, with the civilian sector degenerating into near-chaos, inflation promoted growing discontent and public demonstrations. The official riel-to-dollar currency rate of 55-to-1 more than quadrupled on the black market. The country, which before the war grew enough rice to feed its people and still export around 180,000 tons per annum, now was expected to have to import 100,000 to 200,000 tons of the grain staple in 1972. Rice prices actually doubled in one week.

Cambodia's wounds still were far from fatal. Even with its phantom soldiers, FANK most probably had greater numerical concentrations than and certainly outgunned its foes. It had American and South Vietnamese support. The mid-1971 estimate of Communist troops in Cambodia was about eighty-five thousand, three-quarters of them Vietnamese. To FANK's detriment, they usually selected the battlefield. The North Vietnamese were able to return their attention to the less aggressive Khmers once ARVN's *Toan Thang* offensive petered out. Elements of the PAVN 9th Division occupied patches of high ground in the swampy Tonle Toch area east of Phnom Penh. This move to open an infiltration route aimed at the capital set off a major battle. On May 28, ANK began injecting some two dozen battalions into the area. The government troops not only made no headway during the fighting that ensued, but more than ten thousand of them were pinned down along the Toch River banks by mid-June. To isolate them, the Communists slashed at their supply lines and diverted reinforcements by stepping up assaults along Highway 7 to the north.

In desperation, FANK helicopter-lifted two 7th Brigade battalions of Khmer Krom soldiers into the battle zone on June 25. A twelve-thousand-strong Cambodian offensive, assisted by massive U.S. air power and the onset of the rainy season, gradually cleared the flat lowland of Communists. To mark the accomplishment, a "Victory East of the Mekong" celebration—complete with parade and display of captured arms—was held in Phnom Penh. This type of Khmer advance-then-pull-back tactic, however, permitted the enemy to reinfiltrate once the government forces departed. The result, obviously, was all too often having to reclear a zone.[13]

Summer 1971 "Victory East of the Mekong" parade ceremony, Phnom Penh, with captured weapons in the foreground. Photo by author

With Lon Nol once more in charge of military planning, a decision was made to snatch the initiative from the enemy. The result was Chenla II, a reactivation of the fizzled 1970 offensive to reopen Route 6, the highway connecting the capital and Siem Reap. Its main objectives were to lift the year-long siege of Kompong Thom, seventy-nine air miles from Phnom Penh; to cut enemy infiltration routes; and to ease the economic crunch by reclaiming countryside rich in rice, fish, fruit, and rubber. Secondarily, but perhaps as important, were the needs to revive national and international confidence in the government and to restore shaken FANK morale. Further, the operation would contribute to Lon Nol's program of "general mobilization of the population" by returning additional civilians to friendly control. Nor could it be denied that Chenla II would alleviate Communist pressure on America's Vietnamization of the fighting to the east.

Lon Nol wanted Chenla II to knife through to Kompong Thom, pausing only long enough to take road-controlling terrain features that later could be used to extend FANK control. As in the first Chenla offensive, a smaller diversionary advance would be made up Route 21, less than twenty miles east of and nearly parallel to Highway 6, toward the Chamcar Leu and Chamcar Andong plantations. Another diversionary force, a combined army-navy effort, would move up the Chinit River in the flooded marshlands to the west. Some of the FANK general staff, echoing the views of the U.S. Embassy, suggested a more prudent course—first draw out and then destroy the PAVN divisional elements reported east of the main line of advance. Only then should troops move up Route 6. They pointed out that the units earmarked for the operation, having borne the brunt of the fighting for months on end, now were understrength and in need of refitting, as well. Lon Nol brushed aside the concerns of the naysayers; the offensive would follow his blitzkrieg plan. Brigadier General Hou Hang Sin was put in charge. On August 20, the sixteen-to-twenty-thousand-man (sources differ on the figure) Chenla II offensive ground into first gear from Tang Kauk on Highway 6 just fourteen miles above its junction with Route 7.

Meeting only loose enemy resistance, the miles-long Chenla column of armored and transport vehicles, soldiers' women and children straggling along, wove northward beside misty fields. Overhead, an air umbrella floated across skies that alternated deep gray and bright blue. On August 24, six miles from their starting point, the troops entered Rumlong. Three more days and they secured Baray. There, the ANK G.I.s were received by peasants who showed them the burial pit of 180 inhabitants liquidated by the K.R. "for minor infractions." On September 1, its path eased by ground-controlled air strikes and artillery barrages, the column liberated Kompong Thmar, the unattained stepping stone to Kompong Thom of the first Chenla operation. Bare tree trunks stood above craters and the smoldering foundations of what had been a thriving town of ten thousand. A battalion commander, Captain Lay Chhom, said that the destruction could not be helped. "The Communists fired rockets from the houses. The colonel asked for napalm. Three American planes dropped it." Here the main body of weary troops paused to rest.

On September 2, the garrison of Kompong Thom, twenty miles to the northwest, made a preplanned move to break the enemy encirclement. One of the 5th Brigade Group's two brigades defending the town smashed down Route 6 toward a six-thousand-man Chenla brigade bulldogging its way westward from Kompong Thmar. A linkup came thirty-three days later, after disorganized and intermittent combat. That same day, October 5, the ANK 8th Brigade helicoptered onto 679-foot-high Phnom Santuk, an enemy training and supply center about halfway between the two Kompongs. Two other air-covered brigades slogged up the forested, rock-strewn heights from the south. After eight days of brutal, often hand-to-hand fighting, the Khmer G.I.s reached the pagoda atop the hill. On that same October 5, Marshal Lon Nol, as FANK commander-in-chief and chief of staff, issued an order of the day boasting that "the enemy has been put to flight" by Chenla II, with "3,634 VC/NVA put out of action, of which 952 bodies were left on the battlefield, 287 weapons captured, including 18 crew-served," and stocks of munitions, supplies, and latex seized. Recognizing that "still further sacrifices will be asked" of the army, he ended with the exhortation, "Now, forward to victory."

Earlier, on September 6, the secondary drive along Route 21 cautiously started forward, initially without meeting appreciable resistance. The less mobile, more flexible Communists were focusing their attention on Route 6, probing the widely scattered government positions and harassing ANK patrols. The diversionary advances could be stopped at any time, they knew, and they soon were. In late September, a FANK convoy moving up the Sen River was forced to turn back, preventing a repeat of the successful 1970 efforts to reinforce Kompong Thom by water. All in all, though, the PAVN soldiers believed to be in the nearby plantations were putting up less opposition than expected. An American in Phnom Penh said that "the war has stabilized. The Communists want South Vietnam. They don't want to take over this country." Lon Nol listed the important factors in favor of ultimate victory: "First is our race. Second is our religion. Now we have a third—the way we defend ourselves." In the capital and in the field alike, celebrations were held on October 25 and 26. The successful conclusion of Phase I of Chenla II appeared a good time for a collective anti-Communist sigh of relief. Perhaps Lon Nol's strategy was the right one after all, although MACV commander General Creighton Abrams, Jr. was skeptical. "They've opened a front forty miles long and two feet wide," he remarked.

From their Chamcar Andong plantation headquarters, the Communist commanders had followed the progress of the government advance and gathered troops for a counterblow. The latter was planned to come in three stages, beginning on August 20 with the evacuation of civilians from along Route 6 and the onset of a campaign of guerrilla fighting. Phase two, scheduled for late October, would be a major assault against the center of the ANK column's right flank. This would isolate units and snip supply lines. The final stage, starting in mid-November, would seek to obliterate the Chenla II offensive. Stealthily, using the cover of night and bad weather, the 9th PAVN division's 201st and 500th Regiments, reinforced by the 205th and 207th Regiments of the PAVN-PLAF C40 Division, and including PNLAFK elements, moved westward from their forested high ground. They followed rain-drenched paths and crossed paddies toward the celebrating, thinly-stretched government forces.

Disaster struck Chenla II only hours after the start of its second phase, pacification and consolidation. The Communists materialized out of the 1 A.M. blackness of October 27, slamming against the Chenla column's center. A roughly six-mile stretch of Route 6 between Tang Kauk and Rumlong became a continuous line of muzzle flashes and explosions. Encamped just over half a mile above Rumlong, the understrength ANK 376th Battalion was erased in the first charge; only a handful of G.I.s escaped. PAVN soldiers sliced through the government line and double-timed across the two-laned hardtop south of Rumlong, isolating the 46th Infantry Brigade command post, the 14th Battalion, and a platoon of 105mm artillery. Other assaults bashed Baray and Kompong Thmar. It was the beginning of the heaviest fighting of the war to date. The bridge carrying Highway 6 over submerged flatland southwest of Skoun, a vital link between the Chenla army and its supply bases to the south, was blasted apart by sappers. Staggered by the shocking blows that shattered its revelry, ANK was subjected to unceasing attacks that kept it off balance. Weather, darkness, and chaos on the ground diluted the effectiveness of air strikes.

During the dark hours of October 28, according to General Sin's afteraction report, the North Vietnamese used "toxic gas shells" to chase the 211th Battalion from its position below Rumlong. The survivors fled southward to the 118th Battalion lines in Kroel, which also was assailed. On October 29, the battered remnants of both battalions retreated farther down Route 6 to Tang Kauk. Two nights later, they were joined by the shredded 377th Battalion. The 63rd and 425th Battalions of the 61st Infantry Brigade pulled back to the position held by the 22nd Battalion just south of Rumlong, now surrounded by four PAVN regiments. A four-day hell of gunfire and explosions tore into the flesh of women and children, as well as into the soldier husbands and fathers they had counted on for food and shelter.

Like a snake's head snapping back to protect its injured coils, two ANK brigades turned to strike at the enemy encircling Rumlong. They were restricted to the road by their tactics and equipment, and succeeded only in taking and again losing small parcels of ground. Air supply drops were too little and too widely scattered to do more than prolong the agony of the exhausted and dispirited army, which was losing a reported one hundred men a day. Friendly air attacks inadvertently broke up another attempt to relieve Rumlong. The massive lightning and thunder of two B-52 missions did more damage to the rubber trees than to the Communist long-range cannons in the Chamcar Andong plantation. On November 13, the Rumlong stronghold, pulverized by rocket and shell fire, ceased to exist.

The Chenla column, sliced into pieces no one could rejoin, did not die easily. Throughout the entire month of November, as the dry monsoon season wafted its winds over the brutalized land, cut-off ANK pockets from Phnom Santuk in the north to Prakham in the south fought to survive. Despite intensified U.S. air support, the enisled points of resistance fell silent one by one. For those who weren't slaughtered or captured for an unknown fate, it was "every man for himself." Alone or in decimated groups, many having gone for months without even being paid, the remaining soldiers of Chenla melted into the countryside to return to their homes or to friendly lines. The vacuum they left behind immediately was filled by the Communists. Lon Nol and his staff flew as far north as they safely could on November 30 to "survey the situation as it actually was"; surely it couldn't be as bad as it seemed. The result of the "survey" was inevitable—Chenla II officially was terminated on December 3. FANK's last major offensive of the war had cost, according to Lieutenant General Sak Sutsakhan, the deputy chief of the general staff who was to be the republic's last leader, "on the order of ten battalions of personnel and equipment lost, plus the equipment of an additional ten battalions." He called it "the greatest catastrophe of the war."

Phnom Penh's official figures for the August 20–October 21 period of the offensive listed 156 dead and 656 wounded on the FANK side, with 12 villagers killed and 54 hurt. PAVN-PLAF losses were given as 978 dead, 3,006 wounded, 16 captured, and 3 surrendered. In addition, ANK reportedly seized 322 individual weapons, other arms and munitions, thousands of sacks of rice, hundreds of barrels of fuel, about 100 tons of latex and a number of vehicles. Government statistics were not given for the post–October 21 period. The Communists claimed more than twelve thousand government troops killed, wounded, or captured during the ill-fated campaign. Whatever the actual figures, Cambodian G.I.s proved they could fight long, hard, and well. It was their leaders who failed.

While Chenla II was still optimistically churning northward, other ANK units, able to move freely east of Phnom Penh along elevated roads above the flooded Mekong Basin, acquired a false sense of regaining control of the countryside. Disabuse was not long in coming. Largely in response to Chenla II,

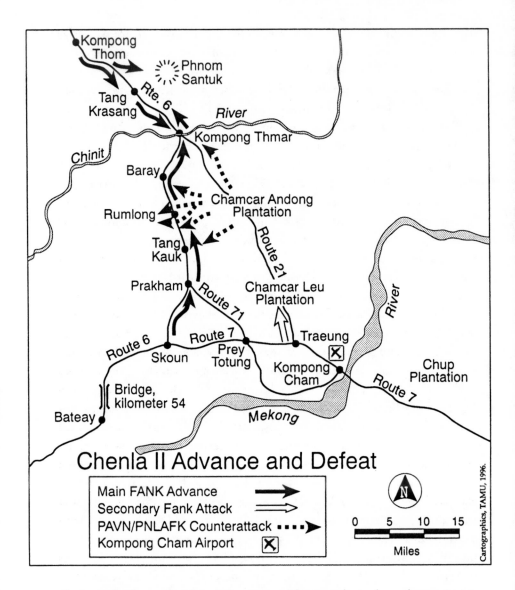

Chenla II Advance and Defeat

Legend:
- Main FANK Advance →
- Secondary Fank Attack ⇒
- PAVN/PNLAFK Counterattack ••••►
- Kompong Cham Airport ⊠

N ▲

0 5 10 15
Miles

Cartographics, TAMU, 1996.

Communist forces struck in other areas with ground attacks and terrorist actions. November assaults by the PAVN 1st Division and K.R. elements along Route 4 to the south, for example, drew away ANK units that otherwise would have been free to temper the Chenla II debacle.[14]

The new round of terrorism, the first to hit the capital since mid-June, began on September 7 with an attempt to assassinate the American ambassador. At 7:30 that Tuesday morning, Coby Swank eased himself into the Checker Marathon in front of his house in the southeastern part of the city.

The bulky sedan swung out to curve southwestward away from the Bassac River for the quarter-mile drive to the embassy. As the car passed the Nuon Monirom pagoda to the right, three men idling on the side road leading to the temple suddenly came alive. One sent a bicycle rolling onto the dual-lane pavement toward the chauffeur-driven Checker. The two-wheeler barely ticked the car before clattering to the macadam as the alert Khmer driver swerved to avoid it. The loiterers roared off on motorcycles. Swank's chauffeur accelerated. Once he had dropped off his passenger, he phoned the military police. The latter found and examined the abandoned bike. Concealed beneath long loaves of bread in a basket hooked onto the back were over twelve pounds of plastic explosive. Only hours later did the ambassador learn of the attempt on his life.

It was the fourth terrorist assault against Americans in Phnom Penh that year. In January, a briefcase bomb flipped from a motorcycle at an American's car failed to explode. On June 1, detonating within fifteen minutes of each other, plastic charges damaged two buildings housing personnel assigned to the defense attaché's office and to the marine embassy guard detail. One of the four servicemen living in the first house received flesh wounds. Fourteen days later, moments after seven embassy-bound MEDTC personnel boarded a vehicle in front of their hotel, a small plastic bomb was flung at them from a passing motorcycle. Badly aimed, the projectile exploded on the sidewalk about twenty-five feet away, injuring two Cambodian passersby. Although the Americans were not hurt, their vehicle suffered a broken window, three flat tires, and several shrapnel holes. MEDTC soldiers shortly afterward moved into a guarded house.

The next terrorist act came in the morning gloom of September 20. Under the cover of mortar shells and B-40 rockets, an estimated twenty-six sampan-borne Communist sappers dashed up the west bank of the Sap River in northern Phnom Penh. Their objectives were the Esso and the Shell company tanks holding most of the nation's gas, diesel oil, and fuel oil supply. Only a week before, the circular tanks had been replenished with more than 1.5 million gallons from a river convoy. The raiders killed four people and wounded six others, planted satchel charges, and left with six kidnapped guards. The ensuing detonations lit the sky and rocked the city. Blazing fuel ignited other tanks until eighteen, containing 1,750,000 gallons, were roaring conflagrations that were to belch greasy black smoke for two days. At least half of the two farms' storage capacity was destroyed. A third tank farm, owned by the Tela Khmer Company, was undamaged, as was the army fuel depot ten miles upriver.[15]

After the attempt to kill Ambassador Swank, his security and the embassy building's were tightened. Elsewhere, however, Americans kept to their insouciant routines. The marine guards, for instance, held regular Sunday afternoon softball games. Americans and curious Cambodians weren't the only ones taking an interest in the playing, however. Also watching were terrorists, who were about to make a mockery of the cocky statement made by a U.S. official after the last failed attempt that "our enemies make so many stupid mistakes."

On the hot, sunny afternoon of September 26, clouds of deep black smoke again were mushrooming over northern Phnom Penh. Earlier that day, three men in ANK uniforms riding in a Jeep slowed down at the river bank adjacent to the tank farms damaged less than a week before. A satchel charge flew at three docked fuel barges, exploded, and set afire ten thousand gallons of diesel fuel. Guards at a checkpoint the terrorists had just passed opened fire but missed. Now, at the other end of the capital, the usual crowd gathered to watch embassy employees play softball on a diamond only about six hundred feet from the ambassador's well-guarded residence.

The cheery enthusiasm changed to screams and shouts as two men tossed explosives onto the playing field. Two Americans, including Marine Security Guard detachment Staff Sergeant Charles Tuberville and a MEDTC soldier, were killed. The CIA station chief was blown unhurt off third base by the shock waves of two or three simultaneous detonations. Ten other mission personnel were wounded. A Cambodian child was killed outright and others were hurt. Another homemade bomb going off an hour later wounded a Khmer military policeman detailed to help secure the killing field. Still another charge, unexploded, was discovered after a search of the grounds. The bombers escaped, riding tandem on a motorcycle. Ironically, nearly forty-three months later as Landing Zone Hotel during Operation Eagle Pull, the sports field would become the stage for the official departure of the Americans from the contemporary Khmer scene.

A bomb blasted the popular Chinese-owned, three-story Thai San Hotel and Restaurant on September 30. Then a second eatery frequented by military personnel was torn by another bomb. Farther afield, the idled Thnaot River dam construction site was attacked. Enough damage was done to write finis to the UN-overseen project. Predictably, the wave of terrorism persuaded the government to cancel an elaborate October 9 celebration of the republic's first anniversary. In early December, three Soviet-made 122mm rockets slammed into downtown Phnom Penh, wounding four women and children. Eight other projectiles killed a pair of soldiers and injured two more when they screamed onto Pochentong Airport. A simultaneous ground assault on the nearby government radio station and telephone exchange was repulsed. On December 21, Prince Sisowath Rattasa died in a grenade explosion on a street near the palace his uncle, the exiled Sihanouk, once occupied. The Chenla II disaster, the Communist hit-and-run tactics, and the terrorist activity assured that ANK would stick close to the urban centers and leave the countryside to the enemy.[16]

The consistent military setbacks for the first time seriously threatened to pull the reins of power from Lon Nol's grasp. Khmer political leaders, including his deputy, Sirik Matak, on December 7 "sought to persuade him to give up not only his close personal direction of military operations but also his active leadership of the government," according to a U.S. report. Nol refused and blamed Chenla II's failure on the "lack of ARVN and U.S. support." It was noted that, since his return from convalescence in Hawaii, Nol's contacts with his advisers were "restricted," that he now surrounded himself with "self-seeking aides who have isolated him from harsh realities." At least one key Cambodian political figure, "considering alternatives to the present situation," apparently was probing for American reaction to and possible support for Nol's removal from power. Washington, still smarting from the 1963 ouster and murder of South Vietnam's Diem, would have none of it. Future, less subtle proposals by plotters to embassy officials for a change of leadership were firmly rejected, their authors told to maintain the status quo or else risk a cutoff of aid.

These rebuffs did not deter high-level Cambodians from allowing themselves to be recruited to one degree or another as embassy sources of information and means of exerting American influence. They were supplemented by other human assets in a growing pool that Swank's embassy could dip into: military and civilian personnel at the middle and lower levels, diplomats, refugees, and ralliers. Even prisoners of war were wrung out by U.S. information seekers. Technologically obtained material rounded out the embassy's intelligence picture. Information was as varied as its origins. Eyewitnesses reported the first serious clashes between Vietnamese and K.R. factions, as well as the beginning of secret Pol Potist purges. Others said that PAVN was grouping tanks in the rubber plantations. Intelligence on enemy concentrations was swiftly translated into air photo or strike missions. Sources told of priceless carvings being removed from the Angkor ruins for sale to Western art markets. There were reports of corruption: ANK and ARVN units selling arms and supplies to the enemy; illicit transfer of funds out of the country; heroin transitting through Cambodia; the diversion of precious pharmaceuticals; stolen U.S. goods moving along the Saigon-to–Phnom Penh black market pipeline; and the overnight enrichment of top-level Khmers.[17]

Cambodia's situation seemed bleaker than ever as 1971 drew to a close. A monthlong ANK-ARVN operation in the Chup plantation area abruptly ended with the withdrawal of the South Vietnamese elements. Phnom Penh–to–Kompong Som Highway 4, opened by Allied cooperation in January, once again was cut. The only upside, whatever small consolation it provided the Khmers, was that FANK's disasters had benefited the Allied war in Vietnam by diverting units of four PAVN divisions and weakening them. Disruption of three of them, the 1st, 7th, and 9th Divisions, apparently was a key cause of the failure of the Communist 1972 spring offensive in South Vietnam. MEDTC's General Mataxis blamed the "poor showing of the 9th Division [the victors of Chenla II] as the reason for the chastisement of its commander and its relief from the siege of An Loc [in South Vietnam] by the 7th Division—which in turn fared no better."[18]

CHAPTER SEVEN

1972:
Attrition

IN CONTRAST TO THE RELATIVE MILITARY LULL that accompanied the arrival of a new year, the Cambodian political scene was as troubled as the witches' bubbling cauldron in Shakespeare's *Macbeth*. Phnom Penh was rife with rumors of Lon Nol's imminent overthrow. Potential successors, so the gossip ran, were Sirik Matak (Washington's favorite), Son Ngoc Thanh, popular general staff officer Sak Sutsakhan, and In Tam. The latter, disliked by the army and dismissed as a vice prime minister the preceding October after clashing with the marshal, was the acting president of the constituent assembly who had called for the vote that ousted Sihanouk nearly two years earlier. He also probably was the most respected of the government figures. The rumors, kept from becoming reality only by American determination to maintain the status quo, accurately reflected the fact that the ardor and wild patriotism displayed by most Cambodians when they entered the war had run smack into a wall of disillusionment. While quietly sending Cambodia the "suggested text" of a letter the marshal should personally address to world leaders for financial and military assistance, the United States also realized that the odds for a Khmer government victory were not improving. Ambassador Swank, for example, rapped the Cambodian chief's "haphazard, out-of-channel and ill-coordinated conduct of military operations." The Chenla II debacle, for one, was owing to "ineffective leadership and tactics."

A new head count of FANK troops after Chenla II resulted in the writing off of thirty battalions (some fifteen thousand men) as existing "on paper alone." The diversion of money by corrupt officers was further illustrated by reports of Chenla survivors begging food from peasants to feed themselves and their families because they hadn't been paid in two months. Results of low-key battlefield activity in January 1972 also gave little cause for optimism. When South Vietnamese units withdrew from Krek in the Fishhook area of eastern Cambodia, the Khmer 22nd Brigade commander apparently panicked at the prospect of facing the enemy alone. His demoralized troops hastily abandoned prepared positions and stored munitions, leaving Highway 7's eastern half to the Communists. Nor was the loss balanced by the success of *Prek Ta,* a modest operation launched that same day, January 10, by eleven ANK and ARVN battalions near Route 1 west of the Parrot's Beak zone of the frontier.[1]

The military spotlight temporarily shifted to northwestern Cambodia as the Vietnamese Communists concentrated on their ill-fated spring offensive in South Vietnam and the K.R. focussed on growth and consolidation. Angkor Wat, completed at the same time the medieval French were preparing to erect Nôtre Dame cathedral in Paris, had come to represent the heart and soul of Cambodia, a symbol of cultural achievement and political power. Its silhouette has graced each of the many variations of the country's flag since the nineteenth century, even under K.R. rule. The temple, built of sandstone during the twelfth century to honor the god Vishnu, is the southernmost and most famous of the more than six hundred ruins in the approximately seventy-two-square-mile complex. It is the only monument in the area to face due west. This connotation of death, west being the direction of the setting sun, leaves unresolved the question of whether the wat was intended primarily as a temple or as the tomb of King Suryavarman II. It was ironic that the past glory of Angkor, revived for the Khmers by the French, provided the focus for the unrealistic aspirations of both Lon Nol and Pol Pot. Their soldiers now faced each other on the southern side of the aged, jungle-embraced ruins.

A PAVN regiment and some PNLAFK battalions controlled the ruins they had overrun three months after Sihanouk's overthrow; about two thousand refugees shared the space with them. Following an early unsuccessful attempt to eject the invaders, three ANK brigades set up a defensive line on the northern outskirts of Siem Reap approximately two miles away. The forty-seven-year-old Cambodia-born French archeologist Philippe-Bernard Groslier, as director of the institution responsible for restoring and maintaining Angkor, appealed to the combatants to spare the ancient temples and monuments. His plea was rewarded with a mutually observed truce, broken only briefly in February 1971 when about a dozen shells were fired at an active Communist gun position near Angkor Wat's south wall. Fortunately, the only noteworthy damage was a hit on the roof of one of the wat's galleries. The shell's shrapnel splattered a bas relief below. Many of the area's trees fell to become part of the Communist defense system of bunkers, interlocking trenches, and tunnels. Most serious was the disappearance of irreplaceable carvings, which were secured to the sides of walked bicycles for shipment outside of Cambodia. Some subsequently reappeared even in the United States after having been illegally bought in the Far East.

In mid-1970, after international negotiations and payment from the French, the Communists permitted several hundred Khmer restoration and maintenance workers to continue their labor under Groslier's direction. Twice a week, on Tuesdays and Fridays, the Frenchman pedaled his bicycle from a modest office in the no-man's-land halfway between the lines to supervise his laborers. Suddenly, in January 1972, additional North Vietnamese troops arrived, work on the old imperial site was halted, and the imperious Groslier was evicted. More than three dozen Khmer workers were arrested, twenty of them being swiftly executed for "giving information to the Central Intelligence Agency."

On January 29, ANK Major General Sar Hor launched Operation *Angkor Chey* (Angkor Victory) to encircle the enemy and interdict his supplies. Moving out along Highway 6 east and west of Siem Reap, a town of ten thousand whose name translated into "Siamese Defeated," Cambodian troops almost immediately came under fire. Shooting also erupted along the 3.5-mile-long, forest-flanked road linking the town and Angkor Wat. Two hotels, a stadium, and an unfinished theater along the arrow-straight road provided mock reminders of a time when tourists were more numerous than armed men. A February 8 PAVN counterattack stymied the slowly advancing Khmers until artillery fire and T-28 strikes reversed the tide. Thirteen days later, at a more than two-mile-long outer dike—with the 190-foot-high, cupola-topped central tower of the world's largest religious building within sight—Angkor Chey was transformed into a stalemate by the well-entrenched Communists.[2]

Meanwhile, after the sun set on January 30, the skies over Phnom Penh brightened with flashes and crisscrossing tracer shells for almost an hour as thousands of rounds slanted skyward from FANK small arms and machine guns. The target was Rehaou, a legendary frog monster whose swallowing of the moon could be stopped only by loud noise. This superstitious reaction to a lunar eclipse caused, in addition to the expenditure of precious ammunition, a number of casualties—between one and seven dead, with sixty to more than two hundred injured, depending on whose figures one accepts—from spent slugs returning to earth. The information ministry interrupted a classical music program to reassure alarmed foreigners that the shooting was "an expression of joy" over the lunar eclipse marking Buddha's birthday. Lon Nol, still using forearm crutches and often a wheelchair to get about, called the episode an "ill-considered action" caused by civilians or subversives, and a "serious blot on the honor of the Khmer Republic."

The republic's leaders, instead of unifying in the face of the brutal realities of the war, stubbornly followed a fatal path paved with petty bickering and individual self-interest. The Lon brothers manipulated this fact to their advantage. Non tried to quell a reporter's unease over the unstable political situation with the comment, "It is difficult for foreigners to understand developments in Cambodia. I would only advise that no one worry too much."

On March 10, the marshal announced that he was taking over as head of state and accepted Cheng Heng's instant resignation. A decree two days later gave him, as supreme commander and chief of staff of the military establishment, "combined policy direction and operational control" of FANK. Over the next few days, with sibling Non orchestrating such backstage details as student demonstrations against Sirik Matak (always a rival for power), Lon Nol shed the chief of state title to become the republic's first president. He also dismissed both Matak and the constituent assembly, which had been in the process of finalizing a new constitution limiting executive power. Nol further confirmed himself as president of the council of ministers (in effect, his own prime minister) and reaffirmed himself as defense minister. Sak Sutsakhan was appointed minister of state for national defense, a title more impressive than its powers.

Lon Nol was inaugurated as president on March 14, 1972, in a short improvised ceremony before a Khmer-only assemblage of military officers, ministers, and bonzes. In April, the freshly minted chief executive unveiled a new constitution, one giving him a still firmer grip on power. A "popular" referendum overwhelmingly approved it. The following month, as a sop to the U.S. and to neutralize him further, Sirik Matak was named Nol's special adviser.[3]

The relative military inactivity in southeastern Cambodia was shattered during the second week in March by Operation *Toan Thang* (Total Victory) VIII, an ARVN stab into Cambodia's Svay Rieng Province. The operation was still in progress eleven days later when, in neighboring Prey Veng Province and against Phnom Penh, the Communists unfettered their first significant action of the year inside the country. The principal reason they had not acted earlier was the redeployment of most of the PAVN 1st, 5th, 7th, and 9th Divisions toward South Vietnam for Hanoi's spring, or Eastertide, offensive. This massive five-and-a-half-month-long attempt to conquer South Vietnam, triggered on March 30, was smashed by resolute ARVN defense and American firepower. A weakened 1st Division afterward returned to southeastern Cambodia, while the 367th Sapper Regiment of the PAVN was ensconced north of Phnom Penh to increase pressure on the capital. The Vietnamese-K.R. C40 Division remained throughout the period in position north of the Tonle Sap Lake.

Coordinated PAVN assaults were launched on the night of March 20–21 against the provincial capital of Prey Veng and the Mekong ferry town of Neak Luong about eighteen miles to the south at the end of Route 15. A barrage of 60mm and 82mm mortar shells, 75mm recoilless rifle projectiles and 120mm rockets descended on Prey Veng. Communist infantrymen then surged southward along Route 15 and westward to occupy the open flatland where the Mekong bows toward Phnom Penh. Cut off, Prey Veng was pounded for two more nights. At Neak Luong, rockets arced into stored FANK-Vietnamese fuel and ammunition, sending fiery fists and broiling smoke high into the air. Finally, ANK reinforcements arrived to relieve pressure on both towns. No sooner was this accomplished than the enemy upgraded the fighting above the harassment level west across the Mekong in Military Region 2.

Simultaneously with the opening attacks in Prey Veng Province, Phnom Penh began its worst ordeal of the war to date, what the U.S. Embassy considered the "first real effort" to strike at the capital. Mortar and rocket rounds punched into seven sections of the city between 1:45 and 5:30 A.M. Hardest hit was a slum area housing refugees and army families. By morning, the area was a smoking ruin strewn with human and animal remains. Other projectiles burst among government positions at Pochentong Airport, destroying a light aircraft and damaging four others. North Vietnamese sappers materialized from the darkness to hit the government radio station across the highway from the airport. In a short, one-sided fight, the Communists killed twenty-five guards, flamed two APCs, and damaged several transformers and antennas. The commandos then burst into the on-site home of the station director, a colonel and close associate of Lon Non named Som Sam Al. Working with cruel precision, the intruders sliced the throats of Sam Al, his French wife, and their son.

An estimated 100 to 200 projectiles had hit Phnom Penh during the night. Casualties were between 60 and 102 dead and 100 to 208 injured (sources vary), with several hundred left homeless. Three attackers were killed. A brief three days after presiding over festivities marking the second anniversary of

Sihanouk's removal, Lon Nol found himself declaring a day of mourning for the capital's dead.

As ANK clearing operations forced low the rocketeers outside Phnom Penh, the Communists loosed terrorist activities inside the stunned city. On March 23, Vietnamese frogmen nestled mines alongside two freighters moored in the Mekong off Chrouy Chang War's naval station. Shortly, two explosions sank one and damaged the second. The next day, a battered French pickup truck slowed to a stop on the three-hundred-foot-long central span of the concrete-and-steel bridge over the Sap River between Phnom Penh and the Chrouy Chang War Peninsula. Built with World War II repatriation money, the aptly-named Japanese Friendship Bridge was only five years old. Moments after the truck stopped, an estimated two hundred pounds of explosives blasted the vehicle into the river through a fifty-foot hole blown out of the roadway. Four passersby were obliterated by the explosion fireball; seven others were hurt. Three days later, patched with Bailey bridging, the thoroughfare reopened. On March 26 and 28, respectively, grenades were tossed into a Khmer military housing area and at a Cambodian soldier-laden bus. In addition to all this, floating mines damaged two fuel barges moored near the navy base.[4]

Despite the war and the terrorism, Phnom Penh remained a detached study in surrealism. The city French culture tailored to the Khmer character was considered by many to be Asia's most beautiful, the "Paris of the East." For Cambodia it was more of a political, economic, and social hub than even Paris is to France. Motor vehicles, bicycles, and bell-tinkling, three-wheeled *cyclo-pousses* propelled by hustling pedalers moved along broad boulevards flanked by flamboyants (red flame trees), bougainvillea, and hibiscus. Ornate pagodas disgorged saffron-robed bonzes carrying white parasols and "begging buckets" early each morning. Moviegoers could watch their favorite stars on the silver screen inside poster-plastered theaters. The world-famous classical ballet continued to rehearse before select audiences in an open, green- and gold-roofed pavilion on the royal palace grounds.

The colonial Phnom Hotel on the city's fashionable near-north side re-mained a star, although the wrinkles and cracks had begun to show through its makeup. Its Cyrene Restaurant still served FANK officers superb bass and tournedos Rossini, papaya as red as the blood of their troops, and flaming baked Alaska. There also was fine dining at the posh, Corsican-owned Café de Paris, at La Taverne and at La Venise. Vintage wine and VSOP cognac were available. Angkor or Bayon beers, although with the same French roots as other Indochina brews, lacked the ghoulish formaldehyde taste of their

Saigon Ba-Mui-Ba (33) counterpart. Bars served drinks chilled with ice made from distilled water; few customers realized that the ice often was hammer-crushed in the communal urinal. Slender bar girls sipped watered-down sixty-riel orange soda while cuddling their light-skinned *cheris*. For more adult entertainment, brothels ran along the highway southeast of town or in house-boats on the three rivers. Prostitutes in pedicabs aggressively offered themselves to the nearest takers. Several newly arrived Americans fell victim to penicillin-resistant venereal disease. For opium, the names were Madame Chantal's or Mère Chum's.

Like all French settlements, Phnom Penh had its *Cercle Sportif* (Sports Circle). This urban country club was situated between the Phnom Hotel and the artificial hill that gave the city its name, and catered mostly to the French. Annual tennis championships still were held there until the Gallic exodus became serious. But it was the Phnom Hotel's poolside that was a people-watcher's paradise. By the dawn's early light, until he moved into a villa, a MEDTC general swam his laps, ending them with a towel and a Coke on a tray held by his waiting aide. Later in the day, reporters congregated at the outdoor bar, while diplomatic personnel and businessmen monopolized the tables. The eye-catcher was an orange-bikinied Czech beauty chaperoned by a brawny, T-shirted bodyguard, both belonging to a Corsican pilot who allegedly flew illicit gold and opiates between Indochinese airfields, Thailand, and Hong Kong.

The capital's university and public schools remained open. Its acclaimed silver roosters crafted by now-rare Vietnamese artisans still could be purchased in usually well-stocked (though decreasing in number) shops before they closed in deference to the stifling afternoon heat. Valuable coins were obtainable on Silver Street. The market places, supplemented by sidewalk vendors, continued to sell their food and nonedibles. Cooking lunch atop curbside charcoal-fueled braziers, the good-natured Khmer sellers squatted on their haunches with small bowls in hand to chopstick fish and rice spiced with *prahoc* paste or *tuk-trey* sauce, fermented fish mixtures often stronger than Vietnam's *nuoc-mam*. Around them, the traffic—including people-jammed, triwheeled taxi buses and Honda-towed mini-trailers—combined the worst of Oriental disorder and French aggressiveness. Cattle, chickens, and naked children, even elephants moving axed tree trunks, staked their claims to the roads beyond the boulevards. Elaborate funerals, with floatlike "hearses" preceded by small bands and with the requisite two to three days of cremation while the ashes were stirred, went on for the affluent.

1972: Attrition

Cambodians tried to forget the war every springtime new year when they filled the streets and the grassy slopes of the monastery-topped phnom ascribed to Lady Penh. It was a time for feasts, traditional *ramvong* dances, spectator and mass-participant sports, entertainers, fortune tellers, and ice cream cones—until the fighting intruded conclusively in 1974. Another annual spring festival was *Visakobochea,* the May 16–17 Triple Anniversary of Buddha, to commemorate the "Great Master's" birth, enlightenment, and death, all occurring during the middle of the month of Visak before the birth of Christ. The celebration in Phnom Penh, involving religious and political leaders, focused on the Square of the Grand Stupa, located just south of the Catholic Cathedral and the Phnom Hotel. Reputed ashes of Buddha brought from Ceylon in 1952 reposed in the pointed stupa. Religious rites were followed by a procession of decorated vehicles and floats depicting events in Buddha's life. The second day was devoted to meditation and catering to monks.

An eyewitness called Phnom Penh an "eerie blend of normalcy and hopelessness." Fatalism, optimism, defense mechanism, or selfish unconcern—whatever the cause of the ostrich-like attitude of the Phnom Penhois, the effects of the war could not be totally ignored. Incoming missiles and terrorist acts were the most shattering intrusions, even if their fickle fall directly impacted only a few at a time. Then, increasingly in 1973 until mid-August, there were the U.S. fighter-bomber strikes that could be watched from a safe distance during the day. These were followed after twilight by soon nightly vibrations from B-52 and artillery bombardments on suspected enemy positions lit by the swaying twinkle of parachute flares. At 9 P.M., police whistles told the remaining Vietnamese to get indoors. An hour later, it was the turn of the Chinese. At 11 P.M., the curfew became general, although foreigners were waved through checkpoints with smart salutes even later. Nor were foreigners the only privileged. Wealthy and influential Khmers, military officers standing out among them, found countless ways to siphon money from the American largess just as they had from the Communists when rice had been diverted from Battambang and military supplies flowed into Sihanoukville. They had Hollywoodesque villas erected either for themselves or to rent at outrageous prices to the foreigners. They assured that their *fils de Papa* (daddys' boys), insolent Mercedes drivers on Phnom Penh's streets, were exempt from military service. And they continued to host elaborate, army-guarded social events.

Surprisingly, the military presence was not what one would expect in an intermittently isolated city at war. Trucks and APCs occasionally rumbled along city thoroughfares. Soldiers demonstrated, threw grenades for fun or to catch fish in the rivers, and shot holes in restaurant ceilings when asked to pay, but these actions seemed unreal. More permanent signs of war were the sandbags and barbed wire protecting government buildings. And, as in Saigon, metal "cages" were installed over nightclub and restaurant windows to deflect possible terrorist explosives. The conflict's replacement of France by the U.S. as the dominant outside influence also was evident. While French families were leaving, Americans were arriving, the military personnel in mufti to keep their low profile. For the affluent Khmers, it was "in" to enroll in one of the many English language "academies" that sprang up. Stateside popular music began nudging aside high-pitched Oriental airs on the radio. Then there was America's powerful Armed Forces Vietnam radio with its strident musical offerings.

With the spate of dollars came stolen goods to swell the black market. Hundreds of civilian and military items came by air, road, and river from Saigon, courtesy of the unwitting U.S. taxpayer. Diversion tainted every level, with even G.I.s' wives selling bottles of bootlegged gasoline beside their ramshackle quarters. Corruption at Enaphar (acronym for *Entreprise Nationale de Produits Pharmaceutiques,* Cambodia's government drug distributor) ensured that medicines generated further illicit profits and reached the K.R. The currency black market, involving Thai bahts as well as dollars and riels, also was mind-boggling. All of which contributed to artificial shortages in the legitimate market and a runaway inflation. If Phnom Penh needed further evidence that its "normalcy" was abnormal, it could be found in erratic electric and water service.

Militarily, despite the influx of American weapons and FANK's large numbers, the Khmers seemed unable to abandon a strategy, in the words of a CIA report, "based on a desire to permit enemy attack and to rely on air power and ARVN to inflict casualties." This resulted in a seesaw warfare in which the Communists took three steps forward for every two they were forced back. Route 15 between Prey Veng and Neak Luong again was severed on April 7. Isolated anew, the provincial capital, Prey Veng, absorbed numerous rocket and shell bombardments during the month. Lightning raids erased twenty-two government outposts along Highway 1, until mid-April considered the safest road in Cambodia. When an ANK relief column plodding along the highway from Neak Luong eastward toward Kompong Trabek bogged down under enemy fire, five Khmer battalions training in South Vietnam had to be pulled out prematurely to prop it up.

Even in southernmost Military Region 2, despite the commitment of their main strength in South Vietnam, the Communists trounced the unaggressive

Cambodians. The agricultural market town Kompong Trach fell to the PAVN 1st Division on April 30. Advancing north of the shattered town on Route 16, the victors threatened the provincial capital of Takeo. Simultaneously moving westward along the curving asphalt highway, they reached and surrounded Kampot, capital of the same-named province sitting astride Route 3 between Phnom Penh and Kompong Som. There were instances of Khmer battalions fleeing in panic and entire companies surrendering without a fight. Intelligence reports indicated that the Communists now were able to land limited seaborne supplies in the coastal area just down the road from Kompong Trach. Perhaps as important were refugee tales of enemy units containing an increasing number of K.R.

In response to this late dry season threat to Military Region 2, American tactical aircraft sorties were beefed up by Arc Light B-52 missions requiring Pentagon approval. On April 25 and May 2 and 8, Secretary of Defense Laird okayed SAC heavy bomber raids against the PAVN 1st Division. On May 10, he signed off on a request to give the U.S. commander in Vietnam "approval authority for future Arc Light strikes" in eastern Cambodia. The authorization, "needed to be more responsive to the changing tactical situation," was to be renewed on a monthly basis. On November 23, Ambassador Swank, at the request of the Cambodians, asked for B-52 sorties "along Route 5 west of Phnom Penh," an area outside the Saigon command's jurisdiction. Laird gave the go-ahead for a three-bomber raid the next day, green-lighting B-52 strikes on December 4 and on January 4 and 16, 1973, as well.

American air operations, already widespread, continued to expand, with the U.S. Southeast Asia command soon empowered to act simply when action was "requested by GOK [Government of the Khmer Republic] and validated by the U.S. Ambassador." Growing harassment of the Mekong supply convoys also required more air power, including fixed-wing gunships. The orbiting 7.62mm and 20mm destruction wrought by air force Spectre AC-130s was so impressive that the gunships were asked to escort river trains for the rest of the year and into 1973.[5]

ANK, in the interim, renewed efforts to retake the Angkor ruins. Two reserve paratroop battalions were dispatched to strengthen the Angkor Chey forces. Two reasons were offered for the timing of the new assault. One was that Lon Nol, in consultation with mystical and religious advisers who had convinced him that victory depended on his army occupying the ruins, wanted them captured in time for the upcoming elections so that he could be sworn in as president at the historical site. The second was that intelligence reports said that the Communists were redeploying some troops out of the Angkor complex.

In the darkness of May 17–18, Khmer soldiers silently slipped across the roughly 6,600 feet separating their lines at Siem Reap Airport from a 600-foot-wide moat west of Angkor Wat. They traversed the obstacle, which shifting monsoon rains soon would fill with water, and moved through the trees northwest of the venerable temple to the base of 217-foot-high Phnom Bakheng. Just to the north, beyond wildly chirping insects and croaking amphibians, lay the south wall of the ancient imperial city of Angkor Thom. The Cambodians crept up the hill. Then, in the blue-gray of dawn, they routed the seven Vietnamese and fifty K.R. guarding the crest. The Khmer flag was raised above the small ninth-century temple that crowned Phnom Bakheng, the highest ground in the area. It is not difficult to imagine the G.I.s chattering in excitement and pointing across the flat-topped jungle canopy to the southeast. Rising above the mist-laced vegetation barely a mile away were the five ornate towers of Angkor Wat, their nation's most precious treasure.

The next phase of the ANK operation began the following night. Infiltrating the enemy outer perimeter, one group of soldiers double-timed between the trees parallel to the 4,800-foot-long northern side of the wide moat surrounding Angkor Wat. Then a right turn and a further 1,400 feet along the Siem Reap River bed brought the troops to an earthen causeway that crossed the moat. Beyond it, at the end of a tree-flanked road and a wall-enclosed grassy area, lay the rear east gate of the great temple. The main body of G.I.s, divided into two groups, warily made their way halfway down the western moat to the temple ground's main entrance, a terrace guarded by stone lions. Directly ahead of them, a stone causeway pointed straight across open space, sliced only by a low outer wall, toward the rectangle and pyramid shapes that provided them their national emblem. Lon Nol's soldiers now stood poised to assault the wat simultaneously from east and west. Shots suddenly replaced the silence. Whether it was the springing of a trap, an alert sentry, or an over-enthusiastic G.I. mattered little as flares popped and floated eerily earthward. A vicious crossfire from camouflaged trenches and bunkers needled through the shocked Khmers. Those who weren't chopped down fled, leaving behind dead and wounded. One group had seventeen dead and twelve injured out of thirty-nine men.

Conventional warfare resumed as ANK kept up its efforts to reclaim the prize of Angkor. The fighting west of the temple continued throughout the week, but courage was no match for automatic weapons concealed in con-

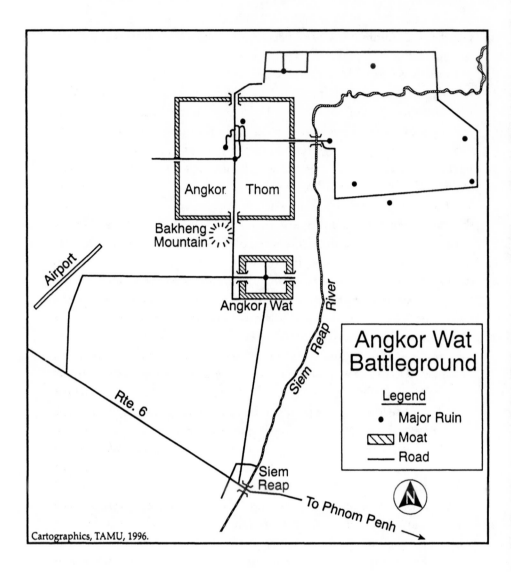

Angkor Wat Battleground

Legend
- Major Ruin
- Moat
- Road

Airport

Angkor Thom

Bakheng Mountain

Angkor Wat

Siem Reap River

Rte. 6

Siem Reap

To Phnom Penh

Cartographics, TAMU, 1996.

crete and wooden emplacements. On the southern Siem Reap–to-Angkor road, after a short-lived ANK advance, the Communists burrowed in around the two demolished hotels less than half a mile below the temple moat. They easily punched back new government attacks. Whenever Khmer T-28s appeared with their napalm and explosives, the defenders ducked into their deep shelters. In August, elements of the PLAF-PNLAFK 203rd Regiment snatched back the Phnom Bakheng heights after heavily shelling the hill. Operation Angkor Chey faded into a stalemate that finally was abandoned in September.[6]

Cambodia's 1972 presidential election campaign essentially was a contest between the Socio-Republican Lon Nol and the independent In Tam, who was backed by the Democrats. It began May 20 and quickly degenerated into a farce marked by ballot tampering, violence (including the murder of an In Tam provincial representative), and other irregularities. Given Cambodia's imperiled state, its obviously rigged election, and America's multifaceted involvement, the official U.S. position of letting the Khmers "play out their hand without outside interference" and the embassy one of not reporting "bad" news were debatable. On June 4, it was announced that Lon Nol had won with 54.92 percent of the 1,059,000 votes cast. In Tam garnered 24.44 percent. The rest went to Keo An, dean of the Phnom Penh University law school, who advocated facilitating the restoration of peace by allowing Sihanouk to return. Ironically, Nol's greatest support came from the rural districts, indicating loss of backing from the urban elite who had helped put him in power. It also indicated that, besides fatalistic detachment from Phnom Penh politics, most rural voters were subject to the influence of the army troops protecting them from the K.R. The troops, of course, were led by Lon Nol's strongest supporters.

Shortly after the voting, Lon Non boasted that, while a pre-election poll "showed 35 percent for my brother," he, Non, had gotten "55 percent for him." The losing candidates filed an official fraud complaint. It was rejected by the Provisional Constitutional Court. When the newspapers kept crying fraud, a new law was enacted to give the government a virtual free hand in suppressing media criticism. The controversial election gave rise to new political parties, most notably the resurrected Republican Party with Sirik Matak as its secretary-general. On July 3, just before his investiture as president, Lon Nol informed Ambassador Swank and visiting White House assistant General Haig that he intended "to emulate the methods of totalitarian indoctrination." The legislative elections under revised electoral laws in September were even more one-sided than the presidential one. The two major opposition parties boycotted them, and the Lon brothers' Socio-Republican Party occupied all 126 seats in the national assembly. An October cabinet shakeup named Hang Thun Hak prime minister, forcing out the old warhorse Son Ngoc Thanh, who returned to Vietnam in retirement. One of the reasons for replacing Thanh, whose name had been associated with the CIA, may have been to facilitate negotiations with the K.R. His successor admitted, "We are negotiating with the Khmers Rouges." The elections had put the capstone on Lon Nol's power, relegating Sirik Matak, Cheng Heng, and In Tam to the political darkside.

The Communists observed Lon Nol's election with a June 5 daytime terrorist attack. A rose-curtained Volkswagen Microbus came to a stop near the defense ministry on the south side of the airport highway in north central Phnom Penh. In bursts of flame and smoke, three Chinese 107mm rockets streaked from a jerry-rigged launcher on the vehicle's roof. Two detonated on the ministry grounds. The third skyrocketed southward over the city to blow up 210 feet from the presidential palace. Three playing girls were killed. The terrorists fled on a motorcycle.

At midday on June 8, eighteen 122mm rockets swooshed into Phnom Penh and its airport, inflicting seven casualties in the third bombardment of the capital since March. At the same time, Takhmau, six miles to the south on Highway 2, was pelted with recoilless rifle fire. Then, Vietnamese Communist commandos, who had canoed up the Thnaot River from the nearby Bassac, assaulted the Kandal Province administrative building, wounding the governor. They also attacked a tire factory and several other key structures. Forced to retreat by ANK troops and an AC-47 Spooky gunship, they left behind fourteen dead comrades. More than fifty Khmers also died. On June 25, two battalions of the six-hundred-man 48th Khmer Krom Brigade clearing Highway 1 southeast of Neak Luong were ambushed by a larger enemy force. Calls for aerial strikes and resupply went unanswered as the crack troops expended their ammunition. An ANK relief effort was blocked by the Communists. In desperation, after three days of fighting, the Khmers Kroms called artillery fire onto their position. Only thirteen men made it back to Neak Luong.[7]

On July 4, after three days of festivities to observe Lon Nol's inauguration as president, the Cambodian army began a limited offensive in the southeast. It was given the name *Sorya*. A major force under Colonel Ith Suong set out from Neak Luong to reopen the sixty-mile-long eastern stretch of Highway 1 cutting through Prey Veng and Svay Rieng Provinces to the Vietnamese border. Phase one of Sorya, which was coordinated with ARVN, broke through to Kompong Trabek, occupied by the enemy since April, after twenty days of fighting. Losses were from 27 ANK dead and 250 wounded, to more than 300 Communists killed. Instead of exploiting the operation's momentum, FANK planners scheduled Sorya's second phase (continuing the advance eastward from Kompong Trabek) for late August. Five battalions of the 11th Brigade Group and three of the 66th Brigade busied themselves digging in along the recaptured portion of the key highway. They then watched and waited.

Fifty-six miles to the north, the more aggressive North Vietnamese rolled over two dozen T-54 and PT-76 tanks from beneath the trees of the Chup plantation and drove them undetected to selected jump-off points. Other weapons and troops assembled beyond the sight of the unsuspecting Khmers. PAVN unleashed its counterblow on August 6 with a predawn rain of shells and rockets. This first Communist use of armor against ANK proved no contest. The high aluminum sides, machine guns, and recoilless rifles of the twelve-ton Khmer M-113 armored personnel carriers posed little challenge for the 35.4-ton, thick-steeled T-54s armed with 100mm cannons. In two and a half weeks, thirty-one APCs were knocked out. ANK claimed that thirty-one enemy tanks also were destroyed. Several attacking regiments cut off elements of the Cambodian 11th Brigade Group and reclaimed 4.5 miles of highway. In still another terrifying surprise, PAVN downed an AAK helicopter with an SA-7 missile on August 8. Fourteen crewmen and refugees died. That same day, a U.S. AC-130 Spectre gunship saved a Khmer position from annihilation by blasting apart a tank and scattering a horde of enemy troops. The partly paralyzed Cambodian president insisted on flying to Neak Luong to confer with Allied officers on the scene.

The result, American-influenced, was the movement of Phnom Penh reserve forces to Neak Luong for the early activation of Operation Sorya's second phase. The goals were to sweep the Communists from the road and to relieve the besieged five battalions around Kompong Trabek. Four ANK M-113–supported brigades and some ARVN troops pushed southeastward from Neak Luong while South Vietnamese units slogged westward from the border to squeeze the enemy between the two forces. Essential to the success of the operation was air power, including American air force and marine jets that, with VNAF aircraft, destroyed or damaged two dozen Communist armored vehicles. It took ten days of air and artillery bombardment to enable ground troops to reach the surrounded Khmer battalions. Plans to reopen Highway 1 beyond the battleground were dropped, however. The Cambodians strengthened defensive positions at devastated Kompong Trabek. ARVN occupied the area south of the town from the highway to the border. An ANK element to the north broke the enemy grip on Route 15 between Neak Luong and Prey Veng.

Meanwhile, on the west side of the Mekong and Bassac Rivers at the beginning of July, the Vietnamese Communists who, with K.R. help, earlier had taken Kompong Trach pounced on and encircled Angtassom forty-seven miles south of Phnom Penh on Route 3. Khmer troops under Brigadier General Kong Chhaith hurried to the rescue as shells and rockets fell on the town. They were stopped, and the general, who also was the governor of Takeo Province, was killed. Relief finally came to Angtassom on July 11. In the national capital, meanwhile, Communist clandestine warriors continued pecking at the city, again hitting the large fuel storage depot on the bank of the Sap River and also sinking another anchored freighter.

Two assassination attempts further roiled Phnom Penh's political waters. The first took place on August 21 as sixty-four-year-old Son Ngoc Thanh, then still prime minister and foreign minister, was being driven to work. Placing two American Claymore antipersonnel mines inside a Citroën *deux chevaux*, the would-be assassins drove the rickety car to the curb across the street from the north wall of the royal palace grounds. They then ran a wire back from the car to a battery-operated trigger in a pedicab parked about 150 feet away in front of the national museum. As Thanh's four-vehicle motorcade drove by just before 8:30 A.M. prior to turning right toward the government buildings facing the waterfront a block away, the explosives' electrical circuits were closed. A thunderous blast sent hundreds of lethal pellets streaking across the street to smack into the yellow stucco palace outer wall; the second device failed. Although the minister escaped unscathed, four startled soldiers were hurt when their escorting jeep leaped a curb and smashed into a tree.

Quietly voiced suspicions circulated that the Communists could not be responsible for such a bungled attempt. Thanh himself said that he suspected "an unnamed someone" (read Lon Non) inside the government. It was pointed out that Thanh, while relatively powerless, remained popular and, as prime minister, stood between Lon Non and the president's chair in the event of Lon Nol's demise before his own removal in October. Interestingly, one of two arrested suspects was a FANK civilian employee.

A similar attempt was made just before 7 A.M. on September 27 against the U.S. Embassy's deputy chief of mission, six-foot-eight-inch-tall Thomas Enders. As his armored limousine—nicknamed the "Al Capone Special"—negotiated the circle southward around the four-legged Independence Monument to the embassy, the pressure wave from about thirty-three pounds of plastic explosive beneath a bundle of charcoal, which had been concealed among motorcycles parked at the curb, slammed into its right front side. Windows of adjacent buildings, including the Polish Embassy, were shattered. A fire broke out in the car's engine compartment. But, once more, the target escaped unhurt. This time, however, an escorting military policeman and a passing bicyclist died; two other people were injured.

The explosive had been detonated by a wire running down a side street from which the terrorists had been able to watch Enders drive away from his nearby house. Again there was talk of an attempt bearing all the earmarks of

The assassination attempt against U.S. Deputy Chief of Mission Thomas Enders in September 1972 quickly drew a crowd of curious Cambodians. To the right of and behind the bombed car is Phnom Penh's Independence Monument. Courtesy William Harben Collection

Lon Non's "goon squads." The motive, it was whispered, was ingratiation with the K.R., with whom the marshal's "little brother" allegedly had business dealings and to whom he might turn if the Communists won.

At about this time, a U.S. Embassy officer mentioned a rumor to a Khmer minister about a possible attempt to assassinate Lon Nol. The Cambodian laughed and replied, "The enemy would burn alive anyone who touched a hair of the marshal's head. He's the greatest asset they have." Even Sihanouk, alluding to Lon Nol's incompetence in a radio broadcast, called the marshal FUNK's "best asset."

September on the battlefield evolved no brighter than August for the Cambodians. On the eighth, three ANK battalions occupying Kompong Trabek fled back along Highway 1 to Neak Luong, leaving behind at least two intact 105mm howitzers. On the eleventh, moving as close as five miles east of the joint FANK-Vietnamese control center at Neak Luong, the Communists pushed off the defenders of Phnom Baphnum, at 482 feet the highest ground

1972: Attrition

in Prey Veng Province. Elements of the 3rd Brigade Group under Colonel Lon Non sped from the capital to spearhead an effort to retake the hill rising above surrounding rice fields. Gains made were rolled back by an enemy counterattack, using tear gas, on September 16. From a foothold on the height's southwest corner, the Khmers launched an uphill frontal assault ten days later. It was repulsed.

A U.S. officer on the scene later remarked that Non "lacked . . . decisiveness, led from the rear, maneuvered in frontal assault with no flanking effort and failed to coordinate fire support" with his offensive. After four weeks, Lon Non's eight battalions, beaten back by an estimated two enemy battalions, were replaced. Non returned to the capital to try his hand at being minister for liberation, nation-building, and rallying.[8]

Phnom Penh received most of its rice, the Khmer staple, from the northwestern province of Battambang (which throughout the war had the nation's highest standard of living) in Military Region 3. However, the loss of acreage to the enemy, illicit diversion, mismanagement, and a drought the year before combined to create a grain shortage in 1972. Much of the rice that was available was sent from Battambang to the capital in large truck convoys along Highway 5; the parallel railroad line had long been neutralized by sabotage and guerrilla raids. Late in August, enemy action closed the highway as well. A seventeen-battalion ANK force tried to reopen it with little success. The result was a food crisis in Phnom Penh and two days of virtual anarchy. On September 7, hundreds of soldiers (in one of numerous instances of G.I.s leaving the battlefield to demonstrate for food and back pay) and civilians broke into a Red Cross depot and stole Japanese-donated bags of rice. More joined in until thousands were looting food shops and storehouses. A Chinese merchant was fatally shot when he resisted. By the following afternoon, the huge X-shaped, midcity *phsar tmey* (new market) was an empty shell of smashed windows and doors and overturned stalls, as looters took everything they could carry off. Finally, other soldiers were trucked in to restore order.

President Nol broadcast an appeal for emergency assistance. Air America and Khmer transport planes flew rice in from Saigon and Battambang, respectively, for ten days pending the arrival of a Mekong convoy. Even after finally being cleared by ANK battalions, Route 5 remained closed because of blown bridges and new PNLAFK attacks until November 18. Then, five truck convoys made it through before additional Communist assaults began on the key landline.

Aggravating the situation in Phnom Penh was the ballooning population. From 600,000 at the outbreak of the war, the population grew to 1.2 million in 1971 and then to almost 1.5 million during the 1972–73 period. The primary reason, of course, was refugees seeking safety from ground fighting, air strikes, South Vietnamese depredations, and Communist tyranny. The first refugees were families escaping Communist occupation and subsequent warfare in the northeast in 1961. The truly massive migrations began with the events of 1970. While the total number of refugees in the country of 7.1 million "is largely conjectural," stated a U.S. Comptroller General report, Washington accepted a Cambodian health ministry approximation of 2 million —150,000 in Phnom Penh and the rest in provincial capitals. The Red Cross said that those living in "thatched shacks on vacant land around Phnom Penh . . . [do] not include those refugees living with relatives" or in four established camps, where living conditions were appalling. Therefore, the number of those in the capital probably was greater than the government estimated. An increasing number of refugees found housing on the ground floor and in the basement of the sprawling, unfinished Cambodiana Hotel at the entrance to the Bassac River.

About another 13,600 Khmers fled to South Vietnam, Laos, and Thailand between 1970 and September 1971. Also to be considered were the fluctuating numbers of military families (5,487 in mid-1971) residing in concentrations throughout the capital. Their numbers varied according to how many accompanied their soldier-providers to the war zones at any one time. The government had no policy guidelines to deal with the population problem and had not requested assistance from the U.S. Embassy, which initially adopted a hands-off policy despite the fact that many of the refugees were fleeing from American bombs. By the fall of 1971, about $4.6 million had been contributed by foreign governments (principally Japan) and private organizations (mainly religious) for refugee aid. American refugee assistance between 1970 and 1973 totaled $1.15 million (far less than the cost of a day's aerial bombardment). One embassy employee was assigned to deal with refugee affairs. Only during the last fifteen and one half months of the war was U.S. aid significant in this area, totaling about 5 percent of the economic assistance program. Refugee funds were channeled through international organizations to avoid diversion by corrupt Khmer government agencies.[9]

The cancer eating out FANK's core went unchecked. Organizational and staff coordination problems persisted. While the army chain of command generally ran from its Phnom Penh headquarters to the commanders of the five military regions, the main force (general reserve) units in the regions remained tightly under headquarters control. So-called territorial forces were under regional commanders. During major operations, general staff personnel were "loaned" to the regions in a feeble effort to speed movement of forces to meet changing needs. Individual soldier recognition—promotions and medals—was awarded on the basis of influence rather than merit. American weapons, munitions, rations, and medicine continued to appear in enemy hands or on the black market. G.I.s went unfed and unpaid. Troop dissatisfaction exacerbated an already present lack of discipline that manifested itself in, among other ways, a cruel disregard for the civilians the troops supposedly were protecting. Property was pillaged and Khmer aircrews bombed and strafed indiscriminately.

After a brief decline under American pressure, FANK's nonexistent personnel, the phantoms, again swelled the ranks to fill the pockets of greedy officers who bought Mercedes for themselves, bought jewelry for their wives and mistresses, and erected luxurious villas. A new U.S.-requested government investigation concluded that 40,000 of FANK's 220,000 troops (a number earlier pared down from nearly 300,000) in mid-1973 existed only on paper. Adding to the problem was the fact that perhaps 4,500 of the army's soldiers were under sixteen years of age. A U.S. Senate report stated that corrupt officers recruited youngsters "because they can pocket their pay and children don't complain." The Khmer president only encouraged further corruption when he raised both the number of men regional commanders could recruit and the military-civil service salaries "of those earning less than 3,500 riels a month" (phantoms were the lower rankers). Cheng Heng's plea to Lon Nol to stamp out military corruption was brushed aside with a reported "calm down" since "the American B-52s are killing a thousand enemy every day and the war will soon be over." William Harben, chief of the U.S. Embassy's political section in 1972, was convinced that "American toleration of military corruption led directly to defeat." Nor was corruption limited to FANK matters. To spread American money further, provincial governorships were sold to allow their purchasers to disburse or keep local funds as they wished. When he ran out of provinces to sell, Lon Nol merely divided existing ones, not the first time Cambodia experienced the practice.

That politics rated over ability in FANK's leadership was proved in the fall of 1972 when Lon Non was promoted to brigadier general to lead the newly created 3rd Division of 13,000 men. Not only was it nearly four times larger than the 2nd Division or three times that of the 7th, but Non, unlike his

U.S.-equipped Khmer army troops included children sometimes barely taller than the weapons they carried. Courtesy William Harben Collection

brother, "does not have the respect or support of the Army . . . The Western diplomatic community holds him in virtual contempt [to quote an official American observation]." Non, "a military dilettante" with "a genius for meddling," lacked meaningful command experience. He was considered responsible for pushing Sirik Matak, In Tam, and Sak Sutsakhan out of the government. The CIA reported at the end of 1972 that Non was working to undermine Prime Minister Hang Thun Hak and Major General Sosthene Fernandez (to whom Lon Nol had bequeathed his chief of staff title in September), the former because of his position and the latter because he promised to reform the army. One of Non's loyalists, Brigadier General Ith Suong, commander of the 1st Division, had been promoted despite panicked flight during Chenla II; his unit began 1973 bogged down on Highway 1 after losing the ground gained in Operation Sorya. The Americans withheld MAP funds from the 1st and 3rd Divisions because of their ineffectiveness.

By the end of fiscal year 1972, FANK's U.S. Military Assistance Program–supported strength was 117 battalions (up 49 from the previous year). This didn't reflect total strength since some units received only payroll assistance. Battalions generally numbered 500 men, although some had only half that number. The American goal was 220,000 MAP-supported troops out of a total of 253,000. Although a December 1972 reorganization attempted to correct many of FANK's weaknesses by limiting strength to 250,000, suspending individual unit recruitment, reapportioning manpower, and streamlining structure, the results were a mixed bag. At the battlefield level, FANK's American contacts encouraged the taking and retaining of prisoners, for intelligence gathering as well as for humanitarian reasons. ANK, like its PNLAFK foes, was reluctant to do this; more than one photograph shows smiling Cambodian G.I.s holding severed human heads. Ancient custom also held that eating a fallen opponent's internal organs transferred his strength to the victor, as well as showing disdain. In one instance, an embassy officer learned that a PAVN captain had been captured. He hurried to question what surely was an intelligence gold mine. Reaching the interrogation site, the American was informed by a Khmer lieutenant that, alas, the Vietnamese "was killed trying to escape." However, the man's head was available.

The U.S. MAP priorities for ANK in 1972 were training and equipping "standardized infantry battalions," as well as reorganizing it into "four divisions comprising 12 brigades, 20 independent brigades, 74 territorial infantry battalions and 465 territorial infantry companies." The emphasis in 1973 was to shift first to increased artillery deliveries and "the introduction of armored cavalry elements into the force structure," and then to the equipping of logistical units to cope with the influx of U.S. equipment. What this all boiled down to was a progressive program to create the U.S. concept of the type of army Cambodia needed. By December 1972, the army officially had been provided with 152,739 rifles and carbines; 4,549 machine guns; 1,366 mortars; 181 howitzers; 53 M-113 and M-106 APCs; 2,094 trucks; 33 recoilless rifles; 7,735 grenade launchers; and thousands of radios and telephones—all of which satisfied bureaucratic requirements. The reality of war requirements was another matter. For one thing, the projected 1973 introduction of mobile armored cavalry elements to permit the relief of embattled units ran afoul of intensified fighting and K.R. assaults on Phnom Penh, which tied ANK into defensive positions. FANK seemed doomed to continue deploying its assets piecemeal in reaction to enemy initiatives.

United States assistance to the *Armeé de l'Air Khmère* was given "to provide it with the simplest, easiest to fly and maintain aircraft [to] accomplish its mission of close air support for ground and naval forces and limited air transport." Reliance on American air power, lack of trained pilots and support personnel, inadequate facilities, and poor leadership and organization kept AAK from rising above mediocrity. Illustrative of the problem was the crash of fourteen T-28s in a twelve-month period, eight of them because of pilot error. It didn't help matters that Lon Nol, like Sihanouk before him, feared airplanes as potential instruments of coup makers. During 1972, AAK grew from 76 to 154 aircraft: T-28s (16 in January 1972 to 48 in January 1973); C-47s (10 up to 15); AC-47s (3 to 6); AU-24 mini-gunships (0 to 14); UH-1 helicopters (14 to 19); T-41 trainers (0 to 14); and light planes (33 to 38). AAK now had three principal airfields; Pochentong, Battambang, and Ream just southeast of Kompong Som. Other airstrips were situated at Kompong Cham, Siem Reap, Phumi Samraong in the far northwest, and, along Route 5, Oudong, Kompong Chhnang and Krakor.

In 1970, the *Marine Nationale Khmère,* Cambodia's navy, had 1,600 men and 11 boats. By February 1972, MNK boasted 5,000 men and 69 craft. The latter were 39 PBRs (patrol boat, river); 19 LCM6s (landing craft medium); 2 ATCs (armored troop carriers); 2 LCIs (landing craft, infantry); 2 tugs; 2 patrol craft; 1 LCU (landing craft, utility); 1 MSB (mobile support base); and 1 drydock. A year later, MNK had 123 vessels. The improved navy was able to take over surveillance of Cambodia's 248-mile-long Gulf of Thailand coastline from the South Vietnamese. Its most critical mission, however, was protection and control of shipping on the Great Lake and 1,116 miles of navigable waterways. The addition of thirty-five armored craft—including monitors, ATCs, minesweepers, and a command-communications boat—soon enabled MNK to assume a greater role in escorting convoys along Cambodia's "umbilical cord," the Mekong line of communication. The primary naval stations were at Phnom Penh, Kompong Som, Ream, and, as of early 1972, Kompong Chhnang on the Sap River.

The American MEDTC team, in daily contact with FANK combat units, continued pumping equipment out of warehouses in Phnom Penh and Kompong Som and trying to "straighten out" the Khmer military establishment. Its new commander was a gung ho brigadier general named John Cleland, who had commanded a battalion in Vietnam. By early 1972, U.S. military personnel in Cambodia numbered 97, of whom 62 were assigned to MEDTC's metal sheds behind the embassy. Later in the year, there were 136 Americans and third-country nationals working on military activities out of the embassy complex: 74 in MEDTC (with an additional 10 in Saigon); 17 in the defense attaché's office; 5 in communications; and 40 as civilian contractors.

Military assistance to the Khmers for the fiscal year ending mid-1972 ran to $220 million, $40 million beyond the previous year's total; $300 million were requested for fiscal year 1973. In October, however, the Senate Foreign Relations Committee voted a $250 million limit. Total American military and civilian personnel in Cambodia already had been capped at two hundred by the Symington-Case Amendment to the Substitute Foreign Assistance Act and Related Assistance Act. In a 1972 agreement, supplementing one reached the previous year, U.S. "surplus agricultural commodities" would be delivered to Cambodia with the understanding that 80 percent of the currency (that is, local currency equal to $18.1 million) raised by their sale would be used to pay FANK salaries, including, presumably, those of the phantom troops.[10]

Nor were the Khmer Republic's adversaries idle. On June 19, 1972, beginning the first international trip since his overthrow, Sihanouk flew from Beijing to Bucharest. During the forty-one days he was using his high profile in Romania, Algeria, Mauritania, Yugoslavia, and Albania to drum up support for the politico-military coalition called FUNK, the Communists behind his back kept chipping away at whatever little power he held. Even the *samdech*'s dignity was not spared. Pressured to attend debasing self-criticism sessions with his wife in China, now he found his media contacts closely controlled by K.R. escorts. The prince, an obsession to avenge his ouster enabling him to swallow his pride, nevertheless questioned his allies' motives. As early as 1970, he had admitted, "For the moment I am still indispensable to [the Communists], but after the liberation [of Cambodia], I probably will not be."

Discreet planning, good timing, and the skewing of circumstances to its advantage enabled Pol Pot's CPK to make 1972 the year it came into its own. Hanoi, realizing that FANK posed no real threat to its strategic goals and needing its own manpower for the war in Vietnam, was able to rely more on the K.R. to keep Lon Nol's forces at bay. In keeping with an agreement reached at the 1970 Indochina Conference, PNLAFK was encouraged to assume a larger role in the Cambodian War. Numbering only about 3,000 when Sihanouk was overthrown, the K.R. had swollen to 120,000–150,000 regular and irregular troops by mid-1972. PNLAFK, formed into battalion- and regiment-sized units under commander Khieu Samphan, continued to grow so that it reached about 200,000 by the new year. Most of these were regional and village-level soldiers who freed the main force mobile elements to strike at selected targets and check government offensive actions around the country. Although North Vietnam's major combat role vis-à-vis PNLAFK virtually was ended by the close of 1972, Lon Nol's mindset enabled him to say that "the Khmer Communist movement does not pose a serious threat."

In contrast to North Vietnamese success with their surrogates in Laos, however, Pol Pot's Communists had a fanatical agenda that left no room for Hanoi's domination. At a summer 1971 two-week meeting, K.R. cadres were told by Pot that the CPK had entered a "new phase in its history," one of "national democratic revolution to overthrow feudalism and imperialism." Thus, while PAVN-PLAF combat strength in Cambodia dwindled to perhaps eight thousand (with another thirty thousand keeping the Ho Chi Minh Trail humming or otherwise supporting the war in Vietnam), K.R. extremists prodded farmers and fishermen into collectives for organization and indoctrination into the "pure communism" exemplified by the "uncontaminated" youth of the countryside. The purge of Sihanouk's Khmer Rumdo faction and those trained in Hanoi, quietly begun the year before, and the undermining of the Vietnamese Communists, all were stepped up. Black shirts and pants began to replace the traditional multihued Khmer sampots and sarongs.

The CPK leaders, still using the shield of a popular front to hide its intentions, adopted the name that would become synonymous with the future killing fields—*Angkar*, the Organization. They divided the country into five geographical zones comparable to FANK's military regions. Their strategy for winning the war, like their foes', was focused on the cities. But whereas FANK was tied to their defense, PNLAFK used the cities to advance elsewhere. If urban centers fell to them, so much the better, but generally the K.R. in 1972 used attacks in and around the towns to undercut government initiatives. This left the K.R. free to solidify a hold on the countryside and gnaw away at Cambodia's lines of communications. If the mystical Lon Nol's belief in an Angkorean revival was grandiose, the fanatical Pol Pot's concept of a Kampuchean utopia—both assuming Khmer superiority over foreigners—was no less illusory. The Communist leader once said that "if our people were capable of building Angkor, they can do anything."[11]

After worsening summer terror attacks against Phnom Penh, Washington ordered a phased evacuation of the dependents of embassy personnel. Six days later, as if to underscore the decision, the Communists made their most devastating hit-and-run raid of the war on the capital. Saturday, October 7, was both *Pchum Ben,* the Buddhist festival of the dead to honor ancestors, and the second anniversary of the legislation creating the republic. In the early morning darkness, 103 commandos of PAVN's *Dac Cong* 367th Sapper Regiment burst into northern Phnom Penh. Explosives-laden Vietnamese dashed

On October 7, 1972, North Vietnamese sappers destroyed three of six sections of the Sap River bridge joining Phnom Penh and the Chrouy Chang War Peninsula (background). Courtesy William Harben Collection

onto the Sap River bridge leading to the Chrouy Chang War Peninsula. A series of detonations tumbled three of the six sections of the city's largest water-crossing roadway. It would be a month before enough of the fallen debris could be cleared to allow shipping to pass. The bridge itself would not be repaired until 1994.

A larger group of attackers, sprinting beneath a cover of shoulder-launched rockets, broke into the municipal stadium just west of the bridge. The sports oval served as an army encampment and M-113 APC parking area. Four tracked vehicles were flamed. Six others were hijacked by the PAVN sappers. The Cambodians reacted with all of the fury of a disturbed apiary. In six hours of fierce combat, eighty-three Vietnamese were slain and seven captured. Ten nearby houses burned, and the facade of the French Embassy on the square adjacent to the stadium was badly nicked by bullets. But the determined ANK reaction scotched PAVN plans to assault other installations in the area. Tracking the stolen M-113s westward toward Route 5, the pursuing Khmers destroyed three and recaptured the other three in damaged condition. Friendly losses were given as thirty-three dead and seventy-four wounded, including several casualties when ten diversionary rockets fell on Pochentong.

Later on, with bodies still littering the battleground, civilians crowded into the square and park between the stadium and the broken bridge to celebrate the dual holiday. Unexpected fireworks came when ANK sent mortar rounds thumping into Kak Lake between the square and the airport road to the southwest in response to a report that enemy soldiers were hiding among the reeds of the shallow lake. The government complained that "it was unfair of the enemy to attack on a religious holiday."

In addition to its other problems, Cambodia faced a challenge of its credentials in the United Nations, of which it had been a member since 1956. Beijing-based GRUNK and FUNK had been working to replace the Lon Nol government in the world body ever since the left-leaning Lusaka (Zambia) Conference of Non-Aligned Chiefs of State in August 1970. About thirty countries, including the PRC, already had swung themselves to Sihanouk's side, compared with just over three dozen, including the USSR, for Lon Nol's. Seating of the GRUNK government-in-exile at the August 1972 Non-Aligned Conference of Foreign Ministers in Guyana shocked the Phnom Penh regime into recognizing that something had to be done to reverse the pro-Sihanouk trend.

In September, the Khmer government prepared to send out international "good will" teams and asked for American assistance. One Washington response was a snowstorm of position papers and cables to its foreign posts containing facts and suggested strategies to support Phnom Penh's claim to legitimacy and to open doors worldwide for Cambodia's lobbyists. On September 29, Khmer Foreign Minister Long Boret delivered an impassioned speech to the UN General Assembly in New York. He described his country's plight, rebutted its critics and asked the organization to "intervene to help to call an immediate halt to a systematic and foolhardy aggression on the part of North Vietnam." Whether or not the whirlwind campaign helped Cambodia avoid Taiwan's 1971 fate, Khmer representation at the UN remained unchanged.[12]

The Cambodian government altered its strategic concept of the Lon Nol Line late in the fall of 1972. While accepting the need to keep Highways 5, 6, and 7 open to the Battambang rice bowl and to Kompong Cham, FANK planners realized that they no longer could effectively protect the large area delineated by the old line. Therefore, in November, they prioritized a southern cone encompassing only about 15 percent of the country. Using Peam

*The bodies of North Vietnamese raiders lie in the street after the October 7, 1972,
commando attack on Phnom Penh. Courtesy William Harben Collection*

Lovek, just above the old imperial capital of Oudong northwest of Phnom
Penh as a pivot point, they drew a line southwest across the Elephant Mountains to Kompong Som Bay and another southeast past Prey Veng to the Vietnamese border in the area known to the Americans as the Angel's Wing. This
sector, along with the Route 5, 6, and 7 corridors, encompassed the most populated areas of Cambodia, as well as Highways 1, 2, 3, and 4.

Divisive political shuffling and military attrition along the government's
lines of communication marked the closing months of 1972 in Cambodia.
U.S. presidential adviser Henry Kissinger, whose name forever would be tied
with Nixon's in formulating America's controversial Cambodia policy, made
a lightning October 22 visit, his only one. In a three-hour meeting, he briefed
Lon Nol on peace talks going on with the North Vietnamese, then flew to
Saigon.

In southwestern Military Region 2, the 1st PAVN Division bulldozed ANK
defenders from six positions between Takeo and the frontier; the Khmer 15th
Brigade Group was obliterated. It took an ARVN incursion to enable the Cambodians to reoccupy the area. In November, the Communists concentrated

on pressuring the provincial capital, Takeo. They enisled Angtassom seven miles to the west on Route 3 and Prek Sandek just to the south on Route 2. U.S. airplanes parachuted ammunition and daily pounded the enemy. AAK helicopters brought in ANK reinforcements. The Allied effort succeeded. On November 30, Cambodian units began clearing Takeo Province's Highway 2 between Phnom Penh and the border. As repairs to artillery-pitted roads permitted the first truck convoys to reach the area since October, a combined ANK-ARVN operation finished clearing the highway. To the west, Khmer troops managed to reopen Route 4 for the first time in two months.

Temporarily stymied in the south, the Communists next struck in the lower section of north central Military Region 4. On America's Pearl Harbor Day, between four and seven thousand PNLAFK and PAVN infantrymen assailed Kompong Thom, the goal of the ill-fated Chenla operations. American jets swooped hawklike to give the reeling three-thousand-man garrison time to reestablish a defense perimeter after ceding ground to the city's west and southwest. As U.S. and AAK aircraft dropped ammunition, the attackers probed the defenses and subjected Kompong Thom to nocturnal mortar barrages. On December 19, reinforcements from ANK's 12th brigade reached the town after a mad drive down Route 6 from Siem Reap. Other troops, from the 77th Brigade, were choppered in from Phnom Penh. A powerful enemy assault on December 23–24 was minced with the help of 7th Air Force jets. The PNLAFK-PAVN operation dissolved completely after a December 27 air-supported ANK counterattack.

The Communists continued displaying their dexterity at terrorist and sabotage activities during 1972's final month. December was less than a week old when two 107mm rockets fired from a pushcart whistled against a government building in Phnom Penh. Damage was slight since the thirty-three-inch, forty-two-pound Chinese missile was strictly a people-killing instrument of terror. Exploding at the slightest contact, it lacked penetrating power, spraying jagged metal in all directions.

Shortly after midnight on December 6–7, two pairs of PAVN frogmen swam into Phnom Penh's anchorage. They attached large plastic explosive bricks to the hull of the 2,881-ton, Panamanian-registered freighter *Bright Star,* which had arrived the day before in a Mekong convoy. At about 1:15 A.M., the saboteurs were spotted and fired upon by shipboard guards. Three were reported slain. Although one explosive charge was safely removed by a MNK specialist, a second detonated just after being detached shortly after 3 A.M. It killed four, injured fourteen onlookers, and sank the still-loaded ship. It was the fourth sabotage action in the capital in as many months. The following week, a fuel barge erupted in flames at the same anchorage.

While raiders strove to fill Phnom Penh's Four Arms waterfront with sunken ships, three U.S. Army doctors flown in to check Lon Nol's health made their report. The president still had difficulty walking and retained a slight speech impediment, they reported, but he was "recovering well" from his stroke. If Nol's physical condition was acceptable, his mental state raised questions. Earlier, to the distress of the nation's mostly mixed-ancestry educated class, he had introduced strong xenophobic references in his public statements to the glory of the "Angkorican era" and to Cambodians being "descendants of the Khmer-Mon" race. Nol also had warped the purposes of the new Mon-Khmer (classification of the population based on the Mon-Khmer language family) Institute by inverting its name to "Khmer-Mon" and using it to strain out foreign influences so as to strive for a pure race and culture. In this context, he tried to stress his dark-skinned Khmer purity by encouraging his G.I.s to call him "black Papa," despite the fact that he was of Chinese-Khmer ancestry. Long a believer in the occult, he leaned heavily on talismans, astrologers, and priests to wage his "holy war" against the Communist heathens. Perhaps the most notorious of the priests was Mam Pram Moni, who professed to be a reincarnation of Angkor's Jayavarman VII and became an ANK officer the U.S. Embassy nicknamed "Friar Tuck."

In December 1972, Lon Nol launched "Neo-Khmerism." It was, according to an American embassy summary, "a new attempt to create a national ideology." Laid out in a brochure, the concept glorified Cambodia and the Khmer-Mon race while castigating the Vietnamese and the Thais. Embassy political officer William Harben saw Neo-Khmerism as combining "vague modern political and economic theories with the revival of ancient Khmer and Buddhist tenets." One of its goals was to prolong the "Buddhist era to 5,000 years as predicted," in part by having Cambodia's population reach thirty million by 2020 A.D.

Another example of the president's thinking came with the issuance of an official decree ordering the arrest of anyone buying live rabbits. The fear was that buyers would be enemy agents who would tie timed explosives to the animals and send them into army positions. Despite all of this, Washington felt that "U.S. interests indicate that we support the present leader . . . because there is no visible alternative to him short of disintegration of the government and the army." Admitting the suppression of negative reporting about the Lon Nol regime, a State Department document encouraged "political conciliation and national reform" to create a broader political base in expectation of "the inevitable future political contest with the Khmer Communists." American leadership both assured that it would receive lopsided reporting from its embassy and greatly underestimated CPK fanaticism.

Perhaps the real achievement of 1972 was the survival of the Lon Nol government and the continued existence of the Khmer Republic. The Communists controlled over half of the country. Six of the seven highways tying the provinces to the capital were severed for most of the year. Inflation had propelled the price of rice 500 percent over that of 1970. CINCPAC Admiral John McCain, Jr., the small, verbose Hawaii-based overseer of America's Southeast Asian fighting, believed that "even with massive U.S. logistical and economic assistance," Cambodia could not defeat a determined Communist effort because of "limited technical skills, leadership potential, management capabilities and manpower base." He felt that "our goal should continue to be to develop an integrated GKR [Government of the Khmer Republic] armed force capable of defending territory held by them while concurrently seeking a solution to hostilities through political negotiations." Barring the success of the latter, almost everyone expected Cambodia to fall to the Communists the following year.[13]

CHAPTER EIGHT

1973:
A Rain of Bombs

ON JANUARY 23, 1973, PRESIDENT NIXON told the American public that "we today have concluded an agreement to end the war and bring peace with honor in Vietnam and Southeast Asia." The cease-fire documents, officially the Agreement on Ending the War and Restoring Peace in Vietnam, signed in Paris on the January 27, took effect the next day. Except for the deleted earlier requirement that Saigon's Thieu regime be replaced by a Communist-approved coalition, it contained basically the same conditions Hanoi had insisted on in 1969, clear evidence of Washington's desperation to end the conflict. Another difference between 1969 and 1973 was the fact that Cambodia now was ablaze in its own conflagration.

During the drawn-out U.S.–North Vietnamese peace negotiations, Henry Kissinger had pushed for a cease-fire that would include Laos and Cambodia. Hanoi negotiator Le Duc Tho agreed to a Laotian cease-fire to take effect within a month of the signing of the agreement. But, he told a skeptical Kissinger, North Vietnamese "influence on the Cambodian Communists was not decisive." Sihanouk himself later said that Hanoi in 1973 "tried to make them [the Khmer Communists] negotiate with Lon Nol, but it would have been too dangerous for them. They would have had to share power and they wanted it all alone." Unable to make headway, Kissinger finally stopped pushing. It was not until years later that the West reluctantly recognized the CPK and its single-minded leaders for what they were.

The K.R. aside, Hanoi made an immediate sham of the Paris agreement by ignoring Article 20 of Chapter VII calling for foreign countries to "end military activity in Cambodia and Laos" and "totally withdraw from and refrain from reintroducing troops, advisers," and war materiel into those nations. The PAVN 1st and 5th Divisions had been side-slipped into Cambodia immediately after the agreement was signed. Whatever the outcome, the Nixon administration, its feet already mired in the morass of the Watergate scandal that would cause the president to resign in 1974, had gotten its "decent interval" between the final withdrawal of U.S. troops and the fall of Saigon.

A day after the Paris agreement went into effect, January 29, FANK guns went silent and the Cambodian skies were bereft of Allied bombers. Lon Nol, nudged by the United States, had called a unilateral cease-fire in vain hope of ending his nation's war. Only "to counter specific hostile acts" against FANK, the Pentagon told CINCPAC, would American air activities resume. In that case, a "simple, rapid request-validation-execute procedure" would be set up between the U.S. Embassy and MACV. Communist offensive action in South Vietnam remained dormant until March, but in Cambodia it never ended. Phnom Penh's request for a PAVN-PLAF withdrawal and the restoration of lost ground was flipped aside by the K.R. as "a deceit engineered by the U.S. imperialists and their allies." Thus, PNLAFK pressure on Kompong Thom in Military Region 4 and on the Route 1—Mekong LOCs in Military Region 1 continued.

On January 6, in what apparently was the K.R.'s first directly unassisted major operation, a couple of PNLAFK battalions surrounded Romeas, a railroad town forty-five miles northwest of the capital in Military Region 3. Enemy jabs and shells gnawed away at the Khmer battalion defending the town. Finally realizing that the dry season attack was more than a harassment exercise, FANK a week later dispatched two columns to the rescue from the Highway 5 towns of Kompong Chhnang, sixteen air miles to the northeast, and Saka Lek Pram, about eighteen miles to the southeast. The eleven-battalion reinforcements, lacking aggressive leadership, inched forward against less than heavy opposition. Desperate field commanders called in helicopters to leapfrog a relief force closer to Romeas. The force's 210 men were scattered by enemy fire soon after landing on January 16. American air drops of supplies kept the decimated G.I.s in Romeas from being overrun while FANK ferried in another 750 troops over a two-day period. Backed by heavy U.S. air strikes, the "cavalry" at last broke through to Romeas on January 23. PNLAFK also took advantage of the one-sided truce by slamming anew against the Mekong LOC, Routes 2 and 3 south of Phnom Penh, and Kompong Thom on Route 6.

Regular American tactical and strategic air sorties screamed back into action on February 7 after an eleven-day hiatus during which it became obvious that the Communists had no intention of respecting the cease-fire. Starting on a relatively modest scale, the aerial effort would build up to one of history's most intensive bombing campaigns. Washington initially authorized missions "only to avert actual loss of positions" by FANK, which was requesting all the help it could get. Two K.R. regiments flanking the Mekong above and below Neak Luong were forced to keep their heads down as circling American aircraft escorted two large Phnom Penh–bound convoys without loss. U.S. planes not only buttressed FANK during February's seesaw warfare along the river but also covered its unsuccessful attempts to break the lengthy siege of Kompong Thom. Other American tactical sorties snapped at the enemy to the southeast along Highways 2, 3, and 15 in Takeo and Prey Veng Provinces.

Indicative of the intensity of U.S. tactical air operations during the first half of 1973 was the participation of the Marine Corps' modest aviation component. Between March and mid-August, Marine Aircraft Group 15 flew 10,215 combat sorties involving, according to corps records, "30,998 flight hours and 24,584 tons of ordnance," and the loss of two F-4 Phantom and three A-6 Intruder jets. Phantoms of Marine Fighter Attack Squadrons 115 and 232 flew between a dozen and twenty daily bombing and strafing sorties assigned by the 7th Air Force. In mid-May, the F-4s were joined by nocturnal predators, the A-6s of Marine All-Weather Attack Squadron 533. The Intruders, using airborne moving-target indicators and ground radar beacons, swept roads in southeastern Cambodia on a nightly average of five sorties.

On February 25 and 26, sixty B-52s unloaded 500- and 750-ton bombs from bays and underwing pylons over the rubber plantations east of Kompong Cham in the northwestern part of Military Region 1. U.S. aircraft were so far-ranging that one Cambodian officer remarked that ANK was afraid to move at night lest it attract the attention of electronically-guided B-52s or F-111s. The escalating air war received official sanction on March 9 when, following a Joint Chiefs of Staff proposal, orders went out to use "the full spectrum of U.S. air strike forces against targets posing a threat to friendly forces and population centers" and against "VC/NVA supply routes, storage areas and transshipment points" in eastern Cambodia.

Air action did not restrict itself to the eastern part of the country, however, but rather went wherever it was felt to be needed. Attaining a daily average of 58 B-52 and 184 tactical and gunship sorties during the last two weeks in March, the air force more than tripled the sortie rate of the preceding fourteen-day period and chalked up nearly nine times the February 16–28 level. The soaring bomb tonnage rates, totaling nearly fifty thousand tons in April alone and affecting chiefly the eastern two-thirds of Cambodia, smeared the countryside with distinctively patterned huge crater scars. The enemy, previously using only 12.7mm machine guns and small arms as anti-aircraft weapons, introduced limited numbers of 23mm and 37mm guns, as well as surface-to-air missiles, to cope with the aerial onslaught.[1]

The torrid spring of 1973 was a hard one for the Khmer Republic. Ceaseless enemy pressure almost everywhere was highlighted by heavy fighting in the southeast, the area closest to the Communist supply depots and the capital's primary LOCs. By March 12, two important government positions on Highway 2, Chambak to the north and Prey Sandek to the south of the provincial capital of Takeo, had fallen. Four days later, after the ANK 7th Division's 45th Brigade bogged down in an attempt to recapture Chambak, division commander Brigadier General Un Kauv took personal charge, brought in the rest of his largely Khmer Krom command, and resumed the effort. Braced by four SAC B-52 missions and ANK 105mm howitzer barrages, the general led his troops into Chambak on March 18.

Elements of Lon Non's 3rd Division moving southward from Phnom Penh to participate in the Chambak relief operation belatedly reached the town two days later, having, if nothing else, assured that the highway from the capital was open. Renewed enemy attacks inflicted major personnel and material losses on the Khmers, who once more saw Route 2 cut above and below Takeo. Only American air support, including supply drops, prevented a complete disaster. Just to the northwest of this battlefield, an entire ANK battalion defected to the Communists. It was the unit's way of protesting not having been paid in months.

Fighting along the Mekong and Highway 1 was equally teeter-totter. By the end of March, having rolled up ANK positions north of Neak Luong, PNLAFK controlled between fifteen and sixteen miles of ground on both sides of the river, thereby also cutting Route 1 between the capital and the highway ferry crossing. ANK 2nd division commander Brigadier General Dien Del was charged with reopening the newly lost stretch of highway. One of the army's more respected officers, Del completed his assignment early in April. A short time later, he lost the retaken ground and was unable to prevent the enemy from enlarging their hold to 70 percent of the river banks in the area.

A nearly twenty-ship Mekong convoy was held back in Vietnam as reinforced government units punched along the west and east banks. Just as they were making progress in clearing the way for the river train, guerrillas struck the convoy's holding area at Tan Chau. Orders were given to move out the vessels. Under heavy covering fire, including aircraft and armored patrol boats, the convoy ran the gauntlet to Phnom Penh in two sections. It already was nearly two weeks late, and the city was desperate for the supplies it carried. Food was scarce for most of the capital's inhabitants. Cars lined up for their 300-riel allotments of gas. Thousands watched the first group of three freighters and two tankers, led by the 3,500-ton *Lucky Star,* reach the city on April 8. Nothing could have been more incongruous or illustrative of Phnom Penh's schizophrenia than the appearance, as the first battle-scarred vessel hove into view, of a pink-bikinied girl waterskiing across its bow. The second section of the convoy consisted of a cargo ship and two tankers. Other ships had turned back.

On April 10, reacting to the land isolation of and limited river access to the capital, the U.S. began a mini-airlift of fuel into Phnom Penh. While the initial gallons were intended for military use, subsequent ones were for civilian consumption. Rationing was in effect and the black market price for gas had shot from thirty-five cents to two dollars a gallon, yet there was no observable decrease in motorized street traffic. Later in the month, another river train came under heavy fire in the frontier zone, below which U.S. warplanes no longer could fly. One night, a MNK tug snuck a sandbag-protected ammunition barge to the capital. The April battle of the Mekong convoys had cost two freighters, one munitions barge and one fuel barge sunk, and eight vessels damaged. To cope with the situation, FANK established a Mekong Special Zone (similar to the Phnom Penh Special Military Zone created in 1971 and corresponding to a military region) under MNK chief Commodore Vong Sarendy.

River traffic harassment increased in May, although the month's three round-trip convoys lost only one vessel. There were seventeen convoy attacks in May, as compared with seventeen during the first four months of the year. Ferocious air strikes and the return of the South Vietnamese to the fray kept river ambushes down to sixteen in June. As part of its waterway protection program, MNK dipped into an existent combat swimmer unit for recruits to set up its own SEAL component in mid-1973. In a year, it numbered ninety men in three teams. They were used for river reconnaissance and as shock troops. Enemy activity along the Mekong-paralleling Highway 1 LOC also was slowed by FANK action, but not before the road changed hands more than once.

Meanwhile, on the western side of the Mekong and the Bassac Rivers, Takeo's defenses held against repeated enemy assaults thanks to reinforcements and American air power. To the southwest, however, the gulf resort and fishing village of Kep, once a playground for the wealthy, fell to the Communists. The latter immediately executed the officers of the defending battalion. The K.R. also reclaimed Chambak on April 2, a day after Un Kauv's bloodied 7th Division was relieved by the 37th Brigade. During the fighting, Lon Non's strong but undermotivated 3rd Division was bullied back up Highway 2 until it was a scant six miles below Phnom Penh. PNLAFK now was within artillery range of the capital, where rationing of electricity had been added to the inhabitants' woes. With sadistic timing, during the hottest part of the year, one of the city's two oil-fed generators caught fire. Half of Phnom Penh blacked out and fans stopped as the temperature reached a steamy 95 degrees.

The proximity of the enemy made the continual thud and thump of bombs and shells another unwelcome part of daily life in Phnom Penh. At night, windows shook as heavy American bombs pounded targets along Routes 1, 2, and 30 just southeast of town. U.S. bombs farther afield to the southwest helped break the three-week Communist control of a twenty-mile-long stretch of Highway 4. The 122mm rockets that the PAVN 367th Sapper Regiment showered on Pochentong Airport in late April, however, came from launchers newly erected to the north. The enemy seemed to be everywhere.

PNLAFK troops were spotted occupying undefended villages on the Mekong's east bank across from Phnom Penh on April 25. FANK ferried over soldiers as American F-4 jets howled in to soften up the villages. The aircraft dives were accompanied by the claps and cheers of Cambodian onlookers lining the west side of the river. These strikes and the nocturnal B-52 and F-111 raids represented the closest, most dramatic fireworks show the capital had ever seen. Nothing to worry about, said General Fernandez, now FANK's chief of the general staff and commander-in-chief. "The enemy cannot concentrate troops on the [flat and open] east bank because of the danger of bombing." The general may not have been worried, but until the K.R. finally withdrew from their freshly occupied positions, U.S. helicopters in Thailand were kept on alert to evacuate the American Embassy staff. By late May, the heightened air campaign appeared to make a dent in PNLAFK's vise grip on three sides of Phnom Penh. The diplomatic community consensus was that the Communists were trying to bring down Lon Nol by constant pressure rather than by direct assault on the capital.

The heavy April fighting boosted FANK casualties to the highest level of the war to date. While the accuracy of government statistics remains open to question, they nevertheless represent a trend. FANK acknowledged its dead as numbering 1,093 in 1971; 2,003 in 1972; and 1,641 during the first five months of 1973, with the enemy dead for the respective periods being 1,853; 2,275; and 1,515. Disturbingly, weapons lost by FANK reached the highest recorded level of the war to date in June 1973, with enemy weapons seized remaining relatively constant in number.[2]

Since the relative cease-fires in Vietnam and Laos, the use of air power over Cambodia temporarily was "the only game in town." As a result, America's Phnom Penh embassy found itself assuming a politically sensitive role. Whereas it previously had played no direct part in controlling air missions, new procedures—to cope with the January unilateral cease-fire situation and to assure adequate communications as U.S. Air Force facilities moved from Vietnam to Thailand after the Paris agreement—changed all that. Apparently these new procedures took on a life all their own, being retained, in the view of the embassy, "in the hope that there would soon be a cease-fire situation." They not only were retained but intensified under White House auspices without the secretary of state's full knowledge. The embassy undertook a triad of interrelated tasks principally affecting the two-thirds of Cambodia where combat was still going on.

A military-civilian panel chaired by Deputy Chief of Mission Thomas Enders[3] screened all B-52 and F-111 electronically controlled sorties, while the defense attaché's office, augmented by temporarily assigned military personnel, validated tactical missions in coordination with the ambassador's office and FANK. Second, the air attaché's office provided equipment for direct radio and telephone links among the Cambodian general staff, the 7th Air Force, and U.S. airborne control elements. Finally, the air attaché oversaw the daily management of FAC and strike aircraft in response to Khmer requests or tactical emergencies. The forward air controller planes, mainly twin-boomed OV-10s, became a regular feature at Pochentong Airport, which they used for such purposes as refueling.

Lieutenant Colonel Mark Berent, an embassy air attaché from mid-1971 to early 1973, recalls a two-to-three-week period when "a few of us literally ran the [tactical air] war out of my office . . . using a radio on my desk, and a generator and antenna on the roof." Berent was in his third Southeast Asia tour, already having logged more than one thousand hours of air combat time and earned the Silver Star and dozens of other decorations. He later wrote five successful novels dealing with the Indochina air war. This "hot phase" of the embassy role, he recalls, occurred during the "lag time" when MACV's successor organization and the 7th Air Force were setting themselves up in Thailand. The 7th Air Force command post directing electronics-loaded air force and navy aircraft used as flying command posts had packed up at Tan Son Nhut Air Base and not yet recommenced operation at Nakhon Phanom Royal Thai Air Force Base. As the Thai-based facility became operational, still another variation in the embassy's air strike role was introduced because of the increasing attacks on Mekong convoys. Beginning on April 6, an embassy air force officer, accompanied by a FANK liaison counterpart, boarded a U.S. airborne command post at Pochentong each morning to become an aerial approval extension of the embassy-coordinated operation.

The end of the embassy's direct combat role coincided with the meeting of two visiting U.S. Senate investigators and a correspondent. James Lowenstein and Richard Moose arrived in Phnom Penh on April 5 during a trip to research the Indochina situation for the Senate Foreign Relations Committee. Declassified State Department cables make it clear that the investigators were given less than candid answers to initial questions about the air war. One day, the Senate visitors entered the United Press International wire service office in downtown Phnom Penh to read incoming news on the teletype machine. There, UPI correspondent Sylvana Foa, who also did work for *Newsweek,* informed them what more than one reporter already knew—that the embassy was relaying air strike requests and validating them to avoid civilian damage. She let Lowenstein and Moose listen to the telltale "Fox-Mike" embassy-aircraft conversations on her sixteen-dollar commercial plastic radio.

The men's ensuing communication with Washington's Capitol Hill had predictable results. Embassy doors opened for them at just about the time the direct tactical air coordination operation was being transferred to a Khmer air support center that had been in the process of being established in FANK headquarters. The embassy kept its strike screening and validation function, however. Dust from the political storm involving the embassy, irate Secretary of State William Rogers and an equally perturbed committee chairman Stuart Symington still was settling when Sylvana Foa left Cambodia on April 20 under a Khmer government expulsion order disguised as a temporary measure. Few questioned the information ministry explanation that the expulsion had been requested by the embassy. Publication of the Lowenstein-Moose report at the end of the month and the harsh congressional criticism that followed obliged the administration to defend its actions. Since the protection of American troops in Vietnam could no longer be used to justify the bombing—the last troop formations left on March 29—the reason given revolved around the Communist failure to observe the cease-fire.

Controversy over effectiveness and threat to noncombatants continued throughout the duration of the U.S. bombing. While maps were augmented by photography and electronic devices, those available to air crews were too small-scale and outdated, that is, not certain to show all existent villages. Regarding B-52 raids specifically, embassy officer Harben reacted to hostile press reports of large civilian casualties with a simple experiment. He "idly cut" to scale a rectangle of paper representing the area hit by a B-52 "box" of bombs and moved it around a large wall map of the country. He "found that I could not orient it anywhere" in central Cambodia "without covering a named population point." While some of the communities may have been abandoned, he allowed, "it was quite clear that we were killing some civilians."[4]

An unusual role for an American-built aircraft was demonstrated on St. Patrick's Day of 1973. Captain So Potra, a flight school washout, hijacked a T-28D fighter-bomber from the AAK flight line on the southeastern side of Pochentong. He circled over Phnom Penh to single out a fenced-in complex from among the clutter of villas in the southern part of the city—Chamcar Mon (Silkworm Fields) Palace, which the semiparalyzed Lon Nol infrequently left. Nosing down, the plane swooped low over the palace grounds and dropped two 250-pound bombs. The fence on the southeastern side of the president's residence was converted into twisted iron. The second bomb detonated sixty feet away in a new barracks building, setting off secondary explosions.

In all, thirty-four persons, mostly civilians, were killed and thirty were hurt by the explosives. Throttling forward as he rumbled over the U.S. Embassy, the would-be assassin then jettisoned two more bombs as he flew northward toward enemy territory. One bomb caused another thirty-one casualties, including a fatality, when it hit the Chrouy Chang War Peninsula. The last bomb splashed into an uninhabited flooded area. Eight of the injured subsequently succumbed to their wounds. The Khmer information minister said that Potra, who was called an "enemy agent," was the husband of Botum Bopha, one of Sihanouk's daughters. A Cambodian air force source stated that Potra was a bachelor and the father of Botum's expected child. Embassy records gave another pilot, Prince Sisowath Chivan Monirak, as Botum's husband. Nixon responded to the event with a cable renewing "our expression of admiration for the Khmer people's courage and steadfastness under your leadership."

Enraged at the "clear attempt to kill me," the Khmer president assumed dictatorial powers after declaring a "state of danger." His brother, stating that the attempt was a royalist plot, ordered mass arrests, including members of the Norodom family and leaders of an ongoing teachers' strike. Short hours before, hand grenades had been thrown into a mass meeting of teachers and students at the Pedagogical Faculty near the Independence Monument. At least two persons were killed and eight injured as the national police looked on.

The grenade throwers, sent by Lon Non, calmly walked away without being challenged. Lon Nol ordered his air force grounded and its commander, So Satto, sacked. Under his rule by decree, civil liberties were shelved, opposition newspapers were shuttered and the curfew was extended to begin at 9 P.M. Sirik Matak temporarily was placed under house arrest. From there, he said that the Nol regime "must not and cannot" survive, that Sihanouk now was more popular than the marshal and should be allowed to return.

If trying to silence Matak risked heaven-only-knows-what-reaction from both the populace and the Americans, striking at the aging politician's associates apparently was deemed an acceptable risk by the vindictive Lon Non. Tep Khunnah, chief of the Independent Republican Association and one of Matak's close collaborators, was driving past the Korean Embassy on March 25 when a Honda motorcycle pulled alongside. One of the Honda's two riders flipped a grenade into Khunnah's jeep. The startled Khmer reflexively palmed the explosive device and tossed it out. Detonating, the grenade sent a metal splinter into his thigh and also injured two bystanders. Khunnah told an American official that an informant in Lon Non's political organization had warned him of "an impending assassination attempt." Khunnah soon afterward received Lon Nol's permission to move to Paris. The attempt against Khunnah lent credence to reports that Lon Non controlled a "dirty jobs" unit whose assignments included murder. Called the Republican Security Battalion, the unit reportedly was led by a Major Kol Long Sen and used yellow Honda motorcycles.

Disillusionment in high Khmer government circles was becoming more widespread. At a social function, a slightly tipsy presidential assistant, Hoeur Lay Inn, criticized both the Americans and his boss to a U.S. Embassy officer and a reporter. America corrupted the Cambodian society, he said, by flooding it with money, and the army by giving road-bound vehicles instead of creating a well-paid army capable of fighting the enemy in its own element. He also said, "If we had known you were going to back a Lon Nol dictatorship, we would have overthrown Lon Nol on March 18 instead of Sihanouk."

During a brief stopover on the first of the preceding month, February, Vice President Spiro Agnew of the United States (whose Uzi-armed Secret Service watchdogs had embarrassed everyone during a 1970 visit) had suggested that Lon Nol relax control a bit and broaden his political base. The marshal took a few meaningless, halfhearted steps in that direction. Pressure for reform was increased in early April by Alexander Haig, jump-stepped to four stars and now army vice chief of staff, during his twelfth trip to Indochina in three years. Haig made it clear to Lon Nol that continued American support hinged on, in the words of an official report, bringing "certain opposition political leaders into his government" and putting "an end to the activities of his brother, Lon Non." Finally, late in April, a High Political Council consisting of "equal-ruling" Lon Nol, Sirik Matak, In Tam, and Cheng Heng came into being. Nol selected In Tam as prime minister. Unfortunately, Nol, Matak, and Tam, in the words of a Cambodian general, "were never in agreement." And Heng didn't really count since he lacked a power base.

Illustrative of U.S. efforts to guide Cambodia, and admittedly to interfere in its internal affairs, on April 28 Ambassador Swank was able to inform Washington that "I left with [Nol] an informal list of actions which I said I hoped the new High Political Council would consider implementing in economic and military spheres." The embassy had been exhorted by the State Department to exert greater "U.S. influence upon the deteriorating leadership situation in Cambodia."

Lon Nol made a further concession to "our foreign friends who provide so much aid" and to his co-council members. He agreed to drop his brother—whom one American diplomat described as "the chief troublemaker of the country, second only to the rebels"—from the cabinet. That still was not enough for the Americans, who fretted over Non's growing power and the possibility that he might take over from his ailing, less earthy sibling. So it happened that the younger Lon, accompanied by his wife and children, left the country with neither substantive title nor assignment on April 30. It turned out to be a nearly seventeen-month-long exile, spent mostly in the United States. The State Department figuratively held Lon Non's hand and literally did everything possible to "entertain" him and neutralize his pernicious meddling during his American stay. Among the Lon Non couple's less noteworthy activities were the establishment of an import-export company, the purchase of two houses in the Silver Spring suburb of Washington, D.C., and the deposit of hundreds of thousands of dollars in at least two bank accounts. More eyebrow-raising was the wife's stopover in Paris, when a French customs inspector examining one of the children's stuffed animals found $170,000 in $100 bills inside. An angry Non flew to France to straighten out the matter personally.

Unfortunately, good U.S. intentions accomplished little as, encouraged by the manipulation of its leading member, Phnom Penh's new political council displayed the most divisive side of the Khmer character by squabbling and assuring the continued supremacy of Lon Nol. As evidence of the government's inability to accept reality and set its priorities accordingly, Nol continued to insist that "there is no civil war in the Khmer Republic . . . If Hanoi removed its invasion forces tomorrow, we would see that the Khmer problem would satisfactorily resolve itself."[5]

Unseen scales tipped in favor of the CPK-dominated K.R. as the political erosion continued in Phnom Penh. Having brushed aside Hanoi's request to observe the 1973 cease-fire because they were convinced they could win the war alone and lacked the confidence to enter the political arena, the K.R. bitterly accused North Vietnam of once more betraying the communist cause. In any case, Pol Pot's ledger seemed much less in the red despite a number of debits.

One K.R. loss, partly self-inflicted, was the withdrawal of full Vietnamese support. By midyear 1973, only about two to three thousand PAVN-PLAF C40 Division, 203rd Regiment, 367th Sapper Regiment and Mekong artillery unit combat troops and two thousand political cadres remained in Cambodia, although outside official estimates at the time were considerably higher. The eighteen to twenty-seven thousand others posted along the Ho Chi Minh Trail supported only the war in South Vietnam. In the fall, Vietnamese elements were removed from the C40 Division and the 1st Division was broken up. The sapper regiment left the country in late 1973, but K.R. engineers went on receiving Vietnamese training until 1974. The diminution of Hanoi's role was offset by the Chinese, who were only too happy for the opportunity to dilute North Vietnam's influence. While Beijing's military presence was minimal, although present, Chinese and Soviet weaponry and munitions flowed down the Ho Chi Minh Trail from the PRC. The North Vietnamese provided logistical support because, among other reasons, they needed China to pursue their own war against Saigon.

Also in the debit column was peasant reaction to the increasingly severe K.R. policies. These policies cracked traditional rural society and quashed Buddhism, frightening thousands of country dwellers to the cities or to South Vietnam. There were discordant rumblings even among K.R. troops, who generally lacked commitment to communism. Problems there ranged from distaste for fighting fellow Khmers to supply allotment inequities and the harshness of population control measures. The Pol Potists frequently found themselves opposed, sometimes violently, by other K.R. Even a breakaway Khmer Saor (White Khmer) movement was reported. Composed of mostly

the Cham Moslem minority, it favored Sihanouk and resisted collectiviza-
tion. The oppositionists, however, lacked the CPK's cohesive and disciplined
singleness of purpose and ruthlessness. Many ended up rallying to the government side. The K.R. loss of considerable popular support partly was coun-
terbalanced by the burden the migration to the cities placed on government
resources and by facilitating the imposition of CPK doctrines on those who
remained.

Still another K.R. debit was the U.S. air might that denied victory and
multiplied casualties. On the other hand, the added civil disruption caused
by Allied bombs accelerated the collapse of rural social order, brought in many
new recruits, and strengthened the hand of Pol Pot, who insisted that compromise was impossible. Anyway, as Sihanouk told a French questioner, "We
have neither ports nor factories nor big cities [so] the B-52s can only bomb
our rivers and forests." Yet another negative, K.R. military organization badly
needed tightening up and refining. Its inability to synchronize attacks nationwide left troops more vulnerable to aerial attack and gave FANK breathing spells and reactive flexibility. The insurgent logistical and communication
systems left a lot to be desired as well.

On their plus side, the Communists soon controlled about 80 percent of
the land and expanded their socioeconomic programs accordingly, although
unevenly. K.R. control of the countryside included around-the-clock patrol-
ling and the planting of booby traps, including mines, to protect encamp-
ments and to slow the more mobile enemy. As Pol Pot later said, "A people's
war, and especially a guerrilla war, depends on mines and grenades." This
chamcar meen (minefield) philosophy, with mines becoming a primary K.R.
weapon in the years ahead, was the reason Cambodia by 1990 would have the
highest percentage of physically disabled inhabitants in the world. Pol Potist
mastery of the K.R. was assured by an accelerated purging of Hanoi-trained
Khmers, Sihanoukists, and other "undesirables." Then, as the K.R.'s greatest
plus, there now was military strength, possibly over 200,000 including 175
main combat battalions. The U.S. Embassy at the time placed insurgent figures
at only around 50,000. Whatever their precise manpower, the Communists
found themselves able to employ, as a CIA report stated, "multi-unit attacks
in widespread areas with good results." This military capability was augmented
by numerous spies in government civilian and armed force circles. K.R. efforts
to recruit urban inhabitants into clandestine apparatuses for various purposes
largely were unsuccessful, however.

Finally, the K.R. racked up telling propaganda victories. They, of course, made good use of the widespread Allied aerial and ground-based bombardments. Their battlefield successes and terrorist acts made them appear disciplined and effective, while the government seemed inept and incapable of providing the protection traditionally expected by the Cambodian masses. More internationally exploitable was what Sihanouk called his "long march," a PRC–North Vietnam effort to enhance the *samdech*'s image that also reflected well on the K.R. Late in February 1973, the prince left his home in the one-time French Embassy on Beijing's Anti-Imperialism Street for North Vietnam. From there, Sihanouk set out in a convoy of Soviet vehicles, destination Cambodia via the Ho Chi Minh Trail. With him were his wife, Princess Monique; Ieng Sary, Pol Pot's longtime crony, who had accompanied him during his flight from Phnom Penh to eastern Cambodia in 1963; and a large Vietnamese escort. The prince's three weeks in Cambodia were recorded by Chinese lensmen—meeting with Pol Pot (without knowing the latter was "Brother Number One," the use of "brother" being common among Cambodian men close in age); attending a theatrical performance with Khieu Samphan and the ubiquitous Pol Pot; and viewing the ruins of Angkor. The *samdech* was not allowed to mingle with the troops, however. Stopping in Hanoi afterwards, the prince said, "A marriage has been realized, uniting Sihanouk and the Red Khmers—uniting the old monarchy, now partly symbolic, and the revolution."

Sihanouk no sooner returned to Beijing than he turned around to undertake a multination tour to drum up diplomatic support for GRUNK. When asked about negotiating a peace with Phnom Penh, he steadfastly maintained that he would not "deal in any way with the Lon Nol government." He would have preferred direct negotiation with Washington, which, however, was not yet ready to negotiate. Nevertheless, there was continuing contact between various K.R. and Cambodian government emissaries. Whether or not they were sincere, these talks benefited the Communists by injecting doubt, dissension, and false hope into high Phnom Penh circles. Given the CPK's subsequently proved intransigence, it must be concluded that, however willing other K.R. factions were to compromise, any Pol Potist efforts had to be aimed at undermining the Lon Nol regime. According to Sihanouk, it was around this time that the K.R. extremists methodically set out to match Lon Nol's xenophobic 1970 pogrom by persecuting ethnic Vietnamese and Chams under their jurisdiction. These minorities were herded into "settlements," and, over the next three years, thousands were slaughtered or forced over the eastern border.[6]

The high level of PNLAFK combat activity had declined appreciably by late June 1973. Taking advantage of the breather, the Allies pushed a large convoy up the Mekong to Phnom Penh. On June 5, ANK shoved aside the enemy troops who had been straddling Route 5 for two months. The rosy spell swiftly snapped when the K.R. attacked up Highway 4 only fifteen and one half miles west of the capital. ANK's 7th, 13th, 28th, and 43rd Brigades, backed by howitzers and M-113s, sped to excise the new cancer. U.S. Thai-based jets and AAK T-28s from Pochentong flew support missions during breaks in the wet monsoon weather. Route 4 was resecured on June 20. But, after only three road convoys reached Phnom Penh from Battambang, Highway 5 again was snipped. What FANK did not initially realize was that the June dwindling of enemy action signified not only that the Communists needed to replenish their strength but also that they were shifting attention to focus on Phnom Penh. About twenty-five thousand soldiers (over 40 percent of PNLAFK's 175 battalions) soon were positioned simultaneously to hit the capital from the north, west, and south.[7]

U.S. air assets now were organizationally and physically realigned to comply with the Paris agreement barring them from Vietnam. The U.S. Support Activities Group (USSAG, successor to MACV), responsible for controlling all (except SAC) American air and naval forces remaining in Southeast Asia, was established at Nakhon Phanom RTAFB in northeastern Thailand. It was joined there by 7th Air Force headquarters, which, moving from Saigon's Tan Son Nhut AB, retained its mission of conducting all non-SAC air force operations. General John Vogt commanded both USSAG and the 7th Air Force. With the fighting muted in Vietnam and Laos, other Thai bases also turned their attention to Cambodia. The Udorn-based 432nd Tactical Reconnaissance Wing, which had not yet overflown the Khmer Republic, for example, sent its F-4 and RF-4 twin-engined jets on 7,557 sorties over Cambodia between February 24 and August 15. A number of nonjet aircraft were declared excess to USAF and SVNAF needs during the American pullout and given to the Khmers.

Many air missions required modified procedures after the U.S. withdrawal from Vietnam. The guidance of B-52 Stratofortresses to their targets during the hush-hush Menu operation, for instance, had relied on a technique called Combat Skyspot. The latter, required because the relatively flat Cambodian wetland frustrated standard airborne radar, used computer-directed MSQ-77 ground radars in Vietnam. With these removed, the air force turned to two other methods to pinpoint targets. One was the loran (long-range navigation) system, wherein position is located by determining the time displacement between radio signals from two known stations. Specially equipped F-4s or B-52s were used as pathfinders, especially at night. The other system, older and most often utilized by the more electronically advanced F-111s, depended on hand-portable ground beacons upon which B-52 radar-navigators based their bomb release points. Since this second method homed in on a beacon usually set up in friendly territory, the radar-navigator or his assistant, after calculations were fed into an onboard computer, flipped a switch telling the computer to guide the bomber beyond the beacon to the bomb release point. Such a mission was scheduled for August 6, 1973, using a high-frequency beacon set atop a pole in central Neak Luong, the embattled Route 1 garrison-and-ferry town southeast of Phnom Penh.

Neak Luong's military and civilian inhabitants began their early morning chores that fateful Monday unaware of a trio of B-52s approaching far above earshot. One of the navigators neglected to flip the offset bomb switch from "out" to "in." A string of bombs one mile long and twenty tons in weight dropped toward the beacon nearly six miles below. Moments after a hideous shrieking, apparently out of nowhere, a series of explosions marched down Neak Luong's main street. They pulverized the central market, homes, and part of a forty-bed hospital; 137 died, mostly soldiers and their families, and 298 were injured. Two days later, "friendly" bombs killed more Khmers in a Mekong island village three miles away. B-52s stopped using the ground beacon system after this, thereafter relying solely on sensor or photographic information that even precluded the need for maps.

Most civilian casualties, inevitable in any war despite the most stringent rules of engagement and ablest military competence, came not from such accidents but rather from the vagaries of war: enemy tactics, imprecise intelligence, target confusion, overenthusiasm, and callousness, to name a few. In Takeo Province, to cite a case described by a rallier, PNLAFK "put our lines up against the enemy, and most of the bombs fell behind us" on a village. A hamlet northwest of Phnom Penh was struck twice by B-52s, four times by 7th Air Force jets and twice by AAK T-28s. The inhabitants had dug trenches, thereby avoiding fatalities but incurring K.R. suspicion of being "CIA agents" who had called in the planes. There were American losses too. The Pentagon admitted to losing eleven aircraft between January 28 and July 8, 1973.

Fortunately for the Allies, with Arc Light sorties increasing from a March average of sixty a day to eighty a day the following month, before later dipping, the bombs were taking a heavy toll on Communist troops. Proof that the BUFFs (Big Ugly Fat Fellows, a polite version of the more common name using another "F" word), as B-52s were called, played a tactical role rather than their traditional strategic one was shown by the fact that their mammoth payloads often were dropped a scant three thousand feet from ground-hugging ANK G.I.s. Between January 27 and April 30, 1973, eighty-two thousand tons of bombs were loosed during more than twelve thousand sorties by B-52s, F-111 swing-wing jets, A-7 Corsair IIs, F-4 Phantoms, F-105 Thunderchiefs, and AC-130 Spectres. So crowded were the Cambodian skies as the bombing spread westward during the spring of 1973 that, as one source said, "the problems of air traffic congestion were considerable."

All this activity, duly reported by the media gathered to witness the country's expected collapse, caused the U.S. House of Representatives on May 10 to vote 219 to 188 to block supplemental appropriation bill funds from being used for bombing. The senators, voting 63 to 19, went further, barring *any* money, even that already appropriated, from being used for combat activities. The resultant resolution was vetoed by President Nixon in his administration's last legislative victory. Capitol Hill's stubborn antibombing offensive forced a compromise. The legislative and the executive branches agreed on an August 15 deadline to bomb the Communists into a cease-fire, without an increase in bombing intensity in the meantime.

On June 30, the president signed Public Law 93-52 to stop funding to finance, "directly or indirectly, combat activities by U.S. military forces in or over . . . or off the shores of Cambodia, Laos, North Vietnam and South Vietnam" after mid-August. Congress moved further to curtail the chief executive's military options with passage, over Nixon's veto, of Public Law 93-148, the War Powers Resolution, on November 7. Ending a privilege started by President Harry Truman's commitment of the country to the Korean War in 1950, the legislation required the president to consult with Congress before introducing troops overseas and to report such action within forty-eight hours. It also limited, with tight exceptions, military commitment to sixty days. The Foreign Assistance Act, effective in December 1973, stipulated that no money be made available for combat operations by "foreign forces" in Southeast Asia, thereby heading off proxy action by the United States. With America's Southeast Asia policy a shambles, Hanoi knew it could now pursue its conquest of South Vietnam with impunity.

Allied tactical sorties over Cambodia soared to the highest level of the war. There were more than 16,700 between April and June as "compared with nearly 6,200 in the first quarter [of the year] and 9,930 in all of 1972," according to a CIA report. B-52 missions, however, declined from their April peak. What was surprising was that the K.R. intensified efforts to overwhelm Phnom Penh between June and early August. Instead of slowing as they usually did when the rainy season limited assault approaches by swelling waterways and muddying the countryside, and instead of husbanding their strength until the August 15 bombing halt, the Communists launched attack after bloody attack against the capital under a thunderstorm of American bombs, rockets, and bullets.

A number of reasons have been advanced for their lemming-like behavior. Having isolated themselves from the mainstream of politico-military reality in the world beyond Cambodia's frontiers, the CPK leadership feared a final North Vietnamese betrayal, Hanoi joining with Washington to somehow force a cease-fire on them. Peace feelers recently had been extended by both Sihanouk and Lon Nol; they initially seemed willing to negotiate, but not with each other. The U.S., aware of the K.R. infighting and overestimating the power of Sihanouk and GRUNK, was prepared to back any reasonable compromise. On May 8, for example, Secretary of State Rogers told the Senate Appropriation Committee that "with our support the Cambodian government is continuing attempts to initiate direct negotiation with its opponents." The following month, the U.S. Embassy reported that GRUNK might accept a "National Union Government" to end the war, provided it included a "neutral" element and excluded the Lon Nol "clique." It was "probably the last chance for a negotiated peace" since the K.R. radicals were "still not in total control," the embassy told Washington. The CPK later complained that Hanoi "entered into negotiation in 1973 in an attempt to swallow us." The *Livre Noir* (Black Book) published by the Pol Pot government in 1978 insisted that "if the Kampuchean Revolution had accepted a cease-fire, it would have collapsed."

Another reason given for the intensified K.R. attacks was the fanatical zeal of Pol Pot Communism, with its doctrine of Khmer superiority, an ability to win against all odds and outshine even the North Vietnamese. In a letter included in a 1979 Henry Kissinger memorandum to the State Department historian, General Vogt wrote of K.R. "direct orders to their forward commanders to take the city before August 1973 so they could prove to the world that they could humble the U.S." Relevant to CPK reasoning and timing is information that Pol Pot put his "politically unreliable" elements in the forefront of the assault, which was poorly coordinated, while Khieu Samphan's "loyal" units concentrated on the east bank of the Mekong.[8]

There is little question that U.S. air power—operating night and day to break up enemy concentrations, resupply ANK, and otherwise support the government forces—saved Phnom Penh from being overrun by the 1973 PNLAFK offensive. The air effort was complemented by stepped-up deliveries of APCs, artillery, smaller weapons, and munitions. Southwest of the capital, ANK's ill-starred 3rd Division and 43rd Brigade were staggered by enemy blows along Route 3. Unable effectively to retaliate, the division was forced into defensive positions north of the Thnaot River about ten miles below Phnom Penh. White-starred aircraft swarmed like furious insects between the brooding clouds to prevent the enemy from advancing farther. West-northwest of the capital, along the rail line to Battambang, the 7th Division and understrength 72nd Brigade, again helped by American aircraft, held fast. Fighting in a third area, to the north-northwest less than twenty miles from the city, went less well. Although air strikes and supply drops averted a rout, PNLAFK swallowed the area's last prepared government positions and, in mid-July, took Prek Kdam at the Sap River crossing where Highways 5 and 6 came together. ANK managed to block an enemy end run from the ferry crossing toward Pochentong Airport in late July. The opposing armies now were like boxers slugging it out, with neither appearing able to land a knockout blow.

Incredibly, even as the battle for Phnom Penh raged around them, a lion's share of the government's military and civilian leaders refused to discard the corrupt practices that were weakening the very forces they needed for survival. Despite various approaches, the American embassy remained nearly as ignorant of FANK's actual strength as it did of PNLAFK's. Commander-in-Chief General Fernandez, insisting "I have killed all the phantoms," claimed his army numbered 250,000. Even counting units failed to provide an accurate estimate because of their varying sizes. A local joke told of a general arriving to inspect a battalion allotted 450 men and, seeing no one, asking, "Where is the battalion?" "Oh, he's in the shower," replied his escort.

A State Department memorandum placed FANK's "present-for-duty strength" at about 150,000, "of which 80,000 to 100,000 have been formally trained." An August 1973 CIA study reported a 12 percent drop in FANK strength during the first half of the year, a payroll total of 242,000 (including "a large number of 'phantoms' and unverified personnel") and an actual manpower of 212,000, maximum. FANK's suicidal phantom army tolerance increasingly contributed, along with a waning ability to find new recruits, to its military defeats. Army units, adequate on paper, more and more found themselves outnumbered. As if this weren't bad enough, two defense ministry officers were discovered soliciting bribes from fighting units to deliver U.S. equipment.

Despite its rotting foundation, FANK had greatly improved organizationally and militarily. As part of a more effective command and control function, to give an example, it set up an Artillery Support Coordination Center and a Direct Air Support Center. Along with the FANK Operations Center, these were integrated into an overall Combat Operations Center. All armed services by 1973 demonstrated enhanced capabilities and performance. Growth in these areas, however, lost meaning as government-held territory shrank before an enemy that also had improved with time.

Earlier in the year, to bolster military effectiveness, Lon Nol had charged his *Direction Générale de Guerre Politique* (DGGP, FANK's General Directorate for Political Warfare) to work with its civilian ministerial counterpart in indoctrinating personnel in the national war goals, improving teamwork and cohesiveness, guarding against subversion, strengthening unit leadership, promoting "patriotism, honor, loyalty and respect for leaders," and developing morale. While on paper Cambodia now had replaced the old French-inspired 5th Bureau (Psychological Operations) with a professional system akin to Saigon's and Taipeh's, there were three things wrong with it. First, with personalities more important than organizational structure in Phnom Penh, the theoretically subordinate and renamed 5th Bureau (now the 2nd Political Bureau) remained the powerhouse. The chief of the 450-person bureau, Colonel Am Rong, had direct access to the president and did as he pleased while his nominal superior, Colonel Pell Nal, watched his DGGP fade as an organization. Second, relying mostly on radio and television, the bureau's efficacy was very limited beyond the capital. Finally, decreeing effectiveness while letting FANK's greatest weaknesses fester was an exercise in futility.

Inside overcrowded Phnom Penh, which shivered from the pressure waves of bomb blasts and all-too-frequent enemy projectiles, the government instituted compulsory military service, requiring all men from eighteen to twenty-five (with deferable exceptions) to serve eighteen months of active duty. House-to-house sweeps were conducted to enforce the belated measure. Otherwise, little in the city had changed. Despite U.S.-encouraged midyear reforms designed to stabilize the economy, the overall quality of life continued to decline. The cost of living spiraled even higher, supplies and public utilities became even more erratic, and the elite went on enjoying their German cars and French wines. While foreigners and Khmers who could buy their way out continued to leave, the average Phnom Penhois, numbed by war, remained optimistic that ultimately all would return to normal regardless of which side won.

Most of the foreign military experts, including the MEDTC chief, expected the capital to fall once the U.S. bombing ceased. Despite this pessimism, the niceties of normal existence continued to be observed. On July 19, in a ceremony attended by government and diplomatic officials, educators, and students, Ambassador Swank made a presentation to the education minister, Keo Sangkim, who would die tragically less than a year later. It was a wooden plaque with a tiny piece of moon rock in a clear bubble set above a miniature Khmer flag that had been aboard the final Apollo lunar flight. The presentation included a personal letter from President Nixon to President Lon Nol.

Even while concentrating forces against Phnom Penh, the K.R. maintained enough of a menacing presence elsewhere to keep government troops off balance. They raised havoc with the highways and the Mekong LOC. Battambang's airport in the far northwest was subjected to its first rocketing of the war. On August 12, Skoun, the razed Highways 6 and 7 junction keystone of the two Chenla operations, fell to the Communists. The first helicopter to leave the embattled town had been the garrison commander's. An all-military Council of War, newly established "to restore discipline and fight against military corruption," made an example of him, stripping the officer of rank and putting him on trial. Loss of the last of the Chenla battlefield cost ANK three battalions, nineteen territorial companies, and hardware that included eight howitzers and stores of ammunition.

The relative easing of direct PNLAFK attacks on provincial capitals while focusing on Phnom Penh was exploited by the government and its American mentors. Defense perimeters, usually series of small forts in the rice fields around a community, were enhanced. Ammunition and supplies were flown in under only sporadic enemy fire. At Svay Rieng, barely five miles from Vietnam, for example, aircraft flew in six or seven days a week to revictual the 4,000-man garrison and the refugee-swollen civilian population of approximately 130,000. The city, situated on a line of communication vital to both sides, had been encircled since April 1972. Military-painted C-123 Provider transports of China Airlines, subcontracted to the CIA's Air America, landed thousands of pounds of rice from Saigon on a widened stretch of Route 1. Too large to use the makeshift landing strip, U.S. C-130 Hercules relied on parachutes to deliver goods ferried from Thailand.

Svay Rieng's provincial capital also was one of a number of sites to receive CIA personnel as part of an intelligence-related program. A journalist reported that it was an operation to run "black commando" information-gathering and strike teams. The State Department insisted that, as part of the embassy's political-military section function, the program "was started in May because of our urgent need to have better information . . . [on which] to base our estimates of the situation, [to determine] real Cambodian needs in these [military equipment and refugee] areas" and to learn more about the insurgents. Given the paramilitary background of the agency personnel, it appeared that their assignment went beyond simple intelligence-gathering to include tasks denied to the embassy's military staff. Their presence necessarily nudged aside less essential embassy employees to comply with the congressionally set limit of two hundred "civilian officers and employees of executive agencies of the United States Government who are United States citizens" allowed in Cambodia at any one time.

On August 5, the Pentagon directed CINCPAC to keep B-52 sorties "at the current level of 39" and tactical strikes at an average of "200 per day during the remainder of the authorized period," that is, until August 15. Metal and explosives, ranging from machine gun slugs to 750-pound earth gougers, poured down daily on Cambodia. On August 14, 48 SAC and 231 7th Air Force combat sorties overflew the country. The ordnance kept bursting after midnight. Early on August 15, high-flying B-52s of the 43rd Strategic Air Wing at Anderson Air Force Base on the Pacific island of Guam brought the heavy bombing crescendo to an end. By that time, the war zone along the Mekong was so bomb-pitted that, according to an embassy officer, it "looked like the valleys of the moon."

Later that Wednesday morning, Major John Hoskins released the tactical air force's last bomb of the war, sending the five-hundred-pounder streaking into a PNLAFK position northeast of Phnom Penh. Moments later, at 10:44 A.M., Captain Lonnie Ratley III completed a 20mm cannon run on an adjacent wooded area. These officially were the shots ending America's Southeast Asian air war. They also ended the U.S. regulation-laden combat role in the Indochina fighting, although more Americans would come under fire and die before the final 1975 evacuation from Saigon. The two A-7D Corsairs of the 388th Tactical Fighter Wing that had made the final air strikes then turned toward Korat RTAFB, their airfield northeast of Bangkok. The last radio sound over Cambodia from one of the planes—after a "see you in the next war" send-off—came from a harmonica playing "Turkey in the Straw."

In all of 1972, American aircraft dropped approximately 53,000 tons of bombs on the Khmer nation. In just over six months of 1973, a recorded 257,465 tons of U.S.-dropped explosives altered the surface of uncounted acres of Cambodian soil and killed an indeterminate number of people in an effort to save Lon Nol's republic. In all, between March 1969 and the bombing cutoff, 87,113 B-52 and fighter-bomber sorties unloaded 539,129 tons of bombs—about 350 percent of the total tonnage released over Japan during the Second World War. While greater tonnages fell on Vietnam and Laos, Cambodia nevertheless was, in the words of air force historian Earl Tilford, Jr., "one of the most intensely bombed countries in the history of aerial warfare."

Phnom Penh was blessed with a sunny sky that August 15 as two F-111s roared low over the city at 10:45 A.M. to mark the end of nine years of air strikes in Southeast Asia. Behind them buzzed a twin-engined OV-10 Bronco FAC aircraft. It ejected a stream of white and blue smoke, maneuvered into a barrel roll, and followed the jets to the west. The only American planes to continue missions over Cambodia would now be cargo carriers and reconnaissance aircraft, including, infrequently, the batlike SR-71 Blackbird based on the Japanese island of Okinawa. Most of the information-seeking overflights were to be made by RF-4 Phantoms out of Udorn just south of the Thai-Laos border. Much of the collected intelligence was passed to the Cambodians.

Although Pol Pot later denied the major adverse impact of the U.S. bombing campaign, a few days before it ceased, the bulk of his troops—exhausted and low in materiel—already had begun pulling back from moonscaped positions around the capital. And while they probably didn't suffer the sixteen thousand fatalities claimed by 7th Air Force commander General Vogt, they had been mauled badly enough to give Phnom Penh its first respite in many months. The PNLAFK soldiers left behind to maintain pressure on their opponents were adequate to prevent ANK's 3rd Division from pushing a southward counterthrust beyond the Thnaot River. However, the pluckier 1st Division managed to advance southeastward to clear Highway 1 as far as Neak Luong.[9]

No sooner had the immediate threat to Phnom Penh lifted than PNLAFK attacks elsewhere indicated that the K.R. were reverting to a strategy of snipping LOCs and besieging the more manageable provincial urban centers. Their key northern target was Kompong Cham, situated nearly eighty miles up the swollen Mekong from Phnom Penh. Its neatly aligned streets and public gardens attested to a rubber- and tobacco-endowed prosperity under the French. Now, though, a great part of the city's significance lay in the fact that it was the capital of a province crisscrossed by Communist supply lines. A hot spot during the 1970–71 fighting, it had since been subjected only to harassment attacks. Its population had been bloated by nearly fifty thousand peasants (the largest outside Phnom Penh) fleeing K.R.-imposed regimentation.

During the preceding period of bated action, some of Kompong Cham's defense units had been transferred southward to protect the Mekong LOC. Highway 7 to the west was, with the river, the city's sole open surface supply line. Three battalions and twenty-three territorial companies were posted along the highway to keep it open. The two-laned hardtop also was patrolled by a unique ANK motorized infantry unit, the *Battalion d'Infantrie Portée*, equipped with Soviet BTR-152 wheeled APCs. The city defense perimeter was manned by two battalions and fourteen territorial companies, supported by a four-piece 105mm battery, under a general named Mhuol Khleng. An estimated nine K.R. and two PAVN regiments were stationed mainly to the north and east of Kompong Cham.

The Communists had begun exploratory attacks outside the provincial capital in mid-May. In June, they interdicted Highway 6, which, linking with Route 7 at Skoun, was part of Kompong Cham's overland umbilical cord to Phnom Penh. Having thus virtually isolated the city for the first time in ten months, the enemy prepared a major assault. It came on August 16, slashing Route 7 and badly denting the provincial capital's defense positions. Under the appraising eyes of U.S. officers from the defense attaché office of the embassy, reinforcements—the 79th Brigade, two battalions of the 5th Brigade, the 1st and 3rd Battalions of the Parachute Brigade, and four howitzers were rushed to T-shaped Kompong Cham. A new commander, Major General Sar Hor, who had led the 1972 attempt to retake Angkor Wat, flew in. The Khmers managed to hold the line but failed to erase the enemy encroachments.

Communist shellfire from mortars and captured field pieces intensified on September 1 as PNLAFK started a major drive from the southwest and north. It cut Highway 7 between the city and its airport, then pushed to within half a mile of the town itself. Arrival of the rest of ANK's 5th Brigade, soldiers sucking good luck amulets as they alit from their aircraft, still failed to reverse the tide. Two Special Forces detachments helicoptered in south of Kompong Cham to spearhead a FANK maneuver to break the tightening Communist grip on the city. Using shoulder-fired M-72 light antitank weapons, they opened the way for the remainder of the Parachute Brigade, which also had been brought in, and a sixteen-boat MNK marine and SEAL force. The weeklong PNLAFK advance—which had neutralized the airport, occupied half of the smoke-covered city, and gotten to within a mere hundreds of feet from the governor's mansion—finally was halted and turned back.

On September 10, after a daylong trip up the sinuous Mekong from Phnom Penh, fighting the current and haphazard enemy fire, the 80th Brigade made an amphibious landing on the west bank behind the Communist lines below the provincial capital. A few days later, resupplied by river convoy, the bridgehead troops and the city defenders joined up. They then proceeded to sweep the invaders out of Kompong Cham and restore water service. The outnumbered Communists continued resisting around the airport to the northwest of town until the end of September. The K.R. took with them as they retreated a half dozen captured howitzers and more than fifteen thousand people, what an official report called the "single greatest increase in population for the Khmer Rouge in 1973." The government said that 185 military and 17 civilians died in the fighting, with 972 soldiers and 41 noncombatants wounded. Other sources placed the dead at closer to 400 troops and 600 civilians. Enemy casualties are not known, although an official Khmer estimate of 2,000 was given.

To the south, Highways 4 to Kompong Som and 5 to Battambang were, in the August 26 words of government spokesman Am Rong, "provisionally cut," each at points only between fifteen and thirty miles from Phnom Penh. If it was of any consolation to the Lon Nol regime, its Khmer opponents also were warring, although in a slapdash manner, with the Vietnamese Communists. On an NBC-TV show, James Schlesinger, Nixon's third secretary of defense, said that "we've had periodic reports of fighting between the North Vietnamese and the Cambodians." Refugees told of skirmishes, often over food supplies, occurring between July and September in the southern provinces of Kampot and Takeo. It was a sign not only of the widening gap between the two allies of convenience but also of the CPK's still imperfect control over its various components. South Vietnamese officials in neighboring Chau Doc Province, although failing to exploit the infighting, were able to report a drop in both border infiltration and attacks on ARVN installations.

The welcome lull around the capital did little to relieve the government's problems. A flurry of explosions ruffled Phnom Penh on Sunday, August 20— first when five pounds of plastic went off in the central market, then when grenades detonated in two downtown movie houses. Casualties numbered around fifty. It was debated whether terrorists or disgruntled soldiers were to blame. More rural refugees entered the city, pushing the population to nearly two million at a time when the government needed more recruits for the army, not homeless to feed and shelter.

But even if it had been able to find new enlistees, would the phantom-riddled army have been able to use them effectively? A case in point: on September 4, troops fighting to reopen Highway 4 east of Kompong Speu abruptly abandoned the battleground and returned to their camp at the Champou Vorn temple outside the capital. The men—more than one thousand from three battalions and an APC squadron—refused to fight until they were paid and allowed to rest after ten days of uninterrupted combat. Some of them became involved in a repeat looting of the city's central market in mid-September. Another of the army's woes was the wounded, whose numbers in Phnom Penh swelled with the boatloads brought in from Kompong Cham. Improperly staffed and equipped, the 600-bed Khmer-Soviet Friendship Hospital in western Phnom Penh, for one, was jammed with about 2,000 patients. The Preah Ket Mealea Hospital, intended for 500, now held 1,200, including the victims of the Neak Luong friendly fire tragedy.

Although three river convoys, protected by the Khmer air force and navy, arrived with little difficulty during the first three weeks after the bombing halt, their cargo manifests all included luxury items for the wealthy. Essential goods, such as rice, became scarcer for most. The Pentagon noted that during September and October, rice stocks dwindled from a supply for more than forty days to a "current [late October] level of five to ten days." This level was maintained "only by dint of heavy U.S. military airlift and air charter" operations that wound down on November 1, 1973. The Cambodian riel was devalued again in the late summer, from 230 to 250 to the dollar. And although the government concurrently instituted a hazardous duty payment for combat personnel, the question remained as to how much of it would actually reach the fighting men.

By September 1973, MEDTC had to request an additional $1.28 million beyond the allocated amount "for reprogramming to support increased munitions consumption." There was more to this increase than simple reaction to the bombing halt. As MEDTC chief General Cleland wrote in his after-duty tour report in 1974, "The FANK depend on firepower to win. Seldom has FANK outmaneuvered the enemy." That observation, however, overlooked American responsibility for Khmer overreliance on firepower. Another downside was the fact that U.S. hardware continued to be diverted to the enemy and other illicit markets.

There were new developments in the diplomatic arena. Ambassador Swank, described by Kissinger as "anything but a hawk," had become a thorn in Washington's side because of his waning enthusiasm for the war and for the administration's policies. Swank felt that "by 1973, the Khmer Republic was embattled, plagued by inept leadership and accelerating dependence on outside support." On September 4, 1975, he gave a farewell press conference. Calling Cambodia Indochina's most useless war, he said that it "is losing more and more of its point and has less and less meaning for any of the parties concerned." He nonetheless believed U.S. aid should continue so that the government could hold out long enough to get "peace with justice" through negotiation. The Khmers, he pointed out, had bought time "for the success of the [American withdrawal] program in Vietnam." The former ambassador was reassigned to Norfolk, Virginia, as political adviser to the North Atlantic Fleet. In 1975, he was informed that the State Department, of which Kissinger now was secretary, had no future assignment for him. Swank was replaced, in duties but not title, by the ambitious DCM, Enders, who was considered a "can-do team player."

In October 1973, most of the Soviet diplomatic staff departed the capital aboard an Aeroflot jet, leaving only three representatives behind in their embassy. East Germany followed suit. It apparently was a way to straddle the fence between the Lon Nol regime and the Third World nations (which Moscow was trying to woo away from PRC tutelage) clamoring for world recognition of Sihanouk's GRUNK.[10]

The 4th Conference of Non-Aligned Heads of State, meeting in Algiers in September, condemned both the United States and the Lon Nol government. Sihanouk, attending the session, was pleased that additional support gained at the conference brought the number of countries recognizing his government-in-exile to forty-four. Revealing a growing angst arising from his ambivalent position, however, the prince indiscreetly expressed doubt in media interviews over his future role in a Communist-controlled political environment. It echoed perhaps his most famous post-1970 interview, when he told reporter Oriana Fallaci that when they finished using him, "the Khmer Rouge will spit me out like a cherry stone."[11] CPK control of the K.R. was confirmed in November 1973, when more GRUNK Sihanoukists were replaced and the exile government's ministerial offices were transferred from Beijing to K.R. headquarters in Cambodia. The next month, in no small part owing to intensive American lobbying, a scant five-vote margin in the UN General Assembly revalidated the Khmer Republic's seat.

Inside Cambodia, the self-defeating political turmoil never ceased. Like the Brownian Motion of liquid molecules, frenetic activity accompanied the reconvening of the suspended parliament. Reactivate parliament in a consultive role and give its leaders cabinet posts or civic parts to play, Enders (now chargé d'affaires) had recommended. But Lon Nol found it more advantageous to pay lip service to his parliament and to work with his less potent political council. The marshal's popularity dropped to an all-time low. Former supporters again began serious planning to replace him. However, the dissidents would not act without U.S. approval. In mid-1973, Sirik Matak, In Tam, and Cheng Heng told embassy officers that their leader's faults were "incorrigible," that "everything would improve without him." Perhaps, they suggested, their president should go abroad for medical treatment. Forget it, they were warned.

The grumbling was not limited to civilian leaders. In late October, in a "heart-to-heart chat," Enders found it necessary to tell General Fernandez that Washington would not "go along with an army putsch." As a State Department October 24 memorandum to the White House stated, the United States was seeking to prevent "political upsets that could affect the war effort." A month later, the embassy could say that Fernandez and 2nd Division commander General Dien Del had "dampened" their anti-Nol campaigning but that the 7th Division's General Un Kauv continued voicing an "implied intent to unseat Lon Nol." A later would-be coup-maker was stilled by the threat of aid cutoff. Upset at the U.S. for quashing their efforts to help themselves and for not using its muscle to correct problems, the change-seekers either joined opposition parties or, in most cases, allied themselves with Nol for the sake of their futures. The divisiveness of Cambodian politics seeped like a contagious disease into the embassy to form keep-Nol and dump-Nol factionalism that was publicly noted and officially denied. And, of course, Washington was told mainly what it wanted to hear.[12]

Pech Lim Kuon, a lieutenant in the Khmer air force with a playboy reputation, expressed his disapproval of the government at about 4:30 P.M. on November 19, 1973. Lon Nol was about to chair a meeting of advisers in Cambodia's White House in southern Phnom Penh when Kuon's T-28 rumbled out of the sunny sky. In his replay of the St. Patrick's Day incident, the lieutenant decided to double his chances of killing the president by dropping four bombs on the palace instead of two. A pair of the twenty-nine-year-old pilot's 250-pounders holed a small private movie house, shattering it and the glass in surrounding buildings and drilling openings into a nearby barracks. The other bombs sent tree limbs and leaves into the air to tumble to the well-groomed grounds. Although the windows in the northeastern side of the palace were blown in, the occupants escaped unscathed. Less fortunate were the dead—a guard, an office worker, and a woman reportedly hit by a badly aimed rifle round—and the injured.

By the time Kuon completed a victory roll and disappeared beyond the Mekong, the ANK lieutenant in charge of the palace's two Chinese-made 37mm antiaircraft guns had given up trying to get his weapons to fire. "We tried to put the shells in," he later explained, "but they wouldn't fit in." In the days ahead, new antiaircraft installations would damage airplanes that accidentally ventured too close to Chamcar Mon Palace.

Government reaction was mild compared to that following the earlier assassination attempt. FANK Commander-in-Chief Fernandez nevertheless reorganized the air force to prevent a recurrence, an action that reduced AAK operations to 66 percent effectiveness. During a three-minute radio speech, Lon Nol vowed his determination "to stay with all of you in order to fulfill the nation's work until the final and permanent victory." In the meantime, Kuon crash-landed his plane in Kratie Province and joined the K.R. After seventeen months of reeducation and manual labor, the would-be assassin was returned by the victorious Communists to Phnom Penh, where he helped four Chinese instructors train student pilots to fly the eleven helicopters abandoned by AAK at Pochentong. He also ferried CPK leaders around the country. Disillusioned, Kuon stole a helicopter in the spring of 1976 and, pursued by four other unarmed UH-1 Hueys, defected to Thailand. The information he gave his interrogators provided the West with one of its earliest detailed insights into the leadership and nature of the new Khmer regime.

On December 9, Prime Minister In Tam submitted his resignation. An attempt to step down in October had been rejected by Lon Nol primarily because of the imminent UN seating crisis. The next day, as big guns boomed to the west along Highway 4, the rest of the government also quit, but agreed to keep things going until a new one was formed. Two weeks later, Foreign Minister Long Boret, just returned from New York after months of pleading his nation's case before the United Nations, took In Tam's place. Through it all, corruption flourished unabated. Still new provinces were carved out of old ones so that U.S. funds could find their way into the hands of political favorites appointed as their governors. The latter then could further profit by selling goods to the K.R. and to the black market. One could only guess how many of the hundreds being killed by the K.R. bombardment of the cities were victims of shells sold to the Communists by venal government officials. Earlier in the year, for example, several truckloads of 105mm artillery projectiles mysteriously disappeared. The incredible official response to a critical newspaper article was that "this traffic, like corruption in general, has been bequeathed to us by the former [Sihanouk] regime."[13]

The Communists, realizing the importance of Mekong convoys to Phnom Penh's survival, struck hard at shipping by attacks on the river trains and by sabotage.
Courtesy William Harben Collection

The last three months of 1973 military action resembled a rusty seesaw— lots of noise and motion, but getting nowhere fast. In October, the focus was on the Thnaot River below Phnom Penh, with ANK's 1st Division reinforcing the 3rd. AAK conducted its first mass air offensive, code-named Thunderstrike, with an impressive fifty-two T-28 strikes on the first day alone. For about a week in late October, Khmer aircraft struck at PNLAFK lines and supply areas around Highways 2 and 3. A planned follow-up operation wallowed in the wake of Lieutenant Kuon's attempt to assassinate Lon Nol.

In late November, the arena for the touted 1971 Victory East of the Mekong campaign (the marshy Vihear Suor area across the river from the capital) was occupied by the Communists after brutal fighting. At the same time, the K.R. stepped up bombardments of Kompong Cham, Siem Reap, Prey Veng, Svay Rieng, and Kompong Chhnang. If that was not enough, frogmen plasticked two transports in Phnom Penh's harbor. The final month of the year was highlighted by mutual grabbing for Highway 4, first between Kompong Speu and

Phnom Penh, then along the rice paddies southwest of Kompong Speu. U.S.-supplied artillery, including four recently-delivered 155mm pieces, and M-113s finally enabled the battered ocean-to-capital road to be reopened on January 6, 1974.

That the Khmer Republic managed to survive the last four and a half months of 1973 after the U.S. bombing halt surprised most. The cost, however, had been heavy. Whatever their accuracy, American embassy figures showed 10,200 government troops slain in 1973, compared with 3,000 in 1972. Ironically, the key to the republic's continued existence lay as much in Washington as in Phnom Penh. With the Nixon administration as fatally embattled as Lon Nol's and the United States anxious to wash its hands of Southeast Asia, even the military and economic assistance Cambodia needed was imperiled. "After the summer of 1973," acknowledged Henry Kissinger, "I knew that Cambodia was doomed." Any optimism over the outlook for the new year was clouded on December 23 when 122mm rockets shrieked into Phnom Penh. These shortly were joined by other projectiles, including swooshing shells from American-manufactured 105mm howitzers. Most, if not all, of these had been captured from the Cambodian army.[14]

CHAPTER NINE

1974: Siege

WITH THE VIETNAMESE ENGAGED almost exclusively in their own war, the fighting in Cambodia had evolved into a civil conflict between Khmers. It was not the first civil war to suffer the interference of other countries that deemed it in their interests to support actively one side or the other. But, unlike most such clashes, the Cambodian tinder had been ignited by outsiders. First and foremost, Hanoi, which created the CPK Frankenstein's monster, trampled Khmer neutrality and fought the nation's government. Second, the PRC and, to a lesser degree, the USSR, which nurtured the Indochinese Communists, supplied them and abetted Hanoi's occupation of eastern Cambodia. And finally, Washington and Saigon, which responded logically but disastrously to the Communist threat to their conduct of the war in Vietnam.

The rockets and shells that began to fall even before the new year marked the onset of yet another K.R. attempt to subdue Cambodia's capital. Between December 23, 1973, and January 3, 1974, twenty-nine of PNLAFK's 102-pound 122mm rockets slammed into Phnom Penh on seven days to kill twenty-two and injure sixty-one. Among the foreigners, the French seemed to have the worst luck. On different occasions, missiles flashing from tripod launchers to the northwest dug up an embassy employee's lawn and then injured the French naval attaché's wife. The Communists also resorted to individualized terrorism. On January 6, an apparently overanxious killer team tried to murder FANK's commander-in-chief. Two B-40 shoulder-launched rockets streaked over General Fernandez's house to detonate in a tree. A follow-up pair of M-79 grenades thumped from their launchers, one hurting a guard when it exploded on the front lawn. Their target untouched, the terrorists fled in a three-wheeled cab that pulled up to meet them.

A seventy-five-battalion assault by Khieu Samphan's PNLAFK began that same day. An estimated two K.R. regiments rushed ANK defenses on the flat, occasionally treed, and village-dotted northwest perimeter of Phnom Penh just above the east-west railroad line. The 28th Infantry Brigade, with two squadrons of M-113 armored vehicles spearheading its counterattack, slowed the enemy advance. Two days later, ANK's 1st Division, including weary units freed from the temporarily successful Highway 4 clearing operation, was thrown into the fight. During the first five days of combat, according to FANK, losses were more than three hundred K.R. dead, with eleven captured, compared with only two government fatalities and fifty-six wounded. An AAK AC-47 Spooky gunship night-spraying the battlefield ahead of the city defenses was shot down in midmonth, killing its five crewmen.

On January 22, the army moved to cut off and annihilate a Communist pocket threatening Pochentong Airport. While the 28th brigade pushed north, the 1st Division moved westward. A 7th Division brigade to the north was ordered to chop southward. Buttressed by napalm-dropping T-28s and artillery cover, the 1st Division punched the enemy from their entrenched positions at the cost of an admitted 31 dead and 175 wounded; PNLAFK losses were given as 200 killed, 26 prisoners, and 70 weapons. Among the prisoners were six black-pajamaed women, aged fourteen to twenty-two, of the all-female 122nd Rifle Battalion armed with American M-16 rifles. ANK's 28th Brigade to the south reported 35 dead and 268 injured to the foe's approximately 300 slain and 121 weapons seized. The 7th Division element failed to make contact. The bulk of the enemy force retreated to the west, which FANK planners had for reasons of their own left open.

In the meantime, the K.R. on January 19 infiltrated a defense line held by the 3rd Division just south of the narrow, winding Thnaot River below the capital. One ANK battalion's panicked reaction triggered a domino effect that quickly involved adjacent units. Within twenty-four hours, under minimal enemy pressure, the division had to a great degree unilaterally repositioned itself on the Phnom Penh side of the river. The division's main problems were obvious: poor leadership and inadequate training. In addition to their other vices, some unit commanders sought the comfort of their Phnom Penh villas at night, leaving their men with make-do sleeping arrangements at the front. Therefore, a number of battalion commanders were not with their malaria and deserter-thinned troops when the 3rd Division dominos began tumbling.

The enemy advanced toward the 15th Brigade command post and an adjacent artillery battery just northeast of the junction of Routes 3 and 201. Army headquarters ordered the 20th Brigade from Highway 4, positioned nearby to the northwest, and two 1st Division battalions just beyond to rush to the

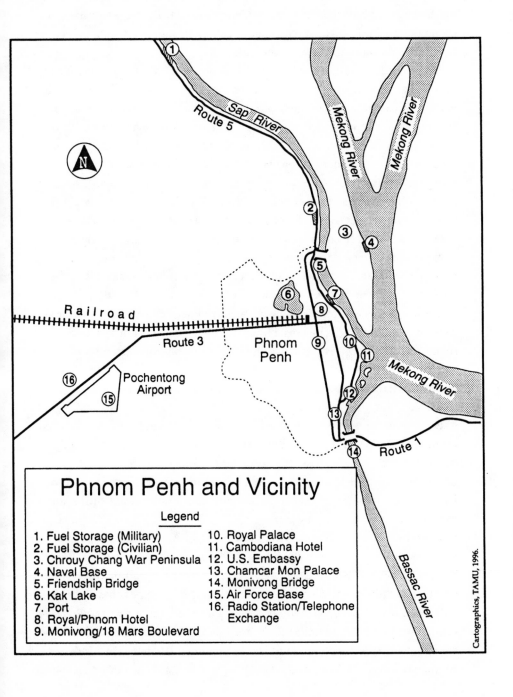

Phnom Penh and Vicinity

Legend

1. Fuel Storage (Military)
2. Fuel Storage (Civilian)
3. Chrouy Chang War Peninsula
4. Naval Base
5. Friendship Bridge
6. Kak Lake
7. Port
8. Royal/Phnom Hotel
9. Monivong/18 Mars Boulevard
10. Royal Palace
11. Cambodiana Hotel
12. U.S. Embassy
13. Chamcar Mon Palace
14. Monivong Bridge
15. Air Force Base
16. Radio Station/Telephone Exchange

Cartographics, TAMU, 1996.

threatened area. Fighting raged there for the rest of the month, with ANK shifting units to block enemy jabs along the bamboo-studded Thnaot River southwest of Phnom Penh between Routes 2 and 3. By early February, the Cambodian army had straightened out its command and control kinks enough to stabilize the situation around the capital.

While combat was flaring to the northwest and south, Phnom Penh continued to be the bull's-eye for numerous rockets and some shells. The projectiles pelted the city almost daily at around 7 A.M., noon, and 10 P.M. On January 15, one of the unguided missiles plummeted into an alley between two apartment buildings; seven died, ten were hurt. Another the next day shattered General Fernandez's anteroom at FANK headquarters. On January 18, fortunately before the arrival of students, thousands of metal shards sprayed the schoolyard of the Lycée Descartes as a rocket hit. Lon Nol's encouraging follow-up radiocasts were belied by the temporary closure of all city schools, the ceaseless fall of hostile explosives, and the loss, once more, of Highway 4.

If the rockets were terrifying, the 105mm rounds from captured howitzers seemed even more destructive. Three straight nights of PNLAFK artillery shelling began at about 8:30 P.M. as Sino-Cambodians were celebrating the Chinese lunar new year on January 24. Although some of the shells arcing the six miles or less from just below the Thnaot River exploded near the presidential palace and the airport, most struck the overcrowded southwestern Tum Pung section of the city, smashing wooden shacks and igniting their splinters. During those three days alone, nearly one hundred died and some three hundred were wounded. More than one person believed that the Communists had somehow come into possession of a fresh supply of the American-manufactured ordnance. Marine guards drew automatic weapons and went on full alert at the sandbagged U.S. Embassy in expectation of an all-out assault on the capital. Since December, the K.R. had been augmenting their indiscriminate killing with fact-twisting radio broadcasts and cannon-delivered propaganda leaflets.

Explosives kept falling from the sky as long as ANK remained unable to shove the enemy back from the edges of Phnom Penh. Frightened refugees, their ramshackle shelters inadequate, ignored the curfew and military checkpoints to surge into the city center. They occupied every possible habitation niche, including the pagodas and houses abandoned by those who could leave Cambodia. Finally, by January 28, the army and air force counterstrokes made enough progress to put an end to the horrendous barrages. It was not soon enough, however, for many of the foreigners who initially had decided to brave the siege. Most notable were the French, Cambodia's colonizers who still considered the country an integral part of their Francophone inheritance and resented the American intrusion. The unnerving bombardment at last pushed them to the limits of their endurance, especially when Paris ordered the evacuation of teachers and dependents. Fistfights broke out at the French embassy for possession of the limited daily number of airline tickets. By the end of January, about half of the city's more than 2,500 French inhabitants had flown to neighboring countries or France. Rockets fell anew on Phnom Penh on January 31, followed the next day by a forty-five-minute barrage of more than one hundred artillery shells.

Former prime minister Son Sann, a neutralist who had made recent trips to Paris in an unrequited search for a peace agreement between the K.R. and the government, stunned everyone in mid-January. He became the first political luminary formally to ask Lon Nol to step down so that the war could end. In a January 9 letter, which he made public three days after the president failed to reply, Sann suggested that Nol turn over control to Cheng Heng and fly to the United States for "medical treatment." One result of the letter was encouragement of increased teacher-student nonviolent agitation. Another was the information ministry riposte, "Our president has no intention of renouncing his duties while the nation is facing danger from the North Vietnamese and the Viet Cong." There was no mention of the Khmers Rouges. Sihanouk made clear what he thought of any peace overtures from Phnom Penh when he told a French journalist, "You can be absolutely certain that we will not accept any contact, other than acceptance by the United States—because it is President Nixon who is making war against us—of a total [K.R.] takeover of . . . Cambodia." On January 30, a government state of emergency proclamation further tightened the vise on civil liberties, that is, mail censorship, warrantless daytime searches, and a numerical limitation on gatherings.[1]

While FANK fought to reclaim the land around Phnom Penh lost the previous month, the Communists reinserted themselves enough in some sectors once more to peck away at the city with intermittent barrages. The incoming ordnance beginning early on February 3 struck hundreds and ravaged working-class dwellings. "International opinion seems not to react to the suffering of the Khmer people," lamented Prime Minister Boret to a *New York Times* reporter. "When American airmen were bombing Hanoi . . . the whole world condemned the action. But when the other side kills our innocent women and children, there is no reaction." The West at the time was more concerned with an international energy crisis that was curtailing its driving habits.

FANK soldiers in front of a "floating village" in central Cambodia. Photo by author

The K.R.'s late February 16 bombardment of the capital was timed to co-
incide with a U.S.-Khmer ceremony during which Chargé Enders was addressing homeless Cambodians next to an enemy-razed site. He told the
displaced survivors about an American gift of over four thousand dollars, including embassy staff donations, as shells thudded in the background. Projectiles aimed at the embassy impacted behind the back fence, hitting the
Nuon Monirom pagoda grounds and wounding two monks. Additional AAK
flights, using flares for night sorties but generally too high to be effective, failed
to stifle the bombardment. During one mission, a T-28 turning out of its
bombing run collided with its spotter plane; neither pilot survived. Contrib-
uting to the air force's weakness were the age of the aircraft and a dearth of
qualified aviators and mechanics.

Despite a commitment of troops and explosives greater than that devoted
to the mid-1973 assault, the K.R. again failed to take Phnom Penh. They now
switched attention to the capital's supply lines, while continuing to keep pressure on both the city and various provincial capitals. Ominously, whereas Com-

munist initiative generally diminished during past wet monsoon seasons, in 1974 it remained at a relatively high level. Efforts to cut the Mekong line of communication intensified now that Highways 4 and 5 were more often than not severed. The eleven February river convoys were attacked by shoreline fire nine times and by mines twice. In the most dramatic action—involving a ten-vessel, Phnom Penh–bound convoy on February 18—the tug *Bannock* and its ammunition barge were hit by recoilless rifle and machine gun rounds. The resultant explosions badly damaged the barge and destroyed $1.4 million of much-needed munitions. The tug *Saigon 240* and its munitions barge received B-40 rockets that ignited more than fifty tons of cargo. MNK, which in January had incurred 19 fatalities and 107 injuries to a reported 52 enemy dead, was presented with a dozen PBRs, the U.S. Navy's primary river patrol craft, to enhance its escort capabilities.

By March 1974, FANK had shown what it could do. Although still performing far below their potential, the republic's armed forces had improved enough to halt a major Communist offensive without outside combat support. The Cambodian army regained its lost ground around the capital, thereby stopping the bombardment, at least for a while. Other all-too-rare feathers in the government's cap were the mass rescue of rural inhabitants from Communist control and the largest rallying of K.R. troops to date. Provincial commanders, taking advantage of PNLAFK concentration on Phnom Penh, had made forays into the countryside to return an estimated thirty-five thousand people to their lines. The downsides were that the accomplishment failed to expand physical area of control and only added to the regime's refugee burden.

On March 8, after over six months of negotiation, 742 former Sihanoukist Khmer Rumdo soldiers pledged allegiance to the Khmer Republic in a Highway 4 ceremony west of Phnom Penh. Their leaders said that there were eight to nine thousand other K.R. troops prepared to join them if they could fight the Communists as an independent nationalist unit. Initial government acceptance was reversed by U.S.-encouraged second thoughts: the ralliers might be a Trojan horse. The defectors would be welcome, it was decided, only if they were willing to be integrated into ANK. That was the last heard of those prospective ralliers.

In Tam, who was in contact with Khmer Rumdo representatives, was an outspoken proponent of the rallier program. He once told an embassy officer that "I could buy off the whole enemy army" with money corrupt FANK officers skimmed off with the phantom army scam. The viability of the program never was put to a real test because both Cambodian and American high-level officials viewed the defection of thousands of K.R. with jaundiced eyes. The Khmer leadership, besides fearing a ruse, saw a sudden infusion of anti–Lon Nol troops into ANK as a threat to its power. In any case, the March ralliers represented a record onetime number, indicative perhaps of increased polarization within the K.R. FANK figures, their reliability diluted by the inclusion of some nondefectors (such as refugees), listed 4,375 ralliers between March 1970 and December 1971; 1,854 in 1972; and 1,024 during the first half of 1973.[2]

In a January 28, 1974, letter to Lon Nol, the politically reeling Nixon said that the U.S. "remains fully determined to provide maximum possible assistance to your heroic self-defense and will continue to stand side by side with the republic in the future as in the past." American aid in 1974 was to include $180 million in alimentary products, including over 200,000 tons of rice, and $2.7 million in riels (at a rate of 377 riels to one dollar) for a semiprivate refugee aid organization established to circumvent government corruption.

Most of the U.S. assistance, however, was war-oriented. The accelerated Military Aid Program—about $414 million and $254 million in fiscal years 1974 and 1975, respectively—achieved an 80 percent completion of the planned Cambodian army force structure. Indicative of ANK's overreliance on firepower, the largest single-item expenditure, ammunition, increased from 37 percent of MAP funding in fiscal year 1972 to 65 percent in 1973 and 87 percent in 1974. MAP's main deficiency was undelivered logistical units to maintain matériel already brought into the country. MAP-supported army formations totaled 166 battalions by mid-1973 and 186 a year later. Although ANK was capable of conducting multibrigade operations, these could be sustained only with difficulty because of understrength elements and the lack of an adequate replacement program.

An inventory of ANK matériel showed APCs (53 in 1973 and 202 in 1974); trucks (2,233 and 4,316); 75mm, 105mm, and 155mm howitzers (181 and 289); 60mm and 81mm mortars (1,366 and 2,726); 106mm recoilless rifles (33 and 304); M-79 grenade launchers (7,735 and 20,481); 30- and 60-caliber machine guns (4,549 and 7,079); 30-caliber carbines (83,515 each year); M-16 rifles to replace older M-1s and Soviet assault rifles (69,224 and 158,115); and communication equipment. All of ANK's weaponry now was furnished by the United States. In addition, the army had a dozen old French AMX-13 and seven U.S. M-24 light tanks, as well as fifteen Russian BTR-152 APCs. By late 1974, ANK consisted of five divisions, each with three brigades; eight autonomous brigades; a parachute brigade; and an armored brigade. Its assigned strength was 218,000.

MNK's inventory comprised 123 craft in 1973 and 171 in 1974. They ranged from patrol boats and troop carriers to a flame-throwing monitor and a dry dock. Commodore Von Sarendy, the Khmer chief of naval operations, now commanded about fifteen thousand volunteers, including nine battalions of marines. AAK's listing went from 154 aircraft to 211 during the same period. The largest numbers of aircraft types were B and D-model T-28s (48 in 1973 and 64 in 1974), O-1 A and D-model Bird Dog spotter planes (31 and 37), and UH-1H Huey helicopters. Most were based at Pochentong. Pilots numbered 298 (a 220 percent increase over 1972) of a total manpower of 9,750. In November 1973, under Brigadier General Ea Chhong, and the following month, under Brigadier General Penn Rannda, AAK was organized into a wing composed of five squadrons (fighter-bomber, FAC, helicopter, transport, and training). Project Flycatcher, as the supply of air matériel to AAK (which had responsibility for all military aircraft) was called, ended on June 30, 1974. In another area, at the beginning of the year, the United States terminated two support operations that weren't paying their way. The Freedom Care and Big Show programs had been disseminating propaganda leaflets over Cambodia.

Sattahip, once a simple fishing community on the gulf-hugged southeastern hip of Thailand, became a primary transshipment point for military and civilian goods destined for the Khmer Republic after the 1973 Paris agreement. Munitions and rice were transferred from freighters to civilian contract barges at the U.S.-built port facilities, located just west of Southeast Asia's largest jetfield, the U Tapao Royal Thai Navy Base that had housed B-52s during the earlier bombing campaign and now hosted airlift aircraft. Selected as the logistics center for the American presence in Thailand in 1962, Sattahip quickly acquired a breakwater, piers for ocean-going vessels, storage facilities, and accommodations for U.S. troops, Thai guards, and Khmer civilian employees. The constant closing of Cambodia's land routes required most Phnom Penh–bound cargoes to be tug-propelled southeastward across the Gulf of Thailand, past Cambodia and northeastward around Vietnam's Ca Mau Peninsula to the Mekong Delta—a more than weeklong, several-hundred-mile voyage. Then the goods ran the Mekong River gauntlet of fire to Phnom Penh. Between forty and fifty thousand tons of U.S. Agency for International Development loads followed that itinerary in March and April 1974. Battambang and Kompong Som remained as the destinations for additional cargoes, the first by land and the second by sea.

American military personnel attached to the embassy defense attaché section and MEDTC (which reorganized along service lines) continued to assist the Cambodians. MEDTC "end item utilization inspections" entailed U.S. officers frequently visiting specific FANK units they had been assigned to monitor. Likewise, defense attaché office personnel commuted between the embassy and Khmer military elements for fact-finding purposes. Since the Cambodians often were involved in combat, the Americans stretched congressional restrictions out of shape. As Kenneth Bowra, a captain attached to MEDTC in 1974–75, pointed out, the U.S. presence "inevitably involved assisting these [Khmer] units with 'suggestions,' although not officially advising." More than one American suffered minor wounds while in the fighting zones.

CIA employees, as well, were caught up in actual combat situations. By the end of 1974, the Phnom Penh station, numbering dozens under its third chief since 1970, was one of the intelligence agency's largest. Then there were the civilian aircrews. Air America, for instance, airlifted Americans (often armed), FANK personnel, and supplies into under-fire sites and, on leaving, evacuated wounded soldiers and civilians. On March 13, 1974, California Democratic senator Alan Cranston said that three laws were violated by U.S. military officers providing advice to FANK. Two days later, Senator Frank Church, an Idaho Democrat, got on the bandwagon. He presented his objections on the subject to Henry Kissinger, who had moved from the White House to the State Department in September 1973. Both to sidestep these legislative protests and to augment their limited number, embassy action offices also relied on a number of third-country nationals (eighty-five were allowed) and technical assistance contracts.

USSAG, the overall American military command for Southeast Asia, oversaw air force supply and reconnaissance missions from its Nakhon Phanom headquarters 375 miles northeast of Bangkok across the Mekong from Laos and only some 20 miles from the Ho Chi Minh Trail complex. Nakhon Phanom was the smallest, most remote of the seven airfields used by the U.S. Air Force in Thailand. The 619 people assigned to USSAG during the spring of 1974 included two air force generals, an army major general, and an admiral, all under General Timothy O'Keefe, who had succeeded General Vogt. An October 1973 change of government in Thailand had made the U.S. presence there a sensitive issue. Reasserted nationalism and resentment of American influence almost overnight reshaped U.S.-Thai relations and imposed a lower profile on U.S. military activities there. In the diplomatic arena, the U.S. Senate on March 13, 1974, confirmed forty-eight-year-old John Gunther Dean as ambassador to the Khmer Republic. The new chief of mission flew into Pochentong eighteen days later.

Phnom Penh began a new conscription drive in early March to fill the gaps left in ANK by casualties, desertions, and phantom soldiers. Draft notices, calling on men between twenty-five and thirty-five because the eighteen-to-twenty-five age bracket was depleted, were based on a February census update. At the end of the month, Lon Nol dissolved the four-man High Political Council created under American pressure the preceding spring. Twenty-four hours later, the Khmer president established a four-man Executive Council for Cambodia. One difference between the old and the new bodies was the replacement of Cheng Heng by General Fernandez. The other members remained Nol, Matak, and Boret. A second difference was the removal of the legislative powers of the earlier council because of the reinstitution of a two-chamber parliament. At the same time, Sirik Matak was named high assistant to the president. On the other side of the battle line, PNLAFK commander Khieu Samphan (who also was GRUNK's deputy prime minister) apparently felt things were going well enough on the battlefield to allow him to lead a K.R. delegation to North Vietnam. It was the first leg in a more than two-month-long goodwill tour of "friendly" nations in Asia, Africa, the Mideast, and Europe. Efforts to displace the Lon Nol government clearly were continuing on more than one front.[3]

Also in March, PNLAFK struck at two widely separated targets—Kampot, a provincial capital just up and astride the Kossla River from the Gulf of Thailand between Kompong Som and Vietnam; and, about ninety-two air miles to the northeast, Oudong, Cambodia's royal capital until the arrival of the French. Attacks on the two cities, one on Route 3 southwest of the national capital, the other on Highway 5 to the northwest near the Sap River, began only a few days apart.

ANK outposts on the northern defense perimeter of the pepper-growing center of Kampot received the opening rounds of the K.R. assault on February 26. The outermost defenders, territorial companies reinforced by components of the 12th Brigade and the 68th Battalion, fell back a few days later, leaving the city water supply and the country's only cement plant in enemy hands. Several hundred government troops deserted during the pullback. Half of Kampot's fifty thousand civilians also fled into the countryside as rockets and shells peppered the city. Only artillery, air force, and naval efforts enabled the infantrymen to hold the wobbly line. After a failed counterattack, ANK adopted a completely defensive mode. Its opponents settled in for a siege by setting up positions in farm settlements to the east and north, and at the base of the Elephant Mountains just to the west.

Whatever factors the Communist planners considered in targeting Kampot, they should have given greater weight to the provincial capital's location adjacent to a body of water they didn't control. The Khmer navy was able to ferry men, weapons, supplies, and precious water from Kompong Som and Ream to the west throughout much of the siege. MNK supply runs up the two arms of the Kossla River were supplemented by AAK and Thai-based U.S. C-130 flights. Between March 2 and 10, two army battalions, marine units, and a half dozen howitzers were brought in to bolster the two-thousand-man garrison against the several thousand attacking K.R. Major General Mhoul Khleng flew in to take command of the city's defense. A March 10 arrival was an American officer temporarily detached from his observer assignment with the ANK 3rd Brigade to the north. Kampot's Sunday open air market remained in operation on the city's left river bank, but most stores were closed as mortar shells continued to fall. The enemy siege lines inched closer. Casualties mounted. In March, according to FANK, 158 government troops died and 828 were wounded. PNLAFK was said to have lost 282 dead and 3 captured.

April did not begin well for Kampot's defenders. They lost the hills dominating the 2,300-foot-long airstrip northwest of town. By the tenth, K.R. soldiers were within a mile of the semi-industrial right bank of Kampot. Their shells, fired at closer range now, thumped into ANK's poorly deployed artillery battery, knocking out eight howitzers and converting thousands of rounds of ammunition into a globe of fire, smoke, and shrapnel. When a marine detachment ceded the southeastern defense sector to the enemy, the latter pushed farther to cut the city's access to the sea. Kampot now was entirely surrounded. To everyone's surprise, the Communists stopped short of administering a knockout blow. The reason was that, lacking their foe's capability of quickly bringing in reinforcements and supplies, they succumbed to the more than five weeks of endless fighting.

By the middle of the second week in April, following the arrival of fresh battalions by air, there were 4,006 government troops in the city. By the twenty-fifth, they numbered 4,561. The 20th and 28th Brigades began to push back the enemy tide that had been eroding their defenses. They reestablished a northern perimeter, punched westward a mile and a half, and fought under ebbing mortar fire to the east and south. On April 30, they reopened the river to the gulf. Official figures for the March 3 to May 3 fighting stood at 416 fatalities (including 25 civilians); 2,363 injuries (88 civilians); and 79 missing (excluding desertions) on the government side. The estimate of more than 2,000 K.R. dead was probably high.

If the outcome at Kampot was gratifying for FANK, the same could not be said for the struggle over PNLAFK's second target. After initial jabs to feel out the defenses of historic Oudong, Communist troops from the K.R. Northern and Southwestern Zones, led respectively by Ke Pauk and Ta (Grandfather) Mok, started their main assault at 3 A.M. on March 3. Within five hours, they had muscled back the outlying territorial battalions from positions northwest and southwest of the city to a hastily improvised perimeter in the small Tep Preanam Temple compound a mile and a quarter to the southeast. Other fleeing G.I.s soon sought refuge in the perimeter, which the attackers isolated while they dealt with the main garrison. Fifteen days after the assault began, Oudong—a laid-back community of public buildings and pagodas that so far had escaped the war's destruction—fell, the first major town to do so in three years. As irony would have it, it was the fourth anniversary of Sihanouk's removal. Only the soldiers in the temple compound still held out.

Oudong's inhabitants almost immediately were subjected to the Draconian PCK philosophy that was to make headlines after they entered Phnom Penh the following year. More than 20,000 civilians were herded into the countryside to be killed or forced to live and work in communes. The K.R. then leveled the deserted town in an apparent attempt to destroy the historical and religious symbol of a civilization they hated. About 1,500 civilians eluded the K.R. roundup and joined the ANK soldiers, estimated at between 700 and 1,750, holding out in their surrounded position southeast of the city.

The ANK 7th Division's 45th Brigade already was being helicoptered the twenty-odd miles from the capital to the U.S.-sponsored supply depot and training center just outside of Peam Lovek a few miles north of Oudong. Loaded into vehicles, these relief troops headed down Route 5 toward Oudong. They were halted short of their objective by enemy fire and a blown bridge. Meanwhile, a second relief effort was launched from the southeast. Elements of the 80th Brigade left Phnom Penh on March 19 in MNK's first major amphibious operation since the Kompong Cham campaign the preceding September. Progress of the soldier-carrying vessels up the Sap River, flowing normally toward the Mekong during this dry season period, was reported to PNLAFK commanders, who correctly surmised that the government troops intended to disembark on the building-lined right bank in an attempt to relieve their embattled comrades.

When the MNK troop carriers turned into the river bank to unload, all hell broke loose. Projectiles from 75mm recoilless rifles and B-40 launchers streaked into the exposed G.I.s, blasting apart metal, cloth, flesh, and morale. With at least thirty-eight dead (including thirteen drowned), eighty-six wounded, a helicopter shot down, and two boats alist, the survivors, firing wildly, pulled back. They continued upriver finally to go ashore at Kompong Luong, only three miles from Oudong. There were further delays as the rest of the 80th Brigade was brought in on March 19–20. They immediately came under fire and dug in. The brigade was reinforced over the next nine days with several battalions from the 28th and 39th Brigades, thirty M-113s, and four howitzers. Only then did the 80th leave its Highway 5 assembly area and move westward under T-28 cover. A full three battalions were left behind for rear area security. When the forward elements became overcommitted and the overcautious brigade commander found himself without reserves, the snail-like advance slowed to a complete stall on March 24. As thousands of orange-robed monks in Phnom Penh demonstrated against the destruction of Oudong's monasteries and monuments, additional reinforcements left the capital. But everything still was "in progress" at the end of the month.

"Dantesque" best describes the situation in the beleaguered perimeter oc-cupied by the Oudong survivors. Pounded night and day, casualties mount-ing, the huddled defenders watched their stocks of ammunition, food, water, and medicine lower. They were torn between the fear of being overrun and the hope of rescue. On the night of March 27–28, more than two thousand refugees appeared and asked for protection. After daylight, an enemy rocket slammed into a munitions storage area. The fiery eruption of 75mm and 81mm shells set off a panic. The enemy rushed the defenses, chaotic with soldiers and civilians madly scrambling for elusive safety. Wounded ANK G.I.s were slaughtered. Others turned their M-1s and M-16s on their own families be-fore killing themselves to avoid capture and torture. The K.R. fired indiscrimi-nately. Of the thousands in the perimeter, only an estimated 650 escaped.

Retake Oudong "at all cost," Lon Nol told his commanders. He was under direct pressure from Buddhist leaders, who feared not only for the ancient city but also for the irreplaceable religious relics that had been packed in pro-tective cases and left behind. On April 21, the insurgents pressed ANK out of Kompong Luong and barricaded the Sap River linking the Mekong and the Tonle Sap Lake. The beaten government troops retreated up Route 41 to join the garrison at Lovek. They left behind four howitzers, two M-113 APCs, all of their mortars and machine guns, ammunition, a fuel truck, a bulldozer, and three boats. About six hundred men also "disappeared." Shaken by the unexpected reversal, FANK headquarters ordered soldiers and civilians at outposts in the area to abandon their positions and go to Lovek to form a single large defensive perimeter. By the end of April, as the enemy moved up to begin bombarding the surrounded Lovek enclave, it held 5,260 troops; 15,488 dependents; 891 paramilitary personnel; and 30,766 civilians. They had to rely on U.S. and AAK aircraft for resupply. Other American aircraft, RF-4 photo-reconnaissance jets, flew high overhead to follow the progress of the fighting and to provide information to FANK.[4]

While the battle for Oudong raged in mid-March, Khmer army and navy forces were wresting two Mekong islands a few miles northeast of Phnom Penh from enemy hands. Conversely, in early April, unable to reinforce them because its reserves were committed to Kampot and Oudong, ANK lost several outposts south of the city between the Mekong and Bassac Rivers. On April 5, rockets once more began to arc into the capital. The Communists delivered their heaviest salvos on *Chaul Chhnam,* the mid-April Khmer New Year celebration. Raiders dashed beneath a 107mm rocket barrage to pass through ANK lines and flip a half dozen grenades into a group of civilian dancers in southern Phnom Penh. Two died and 35 were injured. Rockets alone inflicted between 24 and 91 casualties (announced figures vary) during the three-day holiday. In the first four months of 1974, rockets and shells took a reported 354 lives in the city, leaving another 923 hurt. On April 26, the projectile was a hand grenade and the target apparently was Prime Minister Long Boret. The blast, sundering a wedding reception in the courtyard of a government official's home in the capital, killed 9 and wounded 14. Boret had left only minutes before the attack.

In the south, as April bowed to May, PNLAFK pulled away from the unsuccessful siege of coastal Kampot and turned to an easier prey—the Highway 4 ocean-to–Phnom Penh supply line. Combat surged along the beaten-up roadway throughout May, with ANK surrendering positions on both sides of the Elephant Mountains' Pich Nil Pass. Fighting also flared anew in the southeastern provinces of Prey Veng and Svay Rieng. In the first, it was a case of Communist bombardment of the provincial capital. The warfare in Svay Rieng was more widespread. Air and armor-supported South Vietnamese units crashed over the border into PAVN 5th Division positions and supply lines before pulling back. The North Vietnamese apparently considered the province's capital—K.R.-surrounded but stubbornly holding on—as an armed threat to their own rear. Their 5th division subsequently released its 27th Regiment to join a PNLAFK assault on the city. It failed, but served to prove the mockery Hanoi had made of the 1973 Paris agreement.

The government's most crucial battle of mid-1974 remained that for

Oudong. On May 3–4, PNLAFK assailed the southern and the northwestern sections of Lovek's defenses. The Communists managed to take the army training and supply facilities but were prevented from advancing farther by an 80th Brigade counterattack. ANK retook the training-supply center ten days later. The besiegers made up for the setback with around-the-clock rocketing and shelling. A short distance to the east, on May 28, the Cambodian navy regained full control of the Sap River. MNK seamen dismantled the Communist barricade across the waterway and sailed a convoy of supplies to the provincial capital of Kompong Chhnang above Lovek. During the first two weeks in June, the ANK 5th and 7th Brigades moving north from Phnom Penh toward the Oudong-Lovek area began to make measurable progress in the face of waning enemy resistance. The outcome was decided by the commitment of an additional brigade, the 15th, to the advance.

On June 19, the fresh 15th Brigade bludgeoned the worn-down K.R. and rolled up Route 5 triumphantly to enter Kompong Luong. Nine days later, as the government troops paused to regroup, PNLAFK cut the highway behind them. The ANK brigades, buoyed by the confidence of their recent successes, massed armor and troops. They had the road cleared by the next day. The Lovek garrison, meanwhile, repelled several assaults and, on June 12, began shoving eastward from its perimeter. It quickly reached the Sap about five miles above Kompong Luong. Once there, the soldiers were able to evacuate some ten thousand civilians northward to Kompong Chhnang aboard MNK vessels.

Ground fighting still was in progress north of the capital, near Prey Veng to the east and along Highway 4 to the southwest when a mid-May Mekong convoy was hit hard by the insurgents. The five freighters, five tankers, eight munitions barges, and nine rice barges making up the northbound river train were about eight miles inside Cambodia on the morning of June 13. At Peam Chor, where the still low river narrowed to barely over one thousand feet, they suddenly came under fire from the shoreline. The naval escort vessels, shooting back, hurried their charges through the narrows. A low-lying barge carrying $1.5 million in munitions burst into flame and began to settle. The miraculously unhurt crew was hauled aboard navy craft. A second munitions barge was set afire, but the blaze was smothered before it reached the cargo. The Vietnamese tanker *Vinh Long* also began to burn from the rain of rockets, shells, and automatic weapon rounds. Fire extinguished, the ship was taken in tow. Three crewmen aboard were dead, another fifteen wounded. The luckier supply vessels, many scarred by less serious hits, churned into Phnom

Penh's anchorage at dusk. Although often contested, the convoys were making it through.

Instead of melding into a modicum of substantiality as the republic fought for its life, Phnom Penh's political scene remained unstable. At the end of April, the regime admitted its inability to control the economy by instituting further measures, this time to curb a first annual quarter inflation rate of 40 percent. The riel was devalued from 377 to 420 to the dollar, spending was to be reduced, government income was to be increased, and small enterprises were to be encouraged. Easier legislated than done for most of these. On May 14, the parliament enacted a six-month "nation in danger" law allowing the authorities to suspend the rights of assembly, domicile, and correspondence, but not of the press. The law would be renewed in November. After proceedings asking Long Boret and other ministers to explain their policies and actions, the national assembly on May 30 formally lashed out at government incompetence. Several of Boret's ministers angrily submitted their resignations.

As in the past, renewed public dissatisfaction was displayed first by two of the country's most disparate groups: the common soldiers and the draft-exempt educational elite. At midday on May 21, several hundred G.I.s abandoned their positions northwest of the capital to tramp rowdily through the city. Firing in the air and flipping smoke grenades, they occasionally snatched food from vendors' stands and shouted their grievances. They hadn't been properly fed in days. They hadn't been paid in months. Furthermore, when their understrength 22nd Brigade was disbanded, it was absorbed into the 7th Division's 45th Brigade. In the process, the respected colonel who had recruited them was reassigned elsewhere. No one seemed particularly upset at the noisy disturbance, which soon melted away as had past ones. Resurrected teacher-student activism was announced by the appearance of bannered slogans on secondary school walls and the verbal denunciation of economic conditions and government corruption. Arrests followed.

Early on June 5, 1974, after days of growing tension, Minister of National Education Keo Sangkim and his deputy, Thach Chea, were kidnapped from their offices by students and taken to the center of pedagogic unrest, the Lycée 18 Mars. They were hostages for the release of previously arrested teachers and students. The officials were placed in a second-floor classroom of the secondary school with only an outside door facing a long balcony accessed by stairs at either end. Newly arrived military policemen were greeted with slogans chanted from the school courtyard. Oppressively hot hours passed as Lon Nol and his advisers debated how to react to the situation. Finally, the students were told to release the hostages by 4 P.M. or the police would come in to free them. Upstairs, the forty-eight-year-old Sangkim, photographed earlier in an open-necked white shirt and dark slacks, smiling in the midst of his good-natured captors, was described by witnesses as "joking with the students and eating peanuts." Urged on by their leaders, students armed themselves with sticks, bricks, and rocks. More than two dozen shield-wielding policemen broke into the courtyard, where they were stoned and harangued as they stood in formation. At an angry student leader's request, Sangkim appeared on the balcony and, using a bullhorn, asked the police to leave. They remained.

At about 4 P.M., the boisterous confrontation turned violent. Club-waving students moved toward the policemen in the courtyard, yelling at them to leave. Bricks and stones flew. The police turned to run, but the gate had been locked behind them. Policemen outside charged forward, firing in the air and lobbing gas canisters. As a riot raged below, a youth darted into the second-story classroom and fired three shots from a .45-caliber pistol at the hostages. One slug hit Sangkim in the chest; two others punched into Chea's chest. The assassin brushed past witnesses crouched on the balcony and escaped down a stairway. Only shortly after 6 P.M., following imposition of a citywide eleven-hour curfew, did quiet descend onto the canister and debris-cluttered schoolyard. A couple of students had been fatally shot, others were injured, and seventy-two were arrested.

Sangkim was dead on arrival at a military hospital. His forty-five-year-old deputy, nicknamed "Ringo Starr" by his pupils, died soon afterward. Although accusing fingers were pointed at the students and at the government, the U.S. Embassy believed it had been a Communist provocation. In 1981, one of the witnesses to the event said that an accomplice of the assassin told him the murders were carried out by a hit team from the CPK Eastern Zone. The killings, topping off never-ending factionalism, caused the disintegration of the government cabinet. Almost unnoticed in the day's events were the five 107mm rockets fired into the city. One caused twenty-nine casualties in a crowded movie house. Other missiles slammed into Phnom Penh on June 7, at least two narrowly missing Long Boret. The prime minister was attending an open air religious ceremony on the northern edge of the capital.[5]

The black-haired, bespectacled Boret went from physical close call to political crisis. With his cabinet collapsed around him in the aftermath of the Sangkim-Chea murders, he turned in his own resignation on June 12—only to be almost immediately reinstated. On the sixteenth, he formed a new cabinet composed of seven members of Lon Nol's Socio-Republican Party, seven independents, and two military officers. The opposition Republicans had refused to join it, hoping to exert their influence through an advisory council chaired by the president. Another voice trying to make itself heard above the political agitation was the new American ambassador's. Dean urged internal unity to strengthen the Khmer Republic, to make it stable enough to stalemate the K.R. and force a negotiated peace. He persuaded the government in July to ask its opponents for unconditional talks, a call that Sihanouk immediately and not unexpectedly rejected. More aggressive than his predecessor, Dean was credited with a number of changes adopted by Phnom Penh, including the lifting of four years of press dispatch censorship and the forced retirement of several old generals from the top-heavy FANK ranks. He also ruffled high-level feathers by pressing the corruption issue. For example, the ambassador pushed Khmer authorities to reimburse the United States for $310,000 worth of "missing" aviation fuel. But trying to curb corruption and political backbiting seemed akin to plugging a sieve with bare hands.[6]

Single-mindedly following its own agenda, unhampered by democratic considerations, the CPK acquired new standing. The Chinese, seeing how the leaves were settling in the K.R. teapot and ever ready to counter Vietnamese interests, shifted less than subtly away from the figurehead Sihanouk. On May 26, 1974, publicly admitting having helped them in the past, Beijing announced an open-ended military agreement with the Khmers Rouges. Then, on June 13, Khieu Samphan, GRUNK deputy prime minister as well as PNLAFK commander, was accorded head of state treatment by the Chinese when he completed his seventy-seven-day global goodwill trip. Interestingly, Pol Pot was consistently successful in keeping his leading CPK role in the shadows.

Earlier in the year, the CPK central committee had issued a two-phased strategic blueprint for its field commanders to follow. The first phase addressed the indoctrination of the people under their control in its form of communism. The second was intended to establish the party as the undisputed font of this communism, finally casting aside the original concept of a united front with other K.R. groups. On July 20, the CPK-dominated GRUNK declared its intention to nationalize rubber plantations in areas under its control. One reason the Communists were anxious to recommence rubber production was to pay for such Chinese weapons as antishipping mines to use against the Mekong convoys.

On the battlefield, the struggle for Oudong and Lovek ground on. ANK's

28th Brigade, storming from the east along Route 5, broke the PNLAFK hold on Oudong on June 29 and entered the devastated city. It took another few days under increasingly wet skies to mop up the last insurgent holdouts. The psychological boost of the victory was as vital to the government as its tactical value. Sadly, what had once been a beautiful city now was blackened, body-strewn rubble, where not even vegetation remained. On July 9, the enemy line north of Oudong was punctured, enabling the Oudong and Lovek ANK forces to link up. American military observers felt able to rate the performance of the army's M-113s during the early summer fighting as "outstanding." According to the MEDTC commander, this and "a heavy infusion of U.S.-trained officers" showed "that a U.S. training effort could upgrade the performance of Khmer officers." Total casualties for the April 22–July 9 campaign were given as 890 government losses (104 dead and 786 wounded) and 1,366 PNLAFK dead, with 45 captured and 18 rallying (including the commander of the 114th K.R. Battalion). Renewed confidence enabled ANK to foil an insurgent countermove a week after the end of the campaign.

On July 23, a reinforced government force, M-113s in the vanguard, churned westward from Oudong and Lovek in a limited offensive against a weakened foe. Other troops moved south from Lovek on Route 41 five days later to complete clearing of the right bank of the Sap River. They met up with G.I.s slogging northward from Kompong Luong. MNK simultaneously ferried two battalions of soldiers to the east bank of the river to secure a beachhead across from Kompong Luong.

Another dramatic, though smaller, battle was raging at this time for a tiny community just over seventy air miles southwest of Phnom Penh. Kompong Seila, situated among rice paddies in a valley on the western flank of the Elephant Mountains, was significant solely because it sat on the Highway 4 lifeline between the capital and the ocean. On May 20, PNLAFK troops occupied the forested heights overlooking the village and began the longest sustained siege of the war. Shells from mortars and two captured howitzers showered the approximately one thousand soldiers and six thousand civilians in Kompong Seila. Monitored by U.S. Army attachés assigned to them, ANK units tried to effect a rescue from both sides of the village along the highway. Those pushing southwestward from Kompong Speu temporarily severed a vital K.R. supply route as they moved forward. Only the most optimistic observer, however, expected them to surmount winding, enemy-held Pich Nil Pass seven and a half miles above the town. Government elements on the other side of the mountains barely were able to sweep the highway in the foothills between Kompong Som and its airport north of Ream village. Weeks passed, then months, with no easing of the siege.

Badly punished by K.R. action and malaria, the garrison repeatedly called for help. Unfortunately, a communication mix-up roused FANK suspicion that the radio calls were bogus. Before a team from Khmer Special Forces Group 3 could be helicoptered in to clarify the situation, the besieged had begun to assuage their hunger by resorting to cannibalism. Kompong Seila's plight ameliorated somewhat when U.S. and Cambodian aircraft began parachuting in supplies after the communication problem was resolved. Unfortunately, some of the dropped goods drifted into Communist territory because the planes were flying high to avoid antiaircraft fire. In July, T-28s and gunships blasted away at PNLAFK positions to ease the way for a helicopter evacuation of the injured. The attempt was aborted when machine gun bullets jackhammered into the lead chopper, which then was bracketed by shellfire. It barely made it back to Kompong Speu.

By August, the garrison was down to a few hundred able-bodied men. But when the attackers tried an open assault, they "had their behinds whipped," to quote American air attaché Lieutenant Colonel Douglas Roysdon, who overflew the village in an embassy C-47. During one thirty-six-hour period, over seven hundred rounds of explosives pounded the defenses. Bodies had to be left lying in the street until a lull permitted them to be gathered for burial. It was a tribute to the individual Cambodian G.I.'s ability and determination that the garrison held out until April 1975, when helicopters lifted out about two thousand soldiers and civilians.

The unreliability of road travel and the increased harassment of river traffic made Phnom Penh more dependent than ever on aerial resupply. An American-backed push by the Khmer government to pump up air freight shipments resulted in the creation of small companies that scraped up pilots and hardware wherever they could. Another result was new opportunities for graft, from widespread bribery demands and wholesale gasoline theft to dangerously overloading planes for undeclared personal gain. To the pilots' chagrin, high-ranking FANK officers often used the private aircraft for various purposes without paying, pocketing their allotted money instead. One aviator spoke of flying from Kompong Som to the capital "with a complete load of Hennessy [cognac]." One loser was the American taxpayer, since the United States purchased the aircraft fuel in dollars, sold it to distributors for riels, and gave the riels to the Cambodian government. Physical hazards to the aircrews included unsafe airplanes and gunfire—from the K.R., angry ANK G.I.s, and gunners such as those guarding the restricted zone around the presidential palace since the last aerial assassination attempt.

By mid-1974, at least sixteen airlines, with largely American and Taiwanese pilots flying two- and four-engined, propeller-driven planes, competed with Khmer military aircraft and U.S. Air Force munitions-loaded C-130s for runway space at Pochentong. High-profile Air America and Continental Air Services, both long publicly associated with the CIA, gradually cut back their runs. They were replaced by U.S. AID–chartered Bird Air, whose $1.7 million initial contract called for the use of five air force C-130s with civilian crews between September 1974 and June 1975. The official commencement of Bird Air operations on October 7 also phased out U.S. military aircraft activities. Henceforth, except for a few administrative support missions, only civilians would fly into the country. Bird's contract would grow to $2.6 million and call for a daily thirty planeloads from U Tapao to Cambodia by the following February. Air America remained until the end of the year to assist AAK in servicing its aircraft. Continental continued limited operation with a contract to fly three weekly Bangkok-to-Pochentong round trips. The Cambodian airline also maintained a limited flight schedule.[7]

Nixon's presidency finally succumbed to the Watergate scandal on August 9, when he resigned. Gerald Ford, in his first speech to Congress as the new chief executive three days later, said he hoped "to see an early compromise settlement in Cambodia." Shortly afterward, boding ill for any compromise, Sihanouk told a reporter during a visit to East Europe that he was resigned to giving up political leadership and accepting a representational role when the K.R. took over. In mid-August, Phnom Penh was treated to a monster armed forces day parade marking the year that the Khmer Republic had just completed without U.S. combat air support. The enemy reaction to that was a rocket barrage. It landed well to the south of the festivity area only because an army mini-offensive had shoved PNLAFK lines back beyond effective range.

With the arrival of the southwest monsoon that filled lakes, rivers, and rice fields, things seemed to look up for FANK. But underlying the mid-1974 victories, tactical in nature, were certain undeniable truths. In most cases, it was PNLAFK attacking and FANK, despite a monopoly on air and armored units, reacting usually with inadequately planned and poorly coordinated operations. Equally true, K.R. assaults succeeded, even when later pushed back, because of the chronic FANK deficiencies of poor leadership, corruption, inadequate training, and low morale. Finally, in virtually every case, government triumphs ended in stalemates or reversals with no meaningful inroads being made into enemy territory.

There was fierce action northeast of the capital on both sides of the Mekong in August, with positive results for FANK. Government troops to the northwest crowned their Oudong-Lovek successes with consolidation, reorganization, and modest attempts to expand their holdings. Farther up Route 5, around Kompong Chhnang, minor operations enabled 2,500 refugee families to return to Phnom Penh's control. In mid-September, however, PNLAFK hit ANK north and west of that provincial capital, taking several government positions, cutting the highway and creating some thirteen thousand new refugees. Route 5 was reopened on October 6, only to continue changing hands during the weeks ahead.

Warfare to the southeast was aimed at control of the upper Bassac River, FANK giving high priority to areas used by the K.R. to bombard Phnom Penh. On August 7, ANK's 1st Division set out southward on Highway 1 parallel to the Mekong while the 2nd Division advanced eastward along the left bank of the Bassac. The divisions' scissors blades met at Prek Thmei on the Bassac on August 9. They were prised apart three days later by PNLAFK counterattacks. Reinforcements from the capital stabilized the front and enabled the army to launch the government's first major wet season offensive of the year on August 21. Seventeen infantry battalions and four M-113 squadrons drove to broaden control of the Bassac and to establish a defensive line between that river and the Mekong well below Phnom Penh. The Bassac-hugging main force was delayed by, among other factors, the inundated low ground that often bogged down its vehicles. It stalled completely just over three miles shy of a linkup with elements of the 3rd Division that had just reached the Bassac after a cross-country drive southward from the Mekong.

In September, units of the 1st, 2nd, and 7th Divisions, with an APC squadron and two provincial battalions—together called Task Force Alpha in the best American military tradition—began a yard-by-yard advance from the west along both banks of the Bassac against a well dug-in PNLAFK. At the same time, an M-113–spearheaded 2nd Division formation called Task Force Bravo implemented an effort to slice behind the enemy facing the Alpha force. It sped east on Highway 1 along the Mekong, then swerved south and west. Bravo's attempt to outflank the foe was brutally checked just short of the Bassac. Prek Thmei changed hands twice in the fighting, finally ending up under government control. The Bassac offensive ended in a stalemate in late September about seven air miles from the capital. Efforts by both sides to regain the initiative in October failed.

Far to the northwest, Route 6 between Siem Reap and Sisophon near the Thai border was cleared by ANK on August 11 after nearly a week in enemy hands. The action highlighted the fact that areas west of the Great Lake now were receiving greater Communist attention. Besides having focused their earlier more limited military resources elsewhere, the insurgents had until now kept the northwestern sector relatively quiet because it was a key source of food, medicine, and other goods provided by greedy local officials. On August 23, ANK undertook Operation 802, named for the year when the first Angkor king was crowned. Roaring eight lightly contested miles east of Siem Reap on Highway 6, two motorized brigades slued southward another mile and a quarter to occupy the ancient ruins of Roulos, site of Jayavarman II's crowning. The action, if pulled off successfully, would assure government control of a large rice-growing area and interfere with PNLAFK supply lines. Displaying ANK's well-known weaknesses, their strength sapped by disease and desertions, the defenders of Roulos cracked in the face of enemy attacks at the beginning of October.

Brisk riverbank-clearing sweeps kept assaults on Mekong convoys to a minimum during August and September 1974, most attacks originating from the right bank just above the Vietnamese frontier. One ship was lost in August, none in the four September round trips. Another four river trains completed their journeys in October without fatalities in spite of nine confrontations. The feat was repeated the next month. Five convoys made round trips in December, incurring only ship damage. During 1974, about 57,000 metric tons of ammunition, fuel, rice, and other goods had been delivered via the Mekong line of communication. A river convoy farther upriver trying to reach encircled Kompong Cham, however, met with disaster on November 21. Most of the cargoes were lost when hostile fire sank two ammunition boats, two rice barges, and a MNK monitor, killing eight men.

In mid-September 1974, Phnom Penh had once more tried to match economic policies with wartime realities. Among American-encouraged changes were devaluation of the riel to 1,200 to the dollar, boosted commodity prices, abolished import duties, and raised government military and civilian salaries. On September 21, much to Ambassador Dean's chagrin, forty-four-year-old Lon Non arrived at Pochentong after a more than five-hundred-day sojourn in the United States and France. His return, marked by a welcoming committee of more than 100 officials and military officers, coincided with rumors of his older brother's worsening health, and also with unrest stirred by the government's latest economic measures. Soldiers and civilians in Kompong

Som and Kompong Speu demonstrated, then looted Chinese-owned shops.[8]

If the situation at home was in turmoil, the Khmer Republic at least received another reprieve in the United Nations, again thanks to a large degree to aggressive American lobbying. Lon Nol applauded the UN decision to allow his government to retain its seat and once more offered to hold unconditional talks with the K.R. In all, the Khmer government appealed to the Communists for peace talks four times during the second half of 1974: July 9, August 15, October 9, and November 30. Other well-meaning efforts for negotiation extended into 1975. Involving several countries, they focused on the powerless Sihanouk. The insurgents and their supporters, of course, condemned the pro-Nol resolution, with Khieu Samphan stating that they "forbid the UN to interfere in their internal affairs."

On December 18, the 1975 Foreign Assistance Act was passed by the U.S. Congress. It subjected the Khmer Republic to a $377 million ceiling, including a $200 million limit on military aid. In keeping with the intricacies that place such legislation beyond public understanding, the total was hiked to $452 million with the addition of $75 million under the "drawdown authority" provisions of Section 506 of the Foreign Assistance Act. Interestingly, U.S. aid in 1974 represented about 95 percent of the Khmer Republic's income.

While Phnom Penh set a search for peace as its priority, the insurgents established upcoming dry season goals: attacks against the capital, control of lines of communication, encircling and destroying government positions in the provinces, and increasing their own behind-the-lines production. Late in 1974, Pol Pot, who had been afflicted with malaria and intestinal problems, visited various combat units to insure that all was being done to assure success in the upcoming campaign.

The battle for primacy in the upper Bassac River area blazed through November and December. After taking heavy casualties and losing considerable ground, ANK finally managed to set up a defensive line between the Mekong and the Bassac. It was considerably closer to Phnom Penh than its planners had hoped. The army wound up its Bassac offensive by combining Task Forces Alpha and Bravo for a noisy, multidivision, M-113 line-abreast sweep of a large section of the river's right bank.

Just over nine miles above Phnom Penh, more than two thousand soldiers of the PNLAFK 152nd, 153rd, and 182nd Regiments moved against the ANK defenses at Barrong Khnar on November 10. Although the initial assault was repelled, the K.R. persisted and overwhelmed two northern perimeter positions. Government reinforcements from the 128th Battalion and the 2nd and

4th Airborne Battalions were thrown in. Every day for nearly two weeks, the Communists hurled themselves against the ANK line despite heavy artillery and aircraft fire. By November 27, government troops had retaken the last of their lost ground and begun mopping up operations. The final tally was given (presumably with its usual unreliability) as 16 ANK dead and 185 wounded, and 558 PNLAFK killed and 9 captured. A K.R. victory would have given their rocketeers excellent access to the capital.

Almost everywhere, fighting seemed to wind down with the end of the year. A Communist victory had been averted in 1974 by U.S.-supported FANK resistance and K.R. weaknesses. The latter included tactics assuring heavy losses, recurring munitions shortages, a flawed command and control system, mobility limited by inadequate organization and transportation, and weak communications security that facilitated eavesdropping. Despite its defensive success, however, a critically embattled ANK had, for the first time, been deprived of its annual wet season breathing spell to rest, retrain, and refit. In any case, Lon Nol took advantage of the relative calm to take a year-end vacation in Kompong Som, where he began planning still another cabinet reshuffle.[9] Symbolic of the instability that characterized the Khmer Republic, a nation sucked into a modern war it was unready for, Cambodian G.I.s in December 1974 fired thousands of rounds of ammunition into the sky above Phnom Penh. Spent metal fell back to earth, sometimes hitting people. Sixteen reportedly died. It was a reprise of the January 1972 make-noise-to-save-the-moon episode decried by Lon Nol. And again, as the lunar eclipse ended, the superstitious soldiers believed they had saved the moon from being swallowed by an evil spirit.

CHAPTER TEN

1975:
The Fall

JANUARY 1, 1975, LITERALLY STARTED WITH A BANG. The Communists launched what Pol Pot called their "decisive offensive to liberate Phnom Penh and the whole country." Their strategy, expressed late the year before, was aimed at cutting the capital's Mekong lifeline. If that succeeded, an all-out assault on the city could follow. More than one hundred PNLAFK battalions began a series of attacks within ten miles of Phnom Penh and along the river. At the same time, they started a daily rain of high explosives to terrorize the capital's numbed inhabitants, now numbering over two million. More than a hundred 107mm rockets landed during the first twelve days of the year.

The results of the offensive were almost immediate, startlingly so, for a number of reasons. For one thing, K.R. organization had undergone improvement. Second, so had the insurgent supply situation, materially as well as organizationally. The Khmer Communists had gathered a large inventory of captured guns, munitions, and other items over the past year. In addition, Beijing stepped up support, including artillery and antishipping mines. Hanoi moved the PRC-provided matériel down the Ho Chi Minh Trail and supplemented it with some of its own equipment. Finally, the Khmer Republic's political and military illnesses, after years of neglect, had reached their terminal stages. As the last U.S. MEDTC commander noted in his final report, "In five years of war, the KC [Khmer Communist movement] came into its own as a substantially matured military force. The GKR [Government of the Khmer Republic]/FANK did not . . . The Khmer infantry was consistently outfought, outsmarted and outmaneuvered" during the final days.

ANK's 1st Division, buttressed by the 15th Brigade (taken over by now Brigadier General Lon Non after his return from abroad), was posted west of the Bassac in Phnom Penh's southeast defense sector, one of four zones into which the city had been divided. While these two elements were relatively unmolested, the neighboring 2nd Division in the same sector, was burrowing into its positions between the Bassac and the Mekong under heavy fire. Only the tons of howitzer shells and air-dropped explosives being thrown at them kept the attackers at bay. The 3rd Division, astride Route 4 about six miles beyond the airport in the southwest sector, was worse off. The division's fighting units suddenly found themselves cut off from their Kompong Speu command post by a PNLAFK thrust. In the northwest zone, the 7th Division's front was badly punctured. The division was able to regain ground temporarily and thwart a K.R. attempt to neutralize the airlift into Pochentong, thanks largely to the presence of surviving Khmers Kroms in its ranks. FANK tried to block attacks in the northeast sector by ferrying the 1st Parachute Brigade and Phnom Penh Military Region troops across the Mekong as reinforcements. Downriver, PNLAFK captured several islands and erected strongholds to ambush passing convoys. It also enisled the long-suffering Highway 1 ferry town of Neak Luong in mid-January.

A river convoy, following two smaller ones earlier in the month, limped into Phnom Penh on January 26. Despite South Vietnamese air cover and the flanking of loaded craft with empty anti-rocket–screened barges, three vessels had been lost and six others had scurried back to Vietnam. The two tankers and five munitions barges that made it turned out to be the last to reach the city. Days later, unloaded southbound vessels ran into a freshly laid minefield near the Phu My narrows between Neak Luong and the frontier. They were deluged with gunfire that sank several and blocked the river. FANK gave up efforts to reopen the Mekong in mid-February. Except for two isolated major outposts, the entire waterway in Cambodia below the capital now was under enemy control. The significance of this setback was made clear by the fact that in 1974 the Khmer Republic had received about 90 percent of its supplies through the Mekong line of communication.

Commander Cyrus Christensen, a Vietnam War veteran assigned to the U.S. Navy's Mine Force in South Carolina, was flown to Cambodia late in February to study the Mekong mine problem. He was told to low-profile it and travel in mufti, not a new cosmetic requirement in a war where Congress and the executive branch seemed as mutually antagonistic as the battlefield combatants. Christensen found that the mines were command-detonated by wires leading to shore positions. Their threat could only be neutralized by clearing the river banks so that sweepers could cut the wires and disarm the explosives. This was seconded by MNK, which said it could convert some of its boats into minesweepers but that they would be vulnerable to shore fire. The American officer's attempts to organize and train a mine-countermeasures group proved fruitless since ANK was unable to regain control of the river banks.

MNK, in any case, had been reduced to near impotence. Whereas it had lost only a half dozen craft during the first four years of the war, the Khmer navy saw fifteen go down in 1974. In January 1975, seven vessels were destroyed. February and March were even worse. In mid-February, MNK lost responsibility for the river corridor when the Mekong Special Zone became a joint services operation under army command. Naval missions following closure of the Mekong LOC consisted of providing fire support to the army, conducting patrols, making night-time supply runs to the Neak Luong area, defending the Chrouy Chang War Peninsula opposite Phnom Penh, and performing medical evacuations.

Although the Khmer air force never reached its hoped-for potential, it helped prolong the republic's survival by conducting air strikes, supply missions, FAC and reconnaissance sorties, and troop movements. Its overall performance, how-ever, continued to be marked by unimaginative tactics, lack of aggressiveness, and inadequate technical skill. Flying mostly from Phnom Penh, AAK T-28s op-erated only in daylight with orders not to attack below three thousand feet. Nocturnal sorties were accomplished by the twin-engined AC-47 gunships, high-winged AU-24 mini-gunships, and rotary-winged UR-1Hs. U.S. training pro-grams established in Thailand had given some cause for optimism. By the beginning of 1975, for instance, 60 percent of the T-28 missions were under FAC coordination. This improved the performance of an air arm that had earned a reputation for haphazard bombing often fatal to civilians. New ordnance, such as advanced cluster bomb models, and techniques were introduced as well. One example of the latter was the use of the two-motored C-123 Provider transports for day and night bombing. Explosives were loaded onto wooden pallets and dropped over targets from the open rear doors of the aircraft.

C-123 transport missions were augmented by C-47s and helicopters. By the fall of 1974, AAK had a dozen Providers, but lost two in accidents, one of these a mishap on Svay Rieng's improvised Route 1 landing strip. Maintenance and re-pair requirements usually left only three to five of these transports available at any one time. An additional six C-123s, with crews and mechanics undergoing training in Thailand, were scheduled to make the Khmer air force self-sufficient by mid-1975. AAK airdrops to isolated government positions, flown from 4,500 to 5,000 feet in altitude, were being completed without loss of aircraft to enemy ground fire. These continued until March 1975, when the task was mostly taken over by Bird Air C-130s.

Chronic road cutting, loss of the Mekong LOC, and the uncertainty of the

Battambang–Great Lake–Sap River route to Phnom Penh left no doubt that the greatest resupply airlift since Berlin's in 1948–49 soon would be the only assurance of the republic's continued existence. By the first weekend in January, twenty-three airlines were using Pochentong, with more to come. They flew a total of about forty planes, old DC-3s and DC-4s contrasting sharply with the Bird Air turboprops, to lift an estimated monthly 4,500 tons of goods. The latter represented only about a tenth of the city's needs. The airline owners included Chinese merchants and FANK officers. Profits promised to be phenomenal since the Battambang–Phnom Penh price markup was as high as 300 percent. The older aircraft were joined in February by contracted stretch DC-8 jets hefting forty-five-ton loads of rice or ammunition per plane. The record one-day total of supplies landed at Pochentong was 1,133.9 tons on March 18, 1975. Air Cambodge, the government airline, still scheduled its champagne Flight 142 Caravelle jet from Bangkok. Predictably, passenger flights in were much less crowded than the outgoing ones.

Fortunately for the pilots, many of them ex–Air America or U.S. military veterans chasing high, tax-free pay and adventure, PNLAFK had few antiaircraft weapons. The most dangerous times for the airmen seemed to be while on the ground. Alighting aircraft frequently were followed into Pochentong by one or more Chinese-made rockets fired from the northwest. More than 2,500 projectiles struck the airport area between New Year's Day and April 17. Although two Americans were slightly injured, nine Khmers were killed and forty were wounded in January alone. Proof of the freakish conditions of flying into Phnom Penh was the actual in-flight shelling of a Southeast Asia Air Transport CV-540. The twin-engined Convair, descending into its landing approach, entered airspace shared with ANK artillery shells streaking toward enemy lines. It was a "normal" hazard aviators tried to neutralize with calculations based on observing shell bursts. Suddenly, a 105mm shell ripped through the Convair's cockpit beside the copilot's seat. The round then tore through the roof and exploded above the plane. Shrapnel killed and injured several passengers.[1]

No emergency seemed great enough to temper the infighting in Phnom Penh's political circles. Interparty divisions widened even further. Parliament, asserting itself by investigating cabinet members, loudly decried Lon Nol's performance. The U.S. ambassador himself now favored withdrawing support from Nol and seeking almost any mutually acceptable solution to end the war. Cambodian civilian and military leaders pointed accusing fingers, blaming each other for the nation's woes. On March 12, Lieutenant General Fernandez sadly clinked champagne glasses with his uniform-clad president in a public change-of-command ceremony in Chamcar Mon Palace. The general had come under growing criticism for corruption and refusal to accept direction from the general assembly. Tears flowed from behind his glasses as he kissed his country's flag and had the green-and-red ribbon of the Grand Cross placed around his neck. The general shortly afterward left to reside in France.

The new chief of the general staff and FANK commander-in-chief was Lieutenant General Sak Sutsakhan. Since falling out of favor with the Lon brothers in mid-1972, he had been attached to the foreign affairs ministry as a roving ambassador. Sutsakhan spent considerable time abroad and was in New York as a delegate to the UN when he was summoned home in February 1975. He, at least, seemed free of the taint of defeat that covered most of the military elite. Accepting his new assignment with trepidation, he viewed the nation as "a sick man who had survived only by outside means and that . . . the administration of medication . . . was probably of no further value." He was to be, in effect, the republic's undertaker.

Lon Nol tasked Prime Minister Long Boret with forming a new cabinet. The assignment proved a formidable one as, with the dull thumps of artillery providing background accompaniment, the politicians haggled like bargain seekers at a rug bazaar. The main reason for this divisiveness, according to Western diplomats, was the meddling of Lon Non, who had been doing his utmost to regain influence since his return. Encouraged and abetted by the United States, the Cambodian government stepped up contacts with other countries, especially the fence straddlers, to drum up sympathy for its cause. Given current conditions, while such activities might help the republic keep its UN seat, they showed desperation more than anything else.

American hope for a Laos-type coalition solution to Cambodia's war had wisped away. Ambassador Dean, along with his Saigon counterpart, had failed to persuade Secretary Kissinger to pull the rug out from under Lon Nol. The secretary of state still considered Nol a bargaining chip to be traded for concessions from the other side. As the situation deteriorated still further, Dean spoke of a "controlled solution," an illusive, ill-defined "non-military solution which would take into account the realities," which would end the war "and which would permit us to disengage." Unfortunately, any conceivable "controlled solution" options narrowed with each PNLAFK advance.[2]

In both Phnom Penh, whose overcrowded streets now teemed with beggars, and Battambang, its land links with Thailand snipped by the insurgents, soaring food prices caused students to riot on February 21. Their principal targets were the Chinese dominating the goods trade. This time, in contrast to its part in the

1970 anti-Vietnamese pogrom, the government clamped down. About a hundred students were arrested in Battambang. The protesters retaliated by kidnapping the commander of the provincial capital's airbase. They offered to release him if the arrested students were freed and strict anti-Chinese legislation was enacted. Freeing of the arrestees and a meaningless promise to study the legislation demands defused the crisis.

The sudden disintegration of Cambodia's defensive capability made it evident that evacuation plans for foreigners soon would have to be activated. U.S. planning was complicated by the political unrest in Thailand, previously the most obvious destination for evacuees from Phnom Penh. The only practical alternative, in case of Thai intransigence, was the use of Pacific Fleet units in the Gulf of Thailand. CINCPAC had given the USSAG commander in Thailand responsibility, as far back as April 1973, for the planning and execution of an American evacuation, code-named Eagle Pull, from the Khmer Republic. Six major planning sessions were held between August 1973 and December 1974. Representatives of USSAG and the 3rd Marine Amphibious Force (decision had been made to give the marines the primary role) studied a multitude of factors and numerous alternatives before devising an acceptable final plan. Constant adjustments were incorporated to keep current with developments both in Cambodia and with the rescue force.

In early February, the French and the Japanese embassies ordered the departure of families and nonessential personnel. American diplomatic families, now comprising only about half a dozen wives, received identical instructions a few days later from Washington, where the Ford administration was asking an unsympathetic Congress to okay $222 million more in military aid for Cambodia.

PNLAFK's New Year's offensive steamrollered on, barely checked by demoralized ANK resistance. Oudong, for which the government had fought so hard the year before, fell on February 26. A week later, the insurgents edged close enough to the capital to zero in their captured howitzers on Pochentong for the first time. They almost immediately scarred a rice-ferrying American DC-8 from Saigon. After a temporary respite won by a 7th Division counterattack, the shelling and rocketing resumed. On March 22, rockets hit two U.S. transports. Aircraft flying supplies to other surviving urban centers faced similar risks from enemy fire. The American embassy announced the cessation of the airlift until things improved and prodded FANK to clear the area around the airport. Then, recognizing an obvious catch-22 situation, U.S. officials reinstated the flights two days later.

While the airlift was a salve to the troubled American conscience, seeking to reassure Washington's allies of its sincerity and prolonging the republic's existence on a day-to-day basis, its effectiveness was open to question. The six hundred or more tons of ammunition brought in daily from Thailand didn't seem to affect FANK casualties (4,251 troops were reported killed between January 1 and February 20) and certainly wasn't stemming the erosive Red tide. ANK, losing the equivalent of a battalion a day, shrank along with the republic's chances of survival. PNLAFK had access to additional recruits whereas the government, desperately hiking the draft age to fifty, was scraping the barrel bottom. Owing to the high command's current inability to distribute weapons, even the new recruits often went unarmed. Rising desertions, added to the battle losses, depleted ANK ranks to the extent that infantry units fell in foxhole strength from 50 to 30 percent between January and March.

Unbelievably, military corruption continued unabated. Even the civilian goods flown into poverty-level Phnom Penh from South Vietnam were doled out with favoritism, and luxury items remained available for the privileged few. While a handful of well-fed haves still drove to the Cercle Sportif for nightly sets of tennis on floodlighted courts, truckloads of wounded, most of them starving havenots, were off-loaded onto the basketball court of the capital's sports complex now used as a reception and triage center. In January alone, more than thirteen thousand injured and sick were processed at the site and sent elsewhere for treatment. It was ironic that the victims of PRC-furnished weapons were being received at the sports complex that was an earlier gift from Beijing. The body-jamming at Phnom Penh's seven civilian and four military hospitals led to the requisitioning of other buildings, including the former PRC Embassy.

Communist gains northwest of the capital were capped on April 1 by a victory that trashed any slim hope of reopening the Mekong. That day, five PNLAFK regiments launched a mini-offensive along the river below Phnom Penh. Neak Luong, the battered Route 1 town that had received both enemy fire and friendly bombs, was lost, along with its approximately three thousand G.I. defenders and thirty thousand civilians. Brigadier General Lim Sisaath, who had led the ill-fated Copper project in Laos and now had been charged with defending Neak Luong, was last heard from calling for an air strike on his own overrun position. Over the next two days, PNLAFK lunged against ANK's 1st Division and rolled up the few remaining government strongholds along Highway 1 between Neak Luong and Phnom Penh. The victors, strengthened by six more captured cannons, thus were able to reinforce their deployment around the capital.

From Beijing, meanwhile, Sihanouk in March had announced a list of Phnom Penh's "Seven Traitors," who would be hanged if they remained in Cambodia after certain K.R. victory. The chosen seven were Lon Nol; Prime Minister Long

Boret; former ministers Sirik Matak, In Tam, and Son Ngoc Thanh; Cheng Heng, the former national assembly president and chief of state; and General Sosthene Fernandez. Hope for a negotiated peace settlement, the *samdech* added, "is like wishing that the sun would rise in the west and set in the east." There could be no clearer statement of K.R. intentions. Cheng Heng left for France in late March.

As the Indochina whirlpool swirled faster toward swallowing Phnom Penh and Saigon, Sihanouk wrote a letter that seemed frivolous and incredibly egocentric. He asked President Ford for assistance in obtaining and sending him copies of motion pictures he had made in the 1960s. The prince explained their "unique cultural" value and offered some "of my modest musical compositions" in return. A cable flashed to the Phnom Penh embassy to get the films, which had been stored in the *samdech*'s former home. Sihanouk duly received some of his precious reels, while continuing publicly to castigate the United States and its Phnom Penh "puppets." Kissinger used the occasion to tell his representative in the U.S. Liaison Office in Beijing, future president George Bush, to meet with the prince in an effort to find a face-saving path out of the Cambodian morass. Sihanouk slapped the proffered hand, explaining that his sole purpose in contacting the Americans was to recover personal relics of what was perhaps the most escapist period of his life.

A delegation of Cambodian officials had visited Lon Nol in March to present him with a formal resolution. It asked him, in General Sutsakhan's words, to "leave the country on a temporary basis, while the terms of a cease-fire were worked out." A million dollars in installments were promised to ease his stay abroad. The officials were reacting in part to pressure from Japan and Southeast Asian countries seeking to end hostilities in Cambodia. Officially stepping back despite its obvious interest, the United States preferred that the Association of Southeast Asian Nations take the initiative. Shocked—still not understanding, as former Ambassador Swank put it, "that his survival depended, in the first instance, on mustering internal support"—Lon Nol asked for a few days to mull over the resolution.

Khmer pressure for Nol's stepping down also came from outside the government. It was most vociferously voiced by a group containing some of his severest critics, the students. The multi-thousand-member Association of Students of the Khmer Republic, acting amid rumors of an impending coup, called for dissolution of the national assembly, convening of a congress for Cambodians to "express their true views," and the end of U.S. support for the regime and the war. This may have influenced the marshal to sound out, on an individual basis, members of the delegation that had visited him. Finding them all in agreement that he should leave, he reluctantly agreed. Nol's decision notwithstanding, and unrealistic as it was, the Lon family was determined to keep a hold on political power. Lon Non resigned his army command on March 25 to become acting secretary-general of the controlling Socio-Republican Party.

After a simple, Khmer-only farewell ceremony on April Fool's Day, the country's chief executive, wearing a dark gray suit with a black tie, leaning on his cane, limped to one of three waiting helicopters at Chamcar Mon Palace. His tearful wife joined him, and the aircraft lifted noisily into the air. Other relatives and followers clambered aboard the other copters. They beelined to the airport, where the U.S. ambassador waited to say goodbye. To the whistle-and-crash accompaniment of a few nearby rocket strikes, the twenty-nine-person presidential party then boarded Air Cambodge's only jet to fly to U Tapao RTNAB. An Indonesian plane was waiting to take the group southeastward from Thailand to the island of Bali. There the former Khmer leader met with Indonesian President Suharto, who had provided him with advisory support early in the war. Nol then flew on to Hawaii, ostensibly to resume treatment for the effects of his 1971 stroke. A letter order covering the promised million dollars was dispatched from the National Bank of Cambodia to New York's Irving Trust Company.

Lon Nol's departure was followed by a short-lived period of optimism in Phnom Penh. Saukham Khoy, a sixty-one-year-old lieutenant general and president of the senate, became acting president of the republic. Sihanouk promptly added Khoy to his growing list of traitors to be dealt with after the K.R. victory. Prime Minister Boret flew to Bangkok to meet with K.R. representatives on April 8. It was a futile session.

The survivors of the brutal more-than-ten-month siege of Kompong Seila had been evacuated to Wat Prachum Vong, a settlement just below Phnom Penh named for the temple at its center. They barely had begun to recover from their ordeal than they were ordered to a defense line to the north of the capital. Unpaid for months and bitter over being charged to have their families accompany them out of Kompong Seila, they insisted on being paid before moving. Payroll officer First Lieutenant Pen Samnang said they would be paid after repositioning. An argument ensued between Samnang and the brigade commander. As the dispute heated up, the payroll officer drew a pistol and fired several shots that missed the commander but hit other soldiers. Infuriated troops thereupon shot Samnang and sliced him open with knives. Tossing the mutilated corpse beneath a banyan tree, they cooked the various organs and muscles they had removed and ate them.

Dug in along the Sap River north of Phnom Penh, the 7th Division was being chipped to pieces. Enemy charges, undeterred by around-the-clock air strikes and artillery barrages, came daily despite heavy losses. The ANK position, anchored at Prek Phnou village, its two rows of houses beneath palm and fruit trees left in rubbles by mortar fire, often was infiltrated by PNLAFK soldiers. These then turned to hit the government defenders from behind. It was only a matter of days before Brigadier General Khy Hak's division broke. During the first week of April, Communists poured across the dry stream bed of the Phnou about five and a half miles from the capital and advanced down Highway 5, driving the 7th Division survivors before them.

The 3rd Division led by Brigadier General Prince Norodom Chantarangsey, despite being reinforced, was unable either to expand the perimeter around Pochentong Airport or link back up with its command post at Kompong Speu. To make matters worse, friendly artillery rounds fell on the division as it was launching a counterattack. Other enemy assaults hammered ANK defenses south and east of the city. The Parachute Brigade was ferried back across the Mekong in a fruitless attempt to beef up the 3rd Division. Throughout the fighting, frenzied refugees kept filing into Phnom Penh, which repeatedly was rocked by exploding rockets and terrorist grenades. By mid-April, the government forces were squeezed into an approximately fifty-six-square-mile box reaching from the Mekong west to just beyond Pochentong and from a seven-mile-long dike just above the northern city limit down to once-chic Takhmau on the Bassac River.[3]

On April 2, the green light was given for the dispatch of the Operation Eagle Pull command team from USSAG's Thai headquarters to coordinate the U.S. evacuation from Phnom Penh. Led by Colonel Sydney Batchelder, it arrived aboard a Bird Air flight the next day. The team swiftly finalized its plan in coordination with the embassy, which not only had to ready its local staff but also had to gather personnel from the field. There would be a weeklong C-130 fixed-wing aircraft evacuation phase from Pochentong under Lieutenant Colonel Curtis Lawson, followed by a final rotary-wing aircraft lift. On April 4, the Marine Amphibious Unit's Amphibious Ready Group Alpha in the Gulf of Thailand went into a six-hour response status. By April 10, when heavy enemy fire terminated the fixed-wing evacuation, Hercules turboprop transports had hauled out between seven and eight hundred embassy-connected personnel. Ambassador Dean's staff now was down to fifty, including eighteen marine guards.

Politics intruded into Eagle Pull as Henry Kissinger, after long resisting any dealing with Sihanouk, at the eleventh hour backed a suggested compromise to reinstate the prince as a means to span the gap between Phnom Penh and the K.R. Shortly after Eagle Pull moved into gear, the secretary of state pushed back the April 6 date set for the final evacuation of Americans. The reason was to maintain a U.S. presence as a "stabilizing influence" while Kissinger tried to make a deal with Sihanouk and the Chinese. The worried embassy sent out more than one request for permission to begin the helicopter airlift on April 11 as shelling virtually closed Pochentong. According to an eyewitness, one of these requests involved a "most unusual" angry telephone exchange between an embassy officer and Kissinger. Finally, just hours before it occurred, the secretary gave his consent.

The first marine helicopters already had crossed Cambodia's gulf coast when the Eagle Pull evacuees began gathering at the embassy compound for the second and last phase of the U.S. pullout on April 12. Nearly an hour after the whirlybirds entered Khmer air space, the first Thai-based F-4 Phantom jet assigned to provide cover crossed the frontier. Successfully completing their mission, the marine helicopters returned to the ARG Alpha flotilla, the last one landing shortly after noon. The next day, a DC-7, one of its four propellers idled by shrapnel, landed in Air Cambodge's final Bangkok-to-Phnom Penh champagne flight. It was flown back to Thailand by its American pilot, who had come to save his Khmer wife.

On April 14, the over-six-month-long U.S.-contracted airlift stopped. From its rear base in Thailand, MEDTC arranged six parachute supply drops into Phnom Penh on April 16. The next day, MEDTC's job, and with it all American military assistance, ended. The two-year military-civilian aerial supply effort had chalked up 5,413 airfield-delivery missions carrying 123,631 tons. In addition, the largest airdrop program in U.S. Air Force history had, in more than three thousand missions over a thirty-four-month period, delivered over thirty-eight thousand tons of munitions and food—over three times the amount dropped on besieged Khe Sanh, Vietnam, in 1968—to about two dozen Khmer strongpoints without loss to enemy fire during the drops. The initial airdrop had occurred on June 19, 1972, when four C-130 sorties parachuted ammunition to ANK's Svay Rieng garrison.

The republic's five-year war cost the United States about a million dollars a day—a total of $1.85 billion, $1.18 billion of it military aid—plus another $7 billion for air bombardment. In well-meaning words, President Ford vowed to do "whatever possible to support an independent, peaceful, neutral and unified Cambodia." There no longer was mention of his earlier request to Congress for additional military aid funds. The Khmer Republic was to die alone.

Cambodia's national assembly transferred power to a Supreme Committee composed of seven military officers and civilian officials on the evening following the Eagle Pull evacuation. The next day, General Sutsakhan was named committee president, in effect the nation's chief of state. Long Boret was made vice chairman. The committee, touting its continued control of the provincial capitals and the bulk of the country's population, swore to carry on the struggle. It also proposed a cease-fire, which the K.R. slapped aside.

A pause in the fighting on April 13, as the symbolic tiger gave way to the hare with the start of the Khmer new year, was deceptive. Shooting not only picked up the next day, but the republic was subjected to its third aerial assassination attempt by a disaffected pilot. At 10:25 A.M., a T-28 clattered over FANK headquarters. Four 250-pound bombs were released. The two most accurately dropped ones detonated about sixty feet from the office where Sutsakhan was chairing a cabinet meeting. Whereas the officials were untouched, seven soldiers were killed and twenty others were injured. The trainer-cum-fighter bomber flew on to land in Kompong Cham Province. The cabinet session resumed, its main topic of discussion being the flood of refugees still entering the capital.

April 15. The Communists swarmed over the city's last solid defenses. The east-west dike to the north was overrun. Pochentong Airport succumbed. So did Kandal Province's capital of Takhmau to the south. Counterattacks didn't have a chance. The sky over Phnom Penh glowed red that night as PNLAFK projectiles pounded the city to fire wooden homes and FANK depots. The Cambodian military collapse, in the view of MEDTC's last chief, "involved the complete failure of the United States' security assistance objective of developing a self-sustained armed force capable of defending the GKR from insurgency." The American general, William Palmer, deemed the Khmer G.I. superior to the Lao and on a par with the Vietnamese. He also paid tribute to FANK for lasting as long as it had "under some of the poorest leadership in Asia." In Tam was quoted as saying, "Above all, I blame President Lon Nol [for what happened]. He didn't do anything to help the country, but he wanted to keep all power to himself. The Americans gave enough money, but we failed to help ourselves."

The government threw in the well-known towel on the morning of April 16. A new cease-fire offer, this one to include transfer of power to Sihanouk's GRUNK, was sent to Beijing via the Red Cross and Agence France Presse, the French news wire service. Harassed by an unceasing deluge of explosive-laden metal, the Supreme Committee decided to move the seat of government to the far northwestern province of Oddar Meanchey. The committee members gathered during the wee hours of April 17 for helicopters that never appeared. Their depression only deepened when Sihanouk's cabled reply to their last cease-fire offer arrived at six o'clock that morning. The offer was rejected—and the committee members were told they were on the K.R. list of traitors. The only bright spot came with the arrival of seven evacuation helicopters at the Khmer Special Forces–guarded national stadium. Sutsakhan, his wife and children, and the rest of his party—except for Boret, who last was seen by them going from one remaining aircraft to another—lifted away from the smoke-capped city.[4]

Just after dawn that same ill-fated Thursday, sound trucks rumbled beneath the pall overhanging Phnom Penh to instruct the capital's inhabitants to display the white cloth of surrender. Sheets and pillowcases appeared in windows, on rooftops, and in trees. White also was draped on naval vessels circling at the junction of the three rivers and on army vehicles. Because of their siege-produced agony, the shortcomings of the republic, and the innate Khmer belief that normality inevitably follows turmoil, the majority of the people looked forward with relief to the entry of the K.R. Military and civilian alike, they thought that, with their triumph, the newcomers would accept reconciliation. Countless ANK soldiers exchanged their uniforms for civilian clothes. The hundreds of French who remained were confident that their traditional colonial status, having survived the First Indochina War and the Japanese occupation before that, would remain unchanged. Besides, the French government long had recognized the K.R. regime. The Soviets had taken out insurance on March 28 by ordering the Lon Nol government to shutter its Moscow embassy.

The occupation of Phnom Penh began as a farce. About two hundred black-garbed, smiling youths, armed largely with M-16s, appeared at 7 A.M. on Boulevard 18 Mars. They exchanged joyous greetings with cheering inhabitants as shouts of "Peace" filled the air. The young men then led a victory parade of variegated vehicles eastward along a flame-tree–lined avenue past the Independence Monument to the waterfront. They disarmed bewildered G.I.s while their leader, twenty-nine-year-old "General" Hem Keth Dara established his headquarters at the information ministry. As *New York Times* reporter Schanberg later wrote, "It soon became clear that they were not the real Khmer Rouge—we never did learn who they were, maybe misguided students trying to share in the 'revolution,' maybe part of a desperate ploy by the government to confuse and subvert the Khmer Rouge." Some thirty thousand army troops had begun surrendering to a handful of impostors. In fact, the latter were in great part the same student activists who for years had been demonstrating against Lon Nol and wanted to be in the vanguard of the K.R. revolution. Naively idealistic like their equally privileged counterparts in the Western world, they never paused long enough to realize that they would be among the first to be eliminated by the leftist cause they championed. The entire Dara charade is believed to have been the brainchild of Lon Non, who, in staying behind, obviously intended to be a participant in and not a victim of the new regime. Perhaps he hoped to capitalize on his contacts with the K.R. and on his schooldays friendship with Pol Pot to cut a deal with the Communists.

At midday, the carnival atmosphere was shattered as the real PNLAFK, forces from the K.R.'s various geographical zones, began to enter the capital from the north, south, and west. They, too, largely were young. They were dressed in black, khaki, and green, most with checkered kramas (traditional multipurpose cotton scarves) around their necks and sandals cut from tires on their feet. They nearly all were unsmiling, grimly silent, and robot-like. They were heavily laden with a variety of weapons. "General" Dara, whom they dubbed a CIA agent trying to spread panic, and his misguided followers were relieved of their arms and taken into custody.

A radiocast announcement told officials of the republican government to come to the information ministry grounds. Lon Non, pipe clamped between his teeth, his mustache shaved and no sign of rank on his immaculately ironed uniform, was one of the first to appear. The number of surrendering officials grew to about four dozen. With several journalists present, a PNLAFK officer told the closely guarded men that their "lives would be protected." He also directed his attention to the newsmen, saying that the American people were to be thanked "for putting pressure on their Congress to end the war." Long Boret arrived later that afternoon in a black Mercedes driven by his wife.

Although some of the newcomers were civil to the populace, their behavior was overshadowed by the acts of PNLAFK violence. Valuables and goods were arbitrarily confiscated by K.R. soldiers, many of whom had never before seen a big city or possessed items such as cameras, motorbikes, and automobiles. Telephone and telegraph lines leading to the outside world were cut by midafternoon. At about 5 P.M., loudspeaker-rigged trucks and soldiers with bullhorns circulated throughout most of the capital ordering its inhabitants to leave immediately. Some of the announcements warned of impending American air raids. Shots were fired, often with fatal results, to enforce the order. Not even hospitals were exempt. Operations were interrupted and patients were cast out. These scenes were repeated in all of the country's urban centers. One effect of the mass evacuations was the unexpected dispersal of stay-behind assets the CIA had expected to use in future intelligence-related activities.

While the AK-47 and M-16–wielding conquerors were preparing brutally to herd Phnom Penh's population into the countryside with a bare minimum of possessions, FANK Chief of Operations Brigadier General Mey Sichan was directed to radio formal surrender instructions to government forces outside the capital. The republic's effort to establish a new seat of power in the northwest had failed. Sutsakhan and a handful of weary, frightened officers and their families were obliged to bribe their way onto an airstrip on April 18. They boarded a C-123 for the short hop to Thailand. There was confusion at many outlying government enclaves. In Kompong Chhnang, for example, there was a split between those advocating loyalty to the old regime and those encouraging a switch in sides. The latter faction won. Kompong Cham also rapidly obeyed General Sichan's order, and black-uniformed soldiers entered unopposed the city that for years had repelled one attack after the other. Kompong Som, Siem Reap, Kompong Thom, Prey Veng, and garrisons near the western frontier initially opted to hold out, but swiftly fell. Thousands of civilians and FANK G.I.s fled toward the Thai and Vietnamese borders. Ten crowded air force planes winged to U Tapao from Battambang.

Former Prime Minister In Tam was among the last Khmer Republic officials to reach safety. He crossed from a farm outside frontier-situated Poipet into Thailand with several hundred followers and subsequently moved to the United States. Perhaps the last holdout was the 130-man garrison in the temple ruins of Preah Vihear, the longtime Khmer-Thai bone of contention perched on the south-facing rim of a sheer sandstone cliff in the northwestern Dangrek Mountain Range. The lieutenant in charge, having led a successful defensive action on April 21, two days later still was debating whether or not to go on fighting, the other alternatives being to change sides or to take his men a few steps north into Thailand.

There is no record of precisely how much Cambodian army equipment fell into Communist hands. However, the K.R. inherited about one hundred functioning and thirty-one inoperative naval vessels. Only those able to motor away from the gulf base at Ream and those attached to the South Vietnamese base at An Long remained free, most of the latter soon falling into North Vietnamese grasp. A hundred aircraft, mostly T-28s and helicopters, were left behind; ninety-seven had flown to Thailand by April 18. Most serious, of course, were the human losses. Estimates of the number of Cambodians killed during the 1970–75 war range from about 180,000 to nearly 1,400,000, mostly noncombatants, out of a prewar population of around 7 million.

The Cambodian equivalent of the U.S. Veterans Administration tried to maintain statistics of military casualties and resultant orphanings. Although they are not complete, they nevertheless are historically worth recording.

	1970	1971	1972	1–8/1973
Dead	403	5,649	6,773	3,852
Wounded	2,741	20,480	10,093	4,502
Orphans	6,726	9,186	10,156	4,114

In Paris, a FUNK politburo official standing atop a platform decorated with red roses said that Cambodia now would have "a new society . . . and this is irreversibly, like it or not." That "new society" included the speedy destruction of the national bank building, the Catholic cathedral, and piles of books and papers. Sihanouk, in Beijing, agreed with his Communist handlers that the "victory over American imperialism and its . . . Phnom Penh lackeys" was "the most glorious in Kampuchea's two thousand-year history." The Cambodian embassy on Washington, D.C.'s Northwest Sixteenth Street was a mission adrift, its flagpole empty and its communication with Phnom Penh nonexistent. Un Sim, its ambassador since mid-1973, publicly was at a loss for words. There also was little that the U.S., preoccupied with the disintegrating situation in Vietnam, could say.

As "General" Dara and the K.R. were playing out their star roles at the information ministry's center stage, the remaining "haves" of the Khmer Republic were in the wings seeking sanctuary at two locations only blocks to the north—the Phnom Hotel and the French embassy. The republican government had given UN and Red Cross representatives permission to turn the city's best hotel into a "protected international zone." Others swarmed to the site until there were hundreds, ranging the social ladder from former officials like Sirik Matak to peasant refugees, both healthy and ailing, crowding the once exclusive interior and grounds. Hundreds more overflowed onto the tree-shaded, lawn-separated roadways in front that connected Boulevard 18 Mars and the hill where legend says Lady Penh started the city. At 5 p.m. that April 17, PNLAFK soldiers shouldered their way through the throng, passed beneath large, balcony-hung Red Cross flags, and entered the hotel lobby. The multistory main structure, its outbuildings, and its grounds, they said, would have to be cleared within half an hour. Most refugees trudged westward to the street corner and turned north onto Phnom Penh's main boulevard to join the masses leaving the capital. Only military traffic was allowed in the opposite direction. Those who dared quickly broke from the river of humans to enter the French embassy compound.

There, Counsel Jean Dyrac (temporarily demoted to vice counsel to distance France from the republican government) was sheltering hundreds of French na-

tionals and foreigners on the grounds and in the compound's three or four buildings. They were joined by additional hundreds of Cambodians, including Matak
and national assembly president Hong Boun Hor (who toted a suitcase stuffed
with dollars). PNLAFK soldiers brought in seven Soviets, who had refused to
leave their own embassy until persuaded by bursts of gunfire splattering its walls
and windows. There soon were more than one thousand persons jamming the
fenced-in compound. Two days after the K.R. takeover, its radio batteries exhausted, the embassy lost contact with the outside. Its food and water supplies
also were seriously depleted. As the days passed, even pets, including a U.S. official's
gibbon passed on to a friend, were eaten.

Communist officers rejected requests for food delivery to the isolated embassy.
They also brazenly ignored the universally accepted convention that an embassy
is inviolable foreign territory. This is now a foreign regroupment center, they
told Dyrac, and all the Khmers must leave. On April 21, with the sun intermittently blocked by drizzle-producing clouds, Sirik Matak walked out, head high,
and boarded a flatbed truck. Hor, hysterical, had to be sedated before being turned
over to his captors. The new regime lost no time in executing officials of the
republican government, a fact they publicly confirmed on November 1, 1975.
Sihanouk aides earlier reported being told that Long Boret and Sirik Matak, the
only ones on the original "seven traitors" list to remain in Cambodia, were shot.
Lon Non, they said, had been lynched by an "enraged crowd."

At the beginning of May, U.S. communications intelligence monitoring of
K.R. radio transmissions picked up actual execution orders from Phnom Penh
and field responses that they had begun. Among the first to die were eighty or
ninety FANK officers and their wives, providing, as President Ford said, "very
factual evidence of the bloodbath that is in the process of taking place." That
bloodbath, as the world was to learn, included not only civilian and military republican leaders but also the educated urban classes and Cambodia's minorities.
The country had strode down the path to war and, contrary to the many who
initially denied its existence, now found itself in the killing fields.

France tried to contact the new regime to arrange an airlift when the K.R.
announced the expulsion of foreigners from the French embassy and other locations. Foreign Minister Jean Sauvagnargues complained that "we have nobody
to talk with. The local authorities seem to be closing themselves in and avoiding
any contact with the outside." The exodus of nearly all the foreigners in Phnom
Penh was to be a 250-mile overland ordeal—two convoys of twenty-five to thirty
trucks carrying about 1,150 men, women, and children. The first group of confinees
emerged from the embassy into a ghost city on April 30; more than two million

people had simply vanished. Doorways and windows gaped emptily. Debris—cars with doors wide open, broken furniture and kitchenware, and riel notes—littered the deserted avenues, along which an occasional soldier bicycled or lined-up troops stood bow-headed in a "thought session." Identical scenes on a smaller scale were presented to the evacuees as their trucks trundled them northwestward generally along Route 5 through Kompong Chhnang, Pursat, and Battambang. The first vehicles crossed the frontier bridge into Aranyaprathet, Thailand, on May 3. The second convoy, including four American journalists, arrived on the eighth. A baby died during the trip.[5]

Angkar (or *angkar padevat*, revolutionary organization), the CPK creation that now ruled Cambodia, remained for the most part an enigma to the world, which found it difficult to believe that there was no puppet master in Hanoi. Military commander Khieu Samphan had the highest profile of the K.R. leadership, with Foreign Minister Ieng Sary coming second. Pol Pot was mentioned much less frequently.[6] Sihanouk, who had given the K.R. the respectability they needed to win, was not allowed to return to Cambodia until September 1975. Khmer chief of state in name only, he was in Phnom Penh for only nineteen days before being shooed off on goodwill tours to the UN and to countries that recognized the new Khmer regime. Once back in Cambodia, he began a three-year existence under Pol Potist control that is aptly described by the title of his 1986 memoir, *Prisonnier des Khmers Rouges*. Not until the early 1980s did the *samdech* learn that five of his children and fourteen grandchildren had been killed by the group he had helped overthrow Lon Nol.

It must have been an exhilarated Pol Pot, now believing himself as invincible as Lon Nol had once felt, who secretly returned to Phnom Penh in late April 1975. Against all odds, his forces had gained undisputed control of Cambodia weeks before his North Vietnamese mentors took Saigon. From temporary headquarters in the downtown railroad station, he prepared to pursue "Year Zero" of the K.R. reign with measures designed to create a pure communist state that would resurrect Angkorean glory. All the trappings of capitalism, including private ownership and money, were to be erased. Monasteries and schools would be shut. Ceaseless paranoia would keep prisons and execution grounds busy. Military, economic, and technical ties with Beijing would be strengthened to assure the continued support of a major power. Toward this end, Pol Pot secretly journeyed to Beijing to meet with Chairman Mao Zedong and Prime Minister Zhou Enlai. Talks also were planned with Hanoi on various matters, especially those dealing with border areas (where North Vietnamese troops remained).

K.R. organization remained as unorthodox as its methods and goals. While there had to be more management control than some chroniclers believe for the insurgency to have succeeded, the Communist administration was decentralized to a degree that was unthinkable by Western concepts. Zone and region commanders enjoyed a great degree of autonomy enhanced by compartmentation and inadequate means of communication and transportation. These facts explain a number of things, among them the frequent uncoordinated military actions that delayed final victory, the variance in the behavior of the K.R. toward inhabitants and Vietnamese allies in different parts of the country, and the inability of the outside world to get a clearer picture of the K.R.

In any case, when Pol Pot reached Phnom Penh, the CPK of perhaps fourteen thousand members had yet to centralize all of the components it controlled to create a workable government. PNLAFK had 230 battalions forming thirty-five to forty regiments and twelve to fourteen brigades, all totaling more than sixty thousand main force troops, their numbers cut by the fierce 1974–75 fighting. Although operational planning for these soldiers was done by a general battlefield committee and actions had become increasingly coordinated, they still were controlled to a great degree by regional commanders and did not become a unified national army until July 1975. Thus it was that, with K.R. forces from various geographical areas entering the capital from different directions on April 17, the first hours of Phnom Penh's takeover were confused enough for "General" Dara to perform his charade unmolested for several hours. Once fully in power and no longer in need of the fiction of a common front with other groups, the CPK changed the name of its armed forces to Revolutionary Army of Kampuchea (RAK), the name they had been given when originally formed in 1968.[7]

In January 1976, a Marxist constitution and a new flag and national hymn were adopted. The first stanza of the national anthem, *Glorious April 17,* speaks for itself:

> *Ruby blood that sprinkles the towns and plains*
> *of Kampuchea, our homeland.*
> *Splendid blood of workers and peasants,*
> *Splendid blood of revolutionary men and women soldiers!*

In addition, the country's name was changed to Democratic Kampuchea.

Sihanouk stepped down as chief of state in April. FUNK and GRUNK were dissolved. Pol Pot openly assumed the cloak of prime minister, the key position in Democratic Kampuchea according to the new constitution. Khieu Samphan was made chairman of the state presidium. Ieng Sary became foreign minister. It was in 1976, too, that the K.R. internal purges began in earnest. These created unrest that led to further purges. Unchanged was Angkar's obsessive secrecy. Little was to leak out to the world about what was going on inside the country. Conversely, little was allowed in, even for the xenophobic leadership. Angkar was to be a self-sustaining organism.[8]

One can only speculate on how different Cambodia's recent history might have been if the CPK had not been carried away by its cocksure fanaticism and dreams of glory. No sooner had the 1970–75 battlefields begun to cool than Phnom Penh turned up the heat along its borders against Hanoi and, to a lesser degree, Bangkok. Conflict in the east was a continuation of the chronic Khmer resentment and suspicion of Vietnam, and probably an attempt to reclaim parts of southern Vietnam that in the past had belonged to Cambodia. Much of the latter could be blamed on the long-term failure to internationally define national boundaries that involved not only the mainland but also islands lying just off the coasts of the two countries in the Gulf of Thailand. With Democratic Kampuchea seeking economic self-sufficiency, it didn't help matters that these islands lay in an area believed rich in offshore oil deposits.

It could be argued that Cambodia merely hurried a clash that was inevitable, since Hanoi had made no secret of its ambitious intention to impose its hegemony over all of Indochina. What is beyond question is that, during the spring of 1975, Khmer Communist troops invaded some Vietnamese islands that Phnom Penh's new rulers claimed rightfully belonged to them. This began a series of indecisive skirmishes, each side using U.S.-made weapons. Intermittent clashes spread along the mainland border area before winding down in mid-1976. Then, in 1977, encouraged by a China increasingly hostile to Moscow-backed Hanoi, Democratic Kampuchea launched increasingly ferocious cross-border attacks against Vietnam. Hanoi capped its retaliation with a multidivision invasion of Cambodia on December 26. When the violently resisted Vietnamese pulled back in early 1978, they took with them thousands of Khmers, many of whom were proselytized into a growing anti–Pol Pot movement. The latter included former K.R. army officers Hun Sen and Heng Samrin, who were to become, respectively, prime minister and chief of state of the subsequent People's Republic of Kampuchea (PRK).

Far less consequential, except to a United States still sensitive to its failure in Southeast Asia, was a controversial incident that resulted in the first open ground engagement between Cambodian Communist and U.S. military units. K.R. PCF (Patrol Craft, Fast) "Swifties" in the Gulf of Thailand were unusually busy during the first days of May 1975. Enforcing Cambodia's newly expanded territorial waters limit (ninety miles), they intercepted Thai fishermen and fleeing South Vietnamese boats, fired at a South Korean freighter, and held a Panamanian ship for thirty-five hours. Captain Charles Miller could hardly have been expected to know all this as he skippered the 10,485-ton U.S. container ship *Mayaguez* on a routine cargo run from Hong Kong to Singapore with a stopover at Sattahip, Thailand. The thirty-one-year-old, single-stack ship was a veteran of the South China Sea–Gulf of Thailand run. On May 12, *Mayaguez* was steaming north-westward about six and a half miles south of Poulo Wai, an island claimed by Cambodia, Vietnam, and Thailand. The island, lying smack in the disputed oil-bearing area, sits about sixty miles from the Khmer mainland.

Shortly before 2:30 P.M., *Mayaguez* was stopped by across-the-bow shots fired from one of the wide-ranging K.R. Swift boats. What followed was melodrama in the best Hollywood fashion, although ultimately much more tragic. Distress calls. Seizure of the ship by the bad guys. Aircraft fired at as they searched for the hijacked vessel. National Security Council meetings chaired by an anxious U.S. president. On May 13, the freighter was ordered closer to the mainland by its Communist captors. It dropped anchor about a mile from the porkchop-shaped north end of Koh Tang (Tang Island). Its captain and thirty-nine crewmen were transferred to fishing boats. The fill-in Ford administration in Washington was determined to rebuild America's Vietnam War–battered image and to avoid a replay of the 1968 *Pueblo* incident, when North Korea seized a U.S. spy ship and held its crew hostage. As a result, although diplomatic efforts were initiated, the emphasis was on a military resolution of this latest incident. The first tragedy came when a U.S. Air Force CH-53C helicopter staging from Nakhon Phanom RTAFB to U Tapao RTNAB, the assembly area for a rescue force, crashed. All twenty-three men aboard died.

American aircraft circling Koh Tang were instructed to prevent any vessels from leaving the island. A Khmer PCF tried on May 14 and was blasted apart by cannon fire from two air force A-7Ds. Efforts to keep the *Mayaguez* crew on Tang Island were foiled, however, when warning shots and tear gas failed to keep a seized Thai trawler from carrying the American captives to Kompong Som later in the day. Although airmen reported "possible Caucasians" on the trawler, the rescue coordinators believed most Americans still were on the island. They also didn't know that the local K.R. commander, after radio conversations with Phnom Penh and a discussion with Captain Miller, had agreed to release his captives early the next morning provided that "U.S. aircraft did not fire or bomb Cambodian territory." However, a three-pronged American military operation already was nudging the point of no return. One element of the operation would reclaim the container ship. A second would invade the island to free its crew. Finally, punitive air strikes would be flown against the mainland from the carrier *Coral Sea,* steaming 350 miles southeast of Kompong Som. The operation went into gear during the predawn darkness of May 15.

After a two-hour flight, Thai-based air force HH-53 Super Jollies transferred men of D Company, 1st Battalion, 4th Marines, to the 7th Fleet escort vessel *Harold E. Holt.* Jet fighters sprayed *Mayaguez* with tear gas at 7:10 A.M. Immediately afterward, *Holt* pulled alongside the freighter. In a modern version of pirate-era boardings, gas-masked marines leaped onto the container ship. It was deserted. The CH-53 and HH-53 helicopters ferrying the 2nd Battalion, 9th Marine Regiment, landing team onto nearly four-mile-long Tang Island shortly after 6 A.M. found themselves in a virtual apian nest. Instead of an expected token hostile force, the landing leathernecks were faced with a formidable enemy garrison backed by impressive weaponry and bunkers. The two landing team assault waves were able to get only 231 men on the island instead of a planned 430 because of the heavy ground fire.

A fierce battle—involving even the guided missile destroyer *Henry B. Wilson,* CS gas, FAC-coordinated jet strikes, AC-130H Spectre gunship support, and the largest of America's conventional weapons (the 7.5-ton "Daisy Cutter" bomb)— raged throughout the day. Meanwhile, three waves of Carrier Wing 15 navy jets, seeing their first combat since 1972, began mauling their mainland targets just before 8 A.M. Kompong Som's fuel and harbor facilities were hit. Nearby Ream's naval base and airfield received a pounding. Five of the K.R.'s twelve locally based T-28s were destroyed. A civilian Convair transport, one of those used during the early 1975 airlift but left behind because of engine trouble, also went up in flame and smoke.

While Washington politicians discussed and directed, and soldiers fought and died, a forty-foot Thai trawler sailed serenely southward from Kompong Som beneath a sunlit sky. At 9:23 A.M., the high-altitude EC-130 Airborne Battlefield Command and Control Center monitoring the combat zone spotted the intruder and directed a naval patrol plane to check it out. At about 10 A.M., *Wilson* nosed abreast of the small craft. On board, freed by the K.R. along with the Thai fishermen they had been holding, were Captain Miller and his crew. The Pentagon suspended offensive action at 11:55 A.M. Shooting on Tang Island did not end until after the last live marine was evacuated at about 8:15 P.M. The battle to free *Mayaguez* had been a costly one. American combat losses were fifteen dead, three missing (and presumed dead), and forty-nine wounded. Three helicopters were destroyed, ten others were damaged. Perhaps fifty K.R. were killed, with more injured. The Communists also lost four Swift boats, five smaller patrol craft, a barge, and five aircraft; another four PCFs were damaged. Less than a month after the short-lived conflict, Vietnamese troops invaded and temporarily occupied Poulo Wai Island.[9]

A sequel was provided to the *Mayaguez* incident over two decades later when an American POW/MIA recovery team visited Koh Tang aboard what probably was the first U.S. military vessel allowed into Khmer waters since the war. Starting with the wreckage of a CH-53 helicopter in offshore shallows, the team began recovering human body fragments. On December 4, 1995, the Khmer foreign minister signed papers to permit the flying of these initial remains to a Hawaiian laboratory for DNA analysis.

Epilogue

Déjà Vu

CAMBODIA'S MODERN TRAGEDY DID NOT END after the war of 1970–75, or even after the killing fields. While considerable blame lies with the outsiders who violated its territory, much blame also must fall on the Khmers themselves, as we have seen. Had Cambodian leadership been less venal and incompetent, the Khmer Republic just might have won its war against the Khmers Rouges. Bribery and other forms of corruption had always been a way of life, but, with the disorder of war and the influx of American largess, it was carried to extremes. Cambodia's soldiers—most of the time greater in number and all of the time better equipped than their enemy, but exploited by their own commanders—proved able fighters lacking only motivation and good leadership. It is very doubtful that continued or increased U.S. assistance would have changed the ultimate outcome; it would have only delayed it. As the late Haing Ngor observed, "Our society had lost its moral direction. And that's why we lost the war."[1] An observation other nations should ponder as well.

If the 1970–75 war was an unprecedented cataclysm, it merely was the road to one of the greatest tragedies of history—the Khmer Rouge killing fields that accompanied the harnessing of an entire population into unrealistic rural projects under brutal supervision. François Ponchaud, the French Southeast Asia missionary who in 1977 authored the first of many books about the post-1975 genocide,[2] concluded, "against my will, that the Khmer revolution is irrefutably the bloodiest of our century." A former U.S. official concerned with Southeast Asian affairs, Karl Jackson, suggested "that in the Cambodian revolution a greater proportion of the population perished than in any other revolution during the twentieth century."[3] The exact number of deaths due to K.R. execution or mistreatment between 1975 and 1979 will never be known.

Estimates run from the low figures of 400,000 or 740,000 discussed by Michael Vickery to the State Department highs of 1.5 to 3 million. Although around one million became the most widely accepted number, later research indicated a much higher figure. A Yale University project, subsidized by the State Department under the Cambodian Genocide Justice Act enacted to support efforts to bring the K.R. leaders to justice, by early 1996 estimated the number of Khmer mass graves to be between ten and twenty thousand, each holding an average of 100 to 250 corpses.[4] In any case, the K.R. genocide certainly ranks with the crimes of Stalin, Hitler, and Mao Zedong.

Democratic Kampuchea's internal conduct defied common sense, but its relations with Vietnam were absolutely suicidal. Having failed in negotiations with Phnom Penh, Vietnam late in 1978 invaded a section of southeast Cambodia to create a "liberated zone" for a Kampuchean United Front for National Salvation (KUFNS). It was a replay of the more sophisticated Viet Cong front. On Christmas Day, twenty-three days after establishing KUFNS, more than 100,000 soldiers, including three Khmer regiments, made a five-pronged thrust across democratic Kampuchea's eastern frontier. The Revolutionary Army of Kampuchea was no match for Vietnam's armed forces. True to form, the K.R. destroyed food supplies and forced thousands of civilians into the hills with them, where more "cleansing" massacres occurred.

Within eleven days, overcoming heavy localized resistance, PAVN controlled the eastern bank of the Mekong. On January 7, 1979, the Vietnamese entered Phnom Penh, which had grown to about fifty thousand functionaries and workers under Pol Pot. The latter fled west in a helicopter, while Sihanouk flew out to China. The invaders continued to the Thai border in two columns. The K.R. reformed as guerrillas in the less accessible sections of western Cambodia and the Vietnamese established the People's Republic of Kampuchea (PRK). An angry PRC in turn invaded northern Vietnam on February 17, 1979, pulling back the following month after conducting a less than fully successful campaign. It was ironic, in light of Cold War history, to see Communist regimes fighting each other.

Hanoi apparently did the right thing, if not for the purest of reasons. Most Khmers were glad to be rid of "the contemptible Pot" and overcame any anti-Vietnamese feelings they may have had to accept the PRK. The new government, Hanoi-dominated and Moscow-supported, restored a modicum of normalcy to the ravaged nation. However, there was enough opposition to form two new anti-Hanoi insurgent movements. One was loyal to Sihanouk, who once more shifted his stance according to the political wind. Son Sann, a former prime minister and anti-Communist who had fallen into disfavor during the Lon Nol reign, was leader of the second. Unfortunately, the K.R. remained the largest and most unified group, receiving continuing aid from China and Thailand, as well as being recognized by the UN as Cambodia's legitimate representative. Once again, the biggest losers in the seemingly endless political and military turmoil were the thousands of noncombatant refugees.

External pressures led to the three anti-PRK insurgent factions uniting in a shaky Coalition Government of Democratic Kampuchea (CGDK) in mid-1982. The CGDK, with Sihanouk as president and the K.R. holding the key positions, was granted Cambodia's UN seat and received aid from China, Thailand, and the West. It was ironic that the U.S., still harboring bitter memories of its Vietnam defeat, now found itself, however indirectly, helping the K.R. The fighting in Cambodia evolved into a stalemate, with both sides relying heavily on mine warfare. The stalemate began turning to the CGDK's favor as various factors, especially the breakup of the Soviet Bloc and its economic repercussions on Hanoi, led to a withdrawal of Vietnamese forces from Cambodia. Before the departure of the last Vietnamese troops in September 1989, the PRK attempted some mostly cosmetic reforms to avoid a revolution and economic collapse. Private property was authorized, the country's new natural resources (timber and gems) were exploited for exportation, Buddhism was reinstated, the national flag was changed, and the PRK became the State of Cambodia (SOC). Once again the course of Cambodian history was decided by outside forces pursuing a multitude of interests.

The United States and other countries pressed for an end to the fighting in Cambodia, among other things encouraging the warring parties to meet. Although the guns continued to bark, a decade of international negotiations finally led to the signing of the Paris Peace Accords on October 23, 1991, by Cambodia's Supreme National Council (SNC, composed of the four Khmer factions) and eighteen other states, including the United States. The SNC agreed to delegate "all powers necessary" to the UN for a transition period necessary to install a new government chosen by nationwide elections. It was to be the world body's most ambitious project to date.[5]

As part of its search for a suitable resolution of Cambodia's problems, the United States in August 1990 conducted its first formal talks on the subject with Vietnam, which remained closely tied to the Phnom Penh government. Then, stressing that the contact was humanitarian and did not indicate a change in relations, Americans spoke to the Khmers about the eighty-three

U.S. military and civilian personnel reported missing in Cambodia. In August 1991, an American team flew into Phnom Penh to discuss the MIA issue and to accept the remains of an alleged U.S. citizen. On Veterans Day that year, Charles Twining, America's first diplomatic representative in sixteen and a half years, arrived at Pochentong to head the U.S. Mission in Cambodia. He was followed three days later by Prince Sihanouk, returning after nearly thirteen years in exile to head the UN-overseen interim coalition government. The U.S. travel ban against Cambodia was lifted the following February. In October 1993, a $9 million low-interest loan was granted to Cambodia by the American-dominated International Monetary Fund. A further $120 million loan was approved the following spring. Also in 1994, Twining was confirmed as the first U.S. ambassador to Cambodia since John Gunther Dean. France, anxious to reassert influence over its former possession, appointed a new ambassador as well. A growing American presence included humanitarian aid representatives and the management of the *Cambodia Daily* newspaper.

The delay in deploying the UN Transitional Authority in Cambodia (UNTAC) undermined its credibility and created a period of instability marked by political infighting, public unrest, flagrant corruption and crime, and repeated cease-fire violations. The UNTAC chief reached Phnom Penh on March 15, 1992, followed piecemeal over the succeeding months by his multinational force of 22,000 soldiers and civilians. By September, the UN's disarmament effort showed lopsided results. While the Sihanouk and Son Sann elements of the CGDK were effectively disarmed, the SOC and K.R. armies remained viable fighting forces with, respectively, more than 100,000 and about 12,000 troops. Despite this setback, hand-slapping the K.R. as "the obstacle to peace in Cambodia," UNTAC decided to go ahead with the elections.

The months leading up to the elections were far from trouble-free. Nevertheless, the K.R.-boycotted event was held in May 1993 with nearly 90 percent of the almost five million registered Khmers voting. Although the royalist party of Sihanouk's oldest son, Norodom Ranariddh, came out ahead of the other nineteen parties represented, political maneuvering resulted in a coalition government with two prime ministers. A new constitution was promulgated in September, and Cambodia officially became a monarchy once more as seventy-year-old Sihanouk ascended the throne as king. He remained a figurehead despite his influence and spent most of his time residing abroad, mainly in China and North Korea.

In addition to overseeing the elections, the UN undertook the repatriation of 360,000 Khmers from Thai refugee camps. The organization also introduced, however temporarily, the spirit of democracy. By mid-November 1993, the last of UNTAC's military component, totaling 15,991 at its peak, had withdrawn. The final increment of the rest, approximately 6,000 civilians (including police), was gone by the end of the year. Only small non-UNTAC United Nations elements remained. The UNTAC effort, initially budgeted at $1.7 billion, was the international organization's costliest to date.

The UN mission, despite its accomplishments, showed two of its parent organization's major weaknesses. UN peacekeeping efforts work only when the warring parties want the UN there. This, of course, has its positive aspects. It can enable the opposing sides to arrive at a face-saving compromise that, however exploited, should enhance the peace process. It also can, by introducing an outside party, allow certain actions to be performed that otherwise might not be. In any case, by not enforcing its will in Cambodia, UNTAC failed to attain all of its goals, especially that of military cantonment and demobilization. In addition, UNTAC was accused of covering up assassinations, anti-Vietnamese ethnic cleansing, electoral irregularities, and other human rights violations in the interest of "the bigger picture."

A second weakness is the UN's inability to police itself while policing others. UNTAC's frequent waste and mismanagement could only contribute to the organization's fiscal problems. For example, more than three hundred UN vehicles and countless goods were sold or stolen, with Cambodian officials sharing in the illicit profits. A reported $189.5 million were wasted in unnecessary prefabricated housing units, never-used vehicles, a radio station more sophisticated than London's BBC, and the refurbishing of the UNTAC chief's house. More visible were the smuggling of arms and other items, drug offenses, rape and child molesting, vandalism and theft, reckless driving resulting in Khmer fatalities, widespread drunkenness, nonperformance of duties, and racism indulged in by UNTAC personnel, especially the civilian police components. A leaked January 1993 UNTAC report stated that Cambodians referred to the peacekeepers as mercenaries who "came here only to collect their salaries." It was a sad story to be repeated in 1996 Bosnia.

In a country whose per capita Gross Domestic Product was $130 and whose per capita income was about $150 a year, most UN personnel were allowed a $130 to $145 a day mission subsistence allowance above their salaries. The affect on the already inflationary Khmer economy was predictable. For example, a Royal Hotel manager said that the price of a room would rise from a daily $17 "to $37 after the UN comes." The cheapest room in the Cambodiana, opened in mid-1990 some twenty-five years after it was begun, escalated to $120. The UN arrival sparked an artificial boom and all sorts of get-rich-quick activities. Phnom Penh grew at the expense of the rural economy. Outsiders, including illegally immigrating Vietnamese and Thai workers, flocked in to profit from the new money. For all this action at the top, daily life for the average Khmer, poor in assets and having little control over his own life, remained virtually unaltered.[6]

A year after the elections, Cambodia was described by a writer who had visited it seven times in 1992 and 1993 as "still a semi-feudal country, a place of bargaining, survival and lawlessness. It is a state of patronage." Major fighting went on between the government and the K.R., which continued to receive outside support. In Phnom Penh, the Communist leaders installed by Vietnam retained the upper hand, apparently playing a waiting game aimed at eroding the monarchy and assuming full control. Divisive political infighting, corruption and other crimes, poverty, and disease were widespread. Human rights enjoyed during the UN presence gradually were suppressed in the presence of a legal vacuum. In March 1995, the government asked the United Nations to close its human rights center in the capital. Five months later, First Prime Minister Prince Norodom Ranariddh said, "The Western brand of democracy and freedom of the press is not applicable to Cambodia."

Because of Cambodia's unending violence—owing as much to corruption, banditry, and political scrapping as to the K.R.—the introduction of foreign soldiers was inevitable. In mid-July 1994, a U.S. Army team began assembling to give the Cambodian army noncombat training and assistance. The forty-four-man Special Forces and engineer team, activated in August, was the first such military mission in Indochina since the end of the Vietnam War. Others were expected to follow, provided the initial effort was successful. Australian and French military teams had arrived earlier in the year. North Korea, long a Sihanouk booster (in mid-1994, the king called the late President Kim Il Sung "my best friend"), agreed to train two Khmer Royal Guard divisions.

Theirs would be a difficult task since the Cambodian military (now called the Royal Cambodian Armed Forces) had changed little over the years. Phantom troops existed as they did during the Lon Nol regime. Personal connections and money determined rank to the point that the officer-to-enlisted-man ratio was incredibly lopsided. Many of these officers sold food, supplies, and medicine to their troops, as well as to the K.R. There was military collusion with civil authorities and the K.R. in schemes ranging from train robbery, extortion, and kidnapping to illicit arms, gemstone, and wood sales. To make ends meet, Khmer G.I.s often forced travelers to pay road tolls, something they had done even before the 1970–75 war. Perhaps worst of all, according to a May 10, 1994, UN Center for Human Rights report, army elements dominated by the Vietnamese-installed Communists eliminated political opponents, real and imagined, of the regime.

In January 1995, visiting U.S. Deputy Secretary of State Strobe Talbott responded to Cambodian requests for substantial assistance, including "lethal military aid," by insisting that the Khmer army first be thoroughly reorganized. In the meantime, American service personnel would continue with such humanitarian tasks as mine clearing. No more fazed by the Cambodian challenge than were the MEDTC teams of the 1970s, one of the U.S. Special Forces officers in Cambodia was quoted as saying, "I'm glad we're getting a second chance."

In 1996, the Kingdom of Cambodia's future could be viewed as a glass half full or half empty. The nation finally was distancing itself from the worst period in its modern history, the killing fields. Its population, over half of which was under fifteen years of age and female, had risen to about ten million. The unrepentant K.R. controlled scattered sections of Cambodia and a small percentage of the population but had become greatly weakened since the 1993 elections.

In 1996 there appeared a major fracture in the long cracking K.R. facade. Ieng Sary—whose ties to Pol Pot were through marriage and the establishment of the most radical element of the Khmer insurgency—followed earlier defections by breaking with the K.R. in August. Pol Pot accused Sary, who controlled several divisions and considerable territory in western Cambodia, of being a "traitor" and "an agent of the Vietnamese" and sentenced him to death in absentia. Sary, in turn, called his former partner "the cruellest and most savage murderer." On September 14, 1996, Sihanouk granted Sary amnesty, removing a death sentence that had been imposed by the government. A number of questions posed by the growing K.R. breakup will be answered only by time.

In any case, Cambodia was experiencing its most peaceful, albeit restive, period in twenty-six years and was open to the outside world. Internationally, the country was looking forward to eventual membership in the Association of Southeast Asian Nations. Cambodia even had an embassy in the United States, opened in July 1995.

It was inevitable that Cambodia's undeveloped economy would attract foreign investors once the kingdom's internal situation achieved a modicum of stability. Favored by liberal laws, investors by 1996 had poured $1.97 billion into the country. Most of the money, a whopping 75.6 percent, was Malaysian. Singapore was the second largest investor, with its Olympic Towers high-rise project rearing above the low Phnom Penh skyline. The capital once more was humming with activity. It was hoped that the financial infusion was based more on mutual national interest than on exploitation abusing Cambodia's new reputation as the region's "discount store." International donors and lending groups, led by Japan, pledged additional millions to help rebuild the nation's battered economy.

Another reason for optimism was the upsurge of tourism, a vital source of income for the kingdom. Also a favorable sign was the reinstitution of old traditions and progress in the restoration of the Angkor ruins, which had suffered further deterioration and theft. Once again, the annual Fall Festival of the Reversing Current, *Bon Om Touk,* could be enjoyed, with boats racing both at Phnom Penh's Four Arms and in the moats surrounding Angkor Wat. December 1995 saw dance troupes from seven countries performing before a floodlighted Angkor temple at a well-attended international Ramayana Festival. One scholar said it seemed "to symbolize the rebirth of Cambodia." The country even assembled a team to compete in Atlanta's 1996 Olympics—the first time Cambodia had been able to participate in the games since 1972.

If there was justification for optimism, there also remained grave problems that Cambodia's rulers would have to face if the nation was to thrive. Absolutism is deeply rooted in Cambodia's history and, given the country's post-1970 agony, an authoritarian government may be needed to span a difficult transition period. However, a tight government hand has to be properly motivated and know when it has to relax if it is to benefit its people. Political infighting was as prevalent as ever, especially over the power-sharing issue, and threatened to splinter the already fragile coalition arrangement between Second Prime Minister Sen and First Prime Minister Ranariddh. As for Cambodia's annual budget, at the end of 1995, 40 percent of it derived from foreign contributions.

Corruption remains the primary theme in Cambodia. Deputy Prime Minister Sar Kheng was quoted as saying that the "Khmer Rouge is not the number one issue. It is corruption." He explained that the government's two hundred thousand troops could not defeat five to six thousand K.R. because of the corruption problem "in our ranks—in our army ranks." In the civilian sector, investors found that accomplishing anything involved payoffs at virtually every level. The corruption gave rise to a level of crime that could exist only with high-level abetment. For example, Phnom Penh became a major money-laundering center. An internal government report in the fall of 1995 stated that nineteen of the capital's twenty-nine banks were suspected fronts for washing dirty money, as were the popular gambling casinos. Interpol's Phnom Penh representative officially stated that of his organization's 2,000 most wanted criminals, between 150 and 3,000 were in Cambodia. The country has extradition laws only with Vietnam.

Khmer officials admit that their country has a serious drug trafficking problem, including heroin moving through to America and other countries. That businessmen, military personnel, policemen, and customs officials were involved in the widespread heroin, amphetamine, and marijuana traffic was demonstrated in the August 1995 seizure of seventy-one kilograms of heroin hidden in a speedboat. The largest Southeast Asian heroin seizure of the year, it resulted in six arrests. One of those arrested, a senior police official, subsequently "escaped." Indications were that, with foreign assistance, Cambodia was working to overcome the problems (weak law enforcement institutions and lack of both an effective justice system and antidrug laws) that encourage a flourishing drug trade.

One of Cambodia's most far-reaching crimes is prostitution. It became a major industry when the nationwide number of prostitutes rose to about twenty thousand to meet the needs of UNTAC's blue berets. Poverty and urban growth were other reasons the number of prostitutes of both sexes in the capital increased a reported 50 percent. Morality and police payoffs aside, there were two especially disturbing aspects to the problem. One was child prostitution. With other Asian countries under pressure to suppress it, Cambodia became a pedophile tourist destination. Of Phnom Penh's estimated fifteen thousand "commercial sex workers" in 1995, according to a survey, 31 percent were under eighteen. The second disturbing aspect was the spread of AIDS. A study found "that 39 percent of [Cambodia's] prostitutes were infected with HIV." In fact, by the end of 1996 the country had the highest HIV rate in the Asia-Pacific region.

Allied with corruption was the plundering of the kingdom's limited natural resources, especially the trees needed to maintain Cambodia's water-dependent ecological balance. In only two decades, about half of the nation's hardwood forests were hewn to profit both sides in the ongoing civil war, as well as foreign exploiters. Another downside of the Khmer picture is the recurring flare-up of confrontations with neighbors. Thailand, more specifically some of its military elements, was accused of continuing to support the K.R. and to be involved in the shady export of wood and gems from western Cambodia. The confrontational issues with Vietnam were smuggling, land, and anti-Vietnamese insurgents. There still is no mutually accepted agreement on precisely where the border lies. Certainly the most publicized of Cambodia's problems is that of land mines. With probably more of the lethal weapons in the country than people, land mines averaged 142 per square mile, according to an October 1995 UN report. One of between 236 and 300 Khmers had fallen victim to the waiting traps by mid-1995.

Many of Cambodia's challenges, including a more even distribution of the increasing economic benefits, will, one hopes, be met or at least relegated to a level that will allow the kingdom to regain respect from other nations, as well as in its own eyes. Cambodia has passed a number of milestones in its journey from independence to the present. There was its development as a postcolonial nation followed by the overthrow of its royal leader after failed attempts at neutrality. Then came devastating engulfment in war and ruination under Pol Pot's regime. Renewed warfare involving Vietnam resulted in a limbo that persisted until the international situation made room for an election.

New milestones await the country's move into the future. One will be the role of the monarchy once Sihanouk is removed from the scene. Always believing only he could "save" Cambodia, he has been a larger-than-life figure to most Khmers, a powerful force even when a figurehead ruler. Assailed by cancer (which Chinese physicians claim to have cured), diabetes, a brain lesion, and arterial problems, and afflicted with a minor stroke in May 1996, the controversial monarch still could find the energy to say of the man with whom he had once made a devil's pact to avenge his overthrow—but whom he now reviled as "our Ivan the Terrible, our Stalin"—"Pol Pot is ill. He is 65, so death may be awaiting him . . . in the not too distant future." Another critical milestone will be the conduct and results of the national elections scheduled for 1998.

Cambodia is moving through a period fraught with many dangers that can be overcome only if its leadership can bring itself to face and learn from the obvious lessons of the failed Lon Nol regime. Whether the United States will play more than a primarily financial support and training role remains to be seen. What is clear, however, especially when one recalls the ignominy of Operation Eagle Pull, is the truth behind the words of American Secretary of State Warren Christopher during an August 1995 visit to Phnom Penh. "No doubt, with the benefit of hindsight, the U.S. could have done many things better in Cambodia," he said. "None of us is fully satisfied with the role of the U.S. in this period. But what we need to emphasize now is the future."[7]

CHRONOLOGY

• 1941 •

April 23   Prince Norodom Sihanouk proclaimed king following death of King Sisowath Monivong.

October 29   Coronation of Sihanouk.

• 1945 •

March 13   Sihanouk declares Cambodia independent of France, promises cooperation with occupying Japanese.

October   French return to reestablish protectorate.

• 1946 •

January 7   Cambodia's status changed from protectorate to autonomous kingdom within the French Union.

• 1947 •

May 6   Constitution promulgated by Sihanouk.

• 1949 •

November 8   France grants de jure independence within the French Union. U.S. and 34 other nations soon afterward recognize Cambodia's new status.

• 1950 •

December 23   U.S. signs Mutual Defense Assistance Agreement with France and Associated States of Vietnam, Cambodia, and Laos, thereby increasing American support of war against Vietnamese Communists.

• 1951 •

September 30   People's Revolutionary Party of Kampuchea (PRPK) founded under Vietnamese Communist auspices after dissolution of Indochinese Communist Party.

• 1952 •

June 15   Sihanouk assumes all powers of Cambodian administration.

• 1953 •

February–
November   Sihanouk's "royal crusade for independence."

November 9   Cambodia becomes independent from France.

• 1954 •

July 20–21   Geneva Agreements officially end fighting in Vietnam, Cambodia, and Laos, and, in effect, France's dominant role in Indochina.

• 1955 •

March 2 Sihanouk abdicates in favor of his father, Prince Norodom Suramarit.

March 24 *Sangkum Reastr Niyum* national political movement formed by Sihanouk.

April 17–24 Sihanouk, at Afro-Asian Bandung Conference, adopts neutralist, anti-American stance.

May 16 Cambodia signs military aid agreement with U.S.

December 14 Cambodia joins United Nations.

• 1956 •

Mid-February Sihanouk's first visit to Communist China, a follow-up to meeting with PRC Foreign Minister Zhou Enlai at Bandung.

March Sihanouk begins program of "Khmer Socialism."

April 24 Cambodia signs economic assistance pact with PRC.

Spring U.S. backs anti-Sihanouk Khmers; South Vietnam and Thailand impose temporary economic blockades of Cambodia.

May 18 Cambodia establishes relations with USSR.

• 1957 •

January *Sangkum* approves making neutrality constitutional law; enacted later in the year.

March One-sided legislative election tightens Sihanouk's hold on power.

• 1958 •

April 2 Secret Washington policy directive states U.S. should "encourage" anti-Communist Khmer elements.

Spring Thailand occupies ancient Preah Vihear temple ruins in northwestern Cambodia.

June South Vietnamese incursion into eastern Cambodia.

July 24 Cambodia grants de jure recognition to PRC, establishing full relations in August.

August Sihanouk revisits PRC, receives more aid guarantees with signing of joint declaration.

September 25 PRC embassy established in Phnom Penh.

September–
October First Sihanouk visit to U.S. since independence.

November 28 Cambodia breaks relations with Thailand.

• 1959 •

January Bangkok Plot against Sihanouk exposed.

February 20 Cambodia resumes relations with Thailand.

February 21	Dap Chhuon secession attempt crushed; crackdown on Khmer rightists intensifies.
July	North Vietnam activates military unit to open up previously surveyed Ho Chi Minh Trail; Communist infiltration of eastern Cambodia increases.
August 31	Bomb assassination attempt against royal family.

• 1960 •

April 3	Death of King Suramarit and ensuing succession crisis.
April	Sihanoukville port inaugurated after four years of construction.
June 14	Sihanouk becomes chief of state after 1947 constitution is revised.
August	Communist plot against Sihanouk announced; crackdown on leftists follows.
September 30	Khmer Communist organizational congress convenes; PRPK becomes Workers' Party of Kampuchea and Pol Pot becomes member of central committee.

• 1961 •

| September | Armed clashes between Khmer army and Vietnamese Communists inside Cambodia. |
| October 23 | Cambodia severs diplomatic ties with Thailand. |

• 1962 •

January	First U.S. bombs fall on Cambodia; targeted at Vietnamese Communists in border area.
Early	In anticipation of legislative election, Sihanouk increases oppression of Communists, driving them underground.
November 19	Sihanouk formally requests various countries to recognize Cambodia's independence, neutrality, and territorial integrity.

• 1963 •

January	Nationalization of Cambodia's banking and foreign trade.
February	Pol Pot becomes party general secretary after mysterious disappearance of predecessor; subsequently leaves Phnom Penh for eastern Cambodia.
August 27	Cambodia breaks off diplomatic relations with South Vietnam.
November 20	Sihanouk ends U.S. military-economic assistance effective the following day.
December	Cambodia receives PRC military assistance.

• 1964 •

| January 4–8 | French ministerial visit capped by signing of military assistance agreement. |

March 11	Demonstrators damage U.S. and British Embassies in Phnom Penh.
November 3	Soviet military assistance formally accepted by Sihanouk.

• 1965 •

March 1–9	Sihanouk hosts Indochina People's Conference to condemn U.S. activities in Southeast Asia.
April	Pentagon approves U.S. "self-defense" penetration of Cambodia.
April 28	Demonstrators again attack U.S. Embassy in Phnom Penh.
May 3	Cambodia breaks off relations with U.S.
Summer	Communists begin using Sihanoukville to complement Ho Chi Minh Trail.
Early October	Sihanouk visits PRC and Democratic People's Republic of Korea (DPRK), where he cultivates long-term relationship with North Korean leader Kim Il Sung; relations with USSR cool.
November 21	Pentagon approves "hot pursuit" penetration of Cambodia.

• 1966 •

September	Pol Pot tightens grip on Khmer Communists, including changing organization name to Communist Party of Kampuchea (CPK), following 11-month visit to North Vietnam and PRC.
September 11	First election without Sihanouk's preselection of candidates; rightists gain legislative majority.
October 22	Lon Nol confirmed as prime minister; Sihanouk creates "counter-government" watchdog committee.
December 21	Cambodia severs relations with South Korea.

• 1967 •

January	COSVN, Communist headquarters in South Vietnam, moves from near Saigon to Cambodia.
April	Samlaut uprising begins; Sihanouk blames Communists; Lon Nol resigns.
June 1	Secret U.S. Operation Daniel Boone cross-border activities begin.
June	Cambodia establishes relations with Vietnamese Communist National Liberation Front (NLF)
August 27	North Vietnamese Embassy opens in Phnom Penh, formalizing relations established June 24.
September 11	Sihanouk decries PRC interference in Khmer affairs.
November 2–8	Jacqueline Kennedy visit signals U.S.-Cambodia rapprochement.

• 1968 •

January 4	Cambodia receives major shipment of PRC military equipment.

January 8–12   Chester Bowles mission to Phnom Penh.

January 17   Communist Party's new Revolutionary Army of Kampuchea begins
guerrilla warfare.

February   Formal Khmer-Soviet arms agreement signed.

May 1   Lon Nol enters cabinet as third vice-chairman of the council and defense minister.

• 1969 •

January–   Khmer army operation to drive North Vietnamese out fails as Com-
February   munists increase forces in Cambodia.

March 18   U.S. B-52s begin secret Menu raids on Cambodia.

May 8   NLF representation in Phnom Penh raised to embassy level.

June 11   Sihanouk announces state of war in eastern Cambodia between Khmer
army and Vietnamese Communists.

June 11   Cambodia resumes diplomatic ties with U.S.

June 14   Cambodia recognizes Provisional Revolutionary Government (PRG),
organization created June 10 by NLF to rule South Vietnam.

July   Sihanouk steps down and proposes a Government of National Salvation.

August   U.S. diplomatic mission arrives in Phnom Penh.

August 12   Lon Nol becomes prime minister of newly formed Government of
National Salvation.

September 25   Trade and Payment Agreement between Cambodia and PRC signed.

Late 1969–
May 1970   Pol Pot visits PRC and North Vietnam.

• 1970 •

January 7   Sihanouk leaves for "rest cure" in France.

March 8–9   Anti–Vietnamese Communist demonstrations in Cambodia.

March 11   Vietnamese Communist embassies in Phnom Penh looted.

March 12   Cambodia gives Vietnamese Communists three days to vacate border
sanctuaries.

March 13   Sihanouk leaves Paris for Moscow.

March 14   U.S. ship *Columbia Eagle* hijacked.

March 16   Failed coup against Government of National Salvation.

March 18   Joint legislative session deposes Sihanouk.

Mid-March   COSVN begins move from border area deeper into Cambodia.

March 19   Sihanouk makes popular appeals for return to power; calls for united
political front and liberation army.

March 20
and 23   First coordinated U.S.-Khmer–South Vietnamese military action in
response to Communist attack.

March 21	President Nixon calls for respect of Cambodian neutrality.
March 26–29	Pro-Sihanouk demonstrations brutally quelled by Khmer army.
March 27	Vietnamese Communist embassy staffs leave Phnom Penh.
March 29	North Vietnamese army (PAVN) begins offensive into Cambodia; quickly occupies most of eastern Cambodia.
April	Khmer government conducts anti–Vietnamese civilian pogrom.
April 14	Lon Nol makes international appeal for military aid.
April 23	Initial U.S.-directed aid, with transfer of rifles from South Vietnam to Cambodia.
April 24	U.S. begins Operation Patio, tactical complement to Operation Menu.
April 24–25	PRC sponsors Summit Conference of Peoples of Indochina.
April–May	Khmer Krom troops transferred from Vietnam to Cambodia.
May 1	U.S. incursion into Cambodia begins.
May	Formal U.S. military aid begins with Special Support Group to study needs and with troop training.
May 5	Establishment of FUNK popular front and GRUNK government-in-exile announced in Beijing; PRC severe relations with Cambodia.
May 13	Cambodia renews diplomatic ties with Thailand.
May 26	Operation Menu ends; replaced by Arc Light.
May 27	Military assistance agreement concluded between Cambodia and South Vietnam; diplomatic relations restored.
June	Vietnamese Communists occupy Angkor ruins. First Cambodian War terrorist incident in Phnom Penh.
June 24–27	U.S. and South Vietnam evacuate surrounded Khmer garrisons from northeastern Cambodia.
June 25	Cambodia announces general mobilization.
June 29	U.S. incursion into Cambodia ends.
June 30	Operation Patio ends; replaced by Freedom Deal.
July 24	U.S. Presidential Determination provides $7.9 million for military aid; supplemented by $40 million in Military Assistance Program (MAP) funds.
August 19	U.S.-Cambodian military aid agreement signed.
September 7	Cambodian Chenla offensive begins.
September 12	Emory Swank arrives as U.S. ambassador.
September 13	Chenla offensive blocked at Tang Kauk.
September 25	Khmer army takes Tang Kauk.
October	Pol Pot moves headquarters to central Cambodia.
October 9	Khmer Republic proclaimed.

November 12	U.S. air supply flights to Phnom Penh begin.
December 1	Terrorist bombing of new U.S. embassy.
December 14	First directly war-related cargo via Mekong River reaches Phnom Penn.

• 1971 •

January 5	Congress approves $255 million in military-economic aid to Cambodia; Cooper-Church Amendment enacted.
January 13	Khmer–South Vietnamese operation to reopen Phnom Penh–to-ocean Highway 4 begins.
January 17	First Mekong River convoy arrives at Phnom Penh.
January 18	U.S. announces intent to employ "full range" of air power in Cambodia.
January 22	Communist assault on Pochentong Airport.
January 31	MEDTC activated to take over U.S. military aid program.
February 8	Lon Nol suffers stroke; soon evacuated to Hawaii for treatment.
February 18	Sihanouk's *Sangkum Reastr Niyum* dissolved.
March 2	Communist attack damages Kompong Som oil refinery.
March 2	Another $18.5 million in U.S. military-economic aid approved.
April 12	Lon Nol returns to Phnom Penh.
April 21	Lon Nol promoted to marshal in midst of political crisis.
May 28	Monthlong fight for control of east bank of Mekong across from Phnom Penh begins.
June 6	Khieu Samphan selection as PNLAFK commander announced.
August 20	Operation Chenla II launched.
September 7	Attempted assassination of U.S. Ambassador Swank.
September 20	Communist attack on Phnom Penh fuel storage area.
September 26	Terrorist attack on U.S. Embassy softball game.
October 5	Chenla II forces link up with defenders of Kompong Thom, making successful completion of offensive's Phase 1.
Mid-October	Parliament transformed into constituent assembly; power concentrates in Lon Nol's hands.
October 25–26	Celebrations mark end of Chenla II's Phase 1.
October 27	Communist counterattack begins rout of Chenla II.
December 3	Chenla II officially terminated.

• 1972 •

January 20	French-directed restoration work in Angkor ruins halted by Communists.
January 29	Khmer forces (FANK) launch Operation Angkor Chey to regain Angkor ruins.
February 7	Symington-Case Amendment enacted to limit number of U.S. government personnel in Cambodia.

February 21	Operation Angkor Chey stalls.
March 10	Lon Nol named head of state.
March 18	Lon Nol becomes president.
March 20–21	PAVN assaults Phnom Penh, Prey Veng, and Neak Luong in year's first major Communist action.
May 11	New Khmer constitution promulgated.
May 17–18	Operation Angkor Chey resumes, with limited success.
June 4	Lon Nol wins Cambodia's first presidential election.
June 19	First U.S. Air Force supply airdrop to Khmer army occurs during siege of Svay Rieng.
June 19– July 24	Sihanouk makes first international trip on behalf of FUNK.
July 4–24	FANK completes first phase of Operation Sorya in coordination with South Vietnam.
August 6	PAVN, using tanks and antiaircraft missiles against FANK for first time, counterattacks Sorya forces, making limited gains.
August 11–21	Operation Sorya Phase 2 prematurely conducted to relieve surrounded Phase 1 units; plans to reopen Highway 1 to Vietnam border abandoned.
August 21	Attempted assassination of Prime Minister Son Ngoc Thanh.
September 7–9	Phnom Penh food crisis; U.S. airlift eases situation.
September 17	Sosthene Fernandez becomes FANK chief of general staff.
September 21	Operation Angkor Chey terminated after failure.
September 27	Attempted assassination of U.S. Deputy Chief of Mission Thomas Enders.
October 7	PAVN makes severest raid on Phnom Penh, destroying city's principal bridge.
December 3	Lon Nol launches "Neo-Khmerism" theory.
December 7–27	Major PNLAFK-PAVN attempt to take Kompong Thom fails.
December 31	After year of growth and consolidation, with Pol Potists in ascendancy, K.R. able to take over fighting from PAVN.

• 1973 •

January 6	PNLAFK conducts first significant action without direct Vietnamese Communist participation.
January 27	Paris Agreement signed to bring peace to Southeast Asia.
January 29	Cambodia declares unilateral cease-fire.

February 1	U.S. vice president visits Cambodia and pressures Lon Nol to ease control.
February 7	U.S. air action recommences after 11-day halt.
Late February	Sihanouk leaves Beijing for three-week Cambodia tour.
March 17	Grenade thrown into meeting of striking teachers and their students in Phnom Penh.
March 17	Aerial assassination attempt against Lon Nol; latter assumes dictatorial powers.
March 25	Assassination attempt against leading Lon Nol opponent Tep Khunnah.
March–April	Intensive action to cut lines of communication (LOCs) to Phnom Penh brings PNLAFK into artillery range of the capital; FANK establishes Mekong Special Zone; U.S. conducts mini-airlift.
April 5	U.S. Senate investigators arrive in Phnom Penh; soon bare active embassy air support role, especially during Vietnam-to-Thailand move of U.S. Air Force support facilities.
April 9	U.S. Army Vice Chief of Staff Haig increases pressure on Lon Nol to "democratize" during visit.
April 11	Sihanouk returns to Beijing after Hanoi stopover following Cambodia tour.
April 24	Lon Nol responds to U.S. pressure by creating High Political Council.
April 25	K.R. advance across Mekong from Phnom Penh begins monthlong fight; U.S. Embassy evacuation alert.
April 30	Lon Non, Nol's controversial brother, leaves for extended visit to U.S. and France.
May 10	Sihanouk begins 56-day tour of Africa and East Europe.
May 30	Mass release of royal family members arrested after March 17 assassination attempt and earlier.
Mid-1973	PNLAFK takes over virtually all fighting in Cambodia from PAVN-PLAF.
June 13	Sosthene Fernandez becomes FANK commander-in-chief.
June 30	President Nixon signs PL 93-52, setting August 15 cutoff of all U.S. military action in Indochina.
July 16	Cambodia institutes compulsory military service.
August 6	Accidental B-52 bombing of Neak Luong.
August 15	U.S. bombing in Cambodia ceases.
August 16	Battle for Kompong Cham, Cambodia's third largest city, begins.
September 4	Ambassador Swank gives farewell press conference.
October 4	Kompong Cham battle ends in FANK victory.

	October
25–30	Operation Thunderstrike, first major Khmer air offensive.
November 3	Sihanouk family members leave Phnom Penh for Beijing.
November 7	Congress passes War Powers Resolution over Nixon veto.
November 9	Sihanouk announces transfer of GRUNK to Cambodia.
November 19	Second aerial assassination attempt against Lon Nol.
December 23	PNLAFK begins two-month assault on Phnom Penh with intensive bombardment.

• 1974 •

January 6	Assassination attempt against Sosthene Fernandez.
January 9	Neutralist Son Sann formally asks Lon Nol to step down.
February	FANK provincial operations bring thousands of peasants back under government control.
Late February	PNLAFK switches main effort from Phnom Penh to capital's LOCs and provincial capitals.
February 26	PNLAFK assault on Kampot begins.
March 3	PNLAFK assault on Oudong begins.
March 6	New Khmer army draft drive begins.
March 8	Mass pro-Sihanouk, anti–Pol Pot K.R. defection to government side.
March 18	PNLAFK occupies Oudong.
March 28	GRUNK Deputy Prime Minister/PNLAFK commander Khieu Samphan begins 77-day Asia–East Europe–Africa trip.
March 31	New U.S. ambassador, John Dean, arrives in Phnom Penh.
March 31	Lon Nol dissolves High Political Council upon resumption of two-chamber parliament.
April 1	Lon Nol creates executive council.
April 21	PNLAFK blocks Sap River between Tonle Sap Lake and Phnom Penh.
April 26	Apparent assassination attempt against Prime Minister Long Boret.
April 30	PNLAFK begins siege of Lovek.
May 1	Battle for Kampot ends in FANK victory.
May 20	PNLAFK attacks Kompong Seila, beginning war's longest sustained siege.
May 26	PRC announces open-end military agreement with K.R.
May 28	Khmer navy reopens Sap River.
June 5	Khmer education ministry officials assassinated after being taken hostage by student protesters.
June 12	Lovek garrison breaks siege.
June 13	Khieu Samphan receives head of state treatment from PRC at end of three-continent tour.

June 29	FANK retakes Oudong.
June 30	U.S. supply of materiel to Khmer air force ends.
Mid-1974	Aerial resupply of Phnom Penh becomes major military-civilian operation owing to growing effectiveness of Communist harassment of other LOCs.
August 9	President Nixon resigns.
August 21	FANK initiates offensive for control of Bassac River southeast of Phnom Penh.
August 23	Khmer army begins Operation 802 in Siem Reap area.
September 21	Lon Non returns to Phnom Penh.
Late September	FANK Bassac River campaign stalemates.
October 3	Operation 802 ends in PNLAFK victory.
October 7	Regular U.S. military noncombat air activity in Cambodia ceases.
November 10	PNLAFK launches two weeks of major attacks against Phnom Penh's northern defenses.
December 18	U.S. Foreign Assistance Act limits aid to Cambodia.
December 31	FANK terminates Bassac River operation.

• 1975 •

January 1	PNLAFK launches final offensive against Phnom Penh.
January 26	Last Mekong convoy reaches Phnom Penh, leaving city dependent on massive airlift.
February 21	Student anti-Chinese riots in Phnom Penh and Battambang, Cambodia's second largest city.
February 26	PNLAFK recaptures Oudong.
March 5	PNLAFK advance brings Pochentong Airport into artillery range.
March 12	Sak Sutsakhan replaces Fernandez as FANK commander.
April 1	Lon Nol leaves Cambodia; Saukham Khoy becomes acting president.
April 1	PNLAFK captures Neak Luong.
Early April	Long-besieged Kompong Seila falls as garrison survivors are helicoptered out.
April 4–10	Fixed-wing aircraft evacuation of U.S. Embassy personnel from Pochentong.
April 8	Prime minister Long Boret holds futile peace talks with Khmer Rouge representatives in Bangkok.
April 12	Operation Eagle Pull evacuates last U.S. Embassy personnel and Acting President Khoy.
April 12	Khmer Supreme Committee assumes power.

April 13	Sak Sutsakhan named committee president; peace offer made to Sihanouk.
April 14	Aerial assassination attempt against Khmer cabinet.
April 14	U.S. airlift into Pochentong ends.
April 15	PNLAFK overruns Phnom Penh's last major defenses.
April 16	Khmer government makes final cease-fire offer and prepares move to northwestern Cambodia.
April 17	K.R. enters Phnom Penh; begins evacuation of inhabitants.
April 30–May 8	Overland evacuation of French Embassy occupants to Thailand.
May 12–15	*Mayaguez* incident.

NOTES

Sources for this book fall into four categories: author information, interviews, documents, and published material. The first encompasses personal experience and all that implies, including, as stated in the preface, firsthand observations and notes, documents and other papers perused before undertaking research for this book, and information provided by innumerable persons over an extended period of time. Although "author information" material is used throughout the text, it does not lend itself to formal attribution criteria and therefore is not reflected in the following listings. Instead, since I was obliged to submit this manuscript to government review, where possibly sensitive material appears in the text, in this Sources and Notes section I cite sources that (to use Scott Breckinridge's bibliographical commentary in his 1993 memoir *CIA and the Cold War*) "demonstrate that the topic in question is in the 'public domain' and therefore publishable." This factor is the primary reason for the great number of published sources cited below. I believe readers, especially those familiar with the secrecy aspects of government employment and the unevenness of the document declassification process, will understand. I have been as specific as possible within these limitations.

The initial interviews for this book more accurately fall within the "author information" source category since at the time they occurred I had no idea they would contribute to its writing. The interviewees were, of course, the Cambodians—pro- and anti-government and neutral—who became the sources for the dozens of reports I produced to help inform Washington of the situation in Cambodia. Faced with time and space limitations, I decided that a few selected present-day interviews would serve to fill gaps in and flesh out my information. I focused on participants whose knowledge of the Cambodian War has received little attention. Meeting with those who already have been widely published or quoted admittedly would have been fruitful but probably would have added little new except detail. For the cooperation of those who unselfishly gave me their time and effort and showed me their personal papers—especially Andrew Antippas, Mark Berent, and William Harben —I am truly grateful.

As noted in the preface, I had access in Cambodia and elsewhere to documents produced by the Khmer, American, and French representatives of numerous agencies. Fortunately for me, the Cambodian documents were in French, the language of pre-1975 Khmer officialdom. I also was shown captured documents, which were translated for me. A principal K.R. document, the *Livre Noir,* is available in French and English. Other documents consulted for this book ran the gamut from diary-type journals and oral histories to field communications and formal papers, the latter two either unclassified or shaken free under the Freedom of Information Act. Obviously, many Khmer documents of the pre-1975 period are unavailable because the wartime Pol Pot organization was not an archive-keeping institution and its anti-intellectual drive for "purity" wreaked havoc with the libraries and files it inherited. While a number of federal and private institutions provided documentary contributions to this book, the most responsive were, on the government side, the Army Military History Institute, the Library of Congress, the Marines Corps Historical Center, and the State Department, and, in the private sector, the National Security Archives and the Vietnam Veterans of America Foundation.

I consulted many hundreds of published sources that ran the gamut from primary accounts by participants and historical works to secondary source books, magazines, and newspapers. Articles in the latter two, especially those written by eyewitnesses, can provide a valuable complement to other sources when used judiciously.

PROLOGUE: OPERATION EAGLE PULL

1. Principal sources for description of the evacuation were *The Vietnam-Cambodia Emergency 1975, Part 4, Cambodian Evacuation: Testimony of John Gunther Dean* (Washington, D.C.: Special Subcommittee on Investigations, U.S. House International Relations Committee, May 5, 1976); Brig. General William Palmer, *End of Tour Report, MEDTC, 1974–1975,* Apr. 30, 1975; David Whipple, interview with author, McLean, Virginia, Aug. 25, 1994; Col. Sydney Batchelder, Jr. and Maj. David Quinlan, "Operation Eagle Pull," *The Marines in Vietnam, 1954–1973: An Anthology and Annotated Bibliography;* Maj. George Dunham and Col. David Quinlan, *U.S. Marines in Vietnam: The Bitter End, 1973–1975;* and Edward Marolda and G. Wesley Pryce III, *A Short History of the United States Navy and the Southeast Asia Conflict, 1950–1975.* Whipple is a former high-ranking U.S. government official who served in Africa and in Europe, as well as in Asia. He retired in 1985 and, at the time of the interview, was director of the Association of Former Intelligence Officers.

2. Operation Frequent Wind is described in, among numerous works on the Vietnam conflict, David Butler, *The Fall of Saigon;* Clark Dougan and David Fulghum, *The Vietnam Experience: The Fall of the South;* Stanley Karnow, *Vietnam: A History;* Frank Snepp, *Decent*

Interval; Olivier Todd, *Cruel April;* and in the previously cited Marine histories by Batchelder and Quinlan, and Dunham and Quinlan.

3. Whipple interview; Arnold Isaacs, *Without Honor,* p. 276; Lt. Gen. Sak Sutsakhan, *The Khmer Republic at War and the Final Collapse,* pp. 162–63; William Shawcross, *Sideshow,* p. 361; and contemporary media reporting.

4. Whipple interview; Dougan and Fulghum, *The Vietnam Experience,* p. 122; Shawcross, *Sideshow,* p. 362; Todd, *Cruel April,* p. 260; and Denis Warner, *Certain Victory,* p. 207. Indicative of Matak's relationship with the U.S. Embassy, the ambassador, in a 1972 cable to Washington, used such phrases as "the comprehension Sirik Matak has invariably shown for our policies" and "the cooperative relationships we have enjoyed with him" (Phnom Penh Cable, henceforth PPC, no. 1712, Mar. 23, 1972). While Washington and many of the embassy staff favored Matak, others preferred another former prime minister, In Tam, whom they saw as more in touch with reality and the public.

5. PPC no. 6136 (Apr. 12, 1975).

6. Physical feature descriptions in the prologue derive from author observation; U.S. Marine Corps aerial and ground photographs; and maps (Sheet 5945, Series L7O11, *Phnom Penh,* U.S. Army Map Service; and *Ville de Phnom Penh,* SG/FARK, 1966).

7. Dougan and Fulghum, *The Vietnam Experience,* p. 122; Isaacs, *Without Honor,* p. 277; Arnold Isaacs, Gordon Hardy, and MacAlister Brown, *The Vietnam Experience: Pawns of War,* pp. 111–12; Sydney Schanberg, *The Death and Life of Dith Pran,* pp. 11–32; Todd, *Cruel April,* pp. 260–61; and contemporary media reporting. Ironically, Schanberg was one of the majority of journalists who initially doubted the possibility, foreseen by the embassy, of the Khmer Communist bloodbath. Days before the fall of Phnom Penh, he wrote that "it is difficult to imagine how their [the people of Indochina] lives could be anything but better with the Americans gone."

8. The ambassador's departure description is based on Whipple interview; Isaacs, *Without Honor,* p. 277; Shawcross, *Sideshow,* p. 363; and Marine Corps photographs. A country team was a coordinating body of embassy officers headed by the chief of the diplomatic mission (normally the ambassador) and consisting of the senior members of each represented agency.

CHAPTER 1. A LAND AND ITS PEOPLE

1. David Chandler, *A History of Cambodia,* pp. 13–27; and D. G. E. Hall, *A History of South-East Asia,* pp. 24–33. Readers interested in the history of Cambodia also should see Ian Mabbett and David Chandler, *The Khmers.*

2. The description of Cambodia derives from Department of State Airgram 363, July 3, 1965; David Chandler, *The Land and People of Cambodia;* Russell Ross, *Cambodia: A Country Study;* Donald Whitaker et al., *Area Handbook for the Khmer Republic; Encyclopaedia Britannica;* and U.S. government *Map 77156 7-70.* Uncontrolled deforestation over the years has considerably reduced Cambodia's wooded area and has contributed to increased erosion problems.

3. Chandler, *History,* pp. 11–34; and Ross, *Cambodia,* pp. 3 and 6–9. Illustrative of the haziness of early Cambodian history, Chandler and Ross start the Chenla period with the

seventh century, while David Albin and Marlowe Hood, *The Cambodian Agony*, give the sixth century.

4. The following were consulted for the Angkor period: Albin and Hood, *The Cambodian Agony;* K. Branigan, *The Atlas of Archaeology;* Chandler, *History;* Bruno Dagens, *Angkor: Heart of an Asian Empire;* Michio Fujioka, *Angkor Wat;* Bernard Groslier, *Indochina;* Hall, *History;* W. R. Moore, "Angkor: Jewel of the Jungle," *National Geographic,* Apr. 1960; Ross, *Cambodia;* Peter White, "Ancient Glory in Stone," *National Geographic,* May 1982; and articles in *Historia* no. 545, May 1992.

5. Chandler, *History,* pp. 77–89 and 94–98; Hall, *History,* pp. 233–37, 293, 337, 340, 395, 398–400 and 411–12; Charles Meyer, "Le Cours de l'Histoire," *Historia,* May 1992, pp. 55–59; Ross, *Cambodia,* pp. 12–13; and Whitaker, *Area Handbook,* pp. 28–30.

6. The discussion of Cambodian culture and character is based on author observations and interpretations, and on such works as Sanglim Bit, *The Warrior Heritage,* and the Chandler books.

CHAPTER 2. THE FRENCH CONNECTION

1. Description of nineteenth-century events derives largely from Bit, *The Warrior Heritage,* pp. xvi and 13; Malcolm Caldwell and Lek Tan, *Cambodia in the Southeast Asian War,* pp. 11–13; Chandler, *History,* pp. 140–52; Michael Edwardes, *The West in Asia: 1850–1914,* pp. 55–59, 63, 113 and 176–77; John Fairbank, Edwin Reischauer, and Albert Craig, *East Asia: The Modern Transformation,* pp. 452–55; Hall, *History,* pp. 615–18, 628–29, 634, and 664; Meyer, *Historia,* p. 59; Milton Osborne, *The French Presence in Cochinchina and Cambodia,* pp. 355–74, and *Southeast Asia,* pp. 86–87; and Ross, *Cambodia,* pp. 16–20.

2. Notable exceptions were nonviolent tax protest demonstrations in 1916 and the 1925 murder by an angry mob of *Résident* Félix Bardez when he attempted to tighten the tax screws. Rural disorder, including the banditry common to countries with a great city-rural socioeconomic gap, was locally rife but did not directly challenge French rule. In contrast, between the world wars, Vietnam was seething with political turmoil.

3. Twentieth-century events through World War II descriptions are based largely on *Sihanouk's Dossier,* an unascribed and undated booklet most likely published by the U.S. government, pp. 5–7; Chandler, *History,* pp. 151–64 and 167, and *The Tragedy of Cambodian History,* pp. 14–15; Peter Dunn, *The First Vietnam War,* pp. 34, 209, 252, 254, and 267; Bernard Fall, *The Two Viet Nams,* pp. 44–45; Hall, *History,* pp. 689, 691, and 718–20; Ben Kiernan, *How Pol Pot Came to Power,* pp. 1–39; and Ross, *Cambodia,* pp. 20–21.

4. The following were consulted for Cambodia's post–World War II move to independence: *Sihanouk's Dossier,* pp. 7–10; Michael Carver, *War Since 1975,* pp. 106 and 109; Chandler, *History,* pp. 168–78 and 184–86, and *Tragedy,* pp. 14–47 and 57–71; Dunn, *The First Vietnam War,* pp. 34, 62–65, 209, and 252–57; Hall, *History,* pp. 810–11 and 827–30; Kiernan, *How Pol Pot,* chs. 2 and 3; Ross, *Cambodia,* pp. 22–26 and 245–49; and Whitaker, *Area Handbook,* pp. 33–37.

5. Chandler, *History,* pp. 178–83, and *Tragedy,* pp. 34 and 47–61; Norodom Sihanouk, *My War with the CIA,* pp. 55 and 263; and Ross, *Cambodia,* pp. 25, 35–40, and 315–16. Pol Pot's background is described in David Chandler's biography of the Khmer Rouge leader,

Brother Number One, and in Ben Kiernan's *How Pol Pot* and *The Pol Pot Regime.* Kiernan also provides a summary of French-Khmer versus Vietnamese-Khmer fighting in 1953–54 (pp. 132–34 and 140 in *How Pol Pot*). Ross, *Cambodia,* pp. 35–41, offers a concise description of Communist development during the years preceding the 1970–75 war.

CHAPTER 3. THE SIHANOUK YEARS

1. The cease-fire agreement pertaining to Cambodia appears in *Background Information Relating to Southeast Asia and Vietnam* (June 16, 1965, revision), Document 11, Senate Foreign Relations Committee. See also Bernard Fall, *Viet-Nam Witness,* p. 258; Marvin Gettleman, *Vietnam: History, Documents, and Opinions on a Major Crisis,* pp. 135 and 155; and Ross, *Cambodia,* p. 28. The agreement for setting up the International Commission for Supervision and Control is in Gettleman, *Vietnam,* pp. 146–50, the final Geneva Declaration on pp. 151–55.

2. Remark to French General Paul Ely, June 1954, quoted in Chandler, *Tragedy,* p. 72.

3. Chhang Song, interview with author, Washington, D.C., Apr. 27, 1993, and quoted in Al Santoli's oral history *To Bear Any Burden,* pp. 223–24. Pulitzer Prize–winning reporter Malcolm Browne, comparing Sihanouk to Thailand's King Mongkut of the novel *Anna and the King of Siam,* liked and admired the Cambodian leader. He seemed, wrote Browne in his *Muddy Boots and Red Socks,* "an effective ruler for a country where parliamentary democracy was as alien as military or communist dictatorships."

4. A general description of Sihanouk's rule following his abdication is in *Sihanouk's Dossier,* pp. 15–18; Chandler, *History,* pp. 188–95, and *Tragedy,* pp. 77–98; Milton Osborne, *Sihanouk: Prince of Light, Prince of Darkness,* pp. 89–99; and Ross, *Cambodia,* pp. 28–34. Sihanouk's own views are in his *My War, War and Hope,* and *Souvenirs doux et amers.* Sihanouk's books reflect his highly subjective thinking at the times they were written and are not always accurate. *My War with the CIA* was written "as related to Wilfred Burchett," the Australian-born inveterate propagandist for Communist causes who died in Communist Bulgaria in 1983. In the book, the prince attributes virtually all of his woes to the CIA, which undoubtedly wishes it had been as omnipotent as Sihanouk alleges. Sihanouk's heroes at the time were France's de Gaulle, Yugoslavia's Tito, and China's Zhou Enlai.

5. John Gaddis, *The Long Peace,* pp. 89–94, and Harry Summers, Jr., *Vietnam War Almanac,* pp. 193–95. Gaddis quotes Secretary of State Dean Acheson as stating in a 1949 cable that "Question whether Ho as much nationalist as Commie is irrelevant . . . all Stalinists in colonial areas are nationalists. With achievement national aims (i.e., independence) their objective necessarily becomes subordination state to Commie purposes." Gaddis discusses the monolithic-nationalistic aspects of Communism in his chapter 6.

6. Ken Conboy, Ken Bowra, and Simon McCouaig, *The NVA and Viet Cong,* p. 8; Gettleman, *Vietnam,* pp. 193–95; Peter Macdonald, *Giap,* pp. 247–48; Richard Nixon, *Real Peace/No More Vietnams,* pp. 146–47 and 154; and Ronald Spector, *Advice and Supports: The Early Years, 1941–1960,* pp. 303, 315–16, 325, and 327. Diem's broadcast was published in the Vietnamese Embassy's *Press and Information Service,* vol. 1, no. 18, July 22, 1955.

   There still are those who believe that the Viet Cong were largely self-sustaining and independent, though allied with North Vietnam. The V.C., most of whom honestly thought they were "making a revolution for the people" of South Vietnam, were no more free of Hanoi than was the American Communist Party independent of Moscow. As early as 1965, the U.S. government insisted that the V.C. were "inspired, armed and controlled from the North." This was confirmed by Hanoi after the war. Following the 1954 Geneva Agreements, Ho Chi Minh had two primary goals. The first, turning North Vietnam into a Communist state, started during the winter of 1954–55. The second, absorbing South Vietnam by warfare since diplomacy had failed, began in mid-1956 when Hanoi's Communist Party Politburo ordered a restructuring of the cadre cells implanted in the South. These cells, using mostly appeals for reform to recruit non-Communists, multiplied and stirred up unrest.

In late 1960, North Vietnam ordered the creation of a political framework (the National Liberation Front) for the V.C. Hanoi's next step was assuring a tighter grip on the V.C. movement by reorganizing its chain of command with the Southern Communists. The result was a new Central Office for South Vietnam (COSVN) directed by North Vietnam's Politburo and the Central Committee's Military Affairs Department. Initially, the V.C. bore the brunt of the fighting. This changed in the late 1960s because of increased Allied strength and attrition (especially in the 1967–68 campaign and the 1968 Tet Offensive). See, for example, *State Department Publication No. 7839* (Feb. 1965); Conboy, Bowra, and McCouaig, *The NVA*, p. 8; Michael Lanning and Dan Cragg, *Inside the VC and the NVA*, p. 232; Macdonald, *Giap*, pp. 190 and 201–206; and Douglas Pike, *PAVN: People's Army of Vietnam*, pp. 42–49.

7. Major Kenneth Bowra, *Analysis of U.S. Military Assistance to Cambodia, 1970–1975* (Thesis presented to Army Command and General Staff College, Ft. Leavenworth, Kansas, 1983), available in Bowra Unbound Oral History, vol. 2, U.S. Army Military History Institute, Carlisle Barracks, Pennsylvania (hereafter Bowra Thesis); and Ross, *Cambodia*, p. 32. Of the U.S. assistance total, $309.6 million was economic grant aid and $83 million went into military assistance. Technically, U.S. aid to Cambodia dates back to 1950, a year after a Franco-Khmer treaty accorded the Khmers qualified independence. An American military advisory group gave aid to Cambodia, Laos, and Vietnam through the French in response to the Viet Ninh threat.

8. Anonymous U.S. government source; Caldwell and Tan, *Cambodia*, pp. 97–98; Isaacs, Hardy, and Brown, *Pawns of War*, pp. 52–54; and Maslyn Williams, *The Land in Between*, pp. 98 and 220. Caldwell, a British Marxist, was murdered in his Phnom Penh guest house during a late 1978 visit to Cambodia. Williams quotes Sihanouk as saying that "if I must decide between the annihilation of my country by the Thais and the Vietnamese, and the communization of my country by the Chinese, I will choose communism."

9. Craig Etcheson, *The Rise and Demise of Democratic Kampuchea*, p. 231; Hal Kosut, *Cambodia and the Vietnam War*, pp. 8–9; and Robert Shaplen, *Time Out of Hand*, pp. 310–11. Cambodia was a nonsignatory "protocol state" under SEATO. Actually joining the organization would have been interpreted as a violation of the Geneva General Agreements addressing participation "in a military alliance."

10. 1958 PPC Nos. 46 (July 9), 156 (July 29), 278 (Aug. 26), 300 (Sept. 2), 349 (Sept. 16) and

509 (Oct. 25); Chandler, *Tragedy,* pp. 75 and 98–99; Ross, *Cambodia,* p. 252; Shaplen, *Time,* pp. 311–12; and Sihanouk, *My War,* pp. 76 and 102.

11. The two intrigues are the subjects of 1958 PPC no. 533 (Nov. 3), 1959 PPC Nos. 835 (Jan. 19), 922 (Feb. 2), 1037 (Feb. 16), 1091 (Feb. 24), 1151 (Mar. 2), 1188 (Mar. 9), 1248 (Mar. 23), and 410 (Oct. 4), and 1960 PPC Nos. 5 (Jan. 29), and 6 (Feb. 5); William Colby and Peter Forbath, *Honorable Men: My Life in the CIA,* pp. 149–50; Cecil Curry, *Edward Lansdale: The Unquiet American,* pp. 202–204, 214, and 368; Edward Lansdale, *In the Midst of War,* p. 183; Osborne, *Sihanouk,* pp. 108–11; and Thomas Powers, *The Man Who Kept the Secrets,* pp. 98–99; as well as Sokhom Hing, "The CIA Against Cambodia," in Howard Frazier, *Uncloaking the CIA,* pp. 83–84; and Sihanouk, *My War,* pp. 104–11. In a 1994 interview, former CIA Saigon station chief and later CIA director William Colby said that the South Vietnamese president's "people spent most of the time in '59 trying to stir up trouble in Cambodia . . . and we spent a lot of our time trying to dissuade them from it." Despite agency efforts, the South Vietnamese "wouldn't pay a damn bit of attention to us. They wanted to do it on their own and eventually they got caught." See Sedgwick Tourison, *Secret Army, Secret War,* p. 18. The Soviet forgery was revealed by Richard Helms, then assistant director of the CIA, in June 2, 1961, testimony before a Senate Judiciary Committee subcommittee hearing.

12. The assassination plots are discussed in PPC Nos. 307 (Sept. 8, 1959) and 253 (Feb. 28, 1961); a pouched U.S. Embassy communication dated Oct. 15, 1959; Chandler, *Tragedy,* pp. 106–107; and Sihanouk, *My War,* pp. 109–13. Chandler places Ngo Dinh Nhu, the South Vietnamese president's brother and adviser, behind the mail bombing. A "clumsy attempt by the South Vietnamese to reassert themselves after the Dap Chhuon affair," according to Chandler, the bomb was intended to kill Sihanouk and replace him with Son Ngoc Thanh. Why, however, if Sihanouk was the target, was the lethal package addressed to his mother? Possibly because the prince usually went through the daily mail with his parents.

On December 10, 1992, a U.S. Special Forces veteran engaged in humanitarian work in Cambodia told the author that he had been asked by another ex–Green Beret to tap Sihanouk for an introduction to a book he was writing about his participation in a plot to kill the prince. The first veteran said he was "not about to ask Sihanouk to write something for someone who had tried to kill him." He provided no further information to allow corroboration or debunking of the assassination attempt claim.

13. 1960 PPC Nos. 1312 (Apr. 12), 1642 (June 20), 95 (Sept. 30), and 126 (Oct. 28); 1961 PPC Nos. 316 (Apr. 13), 67 (Aug. 31), 115 (Oct. 12), 180 (Dec. 8), and 187 (Dec. 15); Albin and Hood, *The Cambodian Agony,* p. 81; and Chandler, *Tragedy,* pp. 115–18 and 335.

14. PPC no. 1686 (June 28, 1960); 1961 PPC Nos. 76 (Sept. 7), 135 (Oct. 27), and 145 (Nov. 3); and Kosut, *Cambodia,* pp. 13–15. As Harry Summers points out in his *Vietnam War Almanac,* "Viet Cong was a derogatory term for Vietnamese communists in the South." The term has been used both all-inclusively and to denote the combat arm of the political National Liberation Front/Provisional Revolutionary Government. The failings of the various South Vietnamese regimes, many identical to the Lon Nol government's, assured widespread support for the Viet Cong.

15. Department of State *Background Notes: The Khmer Republic,* Nov. 1973; Albin and Hood,

The Cambodian Agony, pp. 381–82; Elizabeth Becker, *When the War Was Over*, pp. 115–16; Chandler, *Tragedy*, pp. 130–46; Kiernan, *How Pol Pot*, pp. 205–206; Kosut, *Cambodia*, pp. 14–19; Osbourne, *Sihanouk*, pp. 165–66; Sihanouk, *My War*, pp. 114–16 and 269; and Ross, *Cambodia*, pp. 32–34 and 253, all address the termination of U.S. aid and its immediate aftermath. Kennedy's undeveloped initiatives are discussed in David Halberstam, *The Best and the Brightest*, p. 367; and Chandler, *Tragedy*, pp. 134–35. Taiwan's 1963 attempt at assassination in Cambodia was matched by Communist China five years later. The target then was Yugoslav president Josip Broz (Tito). Khmer security police arrested several Chinese and seized four crates of grenades a few days before Tito's official visit. "They were awaiting the moment of the arrival of Tito, at which point they were going to blow all Phnom Penh sky-high in hopes of assassinating Marshal Tito," Sihanouk dramatically announced after the arrests.

16. Becker, *When the War*, p. 112; Chandler, *Tragedy*, pp. 126 and 338, and *Brother*, pp. 63–64 and 206; Kiernan, *How Pol Pot*, pp. 197–98; and Michael Vickery, *Cambodia: 1975–1982*, p. 200. The Sihanouk quotes are from a transcript of a black-tie dinner toast to U.S. Senator Michael Mansfield at Chamcar Mon Palace on August 21, 1969, during a visit by the Montana Democrat. Illustrative of the conflicting material on Samouth's disappearance, Kiernan blames intraparty clashes, with Pol Pot's involvement, while Chandler leans toward the government as the culprit.

17. Chandler, in *Tragedy*, p. 147, quotes Foreign Minister Nguyen Co Thach of Vietnam as saying in 1978 that the North Vietnamese had told Pol Pot to "support Sihanouk while criticizing him, and maintain a political but not a military struggle."

18. Andrew Antippas (State Department political affairs officer in Phnom Penh, April 1970 to February 1972), interview with author, Washington, D.C., Feb. 7, 1994, and his *The Nixon Doctrine Revisited: The Arming of the Cambodians in 1970* (unpublished National War College thesis, henceforth Antippas Thesis), p. 14; Chandler, *Tragedy*, pp. 141–46; René Francillon, *Vietnam: The War in the Air*, pp. 195, 223, and 245; Kosut, *Cambodia*, pp. 19–32; Osborne, *Sihanouk*, pp. 164–65; Sihanouk, *My War*, p. 269; and *Washington Post*, Jan. 5, 1968, describe the deterioration of U.S.-Cambodian relations. The American embassy, down to thirty-three persons by the end of 1964, had been operating without an ambassador since Philip Sprouse was recalled to Washington in mid-December 1963. Nearly three dozen embassy dependents were evacuated to Thailand on October 30 and November 1, 1964, as "a precautionary move taken against possible anti-U.S. demonstrations."

19. Antippas Thesis, p. 15; John Schlight, *The War in South Vietnam: The Years of the Offensive, 1965–1968*, pp. 40 and 105–106; and Summers, *Vietnam War Almanac*, pp. 202–203. Louis Fisher, *Presidential War Power*, pp. 115–18; and John Lehman, *Making War*, pp. 81–83, address the Tonkin Gulf Resolution. Changing rules of engagement also are in Joint Chiefs of Staff message to CINCPAC, Nov. 21, 1965. The first U.S. bombing of Cambodia appears to have occurred in January 1962, when American-piloted T-28s and B-26s flying from Bien Hoa Airbase in Vietnam hit a Khmer village in the border area known as the Parrot's Beak.

20. Antippas Thesis, p. 16; Bangkok Embassy Airgram 363 (July 3, 1969); transcript of Long Boret statement to twenty-seventh session, UN General Assembly, Sept. 29, 1972; Chan-

dler, *Tragedy*, pp. 8–9 and 188; and Sutsakhan, *The Khmer Republic*, pp. 20–21. During this period, according to a CIA report, the Vietnamese Communists were widely proselytizing Vietnamese Cambodians to their cause, recruiting them as soldiers, support personnel, and spies, as well as taxing them.

21. Anonymous Cambodian source; Antippas interview; Henry Kissinger, *White House Years*, pp. 241–42; Powers, *The Man*, pp. 215–19; Sutsakhan, *The Khmer Republic*, pp. 20–21; and Snepp, *Decent Interval*, p. 20. In October 1967, the U.S. Navy's Market Time sea-monitoring operation was expanded to include intercepting Communist shipping to and from Sihanoukville. Until 1970, the Pentagon and the CIA disagreed on the importance of Sihanoukville to the enemy. CIA compilations, based on factors such as radio intercepts, dismissed the port's role as "marginal." The Pentagon, backed by the White House (given the CIA's perceived anti–Vietnam War stance), considered the seaport important enough to justify military action. Ironically, the intelligence agency discounted information from one of its own agents, who had access to actual bills of lading. Documents found during the U.S. incursion into Cambodia showed that since December 1966 the enemy had brought 23,000 tons of goods into Sihanoukville, more even than the military had estimated.

22. Anonymous U.S. government source; State Dept. cable to Bangkok, Saigon and Vientiane, mid-Feb. 1969; Antippas interviews, Feb. 3 and 7, 1994, and thesis; John Clasey, "Twilight Zone East," *Vietnam*, Dec. 1992; John Newman, *JFK and Vietnam*, pp. 208–10; Howard Schaffer, *Chester Bowles*, pp. 310–15; Shawcross, *Sideshow*, pp. 66–73; and Brian Toohey and William Pinwill, *Oyster*, p. 130. The Johnson quote is from J. Thompson, Johnson Oral History, AC 81–58, quoted in John Prados, *Keeper of the Keys*, pp. 167–68. The U.S.-Khmer Phnom Penh meetings are discussed in the May 20, 1968, Bowles mission report of the New Delhi embassy and in the State Department transcript of Secretary Rogers's briefing of the House of Representatives, July 25, 1973. Rogers, on August 3, 1973, told the Senate Foreign Relations Committee that Sihanouk indicated to Ambassador Bowles in January 1968 and to Senator Mansfield in August 1969 that he had no objection to U.S. bombings as long as they did not injure Cambodians. The prince publicly said the same thing in a May 13, 1969, press conference.

23. Description of SOG and CIDG derives from *Cross-Border Operations, Southeast Asia: 1964–1968—Section 2: Cambodia*, Aug. 7, 1973; *JCS Recommendations and SECDEF Actions With Respect to Cambodia, 1 January 1969–15 February 1975*, Feb. 26, 1975 (hereafter *JCS Recommendations*); *Sensitive Operations in Southeast Asia, 1964–1973*, undated, noncredited Joint Chiefs of Staff document; 1983 Oral History interview of Brig. General Donald Blackburn (1965–66 SOG commander); 1989 Oral History interview of Colonel John Crear (1966–67 SOG officer); and Ron Podlaski, interview with author, Washington, D.C., Dec. 10, 1992. A Special Forces veteran, Podlaski subsequently returned to Cambodia to head the VVAF prosthetics clinic there.

The following published material on cross-border activity also was consulted: Gregory Clark, *Words of the Vietnam War*, pp. 60–61, 163, 206, 263–64, 309–10, 367, 396–97, 412–13, 474, 483, and 505; John Dwyer, "Inside Story," *Vietnam*, Dec., 1992; Kevin Generous, *Vietnam: The Secret War*, pp. 189–92; David Knight, *Shock Troops*, pp. 161–73; Peter Macdonald, *Soldiers of Fortune*, pp. 130–53; Charles Reske, *MACV-SOG History: An-*

nex B (2 vols.); Maj. Gen. John Singlaub, with Malcolm McConnell, *Hazardous Duty,*
pp. 292–316 (Singlaub was SOG commander in 1966–68); Charles Simpson III, *Inside
the Green Berets,* pp. 120–23 and 146–48; Shelby Stanton, *Green Berets at War,* chs. 3–7,
10, 11, 13, and 15, *Vietnam Order of Battle,* pp. 59–60 and 251–53, and *Special Forces at War,*
pp. 204–205, 250–53, 281, 290, 319, and 328–31; Jeff Stein, *A Murder in Wartime;* Leroy
Thompson, *The U.S. Army in Vietnam,* pp. 113–16; and *Far Eastern Economic Review,*
Sept. 1992.

24. U.S. Naval activities directly involving Cambodia can be found in Thomas Cutler, *Brown
Water, Black Berets,* pp. 255–56; Commander R. L. Schreadley, *From the Rivers to the Sea,*
pp. 100 and 158–59; and James Watson and Kevin Dockery, *Point Man,* pp. 271–96.
Watson recalls "pulling about eleven operations in Cambodia" without loss. Instances of
Americans captured and vessels confiscated in Cambodia can be found in Bangkok
Embassy Airgram 363, July 3, 1969, and in contemporary media reporting. The $3.6 mil-
lion rain-making program was acknowledged by the Department of Defense to the Senate Foreign Relations Committee on March 20, 1974. See also Seymour Hersh's article
in the May 19, 1974, *New York Times,* and his *The Price of Power,* pp. 182–83.

25. The B-52 bombing campaign is covered in Secretary of State Rogers's testimony to the
Senate Foreign Relations Committee, Aug. 3, 1973; *Bombing in Cambodia,* Senate Armed
Services Committee hearings, July–Aug. 1973, pp. 231–55; *DOD Report on Selected Air
and Ground Operations in Cambodia and Laos,* Senate Armed Services Committee,
Sept. 10, 1973; Walter Isaacson, *Kissinger,* pp. 171–79; Kissinger, *White House Years,* pp.
240–52; John Morrocco, *The Vietnam Experience: Rain of Fire,* pp. 10–14; Nixon, *Real
Peace,* pp. 217–21; Shawcross, *Sideshow,* pp. 19–33 and Appendix; Tad Szulc, *The Illusion
of Peace,* ch. 3; Earl Tilford, Jr., *Crosswinds,* pp. 125–26; and Truong Nhu Tang, with
David Chanoff and Doan Van Toai, *A Vietcong Memoir,* pp. 167–71. A 1970 North Vietnamese rallier, Lt. Colonel Nguyen Van Nang, told questioners that B-52 targets generally were known "24 hours in advance, although warning time is as little as one hour."

26. Isaacson, *Kissinger,* pp. 212–33; Karnow, *Vietnam,* p. 607; Kissinger, *White House Years,*
pp. 246 and 250–54, and *Years of Upheaval,* p. 340; J. Anthony Lukas, *Nightmare,* ch. 3
and pp. 640–41; Nixon, *Real Peace,* pp. 219–21 and 232–34; Shawcross, *Sideshow,* pp. 33–
35 and 105–108; Szulc, *The Illusion,* pp. 52, 55, and 182–89; Brig. Gen. Tran Dinh Tho,
The Cambodian Incursion, p. 151; and David Wise, *The American Police State,* chs. 2 and 3.

27. Cambodian internal strife and its Vietnamese Communist connection descriptions derive from anonymous U.S. and Cambodian sources; Antippas interviews; Bowra Thesis,
p. 207; Becker, *When the War,* ch. 3; Dennis Bloodworth, *An Eye for the Dragon,* pp.
277–78; Chandler, *Tragedy,* ch. 5, and *Brother,* pp. 84–90; Kiernan, *How Pol Pot,* ch. 7;
Kosut, *Cambodia,* pp. 52–58; Ross, *Cambodia,* pp. 254–55 and 318; and Sutsakhan, *The
Khmer Republic,* p. 59.

CHAPTER 4. 1970: CAMBODIA'S TURNING POINT

1. Becker, *When the War,* pp. 117–25; Chandler, *Tragedy,* ch. 5, and *Brother,* pp. 81–83; Isaacs,
Hardy, and Brown, *Pawns of War,* pp. 85–86 and 88; Kiernan, *How Pol Pot,* ch. 7; Marie
Martin, *Cambodia: A Shattered Society,* pp. 121–22; and Ross, *Cambodia,* pp. 41–42 and

254, address the 1967–68 insurgencies. The *Livre Noir* (Black Book), a modest-sized 1978 publication of the Pol Pot regime, provides an anti-Vietnamese, often inaccurate, interpretation of the Khmer Communist rise to power.

2. Antippas Thesis, p. 21; Chandler, *Tragedy*, pp. 166, 178–79, and 187–91; Kissinger, *White House Years*, p. 458; and Shawcross, *Sideshow*, pp. 113–16 and 424. A decade after his ouster, Sihanouk said that if he lost out to Lon Nol, "it was because I tremendously helped the Viet Cong and the North Vietnamese."

3. PPC no. 136 (Feb. 18, 1970); Antippas Thesis, p. 22; Chandler, *Tragedy*, pp. 185 and 189–93; and Warner, *Certain Victory*, p. 161.

4. Confidential U.S. and Cambodian official sources; William Harben, interview with author, Alexandria, Virginia, Nov. 8, 1994 (Harben was chief of the political section of the U.S. Embassy, Phnom Penh, between January 1972 and June 1973); Antippas Thesis, p. 23; Sihanouk interview, *ORTF*, 2me Chaine television, Paris, March 12, 1970; Kissinger, *White House Years*, p. 461; Martin, *Cambodia*, pp. 122–23; Haing Ngor, with Roger Warner, *A Cambodian Odyssey*, pp. 39–40; Shawcross, *Sideshow*, pp. 117–18; and Warner, *Certain Victory*, pp. 161–62.

5. Paris Embassy cable no. 3010 (Mar. 14, 1970); PPC no. 292 (Mar. 20, 1970); Antippas interviews and thesis, p. 23; Harben interview; *Sihanouk's Dossier*, p. 29; Becker, *When the War*, pp. 131–32; Chandler, *Tragedy*, pp. 195–99; Kissinger, White House Years, pp. 461–62; and Shawcross, *Sideshow*, ch. 8. Interestingly, U.S. astronauts had been scheduled to visit Phnom Penh on March 17–18; their trip was canceled by the Cambodians on March 13.

6. *Discussion of Khmer Insurgent Factions and the Implications for U.S. Policy in Cambodia*, State Department memorandum, March 5, 1973; PPC no. 776 (May 6, 1970); Antippas Thesis, p. 30; *Sihanouk's Dossier*, pp. 35–42; Chandler, *Tragedy*, pp. 197–201; Kiernan, *How Pol Pot*, pp. 298–300; Kissinger, *Years of Upheaval*, pp. 123–26; Shawcross, *Sideshow*, pp. 123–26 and 246; Sihanouk, *My War*, pp. 60–61 and 271; and Sutsakhan, *Khmer Republic*, pp. 25–27, discuss Sihanouk's March 1970 presence in Moscow and Beijing.

In 1971, Sihanouk told an American publisher and former ambassador that he didn't return to Cambodia after his ouster because "I had reliable information that he [Lon Nol] was planning to meet me at the airport, pretend to drive me to the palace and then take me to a wooded area . . . and have me shot." See William Attwood, *The Twilight Struggle*, p. 312. The U.S. beat the FUNK radio station to the airwaves when it learned of its creation. Using a Cambodian with a high-pitched voice to imitate Sihanouk, the Americans inaugurated a bogus FUNK station broadcasting from a clandestine transmitter in Laos. Quickly exposed as a phony, the station nevertheless continued its mischief-making to try arousing Cambodian animosity against the North Vietnamese and FUNK. Some details can be found in Kenneth Conboy, *Shadow War*, pp. 281–82. Sino-Soviet involvement in the PAVN training program is in Phnom Penh Airgram A-5, Jan. 13, 1972. PNLAFK also has been called, owing to translation differences, the Cambodian People's National Liberation Armed Forces (CPNLAF) and PFLANK.

7. Author direct knowledge; State Department cable no. 10883 (July 8, 1970); Antippas interviews; State Department Diplomatic Lists and Biographic Registers; Christopher Andrew, "The Growth of the Australian Intelligence Community and the Anglo-Ameri-

can Connection," *Intelligence and National Security,* Apr. 1989; Alexander Haig, with Charles McCarry, *Inner Circles,* pp. 234–35; Kissinger, *White House Years,* pp. 463–67; Nixon, *Real Peace,* p. 228; Tho, *Cambodian Incursion,* pp. 196–203; and Tooey and Pinwill, *Oyster,* pp. 126–31. With ironic timing, a CIA report making a qualified prediction of a coup was circulated in Washington on the very day of Sihanouk's overthrow. It derived from information garnered a week before. A White House investigation of the intelligence lapse was ordered.

8. Author direct knowledge; Mark Berent, interview with author, Washington, D.C., April 27, 1993 (Berent, a retired USAF lieutenant colonel, was in the embassy air attaché office between 1971 and 1973); Chhang Song interview; and Count de Marenches and Christine Ockrent, *The Evil Empire,* pp. 134–35.

9. Numerous State Department communications, including 1970 PPC Nos. 406 (Apr. 2), 467 (Apr. 8), 2606 (Oct. 3), 2909 (Oct. 31), 2565 (Dec. 5), 3414 (Dec. 15), and 3471 (Dec. 18), and State Department cable Nos. 48647 (Apr. 3, 1970) and 204536 (mid-Dec., 1970); Antippas interview; Hing, in *Uncloaking the CIA,* p. 85; Samuel Lipsman and Edward Doyle, *The Vietnam Experience: Fighting for Time,* p. 141; and Sihanouk, *My War,* pp. 58–59.

10. Author's notes, including a June 1993 discussion of arms gathering with a U.S. Vietnam War helicopter unit noncommissioned veteran who requested anonymity; *JCS Recommendations; Chronology of the Vietnam War: 1966–1973,* 15th Air Force, May 30, 1974; Antippas interview and thesis, pp. 27–29; Kissinger, *White House Years,* pp. 465–73; Nixon, *Real Peace,* pp. 228–29; and Tho, *Cambodian Incursion,* pp. 212–13. Laird's concern and suggestions are from a letter dated March 31, 1970. Indicative of U.S. unpreparedness for the 1970 events, PPC no. 322 (Mar. 24, 1970) stated that "one of the greater dangers [of the] present situation exists in possible clashes between Cambodian and NVN/VC troops."

11. The discussion of unofficial U.S. involvement derives from confidential U.S. government source; Antippas interviews, Feb. 3, Oct. 5, and Dec. 1, 1994; T.D. Allman, *Unmanifest Destiny,* pp. 338–43; Hersh, *The Price,* pp. 177–83; Kiernan, *How Pol Pot,* pp. 300–302, and "The Impact on Cambodia of the U.S. Intervention in Vietnam," in J. Werner and L. Huynh, *The Vietnam War,* pp. 219–21; Osborne, *Sihanouk,* pp. 209–10; Shawcross, *Sideshow,* pp. 120–22; Sihanouk, *Souvenirs,* p. 379; and Snepp, *Decent Interval,* p. 19. The Thanh interview was conducted by Henry Bradsher and printed in the *Washington Star-News,* July 29, 1973. It has been suggested (Chandler, *Tragedy,* pp. 193–94) that Nol's contact with Thanh, approved by Sihanouk, was aimed at recruiting Khmers Kroms to fight the Vietnamese Communists in Cambodia. However, the prince was said to have vehemently refused Nol's request for "additional troops to stand up to Vietnamese infiltration." See p. xxiii in Sihanouk, *War and Hope.*

12. Confidential U.S. government source; PPC no. 386 (Mar. 30, 1970); Harben interview; Bowra Thesis, p. 3; Kissinger, *White House Years,* pp. 465–66; Kosut, *Cambodia,* pp. 60–61 and 63–64; Macdonald, *Giap,* p. 326; Ngor, *Cambodian Odyssey,* pp. 41–42; Barry Rubin, *Secrets of State,* pp. 155–56; Sutsakhan, *Khmer Republic,* pp. 14–15 and 59–60; and Tho, *Cambodian Incursion,* pp. 151–53 and 205–207.

1. The preceding chapter paragraphs derive primarily from Nol to Nixon letter dated Nov. 13, 1971; PPC no. 410 (Apr. 2, 1970); Chandler, *Brother*, pp. 88–91; Conboy, Bowra, and McCouaig, *NVA*, pp. 11–12; Kiernan, *How Pol Pot*, pp. 300–303; Kissinger, *White House Years*, pp. 469, 472–73, and 475; Kosut, *Cambodia*, pp. 72–76 and 190; Powers, *Man*, pp. 217–19; Sutsakhan, *Khmer Republic*, pp. 28, 32–49, and 61; and Tho, *Cambodian Incursion*, p. 153. The 5th, 7th, and 9th Divisions originally were PLAF, but devastating losses during the 1968 Tet Offensive caused them to be reconstituted with mostly North Vietnamese replacements. FANK's six numbered military regions as of 1971 were: 1, southeastern three provinces and part of Kandal Province; 2, southwestern four provinces; 3, west central three provinces; 4, north central four provinces; 5, northeastern two provinces; and 6, east central two provinces. There were, in addition, the Phnom Penh Special Military Zone and the Mekong Special Zone, including most of Kandal Province.

2. Etcheson, *Rise and Demise*, p. 237; Kissinger, *White House Years*, pp. 467–86 and 492; and Kosut, *Cambodia*, pp. 67–69.

3. Author direct knowledge; Berent interview, Sept. 28, 1993; Chris Doyle, "What Happened to Sean Flynn?" *Soldier of Fortune*, Jan. 1991; "Le Fantôme de Sean Flynn," *Paris Match*, Apr. 11, 1991; *New York Times*, June 11, 1974; and *Washington Post*, Oct. 6, 1991. Flynn became the model for the hero of one novel (Jean Larteguy's *Enquête sur un crucifié*) and the villain in others (Mark Berent's novels).

4. Author direct knowledge; 1970 PPC Nos. 1483 (July 3), 1484 (July 3), 1495 (July 5), and 1673 (July 21); Chandler, *Tragedy*, pp. 203–204; Kosut, *Cambodia*, pp. 76–85; *Realités cambodgiennes*, Apr. 24, 1970; and contemporary media reporting.

5. The controversial Cambodian incursion has been widely covered. See, for example, J. D. Coleman, *Incursion*; Keith Nolan, *Into Cambodia*; and Tho, *Cambodian Incursion*. The following were also consulted on the subject: *JCS Recommendations*; Cutler, *Brown Water*, pp. 310–11; Lt. Gen. Phillip Davidson, *Vietnam at War*, pp. 624–31; Kissinger, *White House Years*, pp. 489–520 and 986; Kosut, *Cambodia*, pp. 99–119 and 184–85; Lehman, *Making War*, pp. 88–89; Marolda and Pryce, *Short History*; Nixon, *Real Peace*, pp. 227–38; Truong Nhu Tang, *Viet Cong Memoir*, pp. 176–77; and Boston Publishing Company editors, *The Vietnam Experience: War in the Shadows*, pp. 147–48. Nixon's announced 30-kilometer (18.6-mile) limit for penetrating into Cambodia translated into just over 21 miles during the fighting.

   The admission of secret B-52 raids is in Secretary of Defense James Schlesinger's July 16, 1973, letter to the Senate Armed Services Committee. The Patio and Freedom Deal operations are explained in the JCS document *Sensitive Operations in Southeast Asia: Department of Defense Report on Selected Air and Ground Operations in Cambodia and Laos*, Sept. 10, 1973; *Situation Report on Cambodia*, a State Department INR Intelligence Brief dated May 9, 1970; and the Senate's *Bombing in Cambodia*, pp. 175, 361, 482, and 490–91.

6. Description of the U.S. assistance role derives from PPC no. 2185 (Aug. 27, 1970); Brig. General Theodore Mataxis, *End of Tour Report, MEDTC*, Feb. 12, 1972, p. 1; Antippas

interviews and thesis, pp. 35, 38–47, and 54; Frank Margiotta, a 7th Air Force officer on his second tour in Vietnam between September 1970 and August 1971 and subsequently president-publisher at Brassey's (U.S.), interview with author, McLean, Virginia, June 29, 1993; General Yarborough, Oral History interview transcript, Apr. 22, 1975; Bowra Thesis, pp. 10–11, 52–55, 188–90, and Annex E; and the following published works: Kenneth Conboy and Kenneth Bowra, *The War in Cambodia: 1970–1975*, p. 6; Kissinger, *White House Years*, pp. 518–19; Stanton, *Green Berets*, pp. 283–91, and *Special Forces*, pp. 342–43, 354–55, and 357; Sutsakhan, *Khmer Republic*, pp. 50–52 and 55; Tho, *Cambodian Incursion*, pp. 13–14, 32, 118–20, and 223–26; and *Register of Graduates and Former Cadets: 1912–1991*, published by the USMA's Association of Graduates.

    Fred Ladd was described as a "first-class military maverick [who] tried to tell it like it was" in Vietnam. Mark Berent, in a September 1993 interview with the author, confirmed the opinion expressed in a *Vietnam* magazine (June 1993 issue) interview that Ladd was "the only guy in the whole embassy with his head screwed on right." David Halberstam, in *The Best and the Brightest* (London Pan edition), pp. 231–32, called Ladd "typical of the best of the American officers in Vietnam," and an "intelligent, humane, sophisticated officer" who was neither a hawk nor a dove, but thought it was possible to win the war. When Ladd died in Arlington, Virginia, on August 18, 1987, his last words, as recalled by Berent, were, "Bring my horse, I'm going to be knighted."

7. Author direct observation; Antippas Thesis, pp. 35–36 and Appendix B; Conboy, *Shadow War*, pp. 281 and 284; Kosut, *Cambodia*, pp. 112, 116–18, and 137–39; and Tho, *Cambodian Incursion*, pp. 156–58.

8. The fate of the three U.S. fliers is from a French military intelligence *compte rendu* (report) of the rallier's interrogation, dated Jan. 11, 1972. The report rates the rallier as "probably truthful," with verification by a second unnamed source.

9. Information on Pol Pot and internal K.R. developments is from direct author knowledge, including 1971 refugee and rallier interviews in Cambodia; U.S. Embassy Airgram A-5, dated Jan. 13, 1972, pp. 4–5; Chandler, *Brother*, pp. 91–94; and Kiernan, *How Pol Pot*, pp. 308–22.

10. 1970 PPC Nos. 1004 (May 23), 1067 (May 30), 1217 (June 11), 1333 (June 21), 1395 (June 25), and 2133 (Aug. 24); *Cambodian Cabinet Reshuffle*, State Department memorandum, dated July 1, 1970; Colonel Gene Gurney, *Vietnam: The War in the Air*, p. 250; Kosut, *Cambodia*, pp. 101–16; Lipsman and Doyle, *Fighting For Time*, pp. 174–77; Sutsakhan, *Khmer Republic*, pp. 62–69; and Tho, *Cambodian Incursion*, pp. 100–105, 122–24, and 225–27, except for the material covered by the two preceding notes. A colorful account of the fighting in Siem Reap is in Robert Anson, *War News*, ch. 14. Anson, a *Time* correspondent, was one of a number of journalists to be captured and subsequently released by the Communists.

11. Chenla and subsequent military operations are discussed in 1970 PPC Nos. 1333 (June 21), 2297 (Aug. 6), 2325 (Sept. 8), 3217 (Sept. 11), 3234 (Dec. 1), 3248 (Dec. 2), 3424 (Dec. 15), 3440 (Dec. 16), and 3470 (Dec. 18); CINCPAC-to-CJCS cable no. 7738, dated June 1, 1972; the JCS *Sensitive Operations in Southeast Asia*; Kosut, *Cambodia*, pp. 199–208; Sutsakhan, *Khmer Republic*, pp. 69–71; Tho, *Cambodian Incursion*, pp. 230–31; and contemporary media reporting. Although the White House said that its use of air power in

Cambodia after the incursion would be restricted to interdiction against threats to American forces in Vietnam, U.S. aircraft continued to fly in direct support of FANK and ARVN troops. This was brought out in a December 1970 report by investigators of the Senate Foreign Relations Committee.

Sutsakhan, in *The Khmer Republic,* says that the "final objective" of the Chenla operation was Kompong Thmar. If so, this conflicts with virtually all other available evidence, from that received by the U.S. Embassy to that reported by the media. Perhaps Kompong Thmar became the revised objective when the offensive slowed. Surely, the elaborate simultaneous riverine reinforcement of Kompong Thom beyond that required for strictly defensive purposes would have been a wasteful diversion of resources if Kompong Thmar, a relatively small agricultural community, had been the objective. Furthermore, there was no talk at the time of a Kompong Thom–targeted follow-up to Chenla.

12. *Sensitive Operations in Southeast Asia,* Appendix B; Jack Ballard, *Development and Employment of Fixed-Wing Gunships: 1962–1972,* pp. 211, 217, and 263; and Robert Dorr, *Air War South Vietnam,* p. 114.

13. Confidential State Department source; 1970 PPC Nos. 2372 (Sept. 12), 2397 (Sept. 15), 3234 (Dec. 1), and 3593 (Dec. 30); JCS Recommendations; Antippas Thesis, pp. 43–44; State Department *Biographic Register,* July 1969; and contemporary media reporting. The war's first Communist terrorist incident in Phnom Penh occurred in June when a Honda motorcycle rider threw a grenade at a troop encampment near the former PRC Embassy. (Per PPC no. 2341, dated Sept. 9, 1970.)

14. 1970 PPC Nos. 2610 (Oct. 3), 2631 (Oct. 5), 2644 (Oct. 6), 2661 (Oct. 8), 2686 (Oct. 9), 2715 (Oct. 12), and 3032 (Nov. 10); Bowra Thesis, pp. 10–12; and Whitaker, *Area Handbook,* pp. 25 and 182. The Lon Nol–Nixon correspondence can be read at the State Department's FOIA office in Washington, D.C.

CHAPTER 6. 1971: THE DECISIVE YEAR

1. The 15th Air Force's *Chronology of the Vietnam War;* and *The Air War in Indochina,* a 1971 Cornell University report.

2. Peter Kann, in the September 21, 1971, *Wall Street Journal,* recorded an amusing and revealing anecdote about the two generals. The duo, French military academy classmates nineteen years before, occasionally met over lunch in Phnom Penh. "Ah, yes, the Cambodians," mused Dzu. "They do not like to fight. They have no support. No good weapons. No C-rations. No clothing even. They are like the Vietnamese Army in 1954. But we will organize them." Over his pâté and vintage wine, Fernandez complained that his troops had only World War I weapons, while the South Vietnamese received jets, helicopters, and artillery. As the talk turned to the recent Communist capture of the Gulf of Thailand resort-fishing village of Kampot, the Cambodian lamented that the attackers numbered two thousand. "Two hundred," Dzu said quietly. "We resisted with all our strength," continued Fernandez. "The Vietcong came and the Cambodians ran away," corrected the Vietnamese general. Kampot was subsequently retaken.

3. The Allied Highway 4 clearing operation is discussed in 1971 PPC Nos. 34 (Jan. 4), 126

(Jan. 11), 209 (Jan. 18), and 327 (Jan. 25); CINCPAC-to-CJCS cable no. 7738, dated June 1, 1972; Ballard, *Fixed-Wing Gunships*, pp. 170 and 263; Francillon, *Vietnam*, pp. 164–73; General Donn Starry, *Armored Combat in Vietnam*, pp. 197–98; Sutsakhan, *Khmer Republic*, p. 71; Tho, *Cambodian Incursion*, p. 164; and contemporary media reporting.

4. The January 22–24 events are based on author direct knowledge and conversations with Khmer military personnel; 1971 PPC Nos. 288 (Jan. 23), 327 (Jan. 25), and 1092 (Mar. 8); *DRAC-to-MACV Fortnightly Cambodian Reports* (henceforth *DRAC Reports*) for the period; *State Department Announcement*, Jan. 27, 1971; Etcheson, *Rise and Demise*, pp. 110–11; Charles Heckman, *Phnom Penh Airlift*, pp. 5–6; Isaacs, Hardy, and Brown, *Pawns of War*, p. 98; and contemporary media reporting.

5. Discussion of Lon Nol's illness and related events is based on 1971 PPC Nos. 546 (Feb. 8), 584 (Feb. 9), and 645 (Feb. 12); 1971 State Department cable Nos. 24127 (Feb. 12) and (number illegible) (Mar. 9); 1971 CINCPAC cables dated Feb. 12, Feb. 19, and Mar. 9; CUSMACV-to-CINCPAC cable no. 6879 (July 16, 1971); Etcheson, *Rise and Demise*, pp. 110–11; Sutsakhan, *Khmer Republic*, p. 72; and contemporary media reporting.

6. The Lon Nol–related material is from author direct knowledge; Antippas interviews; Conboy, *Shadow War*, pp. 282–84; Sihanouk, *My War*, pp. 263–64; and *Bangkok World*, July 8, 1971. See also PPC no. 3106 (Mar. 31, 1973). The training of FANK troops in Laos continued until late 1971. In addition, fifteen commando detachments were trained there between September 1970 and March 1971. These Toro Teams, sporting leaping bull shoulder patches, were airlifted into Cambodia's northeastern provinces to report on Ho Chi Minh Trail traffic. The last of the teams was extracted and integrated into the Cambodian army in June 1971. See Conboy, *Shadow War*, p. 284.

7. For opiate trafficking: author direct knowledge; Bureau of Narcotics and Dangerous Drugs (BNDD) *Special Report No. 101;* undated *State Department Publication 8996;* Catherine Lamour and Michel Lamberti, *International Connection*, p. 37; and Alfred McCoy, *Politics of Heroin*, pp. 226–34. The author met with Cambodian officials in mid-1971 to examine a giant Duz soap box filled with white powder that had more the appearance of slightly granular, injectable Number 4 heroin than cleanser. It was one of several taken from a Laotian C-47 aircraft by Khmer customs inspectors. Returning to take possession of the shipment for transfer to the U.S. BNDD after going through bureaucratic formalities, the author was told with a smile, "Oh, it was in fact soap. So we released it to the Laotian Embassy."

8. For intensified U.S. air operations: *JCS Recommendations; DRAC Reports*, July 5 and 19, 1971, and Sept. 13, 1971, to Jan. 3, 1972; Cushman-to-Lavelle message, Dec. 1, 1971; State Department *INR Research Study*, Sept. 25, 1970; *Refugee Civilian War Casualty Problems in Indochina*, Senate Judiciary Committee, Sept. 28, 1970, pp. 39 and 44; Ballard, *Fixed-Wing Gunships*, pp. 170 and 230; Isaacson, *Kissinger*, pp. 239–42; Kiernan, *Vietnam War*, pp. 222–26; Kissinger, *White House Years*, pp. 224–25 and 999; and Tilford, *Crosswinds*, p. 127.

9. The paragraphs on the American presence and assistance program are based on author observations and work with various officials; PPC no. 5204 (Oct. 15, 1971); Berent telephone interview with author, June 27, 1993; Harben interview, Jan. 10, 1995; Antippas Thesis, pp. 44–47; Bowra Thesis, pp. 14–16, 44, and 211–13; Lt. Colonel Ted Mataxis, Jr., quoting his father in the paper *Traits and Behavioral Characteristics of a Combat Leader,*

July 14, 1992, pp. 13–14; Ross, *Cambodia,* pp. 255–56; Tho, *Cambodian Incursion,* pp. 231–35; and Whitaker, *Area Handbook,* pp. 326–27. Overall embassy staffing figures are from *The Congressional Record,* vol. 118, no. 71, Mar. 3, 1972.

The MEDTC generals were Mataxis (1971–72), John Cleland (1972–74), and William Palmer (1974–75). While MEDTC was operationally responsible to CINCPAC, its chief was a member of the embassy country team under the ambassador. As the highest ranking military officer in the mission, the MEDTC commander was consulted on all military decisions and amassed considerable embassy-wide clout, especially since the Nixon administration favored Pentagon over State Department viewpoints. One, whose Prussian manner earned him a "von" nickname in front of his own last name, actually censored Washington-bound communications, excising information derogatory to the Khmer government and FANK or reflecting "undue pessimism," and thereby deprived Washington of complete, factual reporting. The administration, in any case, did not welcome bad news and was engrossed in the larger issues of withdrawing from Vietnam, rapprochement with both the USSR and the PRC, and, later, Watergate. The Cooper-Church Amendment, which became law in January 1971, prohibited MEDTC from advising or instructing.

Mataxis retired in April 1972, after thirty-two years of military service. He returned to Southeast Asia in June as a consultant to the Singapore defense ministry and then again as a businessman to Cambodia before returning to the United States in 1975. He later was associated with the Committee for a Free Afghanistan (making a number of trips to Pakistan between 1983 and 1990), the Committee for a Free Cambodia, and a "small think tank" and arms firm in North Carolina. A 1986 India-published book of questionable funding called Mataxis one of the CIA'S "ugly Americans." Autobiographical data on Mataxis are available at the Carlisle Barracks, Pennsylvania.

10. PPC no. 558 (Feb. 8, 1971); *DRAC Reports;* Starry, *Armored Combat,* pp. 177–78 and 198; and contemporary media reporting.

11. PPC no. 3411 (Dec. 14, 1970) and no. 209 (Jan. 8, 1971); *DRAC Reports,* July 19, 1971–Jan. 3, 1972; Ballard, *Fixed-Wing Gunships,* p. 210; Bowra Thesis, pp. 71–77; G. Cosmas and Lt. Col. T. Murray, *U.S. Marines in Vietnam: Vietnamization and Redeployment, 1970–1971,* pp. 21–22; and Tho, *Cambodian Incursion,* p. 164. While the Mekong River long had been the customary means for delivering bulk commercial supplies to Phnom Penh, the first vessel carrying a war-caused emergency cargo (a load of fuel) docked at the capital on December 14, 1970.

12. Description of FANK's problems is from various U.S. and Khmer sources, including author direct contacts with Cambodian government personnel; PPC no. 558 (Feb. 8, 1971); Bowra Thesis, p. 213; Ross, *Cambodia,* p. 257; Shawcross, *Sideshow,* p. 227; and contemporary media reporting. A 1972 U.S. Senate report called the size of FANK Cambodia's greatest mystery. The Cambodian information minister that year admitted "that 100,000 troops were found to be 'nonexistent.'" Illustrative of Khmer-Vietnamese tension is an August 4, 1971, cable from DRAC to MACV regarding looting and raping by 9th ARVN Division soldiers in Cambodia. *Cambodian Political Reactions to ARVN Pillage,* a State Department *INR Intelligence Note* dated September 3, 1971, further discusses the Khmer-Vietnamese tensions.

13. Discussion of Cambodia's internal crisis derives from author observations and contacts with U.S. and Khmer government sources; 1971 PPC Nos. 1859 (Apr. 20), 2120 (May 3), 2171 (May 6), 2494 (May 25), 2792 (June 10), 3151 (June 28), 5337 (Oct. 21), 5338 (Oct. 22), 5412 (Oct. 25), and 5389 (Oct. 26); early June 1971, Phnom Penh Airgram A-78; *Cambodian Cabinet Reorganization*, State Department memorandum, May 5, 1971; Chandler, *Tragedy*, pp. 210–14; and contemporary media reporting. Military situation sources are author direct knowledge; 1971 PPC Nos. 2911 (June 14), 3034 (June 21), 3151 (June 28), and 3515 (July 19); CINCPAC-to-CJCS cable dated June 1, 1972; Conboy and Bowra, *War in Cambodia*, p. 14; and Kenneth Conboy, *South-East Asian Special Forces*, p. 14.

14. Description of Chenla II is from author direct knowledge, including access to Cambodian sources; 1971 PPC Nos. 4854 (Sept. 27), 5515 (Oct. 11), 5693 (Nov. 8), 5819 (Nov. 15), 6100 (Nov. 29), and 6263 (Dec. 6); 15th Air Force *Chronology of the Vietnam War;* "Tchenla II: The Making of an Army," *Khmer Republic* (government magazine edited in Phnom Penh by Chhang Song), Oct.–Nov., 1971, issue; Etcheson, *Rise and Demise*, pp. III–15; J. W. McCoy, *Secrets of the Vietcong*, pp. 425 and 427; Sihanouk, *My War*, pp. 242–43; Sutsakhan, *Khmer Republic*, pp. 72–75 and 184–85; and contemporary media reporting. Former State Department officer Antippas quotes Mataxis as saying he believed "Lon Nol was encouraged by Washington to launch the Chenla II operation as a means of cutting off rice supplies (coming largely from western Cambodia) to the VC/ NVA Units" in eastern Cambodia. Richard Moose, a State Department foreign service officer who was a Senate committee investigator during the Cambodian War, believes American embassy military officers hoped to participate in the Chenla II planning, but the FANK high command wanted to do it by itself.

15. Terrorist act descriptions are from author direct knowledge, including observation; 1971 PPC Nos. 2934 (June 16), 3034 (June 21), and 3515 (Sept. 20); *Bangkok Post*, Sept. 8, 1971; and *Stars and Stripes*, Sept. 22, 1971.

16. Details on the softball game bombing and subsequent terrorist acts are from author direct knowledge, including observation and comments from witnesses; 1971 PPC Nos. 4854 (Sept. 27), 4997 (Oct. 4), and 5819 (Nov. 15); *U.S. Marine Corps Company C Command Chronology* for 1 July–31 December 1971; Bowra Thesis, pp. 76, 91, and 190–91; C. Nelson and C. Arnold, *U.S. Marines in Vietnam: The War That Would Not End, 1971– 1973*, p. 10; and contemporary media reporting.

17. Author direct knowledge, including participation; *Cambodia: Military Reverses Bring Political Problems*, a State Department INR paper, Dec. 10, 1971; and Antippas interview.

18. Theodore Mataxis, "Cambodia: A New Model for Military Assistance," *Army*, Jan. 1973.

CHAPTER 7. 1972: ATTRITION

1. State Department cable, Dec. 8, 1971; State Department spokesman Charles Bray statement, Jan. 11, 1972; Antippas description to author of conversation with In Tam on Jan. 12, 1972; and *Far Eastern Economic Review*, Jan. 8, 1972.

2. Angkor event descriptions are based on author direct knowledge, including a French and a U.S. government source; 1972 PPC Nos. 767 (Feb. 7) and 2397 (Apr. 24); *Khmer*

Republic, Mar. 1972, p. 26; Michael Freeman and Roger Warner, *Angkor;* Sutsakhan, *Khmer Republic,* pp. 100 and 105; and contemporary media reporting.

3. 1972 PPC Nos. 624 (Jan. 31), 1429 (Mar. 11), 1435 (Mar. 11), 1487 (Mar. 13), 1510 (Mar. 14), 1569 (Mar. 16), 1626 (Mar. 18), 1685 (Mar. 22), and 2968 (May 16); State Department cable no. 49335 (Mar. 22, 1972); Harben interviews; Chandler, *Tragedy,* pp. 220–21; and contemporary media reporting. Lon Nol's comment to the reporter is in *Time,* Apr. 3, 1972. Lon Nol created confusion by his ambiguous use of the title of prime minister. Although he named Thanh as *premier ministre,* which can be translated as both "first" or "prime" minister, Nol himself also used the title when, for example, issuing decrees.

4. Military and terrorist activities are discussed in 1972 PPC Nos. 1657 (Mar. 21) and 1810 (Mar. 27); Conboy, Bowra, and McCouaig, *NVA,* p. 12; Summers, *Vietnam War Almanac,* p. 149; Sutsakhan, *Khmer Republic,* pp. 103–104; and contemporary media reporting. Phnom Penh had only two major bridges, the Japanese Bridge and the Highway 1 span crossing the Bassac River at the southern extremity of the city. None crossed the Mekong.

5. Description of wartime Phnom Penh derives mostly from author observations and conversations with U.S. and Cambodian contacts, including Antippas and Harben. The ensuing description of military activities is based chiefly on *JCS Recommendations;* CINCPAC-to-CJCS cable no. 7738, June 1, 1972; and Sutsakhan, *Khmer Republic,* pp. 103–104. The Phnom Hotel subsequently was renamed Hung Vuong (for the mythical founder of Vietnam), then Samakhi (Solidarity) and, after the departure of Vietnamese troops in 1991, once more Le Royal.

6. Harben interviews; *Khmer Republic,* Aug., 1972, pp. 16 and 21, and Dec., 1972, p. 28; Freeman and Warner, *Angkor,* and White, in *National Geographic,* for background on Angkor; Sutsakhan, *Khmer Republic,* pp. 100–106 and 110–11; and contemporary media reporting (especially Boris Baczynsky, "The Rape of Angkor," *Far Eastern Economic Review,* Sept. 2, 1972). The retaking of Phnom Bakheng enabled the Communists to fire down on Siem Reap's airport, forcing AAK to use a new airstrip south of the city.

7. 1972 PPC Nos. 3657 (June 12), 3840 (June 19), and 4025 (June 26); Antippas and Harben interviews; *Khmer Republic,* Dec. 1972, pp. 33 and 40–41; Bowra Thesis, pp. 218–21; Shawcross, *Sideshow,* pp. 231–35; and Whitaker, *Area Handbook,* pp. 184–86. The Socio-Republican Party was formed by anti-Sihanouk government leaders after the dissolution of the prince's Sangkum Reastr Nyum in February 1971. It quickly was dominated by the Lon brothers. The Republican Party was an outgrowth of the split between Lon Nol and Sirik Matak. The Democrats were less than dynamic, regaining momentum only in 1973.

8. 1972 PPC Nos. 5489 (Aug. 21), 6481 (Sept. 26), 6491 (Sept. 27), and 6496 (Sept. 27); Harben interviews; and contemporary media reporting provided information on the assassination attempts. A third assassination attempt was reported after the two widely attributed to Lon Non. This time the target apparently was Non himself. On October 19, 1972, three bullets were fired at the car in which he was being driven to an official dinner. No one was hurt. Typically, given Phnom Penh's conspiratorial politics, appearances may have been deceiving. While it indeed may have been a genuine attempt to kill Non, some said it was staged to divert attention from his role in the two earlier attempts.

To further muddy the water, the car belonged to Prime Minister Hang Thun Hak, leading others to say that Hak was the real target. For the rest, 1972 PPC Nos. 4392 (July 10) and 5359 (Aug. 15); 1973 PPC no. 3016 (Mar. 31); Harben interviews, *Khmer Republic,* Dec., 1972, pp. 26 and 54; Sutsakhan, *Khmer Republic,* pp. 106–108 and 111; and contemporary media reporting address the July through September military activities.

9. A twenty-page report on the refugee situation is in vol. 118, no. 71 of *The Congressional Record,* May 3, 1972. The report, submitted by Senator Edward Kennedy, stated that, as of March 1971, an estimated "20 percent of the 100,000 to 150,000 homes destroyed and other property damaged were a result of Cambodian and Allied air operations." It also presents unverifiable Khmer figures of 1,400 civilians killed and 20,000 military personnel and civilians injured between March 1970 and September 1971. The last Cambodian census, compiled in mid-1962, gave a nationwide population of 5.7 million, 87 percent rural, 3 percent semirural, and 10 percent urban. The 1972 estimate is based on a 2.2 percent growth rate, the lowest in Southeast Asia. Isaacs, *Without Honor,* pp. 250–54, also discusses the refugee situation.

10. Discussion of the internal civilian-military situations, FANK's growth and problems, and the U.S. presence and assistance program are based on 1972 PPC Nos. 103 (Jan. 7), 6057 (Sept. 12), 6268 (Sept. 19), 6443 (Sept. 25), and 7046 (Oct. 16); Bangkok Airgram A-363 (July 3, 1969); Harben interviews; Bowra Thesis, pp. 48–49, 220, 227, and 277–78; Conboy, *South-East Asian,* pp. 14–15; Conboy and Bowra, *War in Cambodia,* pp. 14–18, 20, and 23–24; Kissinger, *White House Years,* p. 1042, and *Years of Upheaval,* p. 1226; Sutsakhan, *Khmer Republic,* pp. 152–55 and 111; and Whitaker, *Area Handbook,* pp. 17–19, 318–21, and 326–27. The material on Lon Non is from author conversations with various U.S. and Khmer sources; PPC Nos. 4368 (Sept. 2, 1971) and 3016 (Mar. 31, 1973); and Antippas and Harben interviews. Factors such as attrition and lack of maintenance removed major equipment provided by other countries from FANK's inventory. For example, France had provided the Cambodians with a number of AMX light tanks.

11. PPC no. 7676 (June 14, 1972); *Sihanouk's Dossier,* p. 42; Chandler, *Tragedy,* pp. 218–19, and *Brother,* pp. 95–98; Etcheson, *Rise and Demise,* pp. 115–17; Kiernan, *Pol Pot Regime,* p. 16, and *How Pol Pot,* pp. 316 and 327–47; Shawcross, *Sideshow,* pp. 251–58; and "Au Revoir Sihanouk?" *Far Eastern Economic Review,* Aug. 8, 1972. Again, the Pol Pot regime's *Livre Noir* is rewritten history and often inaccurate.

12. The terrorist attack is described in 1972 PPC Nos. 6891 (Oct. 10) and 7670 (Nov. 7); *Khmer Republic,* Dec. 1972, p. 34; and contemporary media reporting. Harben interviews provided other details. Information on Cambodia's UN crisis is in the mass of State Department papers, memoranda, and cables between August 1972 and January 1973, e.g., cable Nos. 150874 (Aug. 18), 167100 (Sept. 13), 187687 (Oct. 13), and 218073 (Dec. 1); and in a transcript of Long Boret's speech before the twenty-seventh regular session of the UN General Assembly.

13. The late-year events are described in 1972 PPC Nos. 7892 (Nov. 14), 8453 (Dec. 5), and 8688 (Dec. 12); *Briefing Material for Foreign Service Inspection* in response to a January 9, 1973, State Department memorandum; *Khmer Republic,* Dec., 1972, pp. 37–41; Conboy, *South-East Asian,* pp. 52–53; Sutsakhan, *Khmer Republic,* pp. 67–68 and 112–14; and contemporary media reporting.

Discussion of Lon Nol's xenophobic mysticism is from author direct knowledge; Antippas and Harben interviews; Becker, *When the War*, pp. 134–43; Chandler, *Tragedy*, pp. 205 and 356; and Martin, *Cambodia*, pp. 129–30. Harben, using mostly published Cambodian sources and contemporary books, produced a lengthy discussion of Nol's idiosyncratic thinking. It was sent to Washington in watered-down form as Airgram A-78, dated May 25, 1972, entitled *The Anthropological Lon Nol*. Not unexpectedly, it was not well received and, as of this writing, was still awaiting State Department declassification.

CHAPTER 8. 1973: A RAIN OF BOMBS

1. Description of the events of 1973's opening months derives from PPC no. 882 (Jan. 30, 1973); State Department cable no. 15050 (Jan. 26, 1973); *State Department Bulletin* 68, no. 1755, Feb. 12, 1972; *JCS Recommendations; U.S. Air Operations in Cambodia, April 1973*, Senate Foreign Relations Committee staff report dated Apr. 27, 1973, pp. 1 and 6 (henceforth *U.S. Air Operations*); Antippas interviews; Isaacs, Hardy, and Brown, *Pawns of War*, pp. 99–100; Charles Kamps, Jr., *History of the Vietnam War*, pp. 201–202; Kissinger, *White House Years*, pp. 1354, 1372, and 1414 (his chs. 33 and 34 detail the final days of the peace talks); Melson and Arnold, *U.S. Marines in Vietnam*, pp. 244–45; Shawcross, *Sideshow*, pp. 259–67; Emory Swank, "The Land in Between; Cambodia Ten Years Later," *Indochina Issues*, no. 36, a Center for International Policy publication; Sutsakhan, *Khmer Republic*, pp. 114–16; and Tilford, *Crosswinds*, pp. 176–77.

2. PPC no. 2787 (Mar. 27, 1973); *The Situation in Cambodia, July 1973*, CIA Document no. 7333/73, Aug. 1973; Harben interviews; Conboy and Bowra, *War in Cambodia*, pp. 17–18; and Sutsakhan, *Khmer Republic*, pp. 116–19.

3. A wealthy career diplomat, the Yale- and Sorbonne-educated Enders subsequently served as ambassador to Canada and to the European Economic Community before becoming assistant secretary of state for Inter-American affairs. Considered one of the department's "best and brightest," a hawk in foreign policy and a civil rights advocate at home, he is best known for his involvement in the 1973 Cambodian air bombardment controversy and the 1980s El Salvador–Nicaragua issues. He died of melanoma in New York City on March 17, 1996.

4. Confidential U.S. government source; 1973 PPC Nos. 2747 (Mar. 26), 3341 (Apr. 10), and 4130 (May 1); *U.S. Air Operations;* Berent interviews; Harben interview; Richard Moose, interview with author, Washington, D.C., Jan. 18, 1995; Senator Stuart Symington interview on NBC's *Today Show*, Apr. 27, 1973; Kissinger, *Years of Upheaval*, pp. 344–48 and 1217–30; and Shawcross, *Sideshow*, pp. 265–75. *U.S. Air Operations in Cambodia*, the Lowenstein-Moose report prepared for the Security Agreements and Commitments Abroad Subcommittee of the Senate Foreign Relations Committee, and both the Appendix (1979 memorandum for the State Department historian) and Tabs B and C (1979 letters written at Enders' request) to Kissinger's *Years of Upheaval* offer the best summaries of the embassy bombing role, although the second has to be read with a critical eye.

There is an amusing-in-retrospect aside to the Lowenstein-Moose visit to Cambodia. During a December 1970 visit to Phnom Penh, the Senate investigators were invited by a media representative and his wife to a couscous dinner. "The couscous was laced with some stuff that looked like parsley," Lowenstein later said. The host and hostess apparently thought it was a fine joke, since the "parsley" was cannabis. Lowenstein, less amused, had to see a doctor and "couldn't write my name for two days." Sylvana Foa went on to a managerial job on UPI's international desk and subsequently joined the United Nations as a spokesperson.

5. 1973 PPC Nos. 2436 (Mar. 17), 2442 (Mar. 18), 2478 (Mar. 19), 2507 (Mar. 20), 2787 (Mar. 27), 3016 (Mar. 31), 3905 (Apr. 25), 4018 (Apr. 28), 4046 (Apr. 29), and 5536 (June 5); Sitrep no. 14, Sept. 25, 1973 (State Department situation report); 1973 State Department cable no. 47710; *U.S. Operations,* p. 8; Antippas and Harben interviews (both men dealt directly with Lon Non); Chandler, *Tragedy* (which confuses the March 17 assassination attempt with a later one), pp. 223–24; and Sutsakhan, *Khmer Republic,* p. 87. The forty-six royal family members and others arrested after the assassination attempt were released in May 1973. In September, Princess Bopha Devi, the thirty-year-old favorite daughter of Sihanouk and former prima ballerina of the Royal Classical Ballet, was allowed to leave Cambodia with her husband and five children. Ailing seventy-year-old Queen Kossamak, along with forty other family members and friends, was permitted to rejoin her son in Beijing in November 1973. This was the result of a Beijing request and Washington arrangements.

6. Appraisal of the K.R. is based on author interviews of refugees and ralliers; *The Situation in Cambodia,* pp. 8–9, 21, and 23; State Department *Country Program Memorandum (Cambodia),* Apr. 1973; *U.S. Policy and Programs in Cambodia,* report of the House Foreign Affairs Committee's Subcommittee on Asian and Pacific Affairs hearings, Doolin testimony, June 6, 1973, p. 85 (which mentions early 1973 Hanoi aid to PNLAFK as including advisors, some combat help, logistics, administrative support, and material); PCK *Livre Noir;* Bowra Thesis, pp. 12 and 26–27; Sam Adams, *War of Numbers,* ch. 8; Chandler, *Tragedy,* pp. 226–28, and *Brother,* pp. 99–104; Conboy, Bowra, and McCouaig, *The NVA,* pp. 12–13 and 54; Kiernan, *How Pol Pot,* pp. 350–93; and Sihanouk, *War and Hope,* pp. 21–22. The Cambodian mine problem is discussed in Paul Davies, *War of the Mines;* and *Land Mines in Cambodia,* by Asian Watch and Physicians for Human Rights. U.S. experts disagreed on the numerical strength of the K.R., which was a factor in congressional funding decisions. In a late 1974 military aid conference, the MEDTC commander displayed a briefing chart showing forty thousand K.R. troops in 125 battalions as of January 1973 and sixty thousand troops in 230 battalions in November 1974. The official 1973 Washington stand was that the K.R.'s forty to fifty thousand poorly-organized troops were "responsive" to Hanoi and could be beaten by FANK's two hundred thousand if North Vietnam stopped helping the K.R. Samuel Adams, a bright and feisty CIA ten-year veteran analyst who also had disputed Communist strength figures in Vietnam, insisted that PNLAFK numbers stood at about two hundred thousand (about half in regular units) and that the K.R. were "virtually independent" of Hanoi. Adams quit in protest in May 1973. He became involved in the 1980s *Westmoreland vs. CBS* lawsuit and died of heart failure at the age of fifty-four in October 1988, in his Vermont home. In an April 9, 1973, broadcast, Sihanouk said that K.R. "offensive units" totaled 120,000 men.

7. *Situation in Cambodia*, p. 9; Etcheson, *Rise and Demise*, p. 118; and Sutsakhan, *Khmer Republic*, pp. 119–20.

8. For the 1973 bombing campaign, K.R. disregard of it and peace feelers: PPC no. 6501 (June 29, 1973); State Department cable no. 59091 (Mar. 30, 1973), which mentions Phnom Penh "preliminary contacts with nationalist factions within the Cambodian insurgency"; Secretary Rogers memorandum to the Senate Foreign Relations Committee, Apr. 30, 1973; Secretary Rogers statement, May 8, 1973; *Situation in Cambodia*, pp. 5–8; CIA Foreign Broadcast Information Service report, May 17, 1978; Berent interview; Harben interview; Bowra Thesis, pp. 228–29 and 283; Gurney, *Vietnam*, pp. 254–55; Kiernan, *How Pol Pot*, pp. 354–55; Kissinger, *White House Years*, p. 1415 (which states that "starting in the spring of 1973, we sought to bring about Sihanouk's return based on a cease-fire"), and *Years of Upheaval*, pp. 16–18, 338–39, and 1217–30; Nixon, *Real Peace*, pp. 292–95; Shawcross, *Sideshow*, pp. 271–72, 284–85, 294, and 297–98; and Tilford, *Crosswinds*, pp. 176–77. A bombing beacon erected atop the U.S. Embassy in Phnom Penh was taken down in April 1973, well before the Neak Luong accident. Tilford (pp. 227–28) records allegations of a "targeteer" in the embassy directing B-52s to "fictitious underwater storage areas" because there weren't enough legitimate targets to meet SAC sortie quotas. Discussion of congressional restrictions on presidential power is based in part on State Department Information Memorandum *War Powers Legislation*, May 4, 1973; War Powers Resolution, PL 93-148; Fisher, *Presidential War Power*, pp. 125–32; Lehman, *Making War*, pp. 89–96 and 262–65; and Nixon, *Real Peace*, pp. 294–95.

9. Former U.S. government officer who requested anonymity; Phnom Penh Airgram no. 57 (Apr. 8, 1973); State Department Airgram dated Sept. 27, 1973; *Situation in Cambodia*, pp. 2–3 and 24–26; *Sensitive Operations in Southeast Asia*; *JCS Recommendations*; *Bombing of Cambodia*, Book 2, pp. 88–108; Cleland, *End of Tour Report*, pp. 2–3; Harben interviews; Bowra Thesis, pp. 46–47, 63–64, and 229–34; Orr Kelly, telephone conversation with author, Feb. 7, 1995, and *Never Fight Fair!* ch. 27; Shawcross, *Sideshow*, pp. 218–19 and 297–99; and Tilford, *Crosswinds*, p. 180. Sihanouk, in an interview published in the Paris *Le Monde* on Oct. 26, 1973, said that the failure to take Phnom Penh was owing to the North Vietnamese cutoff of weapons and ammunition to the K.R. The correspondent who reported the controversial "Black Commando" program was Tammy Arbuckle, writing for the *Washington Star-News* (July 24 and 31, 1973). The State Department position is in *Press Guidance* statements, identically dated with the newspaper articles. Photos of the lunar rock presentation ceremony are in *Khmer Republic*, Aug. 1973, pp. 70–71.

10. Former U.S. government officer; 1973 State Department–to–White House Cambodia Situation Report (henceforth SitRep) Nos. 7 (Aug. 31), 8 (Sept. 4), 10 (Sept. 11), 11 (Sept. 14), 13 (Sept. 21), 14 (Sept. 25), and 24 (Nov. 2); Phnom Penh Airgram no. 43 (Mar. 13, 1973); *Situation in Cambodia*, pp. 10–11 and 15–16; Cleland, *End of Tour Report;* Timothy Carney, "Communist Party Power in Kampuchea (Cambodia): Documents and Discussion," a Cornell University paper, Jan. 1977, pp. 20–21 (Carney was a State Department political officer in the Phnom Penh embassy between 1972 and 1975); Kissinger, *Years of Upheaval*, p. 15; Sutsakhan, *Khmer Republic*, pp. 122–23; Swank, in *Indochina Issues;* and contemporary media reporting. The official *Khmer Republic*, Sept. 1973, 318-page special

issue published figures showing 704,758 Cambodians listed with government agencies as refugees. In Phnom Penh, 9,684 lived in and 372,968 resided outside the capital's six camps. Another 292,041 refugees were in provincial communities. Still another 30,101 were abroad, mostly in South Vietnam. Including those not officially declared, the grand total of Cambodians who had been turned into refugees by the war, according to Phnom Penh, was estimated as more than 2,000,000.

11. *New York Times Sunday Magazine,* Aug. 12, 1973.

12. Former U.S. government officer; 1973 SitRep Nos. 7 (Aug. 31), 10 (Sept. 11), 14 (Sept. 25), 22 (Oct. 24), 29 (Nov. 20), 30 (Nov. 23), 31 (Nov. 27), 32 (Nov. 30), and 33 (Dec. 4); PPC no. 5893 (June 14, 1973); and Harben and Whipple interviews.

13. The assassination attempt is discussed in 1973 SitRep Nos. 29 (Nov. 20), 30 (Nov. 23), and 31 (Nov. 27); and contemporary media reporting. The first noteworthy insight into the K.R. world was Ith Sarin's *Sranaoh Pralung Khmer* (Regrets for the Khmer Soul), published in Phnom Penh in 1973. Excerpts are in Carney, *Communist Party Power,* pp. 42–55. Sarin, a leftist primary school inspector, spent most of 1972 with the K.R. before returning in disillusionment to Phnom Penh. The Lon Nol government quickly banned the book as subversive. Carney was one of the few to recognize its significance. Continuing problems and corruption are discussed in *Foreign Assistance Authorization,* Senate Committee on Foreign Relations report, June–July 1974 hearings; and Chandler, *Tragedy,* p. 230.

14. 1973 SitRep Nos. 22 (Oct. 24) and 32 (Nov. 30); *Foreign Assistance Authorization,* p. 129; Bowra Thesis, pp. 236–39; Kissinger, *Years of Upheaval,* p. 369; and Sutsakhan, *Khmer Republic,* pp. 123–25.

CHAPTER 9. 1974: SIEGE

1. The events of January 1974 derive from a onetime French resident of Phnom Penh; Bowra Thesis, pp. 240–41; Sutsakhan, *Khmer Republic,* pp. 125–29; and contemporary media reporting. Although underaged boys had broad fighting roles on both Khmer sides, FANK generally restricted its ten thousand women to administrative and other noncombatant assignments. However, women in the provincial militias were more widely involved in combat. Obviously posed photos of female warriors are reproduced in *Khmer Republic,* Aug. 1972 (p. 37), and Sept. 1973 (p. 164).

2. *Situation in Cambodia,* pp. 9–10; Harben and Whipple interviews; Bowra Thesis, pp. 139–40 and 241–42; Kiernan, *How Pol Pot,* p. 378; Sutsakhan, *Khmer Republic,* pp. 128–29; and contemporary media reporting.

3. *JCS Recommendations;* Berent and Whipple interviews, Bowra Thesis, pp. 101–104, 156, 195–96, 242–44, and 277–88; Conboy and Bowra, *War in Cambodia,* pp. 15–24; Sutsakhan, *Khmer Republic,* pp. 182–83; and contemporary media reporting. A March 13, 1974, *Washington Post* article by Elizabeth Becker, datelined Kampot, described U.S. Army Major Lawrence Ondecker advising Khmer officers in an ANK command post on conducting a counterattack. The reporter wrote that the major, assigned to the embassy's defense attaché office, pored over maps with Cambodian officers while the latter's commanding general was in an adjoining bunker making entries in his diary. Becker quotes Ondecker

as saying, "I want you to respond very quickly . . . If even one mortar falls in your zone, you must answer back with fire immediately." A second American, Chuck Bernard, is described as writing propaganda pamphlets with his Khmer counterpart.

Colorful accounts of embassy-attached Americans in combat roles have been provided by two former naval officers. The flamboyant Lieutenant Commander Richard Marcinko, the country's most famous SEAL, was a naval attaché in Phnom Penh from September 1973 to September 1974. He said that he led a number of MNK combat sorties, despite the fact that restrictions on the activities of military personnel in Cambodia had been tightened because of past media coverage and congressional complaints. In 1990, Marcinko was sentenced to prison and fined after being convicted of conspiracy, bribery, conflict of interest, and making false claims against the government. An even-handed description of the controversial SEAL's activities can be found in chapter 11 of *Brave Men, Dark Waters* by Orr Kelly. Marcinko tells his own story in *Rogue Warrior*, written with John Weisman. Of interest are *Pogue Warrior* by Dale Andradé (*Soldier of Fortune*, Mar. 1994), which attacks Marcinko's exaggerations and falsehoods, though not his overall accomplishments; and the heated rebuttals in the succeeding issue's letters column. Orr Kelly's *Never Fight Fair!* (ch. 27) tells of a Lieutenant William Beck being an "adviser" in Kompong Thom during a 1974–75 tour that included direct combat involvement and being wounded by shrapnel.

Born in Germany (like Kissinger) in 1926, Dean emigrated to the United States before World War II and changed his named from Dienstfertig. He served in the U.S. Army, acquired citizenship, and graduated from Harvard. His State Department postings before Phnom Penh included Laos, Togo, Mali, and France. After a Vietnam tour, he became deputy chief of mission in Laos and was chargé d'affaires there in 1973, playing a key role in forming a coalition government. It was a role some influential Khmers hoped he could repeat in Cambodia. Married, with three children, the six-foot, pipe-smoking Dean was a tennis and bridge player. Cambodia was his first ambassadorship. He went on to become ambassador to Lebanon, Thailand, India, and Denmark. The CIA chiefs of station were John Stein (1970–72), Kinlock Bull, Jr. (1972–73), and a third man the author has been asked not to identify as chief of station.

4. For the Kampot-Oudong battles, see Palmer, *End of Tour Report*, pp. 8–10; Bowra Thesis, pp. 154–61 and 242–44; Conboy and Bowra, *War in Cambodia*, pp. 8 and 9; Kiernan, *How Pol Pot*, pp. 364–85; Sutsakhan, *Khmer Republic*, pp. 129–35; and contemporary media reporting. Except where otherwise noted, the description of military operations in the rest of this chapter is based on author discussion with various sources; Bowra Thesis, pp. 245–57 and 321; Chandler, *Tragedy*, pp. 231–32; Conboy and Bowra, *War in Cambodia*, pp. 9 and 15; Conboy, Bowra, and McCouaig, *NVA*, p. 13; Sutsakhan, *Khmer Republic*, pp. 136–48 and 151–52; and contemporary media reporting.

5. Bowra Thesis, pp. 247 and 250; Chandler, *Tragedy*, pp 231–32 and 362–63; and contemporary media reporting. One of the witnesses to the schoolyard events was a twenty-one-year-old American who taught English at a private school and was on the balcony at the time of the double murder. On September 1, 1974, Thuch San Khy was sentenced to death in absentia by a military court for the killings. A second student also was given an in absentia death sentence. Others received varying sentences or acquittal.

6. Dean in May 5, 1976, testimony before the House Internal Relations Committee described U.S. efforts to arrive at a nonmilitary solution to the war. Even hawkish optimists were acknowledging the increasing hopelessness of the Khmer government's position. The only hope for Cambodia was a negotiated settlement, wrote an outgoing MEDTC chief. "No military solution appears possible." (Cleland *End of Tour Report*, p. 16.)

7. Nonmilitary air operations in Cambodia during 1974–75 are described in Charles Heckman, *Phnom Penh Airlift*, and Christopher Robbins, *Air America*, ch. 10. Air America was beset by aircrews protesting the October 1973 cutoff of combat pay and questioning the U.S. role in the Southeast Asian warfare. The airline again was summoned to Cambodia to participate in the evacuation of U.S. Embassy–attached personnel in 1975. That flying into Pochentong even by commercial airliner differed from normal operations was demonstrated to the author during an Air Cambodge flight from Bangkok. There were no stewardesses, only a cockpit crew composed of moonlighting Air France personnel. The in-flight food service was limited to orange juice served in Dixie cups by the copilot. The final approach into Phnom Penh apparently was not steep enough to avoid one or two metallic sounds, which a crewman said were caused by small arms ground fire.

8. Antippas, telephone interview with author, Aug. 24, 1994. Non's family and three advisers remained in the United States.

9. PPC no. 17412 (Dec. 31, 1974); Bowra Thesis, pp. 26–27; and Cleland *End of Tour Report*.

CHAPTER 10. 1975: THE FALL

1. Beginning-of-the-year events as described are based principally on *Foreign Assistance and Related Agencies Appropriations for 1975*, Part 3, U.S. House Subcommittee on Foreign Operations and Related Agencies, 1975, pp. 9–12; PPC no. 692 (Jan. 13, 1975); Palmer *End of Tour Report*, pp. 3–4 and 8–19; Bowra Thesis, pp. 26–27, 147–49, 257, 321–24, and 328–31; Batchelder and Quinlan, in *Marines in Vietnam*; Isaacs, *Without Honor*, pp. 241–44; Shreadley, *From the Rivers*, pp. 371–72; Sutsakhan, *Khmer Republic*, pp. 155–56; and contemporary media reporting. The question of North Vietnamese participation in the final K.R. offensive remains to be answered. While most sources deny the presence of PAVN, some (e.g., Chandler, *Brother*, p. 217, note 38) aver a limited Vietnamese involvement. Snepp, *Decent Interval*, p. 341, and Conboy, Bowra, and McCouaig, *NVA*, p. 13, record indications that a PAVN division may have been diverted to eastern Cambodia in case the K.R. needed assistance in their assault on Phnom Penh.

2. Dean testimony, House International Relations Committee, May 5, 1976. Former foreign service officer Antippas believes that Washington's stubborn embracing of Lon Nol, which MEDTC chiefs fully endorsed, "was a serious miscalculation which probably cost the Cambodians the war." Antippas said that Nol, after his illness, "paralyzed the decision-making process and could not or would not discipline his worst officers." (Antippas Thesis, pp. 49 and 56.)

3. 1975 PPC Nos. 5368 (Mar. 24) and 5857 (Apr. 1); Dean testimony, May 5, 1976; Bowra Thesis, pp. 187 and 257–58; Isaacs, *Without Honor*, pp. 247–49 and 259–63; Sutsakhan, *Khmer Republic*, pp. 152–61; Swank, in *Indochina Issues*, p. 2; Warner, *Certain Victory*, pp. 47–53; and contemporary media reporting. Sihanouk's request for help in recovering

his films appears in Chandler, *Tragedy,* p. 234; Osborne, *Sihanouk,* p. 226; and Shawcross, *Sideshow,* p. 360. Lon Nol arrived in Honolulu with his entourage on April 10, 1975. After a short stay at Hickam Air Force Base, he bought an expensive suburban house. Nol moved to southern California in 1979 and died of heart failure there in 1985, four days after his seventy-second birthday.

4. Whipple interview; Dean testimony; Palmer *End of Tour Report,* pp. 14 and B-1; Bowra Thesis, pp. 47–48, 147–55, 185–93, and 258–59; Dunham and Quinlan, *U.S. Marines in Vietnam,* pp. 42–54 and 102–12; Isaacs, *Without Honor,* pp. 278–80; Snepp, *Decent Interval,* pp. 303 and 338; Sutsakhan, *Khmer Republic,* pp. 158 and 162–70; and contemporary media reporting. The U.S. companies flying into Pochentong just prior to the capital's fall were Airlift International, Bird Air, Flying Tiger Line, Seaboard World, Trans-International Airlines, and World Airways. These carried the bulk of the airlifted material, with smaller, officially Khmer-owned carriers flying in smaller amounts. Sutsakhan's monograph, pp. 168–71, describes his two-day flight from Phnom Penh to U Tapao. Others fleeing, mostly air force officers and their families, joined his party in Oddar Mean Chey Province before the final hop to Thailand. The general's group nearly was arrested by turncoat officers and barely escaped from the angry inhabitants of the town of Samrong. Sutsakhan was to play a key military-political role during Cambodia's post–killing fields period.

5. Description of the republic's final days derives from Whipple interview; Palmer, *End of Tour Report;* Ford press conference, May 5, 1975, transcript (for "bloodbath" quote); Bowra Thesis, pp. 324–25 and 331; Chandler, *Tragedy,* p. 215, and *Brother,* pp. 108–109; Etcheson, *Rise and Demise,* pp. 93–95; Kiernan, *Pol Pot Regime,* pp. 31–64; Ngor, *Cambodian Odyssey,* chs. 7 and 8; R. J. Rummel, *Death by Government,* pp. 175–80; Schanberg, *Death and Life,* pp. 18–34; Sihanouk, *War and Hope,* p. 37; Snepp, *Decent Interval,* p. 339; Sutsakhan, *Khmer Republic,* pp. 170–71; and contemporary media reporting. The official casualty-orphan figures are from *Khmer Republic, 100 Days of National Resistance,* Sept. 1973, special issue, pp. 246–47. Kiernan's *Pol Pot Regime* estimates the death toll from the evacuation of Phnom Penh to be "around twenty thousand." The CIA's 1980 *Kampuchea: A Demographic Catastrophe* estimates urban evacuee deaths to have been between 280,000 and 400,000. In June, 1978, Kampuchea's deputy prime minister, Ieng Sary, told reporters during a Tokyo visit that the evacuation of Phnom Penh "was a necessary measure in order to prevent people from dying [of disease]." Schanberg, unable to bring Pran along, was aboard the first Phnom Penh-to-Thailand convoy.

6. Illustrative of the confusion engendered by the reclusive K.R. regime is the *Asia 1977 Yearbook* of the respected *Far Eastern Economic Review.* It noted (p. 139) that a "defecting pilot" (presumably Pech Lim Kuon) said that the "real heavyweights were Party Secretary Solath Sar, Ieng Sary, Son Sen" and two others, with Khieu Samphan as a second-ranker. It also noted that the April 17, 1976, first-anniversary celebration keynote speaker was Sar. The *Yearbook* also quoted Pol Pot and reproduced his photo with the caption: "Premier Pol Pot: Real Name?" The publication, stating that "newly-appointed Premier Pol Pot was a complete unknown outside Cambodia, as were most other members of the cabinet," went on to say that photographic evidence tends "to disprove the two favourite theories that Pol Pot is actually Saloth Sar or Non Suon—the two known com-

munist veterans." In any case, most Western observers continued to believe that Samphan was the real power in Cambodia until April 1977. Even then, although some Cambodia watchers had in 1976 insisted that the two were identical, there still was confusion over whether Pol Pot was Saloth Sar. To obfuscate the situation further, the CPK did not announce its existence until September 1977. The K.R. was to continue its paranoid secrecy into the 1990s.

7. Palmer *End of Tour Report,* p. 2; Bowra Thesis, pp. 25–26; Timothy Carney, "The Unexpected Victory," in Karl Jackson, *Cambodia: 1975–1978;* Kiernan, *How Pol Pot* and *Pol Pot Regime;* and Vickery, *Cambodia,* make clear the unusual organization of the K.R. war machine. Regarding the date of Pol Pot's return to Phnom Penh, Chandler (*Brother,* p. 109) gives April 23, while Kiernan *Pol Pot Regime,* p. 54) records April 24. Pol Pot, in an October 2, 1977, Beijing press conference, said that the reason for evacuating the cities, a decision made three months before the end of the war, was to break up "enemy spy organizations" that could undermine the new regime and open Cambodia to outside (presumably Vietnamese) invasion. (See note 5 above for Sary's stated reason.)

8. Chandler, *Brother,* pp. 116–17, says that while Saloth Sar used the pseudonym "Pol" as early as the 1950s, "no pre-1976 references to 'Pot' have come to light," and that the April 1976 announcement of his assumption of the premiership "marked the first public appearance of 'Pol Pot' as a person and as a name." The K.R. leader first publicly admitted the Saloth Sar–Pol Pot link in 1979. Marie Martin, research director at the *Centre national de la Recherche scientifique* (France's National Scientific Research Center), says that, prior to 1970, "Sar called himself *bâng* Pol [*bâng* is a kinship term signifying 'elder']. As he gained recognition . . . he felt obliged to complete the name. He added Pot, a doublet of Pol" (p. 160 of her *Cambodia: A Shattered Society*). Translation of the Democratic Kampuchean anthem is by Khing Hoc Dy, a Cambodian scholar living in Paris. See Dy's "Khmer Literature Since 1975," pp. 27–28, in *Cambodian Culture Since 1975,* edited by Ebihara, Mortland, and Ledgerwood.

9. Detailed accounts of the *Mayaguez* incident can be found in *Seizure of the* Mayaguez, Parts 1–4, House Committee on International Relations, 1975; CIA *Post Mortem Report: An Examination of the Intelligence Community's Performance Before and During the* Mayaguez *Incident in May 1975,* Aug. 8, 1975; Daniel Bolger, *Americans at War;* Dunham and Quinlan, *U.S. Marines in Vietnam,* ch. 13; John Guilmartin, Jr., *A Very Short War;* Roy Rowan, *Four Days of the* Mayaguez; and Lucien Vandenbroucke, *Perilous Options,* chs. 5 and 6. In September 1975, during a visit to the UN in New York, Deputy Prime Minister and Defense Minister Ieng Sary said that his government first learned of the *Mayaguez* seizure from a monitored American radiocast. He said that Phnom Penh then told the local naval commander to "return to the area where the ship had been captured and release it," even though it had violated Cambodia's "12-mile" territorial limit. U.S. forces attacked before the order could be carried out, he said. Chandler, *History,* pp. 219–23; and Kiernan, *How Pol Pot,* pp. 414–16, and *Pol Pot Regime,* chs. 9 and 10, discuss the K.R.-Hanoi rift and the question of K.R. designs on southern parts of Vietnam. During 1977, Democratic Kampuchea also initiated bloody cross-border raids into Thailand and Laos.

1. Ngor, *Cambodian Odyssey,* p. 69. Ngor, an affluent doctor before the K.R. takeover and a survivor of the killing fields, had the lead Khmer role in the award-winning film *The Killing Fields.* He afterwards pursued humanitarian goals in Cambodia and settled in California to work for a Chinatown refugee center. Ngor was shot to death on February 25, 1996, at age fifty-five, in his Los Angeles carport during a robbery by members of an Oriental street gang.

2. *Cambodge année zéro,* with a U.S. edition published in 1978 by Holt, Rinehart, and Winston as *Cambodia: Year Zero.*

3. Jackson, *Cambodia,* p. 3.

4. *Kampuchea (Cambodia), Background Notes,* State Department, May 1984; Kiernan, *Pol Pot Regime,* pp. 456–63; Vickery, *Cambodia,* pp. 186–87; and *Economist,* Apr. 6, 1996. See also Edward Doyle, *The Vietnam Experience: The Aftermath,* pp. 50–64. Rummel, *Death by Government,* pp. 192–93, using a number of sources, says "that the domestic democide lies between 600,000 and 3 million dead. A most prudent estimate is 2 million."

5. Chandler, *History,* pp. 223–39, and *Khmers,* pp. 252–56; Doyle, *Aftermath,* pp. 64–90; Trevor Findlay, *Cambodia: The Legacy and Lessons of UNTAC,* pp. 1–20; Ross, *Cambodia,* pp. xxxii–xxxvi, 69–70, and 263–98; and D. R. SarDesi, *Vietnam: The Struggle for National Identity,* pp. 118–24 and 130–31. *Brother Enemy* by Nayan Chanda also provides an informative account of the Khmer-Vietnamese conflicts. For UN involvement, see *The United Nations and Cambodia: 1991–1995,* UN Blue Book Series, Vol 2, 1995, pp. 5–9, and subsequent texts of documents. China and Sihanouk, among others, insisted that thousands of Vietnamese soldiers pretending to be PRK troops remained in Cambodia after the official 1989 departure. See, for example, Robert Sutter, *The Cambodian Crisis and U.S. Policy Dilemmas,* p. 107. Former CIA director Robert Gates touches on covert assistance to the Khmer resistance in his *From the Shadows,* p. 322.

6. Confidential Phnom Penh resident, author interview, December 1992; *The United Nations and Cambodia,* pp. 10–55 and 64–72; Chandler, *History,* 2nd ed., pp. 239–42, and *Khmers,* pp. 256–57; Findlay, *Cambodia,* pp. 46–112; William Shawcross, *Cambodia's New Deal,* pp. 1–4 and 12–68; and contemporary media reporting. See also Steve Heder and Judy Ledgerwood, editors, *Propaganda, Politics, and Violence in Cambodia.* Several former officials of the Khmer Republic survived to become candidates in the election: Sak Sutsakhan (Liberal Democratic Party, an offshoot of Son Sann's group) and In Tam (Parti Democrate), for example. Sutsakhan died of a heart attack in Phnom Penh in April 1994.

7. The concluding paragraphs rely in part on conversations with a number of individuals in and outside the U.S. government; *International Narcotics Control Strategy Reports,* State Department, March 1995 and March 1996; Chandler, *History,* pp. 242–45; Shawcross, *Cambodia's New Deal,* pp. 69–103; Lewis Stern, "Cambodia," in William Carpenter and David Wiencek, editors, *Asian Security Handbook,* pp. 121–32; and media reporting. On foreign investments, see Salil Tripathi, "The Good, The Bad and The Ugly," *Asia, Inc.,*

Apr. 1996. Despite Sihanouk's affinity for North Korea, which long centered its Southeast Asian diplomatic and clandestine activities in Phnom Penh, Second Prime Minister Hun Sen spearheaded a shift from Pyongyang to Seoul. The primary reason for this was the economic advantage that Cambodia could gain through a rapprochement with South Korea.

ABBREVIATIONS

AAK	Armée de l'Air Khmère, FANK's air force
ANK	Armée Nationale Khmère, FANK's army
APC	Armored personnel carrier
ARK	Aviation Royale Khmère, FARK's air force
ARVN	Army of the Republic of Vietnam
CGDK	Coalition Government of Democratic Kampuchea
CIDG	Civilian Irregular Defense Group
CINCPAC	Commander-in-Chief, Pacific Command
CJCS	Chairman, Joint Chiefs of Staff
COSVN	Central Office for South Vietnam
CPK	Communist Party of Kampuchea; also called Khmer Communist Party
DRVN	Democratic Republic of Vietnam; North Vietnam
FAC	Forward air controller
FAG	Forward air guide; Khmer FAC
FANK	Forces Armées Nationales Khmères; the Khmer armed forces
FARK	Forces Armées Royales Khmères; Cambodia's pre-1970 armed forces
FULRO	Front Unifié de Lutte des Races Opprimées; the United Front for the Struggle of Oppressed Races
FUNK	Front Uni National de Kampuchea
GRUNK	Gouvernement Royal d'Union Nationale de Kampuchea
ICC	International Control Commission
K.R.	Khmer Rouge
KUFNS	Kampuchean United Front for National Salvation
LOC	Line of communication
L.Z.	Landing zone
MACV	Military Assistance Command, Vietnam
MAP	Military Assistance Program
MEDTC	Military Equipment Delivery Team, Cambodia
MNK	Marine Nationale Khmère, FANK's navy
PAVN	People's Army of Vietnam; also called North Vietnamese Army (NVA)
PLAF	People's Liberation Armed Forces; also called Viet Cong (VC)
PNLAFK	People's National Liberation Armed Forces of Kampuchea, FUNK's military arm

PRC	People's Republic of China
PRG	Provisional Revolutionary Government, PLAF's political counterpart
PRK	People's Republic of Kampuchea
RAK	Revolutionary Army of Kampuchea
RVN	Republic of Vietnam; South Vietnam
SEATO	Southeast Asia Treaty Organization
SOC	State of Cambodia
SOG	Studies and Observation Group
SVNAF	South Vietnamese Air Force
U.N.	United Nations
UNTAC	U.N. Transitional Authority in Cambodia
USSAG	United States Support Activities Group

BIBLIOGRAPHY

OFFICIAL AND PRIMARY SOURCES

Countless official cables, reports, memoranda, letters, transcripts, publications, and other documents from American and foreign government agencies and other organizations provided input for this book. Although many are listed in the Sources and Notes section, they are too numerous (or not listable) to record in a bibliography. I also was able to turn to notes I had made and to personal informal records, such as journals kept by others. Among the many interesting and valuable documents are the Lon Nol–Richard Nixon letters and the 1978 Democratic Kampuchea Ministry of Foreign Affairs Black Book (or Black Paper), all available at the Department of State in Washington, D.C. Informative Department of Defense documents include *Cross-border Operations, Southeast Asia; 1964–1968—Section 2: Cambodia,* August 7, 1973; *Sensitive Operations in Southeast Asia, 1964–1973,* undated; *DOD Report on Selected Air and Ground Operations in Cambodia and Laos,* September 10, 1973; *DRAC-to-MACV Fortnightly Cambodian Reports* for the period; *SAC in Southeast Asia: 1965–1973,* Office of the Historian, Headquarters SAC, August 15, 1974; and *Chronology of the Vietnam War,* March AFB, Office of the 15th Air Force Historian, May 30, 1974. Among the CIA's many declassified documents are *The Situation in Cambodia* monthly reports; *Communism in Cambodia,* May, 1972; *Post Mortem Report: An Examination of the Intelligence Community's Performance Before and During the* Mayaguez *Incident in May 1975,* August 8, 1975; and *Kampuchea; A Demographic Catastrophe,* May, 1980. UNTAC's role is favorably recorded in *The United Nations and Cambodia: 1991–1995,* UN Blue Book Series, vol. 2, 1995.

Oral histories and publicly available papers of the following individuals were examined at the U.S. Army Military History Institute, Carlisle Barracks, Pennsylvania: Brigadier General Donald Blackburn; Lieutenant Colonel Kenneth Bowra; Colonel John Crerar; General Michael Davison; Brigadier General Theodore Mataxis; General William Yarborough. There also are the tour end reports of Generals Mataxis, John Cleland, and William Palmer, dated February 12, 1972; February 20, 1974; and April 30, 1975, respectively. Unpublished papers used in my research included Andrew Antippas, *The Nixon*

Doctrine Revisited: The Rearming of the Cambodians in 1970; Kenneth Bowra, then a major, *Cambodia: Analysis of U.S. Military Assistance to Cambodia, 1970–1975;* and Lieutenant Colonel Ted Mataxis, Jr., *Traits and Behavioral Characteristics of a Combat Leader.* The last two are available at Carlisle barracks.

Those with whom I had conversations (in some cases, numerous ones) and can name are Andrew Antippas, Mark Berent, Chhang Song, William Harben, Orr Kelly, Frank Margiotta, Richard Moose, Ron Podlaski, and David Whipple.

BOOKS

The published book sources listed below comprise the majority consulted to complement and supplement my other sources by confirming facts, permitting balanced assessments, filling in admittedly wide gaps in my knowledge, and providing public sources for descriptions that otherwise would not have been allowed because of my employment agreement with the U.S. government. Naturally, the following material varies in historical value and reliability, even when written by participants in the events described. Some works deal specifically with Cambodia, others only touch upon the subject. All, however, contributed something to my final product. Articles from magazines and journals are cited in full in the notes section.

Adams, Sam. *War of Numbers.* South Royalton, Vt.: Steerforth, 1994.
Albin, David, and Marlowe Hood, editors. *The Cambodian Agony.* Armonk, N.Y.: M. E. Sharpe, 1987.
Allen, Douglas, and Ngô Vĩnh Long. *Coming to Terms.* Boulder, Co.: Westview, 1991.
Allman, T. D. *Unmanifest Destiny.* New York: Dial, 1984.
Anson, Robert. *War News.* New York: Simon and Schuster, 1989.
Asian Watch and Physicians for Human Rights. *Land Mines in Cambodia.* September 1991.
Attwood, William. *The Twilight Struggle.* New York: Harper and Row, 1987.
Ballard, Jack. *Deployment and Employment of Fixed-Wing Gunships: 1962–1972.* Washington, D.C.: Office of Air Force History, 1982.
Barron, John, and Anthony Paul. *Murder of a Gentle Land.* New York: Reader's Digest, 1977.
Batchelder, Col. Sydney, Jr., and Maj. David Quinlan. "Operation Eagle Pull." *The Marines in Vietnam, 1954–1973: An Anthology and Annotated Bibliography.*

Washington, D.C.: USMC History and Museums Division, 1985. Pp. 203–39.

Becker, Elizabeth. *When the War Was Over.* New York: Simon and Schuster, 1986.

Beckett, Ian, editor. *The March of Communism: 1939–Present.* New York: Military Press,1985.

Berger, Carl, editor. *The United States Air Force in Southeast Asia, 1961–1973.* Washington, D.C.: Office of Air Force History, 1984.

Bit, Sanglim. *The Warrior Heritage.* El Cerrito, Calif.: Bit, 1991.

Bloodworth, Dennis. *An Eye for the Dragon.* New York: Farrar, Straus and Giroux, 1970.

Blum, William. *Killing Hope.* Monroe, Maine: Common Courage, 1995.

Bolger, Daniel. *Americans at War.* Novato, Calif.: Presidio, 1988.

Branigan, K. *Atlas of Archeology.* New York: St. Martin's, 1982.

Brown, Ashley, editor. *The U.S. Marines in Action.* New York: Villard, 1986.

Brown, Frederick. *Rebuilding Cambodia.* Washington, D.C.: Foreign Policy Institute, 1993.

Brown, Louise. *War and Aftermath in Vietnam.* London: Routledge, 1991.

Browne, Malcolm. *Muddy Boots and Red Socks.* New York: Times, 1993.

Butler, David. *The Fall of Saigon.* New York: Simon and Schuster, 1985.

Caldwell, Malcolm, and Lek Tan. *Cambodia and the Southeast Asia War.* New York: Monthly Review, 1973.

Carhart, Tom. *Battlefront Vietnam.* New York: Warner, 1984.

Carney, Timothy. *Communist Party Power in Kampuchea (Cambodia).* Ithaca, N.Y.: Cornell University Press, 1977.

Carpenter, William, and David Wiencek, editors. *Asian Security Handbook.* Armonk, N.Y.: M. E. Sharpe, 1996.

Carver, Michael. *War Since 1975.* New York: G. P. Putnam's Sons, 1981.

Chanda, Nayan. *Brother Enemy.* San Diego, Calif.: Harcourt Brace Jovanovich, 1986.

Chandler, David. *Brother Number One.* Boulder, Co.: Westview, 1992.

———. *A History of Cambodia.* Boulder, Co.: Westview, 1996.

———. *The Land and People of Cambodia.* New York: HarperCollins, 1991.

———. *The Tragedy of Cambodian History.* New Haven, Conn.: Yale University Press, 1991.

Chandler, David, and Ben Kiernan, editors. *Revolution and Its Aftermath in Kampuchea.* New Haven, Conn.: Yale University Press, 1983.

Chantrabot, Ros. *La République Khmère.* Paris: L'Harmattan, 1993.

Chirot, Daniel. *Modern Tyrants.* New York: Free Press, 1994.

Christian, David, and William Hoffer. *Victor Six.* New York: Pocket Books, 1990.

Clark, Gregory. *Words of the Vietnam War.* Jefferson, N.C.: McFarland, 1990.

Colby, William, and Peter Forbath. *Honorable Men: My Life in the CIA.* New York: Simon and Schuster, 1978.

Colby, William, with James McCargar. *Lost Victory.* Chicago: Contemporary, 1989.

Coleman, J. D. *Incursion.* New York: St. Martin's, 1991.

Committee of Concerned Asian Scholars. *The Indochina Story.* New York: Bantam, 1970.

Conboy, Ken. *South-East Asian Special Forces.* London: Osprey, 1991.

————. *Shadow War.* Boulder, Co.: Paladin, 1995.

Conboy, Ken; Ken Bowra; and Simon McCouaig. *The NVA and Viet Cong.* London: Osprey, 1991.

Conboy, Kenneth, and Kenneth Bowra. *The War in Cambodia.* London: Osprey, 1989.

Cosmas, G., and Lt. Col. T. Murray. *U.S. Marines in Vietnam: Vietnamization and Redeployment, 1970–1971.* Washington, D.C.: USMC History and Museums Division, 1986.

Curry, Cecil. *Edward Lansdale: The Unquiet American.* Boston: Houghton Mifflin, 1988.

Cutler, Thomas. *Brown Water, Black Berets.* New York: Pocket Books, 1989.

Dagens, Bruno. *Angkor: Heart of an Asian Empire.* New York: H. N. Abrams, 1995.

Davidson, Lt. Gen. Phillip. *Vietnam at War.* Novato, Calif.: Presidio, 1988.

Davies, Paul. *War of the Mines.* Boulder, Co.: Pluto, 1994.

Dorr, Robert. *Air War South Vietnam.* London: Arms and Armour, 1990.

Dougan, Clark, and David Fulghum. *The Vietnam Experience: The Fall of the South.* Boston: Boston Publishing, 1965.

Doyle, Edward. *The Vietnam Experience: The Aftermath, 1975–1985.* Boston: Boston Publishing, 1985.

Dunham, Maj. George, and Col. David Quinlan. *U.S. Marines in Vietnam: The Bitter End, 1973–1975.* Washington, D.C.: USMC History and Museums Division, 1990.

Dunn, Peter. *The First Vietnam War.* London: C. Hurst, 1985.

Ebihara, May; Carol Mortland; and Judy Ledgerwood. *Cambodian Culture Since 1975.* Ithaca, N.Y.: Cornell University Press, 1994.

Editors of the Boston Publishing Company. *The Vietnam Experience: War in the Shadows.* Boston: Boston Publishing, 1988.

Edwardes, Michael. *The West in Asia: 1850–1914.* London: B. T. Batsford, 1967.

Esterline, John and Mae. *"How the Dominoes Fell."* Lanham, Md.: Hamilton, 1986.

Etcheson, Craig. *The Rise and Demise of Democratic Kampuchea.* Boulder, Co.: Westview, 1984.

Fairbank, John; Edwin Reischauer; and Albert Craig. *East Asia: The Modern Transformation*. Boston: Houghton Mifflin, 1990.

Fall, Bernard. *The Two Viet Nams*. New York: Praeger, 1975.

———. *Viet-Nam Witness*. New York: Praeger, 1966.

Findlay, Trevor. *Cambodia: The Legacy and Lessons of UNTAC*. New York: Oxford University Press, 1995.

Fisher, Lewis. *Presidential War Power*. Lawrence: University Press of Kansas, 1995.

Francillon, René. *Vietnam: The War in the Air*. New York: Arch Cape, 1987.

Frazier, Howard. *Uncloaking the CIA*. New York: Free Press, 1978.

Freeman, Michael, and Roger Warner. *Angkor*. Boston: Houghton Mifflin, 1990.

Fujioka, Michio. *Angkor Wat*. Tokyo: Kodansha, 1972.

Gabriel, Richard. *Military Incompetence*. New York: Hill and Wang, 1985.

Gaddis, John. *The Long Peace*. New York: Oxford University Press, 1987.

Gates, Robert. *From the Shadows*. New York: Simon and Schuster, 1996.

Generous, Kevin. *Vietnam: The Secret War*. New York: Gallery, 1985.

Gettleman, Marvin. *Vietnam: History, Documents and Opinions on a Major Crisis*. New York: Fawcett, 1965.

Groslier, Bernard. *Indochina*. Cleveland, Ohio: World, 1966.

Guilmartin, John, Jr. *A Very Short War*. College Station: Texas A&M University Press, 1995.

Gurney, Gene. *Vietnam, the War in the Air*. New York: Crown, 1985.

Haas, Michael. *Cambodia, Pol Pot and the United States*. New York: Praeger, 1991.

———. *Genocide by Proxy*. New York: Praeger, 1991.

Haig, Alexander, with Charles McCarry, *Inner Circles*. New York: Warner, 1992.

Haing Ngor, with Roger Warner. *A Cambodian Odyssey*. New York: Warner, 1989.

Halberstam, David. *The Best and the Brightest*. New York: Penguin, 1987.

Hall, D. G. E. *A History of South-East Asia*. London: Macmillan, 1965.

Hatcher, Patrick. *The Suicide of an Elite*. Stanford, Calif.: Stanford University Press, 1990.

Head, William, and Lawrence Grinter. *Looking Back on the Vietnam War*. Westport, Conn.: Praeger, 1993.

Heckman, Charles. *The Phnom Penh Airlift*. Jefferson, N.C.: McFarland, 1990.

Heder, Steve, and Judy Ledgerwood, editors. *Propaganda, Politics and Violence in Cambodia*. Armonk, N.Y.: M. E. Sharpe, 1996.

Hein, Jeremy. *From Vietnam, Laos and Cambodia*. New York: Twayne, 1995.

Hersh, Seymour. *The Price of Power*. New York: Summit, 1983.

Hudson, Christopher. *The Killing Fields*. London: Pan, 1984.

Isaacs, Arnold. *Without Honor*. New York: Vintage, 1984.

Isaacs, Arnold; Gordon Hardy; and MacAlister Brown. *The Vietnam Experience: Pawns of War.* Boston: Boston Publishing, 1987.

Isaacson, Walter. *Kissinger.* New York: Simon and Schuster, 1992.

Jackson, Karl, editor. *Cambodia; 1975–1978.* Princeton, N.J.: Princeton University Press, 1989.

Kalb, Marvin, and Bernard Kalb. *Kissinger.* New York: Dell, 1975.

Kamps, Charles, Jr. *The History of the Vietnam War.* New York: Military Press, 1988.

Karnow, Stanley, *Vietnam: A History.* New York: Penguin, 1991.

Keegan, John, and Andrew Wheatcroft. *Zones of Conflict.* New York: Simon and Schuster, 1986.

Kelly, Francis. *The Green Berets in Vietnam, 1961–71.* Washington, D.C.: Brassey's (U.S.), 1991.

Kelly, Orr. *Brave Men—Dark Waters.* Novato, Calif.: Presidio, 1992.

———. *Never Fight Fair!* Novato, Calif.: Presidio, 1995.

Kiernan, Ben. *How Pol Pot Came to Power.* London: Verso, 1985.

———. *The Pol Pot Regime.* New Haven, Conn.: Yale University Press, 1996.

Kissinger, Henry. *White House Years.* Boston: Little, Brown, 1979.

———. *Years of Upheaval.* Boston: Little, Brown, 1982.

Knight, David. *Shock Troops.* New York: Crescent, 1983.

Kosut, Hal, editor. *Cambodia and the Vietnam War.* New York: Facts on File, 1971.

Kraus, Max. *They All Came to Geneva.* Cabin John, Md.: Seven Locks, 1988.

Laffin, John. *War Annual,* series 1–5. London: Brassey's, 1986–91.

Lamour, Catherine, and Michael Lamberti. *The International Connection.* New York: Pantheon, 1974.

Landau, David. *Kissinger.* Boston: Houghton Mifflin, 1972.

Lanning, Michael, and Dan Cragg. *Inside the VC and the NVA.* New York: Fawcett Columbine, 1992.

Lansdale, Edward. *In the Midst of War.* New York: Fordham University Press, 1991.

Lehman, John. *Making War.* New York: Scribner's Sons, 1992.

Lentz, Harris, III. *Assassinations and Executions.* Jefferson, N.C.: McFarland, 1988.

Leslie, Jacques. *The Mark.* New York: Four Walls Eight Windows, 1995.

Lipsman, Samuel, and Edward Doyle. *The Vietnam Experience: Fighting for Time.* Boston: Boston Publishing, 1983.

Lukas, Anthony. *Nightmare: The Underside of the Nixon Years.* New York: Penguin, 1988.

Mabbett, Ian, and David Chandler. *The Khmers.* Cambridge, Mass.: Basil Blackwell, 1995.

Macdonald, Peter. *Giap.* New York: Norton, 1993.

————. *Soldiers of Fortune.* New York: Gallery, 1986.

Manne, Robert. *Agent of Influence.* Toronto: Mackenzie Institute, 1989.

Marcinko, Richard, with John Weisman. *Rogue Warrior.* New York: Pocket Books, 1992.

Marenches, Count de, and Christine Ockrent. *The Evil Empire.* London: Sidgwick and Jackson, 1988.

Marolda, Edward, and G. Wesley Pryce III. *A Short History of the United States Navy and the Southeast Asia Conflict, 1950–1975.* Washington, D.C.: Naval Historical Center, 1984.

Martin, Marie. *Cambodia: A Shattered Society.* Berkeley and Los Angeles: University of California Press, 1994.

McCoy, Alfred. *The Politics of Heroin.* New York: Lawrence Hill, 1991.

McCoy, J. W. *Secrets of the Vietcong.* New York: Hippocrene, 1992.

McNeely, Jeffrey, and Paul Wachte. *Soul of the Tiger.* New York: Paragon, 1990.

Melson, Maj. Charles, and Lt. Col. Curtis Arnold. *U.S. Marines in Vietnam: The War That Would Not End, 1971–1973.* Washington, D.C.: USMC History and Museums Division, 1991.

Messegee, Commander J. A., et al. "'Mayday' for the *Mayaguez.*" In *The Marines in Vietnam, 1954–1973: An Anthology and Annotated Bibliography.* Washington, D.C.: USMC History and Museums Division, 1985.

Morrison, Wilbur. *The Elephant and the Tiger.* New York: Hippocrene, 1990.

Morrocco, John. *The Vietnam Experience: Rain of Fire.* Boston: Boston Publishing, 1985.

Moser, Charles, editor. *Combat on Communist Territory.* Lake Bluff, Ill.: Regnery Gateway, 1985.

Nair, Kunhanandan. *Devil and His Dart.* New Belhi: Sterling, 1986.

Neher, Clark. *Southeast Asia in the New International Era.* Boulder, Co.: Westview, 1991.

Newman, John. *JFK and Vietnam.* New York: Warner, 1992.

Nixon, Richard. *Real Peace/No More Vietnams.* New York: Touchstone, 1990.

Nolan, Keith. *Into Cambodia.* Novato, Calif.: Presidio, 1990.

Norodom Sihanouk. *My War with the CIA.* London: Penguin, 1973.

————. *Souvenirs doux et amers.* Paris: Hachette/Stock, 1981.

————. *War and Hope.* New York: Pantheon, 1980.

O'Ballance, Edgar. *The Wars in Vietnam: 1954–1980.* New York: Hippocrene, 1981.

Osborne, Milton. *The French Presence in Cochinchina and Cambodia.* Ithaca, N.Y.: Cornell University Press, 1969.

————. *Sihanouk.* Honolulu: University of Hawaii Press, 1994.

———. *Southeast Asia.* St. Leonards, Australia: Allen and Unwin, 1995.

Palmer, Dave. *Summons of the Trumpet.* Novato, Calif.: Presidio, 1978.

Peterzell, Jay. *Reagan's Secret Wars.* Washington, D.C.: Center for National Security Studies, 1984.

Pike, Douglas. *PAVN: People's Army of Vietnam.* Novato, Calif.: Presidio, 1986.

———. *Viet Cong.* Cambridge, Mass.: M.I.T. Press, 1966.

Podhoretz, Norman. *Why We Were in Vietnam.* New York: Simon and Schuster, 1982.

Ponchaud, François. *Cambodge année zéro.* Paris: René Julliard, 1977; U.S. edition, *Cambodia: Year Zero.* New York: Holt, Rinehart and Winston, 1978.

Powers, Thomas. *The Man Who Kept the Secrets.* New York: Knopf, 1979.

Prados, John. *The Hidden History of the Vietnam War.* Chicago: Ivan R. Dee, 1995.

———. *Keepers of the Keys.* New York: Morrow, 1991.

Radu, Michael. *The New Insurgencies.* New Brunswick, N.J.: Transaction, 1990.

Reske, Charles. *MACV-SOG History: Annex B* (2 vols.). Sharon Center, Ohio: Alpha, 1990.

Robbins, Christopher. *Air America.* New York: Putnam's Sons, 1979.

Rogers, Anthony, Ken Guest, and Jim Hooper. *Flashpoint!* London: Arms and Armour, 1994.

Ross, Robert. *The Indochina Tangle.* New York: Columbia University Press, 1988.

Ross, Russell. *Cambodia: A Country Study.* Washington, D.C.: U.S. Government Printing Office, 1990.

Rowan, Roy. *The Four Days of the* Mayaguez. New York: Norton, 1975.

Rummel, R. J. *Death by Government.* New Brunswick: N.J.: Transaction, 1995.

Sak Sutsakhan, Lt. Gen. *The Khmer Republic at War and the Final Collapse.* Washington, D.C.: U.S. Army Center of Military History, 1980.

Santoli, Al. *Leading the Way.* New York: Ballantine, 1993.

———. *To Bear Any Burden.* New York: Dutton, 1985.

Sar Desai, D. R. *Vietnam: The Struggle for National Identity.* Boulder, Co.: Westview, 1992.

Schaffer, Howard. *Chester Bowles.* Cambridge, Mass.: Harvard University Press, 1993.

Schanberg, Sydney. *The Death and Life of Dith Pran.* New York: Penguin, 1985.

Schlight, John. *The War in South Vietnam: The Years of the Offensive, 1965–1968.* Washington, D.C.: Office of the Air Force Historian, 1988.

Schneider, J.-Martina, editor. *Cambodia, Laos.* Munich: Nelles, 1994.

Schreadley, Commander R. L. *From the Rivers to the Sea.* Annapolis, Md.: U.S. Naval Institute, 1992.

Sesser, Stan. *The Lands of Charm and Cruelty.* New York: Knopf, 1993.

Shain, Yossi, editor. *Governments-in-Exile in Contemporary World Politics*. New
 York: Routledge, 1991.

Shaplen, Robert. *Bitter Victory*. New York: Harper and Row, 1986.

———. *Time Out of Hand*. New York: Harper and Row, 1969.

———. *A Turning Wheel*. New York: Random House, 1979.

Shawcross, William. *Cambodia's New Deal*. Washington, D.C.: Carnegie Endow-
 ment, 1994.

———. *The Quality of Mercy*. New York: Simon and Schuster, 1984.

———. *Sideshow*. New York: Touchstone, 1987.

Simpson, Charles, III. *Inside the Green Berets*. New York: Berley, 1984.

Singlaub, Maj. Gen. John, with Malcolm McConnell. *Hazardous Duty*. New York:
 Summit, 1991.

Snepp, Frank. *Decent Interval*. New York: Random House, 1977.

Spector, Ronald. *Advice and Support: The Early Years, 1941–1960*. Washington,
 D.C.: U.S. Army Center of Military History, 1985.

Stanton, Shelby. *Green Berets at War*. Novato, Calif.: Presidio, 1985.

———. *Special Forces at War*. Charlottesville, Va.: Howell, 1990.

———. *Vietnam Order of Battle*. New York: Exeter, 1987.

Starry, Gen. Donn. *Armored Combat in Vietnam*. New York: Arno, 1980.

Stein, Jeff. *A Murder in Wartime*. New York: St. Martin's, 1992.

Summers, Harry, Jr. *Historical Atlas of the Vietnam War*. Boston: Houghton
 Mifflin, 1995.

———. *Vietnam War Almanac*. New York: Facts on File, 1985.

Sutter, Robert. *The Cambodian Crisis and U.S. Policy Dilemmas*. Boulder, Co.:
 Westview, 1991.

Szulc, Tad. *The Illusion of Peace*. New York: Viking, 1978.

Thompson, Leroy. *The U.S. Army in Vietnam*. Devon, UK: David and Charles,
 1990.

Thornton, Richard. *The Nixon-Kissinger Years*. New York: Paragon House, 1989.

Tilford, Earl, Jr. *Crosswinds*. College Station: Texas A&M University Press, 1993.

Todd, Olivier. *Cruel Avril*. Paris: Robert Laffont, 1987; U.S. edition, *Cruel April*.
 New York: Norton, 1990.

Toohey, Brian, and William Pinwill. *Oyster*. Port Melbourne, Australia: William
 Heinemann Australia, 1989.

Tourison, Sedgwick. *Secret Army, Secret War*. Annapolis, Md.: U.S. Naval Institute,
 1995.

Tran Dinh Tho, Brig. Gen. *The Cambodian Incursion*. Washington, D.C.: U.S.
 Army Center of Military History, 1979.

Truong Nhu Tang, with David Chanoff and Doan Van Toai. *A Vietcong Memoir.* New York: Vintage, 1986.

Vandenbroucke, Lucien. *Perilous Options.* New York: Oxford University Press, 1993.

Vickery, Michael. *Cambodia: 1975–1982.* Boston: South End, 1984.

Walker, Greg. *At The Hurricane's Eye.* New York: Ivy, 1994.

Warner, Denis. *Certain Victory.* Kansas City, Mo.: Sheed Andrews and McMeel, 1977.

Watson, James, and Kevin Dockery. *Point Man.* New York: Morrow, 1993.

Werner, Jayne, and Lun Doan Huynh, editors. *The Vietnam War.* Armonk, N.Y.: M. E. Sharpe, 1993.

Whitaker, Donald, et al. *Area Handbook for the Khmer Republic (Cambodia).* Washington, D.C.: Government Printing Office, 1973.

Williams, Maslyn. *The Land in Between.* New York: Morrow, 1970.

Wise, David. *The American Police State.* New York: Random House, 1976.

INDEX

AAK *(Armée de l'Air Khmère)*, 151, 162, 186, 190, 196, 213; assassination attempts and, 163, 182, 183; establishment of, 71; Operation Thunderstrike and, 183; strength of, 71, 83, 99, 108, 144–45, 193; U.S. training of, 81, 213

Abrams, Gen. Creighton, Jr., 115

Acheson, Dean, 41

aerial supply, 92, 110, 151, 155, 157, 158, 174, 179, 196, 199, 205, 212, 213, 221; during 1974–75, into Pochentong, 205–206, 212, 216

Agnew, Spiro, 163

Ahern, Thomas, 63

Air America, 140, 174, 194, 206, 214

Air Cambodge, 99, 214, 219, 221

Amos, Col. Harry, 107

Am Rong, Col., 83, 173, 178

Ang Duong, 18, 22

Angkor Borei, 105

Angkor empire, 14–17

Angkor ruins, 22, 25, 27, 45, 121, 124–26, 132–34, 167, 241; as occupied, by Communists, 72

Angtassom, 137, 151

ANK *(Armée Nationale Khmère)*: at Angkor Chey, 125, 132–34; at Angtassom, 137, 151; at Barrong Khnar, 209–10; at Bassac, 207, 209; at Chambak, 157, 159; at Chenla I, 87–92, 96; at Chenla II, 113–18, 121, 123, 143; at Chup, 84–85, 122; establishment of, 71; at Highway 4, 96–99; at Kampot, 195–96, 199; at Kompong Cham, 84, 176–78; at Kompong Seila, 204–205, 219; at Kompong Speu, 85; at Kompong Thom, 151, 155, 156; at Neak Luong, 78, 127, 131, 217; in Operation 802, 208; at Oudong-Lovek, 195, 197–200, 203–204, 207, 216; at Phnom Penh, 171–72, 185–90, 211–23; at Prey Veng, 127, 131; at Romeas, 155; at Saang, 74; at Siem Reap, 85; at Sorya, 136–37, 143; strength of, 71, 108, 143–44, 192; at Takeo, 151, 157, 158; U.S. incursion and, 77–79; U.S. training

of, 81–82, 103; at Victory East of the Mekong, 112–13, 183

Antippas, Andrew, 63

ARK *(Aviation Royale Khmère)*, 39, 42

Armée de l'Air Khmère. See AAK

Armée Nationale Khmère. See ANK

ASEAN (Association of Southeast Asian Nations), 218, 240

assassination attempts, 37–38, 40, 94, 111, 118–19, 121, 127, 138–39, 162–63, 185, 199, 202, 222

Australia, 18, 43, 45, 47, 62, 63, 68, 82, 239

Aviation Royale Khmère. See ARK

Bangkok Plot, 36

Baray, 114, 116

Barrong Khnar, 209

Bassac River, 4, 13, 136, 199, 207, 220

Batchelder, Col. Sydney, 4, 7, 220

Battambang, 87, 140, 145, 149, 168, 174, 193, 214, 215–16, 225, 228

Beecher, William, 50

Berent, Lt. Col. Mark, 160

Big Show program, 193

Bird Air, 206, 213, 214, 220

Blackjack missions (U.S. military), 47

blame, for Cambodian War, 185

Bolton, Lt. Col. James, 7

Botum Bopha. *See* Norodom Sihanouk: Botum Bopha (daughter) and

Boun Oum, 84

Bowles, Chester, 45, 50

Bowra, Capt. Kenneth, 194

Bright Light sorties, 48. *See also* SOG

Bright Star, SS, 151

Bush, George, 218

Cambodia: attacks by, against Vietnam, 230; compulsory military service in, 173, 195; cultural beliefs in, 18–21; drug smuggling in, 103–104, 129, 242; early history of, 14–18; elections in, 26, 32, 33, 54, 134–35, 237,

Cambodia, *(continued)*
243; foreign investments in, 33, 56, 240–41;
French rule in, 22–28; general description
of, 11–14; independence won by, 28; invaded by PAVN-PLAF, 72, 73; killing fields
of, 234–35; K.R. anthem and, 229; land
mines in, 166, 236, 240, 243; mobilization
of, 87; 1975–77 Paris Agreement and, 154–
55; pogrom in, against Vietnamese civilians,
74–75; postwar corruption in, 239–40, 241–
42; refugees and, 87, 90, 141, 177, 178, 188,
207, 222, 226, 237; renamed Democratic
Kampuchea, 229; renamed People's Republic, 235; renamed State of Cambodia, 236;
republic established in, 94–95; returns to
monarchy, 237; seeks cease-fire, 155, 171,
209, 219, 222; superstitions in, 19–20, 69,
88–89, 102, 125–26, 144, 177, 210, 219; UN
and, 35, 42, 72, 149, 180, 209, 215, 236, 237–
39, 240, 242; U.S. aid to, 34, 38–39, 65–66,
80–82, 93–94, 100, 103, 106–108, 110, 143–
46, 172, 179, 190, 192–94, 209, 214, 216–17,
221; Vietnamese invasion of, 235; war casualty figures in, 44, 105, 106, 225; wartime
political turmoil in, 111–12, 121, 123, 126,
134–35, 162–65, 195, 201–203, 208–209,
214–15, 218. *See also specific places, military,
governmental, and political branches and organizations*
Cambodian armed forces. *See specific military
organizations*
Cates, Maj. George, 5
Cedar Walk project (U.S. military), 48
Central Intelligence Agency. *See* CIA
Central Office for South Vietnam. *See* COSVN
CGDK (Coalition Government of Democratic
Kampuchea), 236, 237
Chambak, 157, 159
Chamcar Andong plantation, 91, 114, 115, 117
Chamcar Leu plantation, 88, 114
Chandler, David, 58, 111
Cheng Heng, 59, 83, 94–95, 126, 135, 142, 164,
181, 189, 195, 218
Chenla I campaign, 87–92, 96
Chenla II campaign, 113–18, 121, 123, 143
Chenla states, 14
Chhang Song, 31
China, 44, 49, 52, 149; aids Sihanouk, 32, 35,
41–42; ancient role of, 11; creation of

FUNK-GRUNK and, 60; reaction of, to
Sihanouk overthrow, 68; supports K.R., 41–
42, 51, 61, 165, 203, 211, 217, 228, 230, 236;
at war with Vietnam, 235
Chinit River, 86, 114
Christensen, Cmdr. Cyrus, 212
Christopher, Warren, 243
Chup plantation, 12, 84, 109, 122, 136
Church, Frank, 194
CIA (Central Intelligence Agency), 8, 28, 35, 37,
38, 46, 47, 62, 64, 66, 68, 73, 82, 103, 120,
131, 143, 171, 172, 174–75, 194, 206; lost hu-
man assets of, 224; opens Cambodia station,
63; Son Ngoc Thanh and, 67, 135
CINCPAC (Commander-in-Chief, Pacific
Command), 46, 94, 107, 153, 155, 175, 216
Cleland, Brig. Gen. John, 145, 179
Cleveland, USS, 98
Coalition Government of Democratic Kam-
puchea. *See* CGDK
Colby, William, 67
Columbia Eagle, SS, 63–64
Commander-in-Chief, Pacific Command. *See*
CINCPAC
Communist Party of Kampuchea, 51, 86, 146,
147, 154, 171, 178, 228, 229, 230; dominates
K.R., 147, 166, 167, 180, 203
COMUSSAG/7th AF, 6, 160, 168, 194, 216, 220
congressional amendments. *See specific amend-
ments*
Continental Air Services, 82, 206
Cooper-Church Amendment, 79
Coral Sea, USS, 232
COSVN (Central Office for South Vietnam),
12, 44, 50, 57, 72, 78
Cranston, Alan, 194
Cushman, Maj. Gen. John, 105

Da Nang, 7
Dap Chhuon, 36–37
Dean, John Gunther, 4, 5, 6, 8, 10, 194, 203,
208, 214, 215, 219, 220, 237
Defense Intelligence Agency. *See* DIA
defoliation, 49
de Marenches, Alexandre, 63
Deschamps, Noel St. Clair, 45
DGGP *(Direction Générale de Guerre Politique),*
173
DIA (Defense Intelligence Agency), 66

Dien Del, Brig. Gen., 157, 181
Direction Générale de Guerre Politique. See
DGGP
Dith Pran, 8
Do Cao Tri, Lt. Gen., 108, 109
drug trafficking, 103–104, 129, 242
Dulles, John Foster, 27, 34, 36
Dyrac, Jean, 226, 227

Ea Chhong, Brig. Gen., 193
Eagle Pull evacuation, 3–10, 120, 216, 220–21,
243
Eisenhower, Dwight, 27, 36, 38
Enders, Thomas, 138–39, 160, 180–81, 190

Fallaci, Oriana, 180
FANK *(Forces Armées Nationales Khmères)*, casualty figures of, 73, 91, 99, 117, 136, 149,
159–60, 178, 184, 186, 191, 196, 204, 210, 217,
225–26; corruption in, 20, 108, 110, 112, 121–
22, 123, 130–31, 141–43, 172–73, 179, 182, 186,
205, 206, 217; establishment of, 71; matériel
of, left to K.R., 225; organization and
strength of, 71, 72, 94, 143–45, 172; performance improvement of, 173, 191; troop indoctrination in, 173
FARK *(Forces Armées Royales Khmères)*, 28, 40,
44, 51–52, 56, 60, 70
Fix, Lt. Col. Herbert, 8
Flynn, Sean, 73–74
Foa, Sylvana, 161
Forces Armées Nationales Khmères. See FANK
Forces Armées Royales Khmères. See FARK
Ford, Gerald, 6, 206, 218, 221, 227
France, 65, 85, 131, 185, 189, 216, 223, 237, 239;
colonial period of, 22–28; during Sihanouk's
first rule, 30, 33, 39, 41; embassy of, as ref-
uge, 226–27; intelligence of, 63
Freedom Care program, 193
Freedom Deal, 76
Front Unifié de Lutte des Races Opprimées. See
FULRO
Front Uni National de Kampuchea. See FUNK
FULRO *(Front Unifié de Lutte des Races Op-
primées)*, 46
Funan states, 14
FUNK *(Front Uni National de Kampuchea)*, 60,
61, 146, 149, 226, 229

Geneva conferences, 28, 30–31, 33
Glatkowski, Alvin, 63–64
*Gouvernement Royal d'Union Nationale de
Kampuchea. See* GRUNK
Groslier, Philippe-Bernard, 124, 125
GRUNK *(Gouvernement Royal d'Union Na-
tionale de Kampuchea)*, 60, 149, 167, 171,
180, 203, 222, 229

Haig, Alexander, 80, 135, 164
Haing Ngor, 234
Hak Ly, 44
Hall, Richard, 66
Hancock, USS, 3, 8
Hang Thun Hak, 135, 143
Harben, William, 142, 152, 162
Harriman, W. Averill, 43
Hem Keth Dara, 223, 224, 226, 229
Heng Samrin, 230
Henry B. Wilson, USS, 232
Herz, Martin, 35
Highway Route 1, 12, 73, 74, 75, 110, 131, 136,
137, 139, 143, 150, 155, 157, 158, 159, 169, 174,
176, 207, 213, 217
Highway Route 2, 136, 150, 151, 156, 157, 159,
183, 188
Highway Route 3, 132, 137, 150, 151, 156, 172,
183, 186, 188, 195
Highway Route 4, 7, 13, 44, 85, 92, 104, 110,
122, 150, 151, 159, 168, 178, 179, 182, 183, 186,
188, 199, 200, 204, 212; joint operation on,
96–99
Highway Route 5, 85, 87, 104, 110, 132, 140, 145,
149, 150, 168, 172, 178, 195, 197, 198, 200,
204, 207, 220, 228
Highway Route 6, 87, 88, 90, 92, 96, 114, 115,
116, 125, 149, 150, 151, 155, 172, 174, 177, 208
Highway Route 7, 88, 92, 114, 124, 149, 150, 174,
177
Ho Chi Minh, 26, 27, 29, 33, 44
Ho Chi Minh Trail, 34, 36, 44, 49, 52, 79, 86,
103, 147, 165, 167, 211
Hoeur Lay Inn, 163
Hong Boun Hor, 227
Hoskins, Maj. John, 175
Hou Hang Sin, Brig. Gen., 114, 116
Humphrey, Larry, 64
Hun Sen, 230, 241

Kossla River, 195, 196
Kosygin, Alexei, 60
K.R. *See* Khmers Rouges
Kratie, 11, 73, 78
Kudryavtsev, Sergei, 63
KUFNS (Kampuchean United Front for National Salvation), 235

Ladd, Jonathan, 80–81, 93–94, 106, 107
Laird, Melvin, 64, 104, 106, 132
Laos, 11, 16, 23, 25, 30, 34, 43, 45, 46, 62, 103, 108, 147, 154, 160, 168, 217; drug smuggling and, 104; offer of aid by, 84; Thai soldiers in, 84
Lavelle, Gen. John, 105
Lawson, Lt. Col. Curtis, 220
Lay Chhom, Capt., 114
Leclerc, Gen. Phillipe, 26
Le Duc Tho, 72, 154
Lim Sisaath, Lt. Col., 103, 217
Lindley, Capt. Forrest, 66
Long Boret, 5, 149, 189, 195, 199, 201, 202, 215, 217–18, 219, 223, 224; becomes prime minster, 182; execution of, 227
Long Botta, 5
Lon Nil, 69
Lon Nol, 20, 21, 27, 36–37, 38, 52, 56, 67–68, 87, 94–95, 99, 111–12, 121, 137, 139, 142, 163–64, 195, 198, 201, 210, 215, 217; appeal of, for aid, 65; assassination attempts against, 162, 181–82; becomes president, 126; in Chenla I, 91; in Chenla II, 114–15, 117, 121; correspondence of, with Nixon, 95; during French colonial period, 28–29; as FANK commander-in-chief, 71; leaves Cambodia, 5, 218–19; major demonstration against, 69; meets Kissinger, 150; meets Vietnamese leaders, 82–83; mysticism of, 89, 132, 152–53; named prime minister, 54–55; and Neo-Khmerism, 152; in 1972 elections, 135; orders sanctuaries out of Cambodia, 57; rejects Laotian aid, 84; role of, in Sihanouk ouster, 58–59, 67; suffers stroke, 101–102, 126, 152
Lon Nol Line, 87, 88, 149–50
Lon Non, 29, 54, 57, 58, 65, 83, 84, 95, 126, 138, 139, 162, 223, 224; description of, 102–103; "dirty jobs" unit of, 139, 163; execution of, 227; 15th Brigade and, 211; leaves Cambodia, 164; in 1972 elections, 135; at Phnom

Baphnum, 140; renews political activities, 215, 219; returns to Cambodia, 208; 3rd Division and, 142–43, 157, 159
Lovek, 150, 197, 198, 200, 203–204, 207
Lowenstein, James, 65, 161
Lucky Star, SS, 158

MAAG (U.S. Military Assistance Advisory Group), 34
MACV (U.S. Military Assistance Command, Vietnam), 46, 80, 81, 82, 94, 155, 160, 168
Mam Pram Moni, 152
Mansfield, Mike, 51
McCain, Adm. John, Jr., 153
McClintock, Robert, 35
McKay, Clyde, 63–64
Mao Zedong, 42, 228, 235
Marine Nationale Khmère. See MNK
Mataxis, Brig. Gen. Theodore, 106, 107, 122
Matthews, Rear Adm. Herbert, 109
Mayaguez, SS, 231–33
MEDTC (Military Equipment Delivery Team, Cambodia), 8, 93–94, 106–107, 110, 119, 120, 145, 179, 193–94, 204, 211, 221, 222
Mekong River, 4, 11, 12, 13, 35, 168, 178, 199, 208; attacks on, against convoys, 73, 128, 132, 151–52, 155, 156, 157–58, 174, 179, 191, 200–201, 205, 207, 208, 212; closing of, 212; as LOC, 109–10, 193, 212; mines in, 191, 203, 211, 212–13
Melton, Capt. William, 9
Mey Sichan, Brig. Gen., 224, 225
Mhoul Khleng, Brig. Gen., 177, 196
Military Equipment Delivery Team, Cambodia. *See* MEDTC
Miller, Capt. Charles, 231, 232
mines: land, 166, 236, 240, 243; marine, 191, 203, 211, 212–13
MNK *(Marine Nationale Khmère),* 158, 191, 200, 208, 212–13; amphibious operations of, 177–78, 197; Chrouy Chang War base and, 64, 71, 99, 128; establishment of, 71; strength of, 71, 108, 145, 193, 196
money-laundering, 241–42
Monivong, 24
Moose, Richard, 65, 161

Nakhon Phanom RTAFB, 161, 168, 231
National Liberation Front. *See* NLF

Neak Luong, 12, 75, 78, 83, 84, 110, 127, 131, 136, 137, 139, 157, 176, 212, 213; bombing of, 169, 179; fall of, 217

Neak Sam, Brig. Gen., 89, 91

Nehru, Jawaharlal, 34

Ngo Dihn Diem, 33, 39, 40, 41, 121

Ngo Dzu, Lt. Gen., 97

Nguyen Cao Ky, 82

Nguyen Van Thieu, 83

Nixon, Richard, 49, 50–51, 61–62, 63, 64, 65, 73, 77, 106, 150, 154, 189, 206; Congress and, 79–80, 170, 194; correspondence of, with Lon Nol, 95, 174, 192. See also Nixon Doctrine

Nixon Doctrine, 106, 107

NLF (National Liberation Front), 44

non-aligned states conferences: at Algiers, 180; at Bandung, 35; at Guyana, 149; at Lusaka, 149

Nop Bophann, 38

Norodom Chantarangsey, Brig. Gen., 220

Norodom Ranariddh, 237, 239, 241

Norodom Sihanouk, 18, 19, 50, 54–55, 111, 139, 149, 166, 171, 209, 226, 235, 243; abdication by, 32; accepts French aid, 41; accepts Sino-Soviet aid, 32, 36; accepts U.S. aid, 34; as allied with K.R., 60, 167; background of, 31; becomes prime minister, 35; Botum Bopha (daughter) and, 162; calls for uprising, 61; cedes power to K.R., 229; during colonial period, 24–29; ends U.S. aid, 39; establishes relations with DRV and PRG, 44; family losses of, 228; flees to China, 235; letter of, to Ford, 218; meets Pol Pot, 167; Monique (wife) and, 31, 56, 75, 167; 1991 returns to Cambodia, 237; 1970 takes trip to Europe, 55–56, 58, 59–60; ouster of, 59–60, 123; "peace feeler" and, 171; postwar return of, to Cambodia, 228; president of CGDK, 236; prewar rule by, 31–46, 49–55; reascends throne, 237; rejects peace overtures, 189, 203, 218, 220–21, 222; sentencing of, in absentia, 75; severs relations with Thailand/S. Vietnam, 39; severs relations with U.S., 43; traitor list and, 217, 219, 222; trips of, from Beijing, 146, 167; undermining of, by K.R., 146, 180, 206, 229; visits U.S., 27, 36, 38

Norodom Suramarit, 31, 38

North Korea, 237, 239

North Vietnam: allows dominant war role of K.R., 146–47; embassy of, closed, 67; embassy of, sacked, 57; invades Cambodia, 72, 73; reaction of, to Sihanouk ouster, 68; sanctuaries of, in Cambodia, 34, 36, 39, 43–44, 45, 46, 50, 51–53, 56, 57, 67, 68, 72, 74, 78, 79; violates Paris agreement, 154–55, 199. See also COSVN; Ho Chi Minh Trail; PAVN; PLAF; Viet Minh

O'Keefe, Gen. Timothy, 194

Okinawa, USS, 3, 5, 10

Operation Arc Light, 76, 78, 93, 132, 169

Operation Daniel Boone, 47, 50

Operation Eagle Pull, 3–10, 120, 216, 220–21, 243

Operation Frequent Wind, 5

Operation Menu, 50–51, 52, 76, 78

Operation Patio, 76

Operation Salem House, 47

Oudong, 145, 150, 195, 197–200, 203–204, 207; fall of, 216

Oum Mannorine, 57, 58

Palmer, Brig. Gen. William, 8, 222

Paris Agreement, 82, 154, 168, 193, 199

Paris Peace Accords, 236

Paris peace talks, 50, 72, 82, 150, 154

PAVN (People's Army of Vietnam), 30, 39, 43, 44, 52, 61, 67, 72, 151, 165, 177, 228, 235; at Angkor ruins, 72, 124–25; C40 Divison of, 72, 85, 116, 127, 165; in Chenla II, 114–17; commando raids by, 99–101, 127–28, 136, 138, 147–50, 151–52; 5th Division of, 72, 92, 126, 155, 199; 1st Divison of, 72, 92, 97, 118, 122, 126–27, 132, 150, 155, 165; 9th Division of, 72, 74, 84, 90, 92, 112, 115, 122, 126; 7th Division of, 72, 92, 122, 126; 367th Sapper Regiment of, 127, 147–48, 159, 165; use of tanks by, 48, 121, 136–37

Pech Lim Kuon, 181–82, 183

Pell Nal, Col., 173

Penn Rannda, Brig. Gen., 193

Pen Samnang, 1st Lt., 219

People's Army of Vietnam. See PAVN

People's Liberation Armed Forces. See PLAF

People's National Liberation Armed Forces of Kampuchea. See PNLAFK

Sap River, 13, 90, 92, 145, 195, 197, 200, 204, 214, 219; attacks on bridge over, 128, 147–48
Sar Hor, Maj. Gen., 125, 177
Sarit Thanarat, 37, 41
Sattahip, 193
Saukham Khoy, 5, 8, 219
Sauvagnargues, Jean, 227
Schanberg, Sydney, 8, 223
Schlesinger, James, 178
SEATO (Southeast Asia Treaty Organization), 34–35
Sen River, 88, 90, 115
Shawcross, William, 66
Siam. See Thailand
Siem Reap, 14, 36, 85, 87, 124, 125, 133, 145, 151, 183, 208; fall of, 225
Sihanoukville. See Kompong Som
Sisophon, 208
Sisowath Rattasa, 121
Sisowath Sirik Matak, 6, 54–55, 57, 58, 67–68, 83, 87, 95, 101, 123, 126, 143, 164, 195, 218, 226; dissatisfaction of, with Lon Nol, 102, 121, 163, 181; during French colonial period, 28–29; execution of, 227; as Republican Party secretary-general, 135; role of, in Sihanouk ouster, 58–59, 67
Skoun, 88, 90, 91, 92, 93, 111, 116, 174, 177
Slade, Lt. Col. George, 7
Snepp, Frank, 66
Soeung Kimsea, Maj., 83
SOG (Studies and Observation Group), 46–48, 66. See also Bright Light sorties
Som Sam Al, 127
Son Ngoc Thanh, 24, 25, 26, 28, 35, 36, 38, 56, 67, 123, 218; assassination attempt against, 138; retirement of, 135; returns to Cambodia, 75–76
Son Sann, 38, 189, 235–36
So Potra, Capt., 162
So Satto, 163
Sosthene Fernandez, 58, 74, 96, 105, 143, 159, 172, 181, 182, 188, 195, 218; removal of, from command, 214–15
Southeast Asia Treaty Organization. See SEATO
South Vietnam: aids Lon Nol, 83; diplomatic ties of, with Cambodia, 39, 83; drug smuggling and, 104; during Sihanouk rule, 34, 35–36, 37, 39, 40, 42, 44, 45, 46; forces of,

in Cambodia 1970–75, 70, 71, 77, 83, 84, 85, 92, 96, 97–98, 108–10, 111, 122, 124, 126, 137, 151, 199; reaction of, to Sihanouk ouster, 68; repatriates civilians, 75, 78
Soviet Union, 45, 50, 56, 60, 149, 223, 227; aids Sihanouk, 32, 61; cuts embassy staff, 180; intelligence of, 63; reaction of, to Sihanouk ouster, 68; supports PRK, 235
Stein, John, 63
Stone, Dana, 73–74
Studies and Observation Group. See SOG
Suharto, Raden, 219
Summit Conference of Peoples of Indochina, 61
Supreme National Council, 236
Suryavarman II, 15, 16, 124
Svay Rieng, 74, 174, 183, 199, 213, 221
Swank, Emory, 93, 123, 132, 135, 174, 218; influence of, on Lon Nol, 164; replacement of, 179–80
Swann, Capt. Donald, 64
Symington, Stuart, 161
Symington-Case Amendment, 146

Taiwan, 40, 149, 206
Takeo, 132, 150, 151, 157, 158
Takhmau, 136, 220, 222
Talbott, Strobe, 240
Ta Mok, 197
Tan Chau, 109, 157
Tang Island, 231–33
Tang Kauk, 86, 89–90, 91, 114, 116
Tan Son Nhut, 92, 161, 168
Tep Khunnah, 163
Tep Phan, 30
Thach Chea, 201–202
Thailand, 5, 6, 9, 10, 11, 16, 17–18, 82, 174, 194, 213, 216, 219, 221, 225, 228, 231, 242; aids Lon Nol, 83–84; diplomatic ties of, with Cambodia, 39, 83; drug smuggling and, 104; during French colonial period, 22–24, 26; during Sihanouk rule, 35, 36, 40, 45; supports K.R., 236, 242; U.S. bases in, 81, 160, 161, 168, 175, 176, 193, 206, 219, 231
Thlok Trach, 43
Thnaot River, 136, 172, 176, 183, 186, 188; dam project, 85, 120
Thong Van Phan Moeung, Brig. Gen., 91
Tilford, Earl, Jr., 176

Tonkin Gulf incident, 43, 48
Tonle Sap (Great Lake), 13, 90, 127, 145, 214
Tou Samouth, 41
Traeung, 88
Tran Thien Khiem, 111
Tran Van Phouc, 99
Truong Nhu Tang, 50
Tuberville, S.Sgt. Charles, 120
Twining, Charles, 237

Udorn RTAFB, 81, 168, 176
Um Savuth, Brig. Gen., 88
United States: aerial bombing by, 40, 43, 44, 49, 77, 86, 88, 90–92, 97–98, 105–106, 109, 112, 114, 116, 117, 132, 151, 155–57, 159–62, 166, 168, 175–76, 232; aids Lon Nol, 65–66, 80–82, 93–94, 100, 103, 106–108, 110, 141, 143–46, 172, 179, 190, 192–94, 209, 214, 216–17, 221; aids Sihanouk, 34, 38–39; antiwar demonstrations and, 79; assists Cambodia at UN, 149, 180, 209; bombing guides of, 168–69; bombing halt by, 175–76; citizens of, in combat zones, 98, 107, 140, 145, 174–75, 177, 194, 196, 204, 205; clandestine cross-border operations of, 45–49, 50; during French colonial period, 27; evacuation of, from Cambodia, 3–10, 147, 159, 216, 220–21; incursions by, 77–79, 84; MIAs and, 236–37; opposes efforts to depose Lon Nol, 121, 181; Paris Agreement and, 154; postwar military mission to, 239; reestablishes relations with Cambodia, 236–37; role of, in Sihanouk ouster, 61–67; supplants France, 131; supports CGDK, 236; urges Lon Nol reform, 163–64, 195. *See also specific military and governmental branches, organizations, projects, and operations*
Un Kauv, Brig. Gen., 157, 159, 181
Un Sim, 226
UNTAC (UN Transitional Authority in Cambodia), 237–39, 242
UN Transitional Authority in Cambodia. *See* UNTAC
U.S. Air Force, 40, 42, 43, 49–51, 68, 70–71, 76, 81, 86, 88–93, 97–98, 104–105, 109, 110, 112, 114, 116, 117, 132, 137, 151, 155–57, 159–62, 168, 175–76, 194, 196, 199, 205, 206, 221; in Eagle Pull, 5, 7, 9, 220–21; in *Mayaguez* incident, 231–32

U.S. Army, 49, 70–71, 77, 93, 97–98, 100–101, 105, 109, 194; special forces of, 46–48, 66, 80, 81–82, 103, 239, 240
U.S. bases, in Thailand. *See individual bases*
U.S. Embassy: intelligence gathering by, 68–69, 121, 174–75; role of, in U.S. bombing missions, 155, 160–69. *See also* CIA
U.S. Marines: air activities of, 137, 156; in Eagle Pull, 3–10, 216, 220–21; as embassy guards, 94, 120, 220; *Mayaguez* incident and, 232
U.S. Military Assistance Advisory Group. *See* MAAG
U.S. Military Assistance Command, Vietnam. *See* MACV
U.S. Navy, 3–4, 8, 10, 38, 48–49, 77–78, 98, 104–105, 194, 212–13; *Mayaguez* incident and, 232
U Tapao RTNB, 193, 206, 219, 225, 231
U.S. Congress. *See specific congressional amendments*

Vakrivan, 37–38
Vancouver, USS, 3
Vesuvius (U.S. intelligence operation), 45
Viet Cong, 34, 56. *See also* PLAF
Viet Minh, 25, 26, 28, 31, 56
Vietnam, 11, 30, 168, 185, 231, 242, 243; ancient role of, 15, 17–18; during French colonial period, 22–29; 1989 withdraws from Cambodia, 236; and Paris Agreement, 154–55, 160; pogrom against citizens of, 74–75; at war with China, 235; at war with Democratic Kampuchea, 230, 235. *See also* North Vietnam; South Vietnam
Vogt, Gen. John, 168, 171, 176, 194
Vong Sarendy, Commodore, 158, 193
Vo Nguyen Giap, 52

War Powers Resolution, 170
Watergate scandal, 50–51, 155, 206
Watson, James, 48
weather alteration, 49

Yarborough, Gen. William, 81
Yasovarman I, 15

Zhou Enlai, 35, 60, 228

Printed in the United States
101101LV00007B/212/A